computer-assisted theory building

To Pat

computer-assisted
theory
building
MODELING DYNAMIC
SOCIAL SYSTEMS

by
ROBERT A. HANNEMAN

SAGE PUBLICATIONS
The Publishers of Professional Social Science
Newbury Park   Beverly Hills   London   New Delhi

For information address:

SAGE Publications, Inc.
2111 West Hillcrest Drive
Newbury Park, California 91320

SAGE Publications Inc.
275 South Beverly Drive
Beverly Hills
California 90212

SAGE Publications Ltd.
28 Banner Street
London EC1Y 8QE
England

SAGE PUBLICATIONS India Pvt. Ltd.
M-32 Market
Greater Kailash I
New Delhi 110 048 India

Printed in the United States of America

Library of Congress Cataloging-in-Publication Data

Hanneman, Robert.
    Computer-assisted theory building.

    Bibliography: p.
    Includes index.
    1. Social systems—Mathematical models. 2. Social
action—Mathematical models. I. Title.
H61.25.H36 1987   301'.072'4   87-12870
ISBN 0-8039-2961-7

Contents

Preface

This book has the immodest goal of reorienting how many social scientists go about building and working with theories. There are three points in my proposals. First, I believe that we would benefit from a shift in substantive focus toward less concern with statics to a more explicit concern with dynamics. Second, I believe that social scientists' theoretical work would be much advanced by the use of powerful and flexible formal languages for expressing theory, as opposed to the current practices of using either "everyday" language or mathematics. Third, I am advocating the use of computer-assisted simulation methods as a useful way for theorists in the social sciences to explore the implications of their newly developed theories of complex dynamic processes.

Examples are often far more convincing than advocacy in the abstract, and this volume is primarily devoted to the development and analysis of formal language models that represent both new and existing social science theories of dynamic processes. There are three stages in the presentation. In the first part of this volume the necessary ideas about "systems" as a way of thinking about dynamic processes are introduced, along with one "semimathematical" language for formalizing theoretical statements about systems. In this section as well, an outline of the strengths, weaknesses, and methods of simulation analysis for theorists is given. In the second part of the book we show how these ways and means can be used to represent and work with large classes of dynamic models that are already in wide use in the social sciences. In the third section we offer some more complex and speculative theoretical statements that illustrate how much further social scientists can go in theorizing dynamics than most currently do.

The approaches and tools presented here are widely used in applied disciplines (engineering, administration, urban planning, etc.), and are not original to the author. These concerns, methods, and approaches, however, have been very unevenly adopted in the social sciences. Some economists will find many of the approaches offered here rather familiar, as both formal theorizing and the use of simulation methodology are widely used in that discipline. The emphases in the current work on dynamics (rather than "equilibrium" analysis) and on use of "friendlier" semimathematical languages should, nonetheless, be of interest. A smaller number of political scientists and still fewer sociologists and psychologists will find the approaches familiar and noncontroversial. That they have not been widely adopted in these disciplines is, in my view, quite unfortunate, for they bridge major gaps between those who study "structures" and those who study "processes" and gaps between those who use "natural" language to present their theories and those who use formal languages (often mathematics or symbolic logic). They allow far more powerful and rigorous ways of "doing theory" than are often practiced. Still fewer practitioners of anthropology and history will find the contents of this volume familiar. But the methods of representing patterns of social dynamics in formal models and understanding their implications by computer-assisted experiments have a great deal to offer. The focus of the methods advocated in this volume on the study of over-time processes is completely sympathetic with the needs and interests of many workers in these disciplines.

Because the approach to building theories advocates a "middle way" between purely verbal models on one hand and mathematical models on the other, practitioners of either approach in any of the social science disciplines may find things here that are of interest and use. Through the development of increasingly complex and nuanced models as we proceed through the chapters, those who fear that the richness and complexity of natural language models will be lost in formalization will see that the current approach does not sacrifice richness for representational rigor. For practitioners of graph theory, differential equations, game theory, Markov models and other forms of mathematical modeling, the payoff is different. The freedom of model form allowable by the use of "semimathematical" languages for stating theories and the use of simulation methods for their analysis allows for the development of more complex and realistic models of forms of social action.

A large number of people have made important contributions to parts or all of this book. The most critical of these contributions has been by my wife Patricia who has not only motivated and supported me while I've worked on the project, but has also served as my main critic, editor, graphic artist, and production assistant. Without this support the book would simply not exist. Debts of this magnitude cannot be adequately acknowledged. The dedication of this volume to her is the best that I can do.

A number of my colleagues have also made direct and immediate contributions to the development of this volume. Randall Collins, who has been both a teacher and occasional student, contributed much of the work on Marx in Chapter 13, as well as continuing encouragement, and extremely useful critical commentary and suggestions on the manuscript. Jonathan Turner has been of immeasurable assistance in encouraging and supporting the enterprise and by his useful editorial and critical commentary. Another current colleague, David Morgan has contributed to the ideas on stress, coping, and social support in Chapter 12, and to their development into that chapter. To David as well go thanks for support, encouragement, and useful insights and commentary throughout the project. The materials in Chapter 13 on the work of Vilfredo Pareto are the direct outgrowth of earlier work done by Charles Powers, and owe much of whatever value they may have to his contributions to both interpreting and formalizing Pareto's works. Less immediate, but extremely important contributions to the development of this work have been made by two of my former mentors and now colleagues. Jerald Hage first interested me in problems of theory construction, formalization, and dynamics years ago as a graduate assistant. I can only hope that he is not too displeased by the results. J. Rogers Hollingsworth has also been important in the development of this work both through his friendship and through his help in developing and refining many of the ideas on the methods presented. Work that we have done together related to this volume and to other projects have provided a continuing source of stimulation and encouragement. Direct thanks are also due to the staff of the Department of Sociology at the University of California, Riverside for their patience and help, and to large numbers of students who have suffered, willingly and not, through the development and trial runs of many of the elements of this manuscript.

Part I

Social Dynamics

This book is intended to give practicing theorists in the social sciences a new set of tools for creating and analyzing theories about processes of complex social action. The dynamics studied by economists, political scientists, sociologists, anthropologists, psychologists, and historians are composed of multiple simultaneous causal processes, operating along multiple dimensions, and occurring both within and between social actors. Such processes are inherently complicated.

With few exceptions, the task of creating coherent and useful theories about the dynamics of such systems of action has tended to overwhelm us. In efforts to cope, we focus on long-run equilibrium tendencies and comparative statics, rather than on the often more complicated dynamic processes; we progressively simplify problems by assumption until what remains can be dealt with systematically; and, often, we resort to the use of statements at such high levels of generality and abstraction that our theories, however insightful, complete, and consistent, are difficult to verify and offer little guidance in explaining real events.

Effectively creating and analyzing theories about complex processes of social action requires the use of new intellectual tools. At present, theorists concerned with dynamics tend to be divided into two methodological camps (and into numerous factions within each camp). These groups and factions exist in each of the social sciences, with one approach more common in one discipline, and another being the "normal" way of theorizing in another. One group utilizes "everyday" language for constructing theories, including special rules for the definitions of concepts and for making statements about relations among them. Theories are formulated and their properties and implications explored using rules of logic (e.g., axiomatic deduction). Another large group of scholars utilize formal mathematical language tools (e.g., differential equations, Markov processes, etc.) to state theories of dynamic social relations and to analyze and explore their theories.

Everyday language and mathematics are both less than perfect tools for describing and analyzing complex social action. Purely verbal formulations are often insufficiently specific; mathematical formulations tend to be too restrictive. In this volume we will show how the use of specialized formal languages that lie between the everyday and the mathematical can build on the strengths of each and become a powerful tool for stating formal theories of even relatively complex social dynamics. We will also show that computer assisted simulation of dynamic theories provides a "third way" of analyzing and understanding the implications of theories about complex action that is in some ways more powerful than the logical deductive approach associated with "everyday language" formalization and the direct solution approach associated with mathematical formulations.

Our argument proceeds in three main stages, which constitute the major sections of the book. In this first section we will introduce the basic elements of a "systems" approach to creating formal theories of social dynamics, and discuss the use of simulation methods in the theory construction process. In the second section of the book we examine a number of "simple" systems that include many of the major mathematical dynamic models commonly used by social scientists. In the third section we explore some of the applications of semimathematical languages and computer-assisted simulation for dealing with social dynamics that are more complex than most of the mathematical models currently in use, and approach the level of complexity of some everyday language models. These models are extremely rich in the kinds of processes that they can represent while retaining much of the analytic rigor of less complex mathematical models.

The first order of business (and the first chapter) is to get a grasp on the problems of theorizing in the social sciences that this book is intended to address, and to outline our proposed solutions. In this book we stress the importance of theory about dynamic processes as well as about comparative statics, emphasize the need for formalization of such theories using semimathematical language, and advocate a "systems" approach to conceptualizing complex social action. The purpose of the first chapter is to explain these emphases.

The remainder of the first section (i.e., Chapters 2 through 5) explains our approach and acts as a primer on the concepts and language that will be used throughout the volume. In the second chapter the basic elements of systems thinking and formal languages for representing dynamic processes are discussed. In the third and fourth chapters the necessary specifics of one particular semiformal language for continuous state continuous time dynamics (DYNAMO) are explained. In the fifth chapter the notions of systems complexity and the use of simulation methods for working with complex systems are discussed. Taken together, these chapters provide all the tools that the reader will need to understand the models developed in the second and third parts of the volume, and to begin translating their own theories into formal dynamic models.

1

Dynamics, Formal Theory, and the Systems Approach

What social scientists do when they theorize is remarkable in its diversity. They have a variety of goals, ranging from creating time- and space-invariant general laws of social behavior to seeking to uncover and understand the "deep structure" of everyday life. Theorists use a variety of theory-building methods, ranging from deductive reasoning by rules of formal logic to efforts to understand and offer "thick" descriptions of the patterns of meanings and definitions of situations of people in everyday settings. Social scientists are concerned with both large-scale and small-scale human behavioral patterns, are concerned with economic, political, and cultural phenomena, and approach their subjects from a wide range of paradigms.

One of the main goals for all theorizing, regardless of specifics of problem and perspective, is the creation of a mental model of the phenomenon to be understood and/or explained. The models that social scientists build are quite varied in form. Most describe and classify patterns of social action, and identify traits that tend to covary. Fewer take as their problem the processes that create these patterns of co-occurrence. Most social scientist's models are stated in everyday language, and are rich in their ability to evoke analogies and create insights. Fewer are stated with the precision and rigor of formal languages. Most social scientist's models deal with particular phenomena, or narrow classes of phenomena. That is, they are theories of the "middle range." Fewer of our models are useful for understanding the similarities and differences across wide ranges of patterns of social behavior.

We believe that social scientists give too little attention to the tasks of building models useful for understanding social dynamics, relative to the emphasis on comparative statics. We also believe that too little use is being made of the power of formal languages in stating and analyzing theories, relative to the emphasis on narration and description. And we believe that too little attention is given to building theories of broad classes of social behaviors, relative to the emphasis on theories of this, that, and the other specific phenomena.

In this volume we are going to advocate, by discussion and example, some different emphases for theory builders in the social sciences. Our emphasis is on the creation of theoretical models for the analysis of social dynamics, rather than statics. Our emphasis is on the use of formal languages and computer-assisted simulation as a means of theoretical analysis, rather than everyday language. And, our emphasis is on theoretical models as realizations of the more general systems principles, rather than as unique to each phenomenon.

The first task, to which we will devote the remainder of this chapter, is to explain the returns that can be had from an investment of effort in constructing theoretical models about dynamics, using formal languages, and approaching the task of theory building from a systems perspective.

From Comparative Statics to Dynamics

The most common kinds of theoretical statements in the social sciences have the following form: The greater the X, the greater the Y.[1] This type of theoretical statement is an assertion about patterns of hypothesized covariation among the properties described by the concepts. As such, it is a statement of comparative statics.

Theories of comparative statics are tremendously important in the social sciences. They serve to map the territory by providing definitions and classifications. Mapping the patterns of covariation among the parts of a phenomenon helps us to understand that certain forms of behavior or action are unlikely to occur and that other patterns are more likely to occur. Assertions that properties tend to covary and to co-occur imply that causal mechanisms are at work to produce this end. Comparative statics then lead in the direction of a search for the causes of patterns of co-occurrence, and often provide considerable insight into causal mechanisms.

Theories of social dynamics differ from theories of statics in that they focus on the process of change as the thing to be explained rather than the structures themselves. The difference can be subtle. Compare the statements "the greater the centralization, the greater the formalization" and "an increase in centralization produces an increase in formalization." The former statement clearly focuses attention on the assertion that centralization and formalization tend to co-occur, but does not give us any guidance as to why this is the case; the latter statement clearly asserts that a change in centralization produces a change in formalization. Here, as in theories of dynamics generally, attention is focused on the causal mechanism rather than the covariation itself.

The building of theories of statics and of dynamics are closely related and mutually dependent activities. While the focus of theories of comparative statics is not on the processes that produce and reproduce the structures, such theories almost always (but often implicitly) are accompanied by a mental model of where structures come from and how they change. Indeed, one of the key ways in which types of structures are distinguished from one another is through differences between the processes that produce and reproduce them. Similarly, theories that focus on "process" or social dynamics must have (at least implicitly) models of structure embedded in them. There is little meaning in assertions about change in general (though we can make assertions about processes of change that we believe have wide application), without referring to the structures that are connected by such processes.

Greater emphasis has been given to statics than to dynamics in most social science theorizing. And, while comparative static analysis is a necessary and important task, too much emphasis can deflect attention from other important theory-building tasks.

To the extent that social scientist's theoretical activities seek to build explanations of phenomena, rather than descriptions, they must focus on causal processes that occur over time. In the life sciences we see elaborate and effective taxonomical systems for mapping and describing organisms. These systems are remarkable intellectual achievements, but are useful only because they are closely tied to causal theories about the origin, selection, and retention of species differences. That is, the static taxonomy is closely connected to the theories of selection dynamics.[2] Similarly, the distinction between the "extended family" and the "nuclear family" is useful primarily because it is tied to (and helps us to build theories about) the causes and consequences of patterns of variation in interpersonal relations. The distinction between a "market" and a "hierarchy" similarly is useful primarily in the context of explanations about the processes that cause the emergence of these forms, or the consequences of these forms of coordination. Static comparisons in the social sciences, then, are usually no less grounded in dynamic theories than the physical or life sciences are—though social scientist's dynamic theories are often poorly developed, leading to poorly developed and competing static models.

Dynamics, then, should be a top priority in social science theorizing because of the role that they play in motivating comparative and static analyses. But dynamics can (and should) be a central object of theorist's concern in their own right. It is often the case that the phenomenon that needs explanation is the rate of change in some pattern of social action, rather than variability in the pattern itself. Some examples will make the point. A psychologist may be interested in the rate of cognitive development (i.e., change in the level of the construct with respect to time) as it is affected by life experiences. A social psychologist might focus attention on changes in the rates of communication or of affective support among members of a social network over time. An anthropologist may wish to explain the rate of diffusion of a belief pattern within and among the tribal units in an area. Sociologists may wish to account for changes in the level of income and occupational prestige of individuals over their life-cycles. The interest of political scientists may be drawn to the processes that generate changes in the level of support for parties or candidates over time. Economists focus attention on rates of growth and changes in prices. In each of these cases (and clearly many more could be cited), the central theoretical problem is one of understanding change per se, rather than patterns of covariation or the equilibrium realization of the systems.

Where the goal of the theory building enterprise is to provide mental models for understanding change, theorizing that deals explicitly with dynamic processes may be more appropriate than theorizing in the static mode. Building theories about dynamic processes may also have some practical advantages in the continuous movement back and forth between theory formalization and observation. In making observations about social action, either during the process of constructing theories or of verifying them, we are often able to observe the dynamic behavior of systems, but rarely able to observe systems in their static or equilibrium states.

In the process of making theoretical generalizations on the basis of observations, we are sometimes in a position to identify causal connectedness among properties, but do not have available cases in which all the causal processes have reached their full realizations. That is, we may not have examples of the "normal," or "stable," or "ideal-typical" ways that the elements fit together. It may also be the case that we wish to create a theory to understand the workings of processes that occur only once (e.g., the rise of the capitalist world economy). In this instance we do not have multiple cases to compare in order to attempt to uncover the nature of the processes that generate variability in outcomes. In either of these circumstances, we can still use our observations to attempt to formulate theoretical statements about variations in the rates of change in properties of the social system. That is, it is possible to create a theory of dynamics, or change with respect to time, even when events are not repeated and do not ever reach an equilibrium condition.[3]

The verification of theories of comparative statics is often difficult because of the requirement of comparing multiple cases and the requirement that the cases be in their final or "equilibrium" conditions. In experiments we are often able to observe multiple comparable examples of fully realized dynamic processes. Most other forms of observation (participant and systematic observation, use of archival and statistical records, questionnaires and surveys, etc.) yield data that are more problematic. The multiple observations (cases) are rarely "equivalent" in important ways, they are not randomly selected into treatment groups, and the effects of independent variables on change in the dependent variable have not necessarily been equally or fully realized across observations. All of these realities about the data arising from observational methods in the social sciences can raise difficulties for using observations to build good static theories. Theories about dynamics, because they imply observation across time, rather than across cases, are less subject to certain of these problems (and are more subject to others). Data on event histories or time series may be easier to come by in the nonexperimental branches of the social sciences than truly comparable cross-sections, and hence may bring observation and theorizing closer together.

The argument for a greater concern with theories of social dynamics and hence for techniques tailored to building them is relatively simple, but, we hope, convincing. Many of the fundamental theoretical questions of social scientists are explicitly questions about rates of change in patterns of social action. For such processes as growth, decline, status transition, modification and elaboration of form, the most powerful and direct way of stating theory is in terms of dynamics. Theories stated in terms of rates of change may also be more useful than those stated in terms of patterns of static covariation in certain cases for more practical reasons. There are many phenomena about that social scientists may wish to theorize that either fail to ever reach equilibrium or else are not repeated. In these cases, theory formulation and/or verification by means of static comparisons are simply not possible, and observations of rates of change in one or more realizations must form the empirical base for theorizing.

Formalization: The Languages of Theory Building

One of the issues about theory-building methods that most deeply divides practitioners is the question of the most useful languages for creating theory. At one extreme, some would argue that theories about social action must be stated in the language of the actors and settings about which the theory is written. Near this extreme position is the view of "historicist," "ethnographic," and "institutionalist" scholars in the various social sciences. These positions all emphasize the virtues of rich, evocative, and "thick" description of phenomena. Practitioners in these traditions have, not surprisingly, strong preferences for the use of "everyday" language in making their theoretical statements. At the opposite extreme, some social scientists argue that theories of social action ought be constructed using the most abstract and general languages possible. Social science historians, social network analysts in sociology and anthropology, mathematical sociologists, and others of their ilk in political science, economics, and the applied social sciences display strong preferences for the use of restrictive formalisms (e.g., statistical and mathematical tools) for making theoretical statements.

At the root of much of the diversity of views about the language appropriate for building theory in the social sciences are important epistemological debates about empiricism and about the possibility of general laws in social and cultural sciences.[4] Our concern with language choice here, however, is far narrower.

There are a variety of different ways of talking about economic, political, and cultural dynamics, and for stating theories about them. In practice, models about dynamic relations are most frequently formulated utilizing either everyday ("natural") language, causal models based on linear structural equations ("statistical") language, or differential equations ("mathematical") language. Each of these languages for describing dynamic relations has certain strengths and limitations, and each tends to create habits of thought affecting the types of theories that we build. In this volume we advocate a language for constructing theories about continuous state dynamics that is a hybrid of natural and mathematical language. Since we will ask the reader to become familiar with the basic vocabulary and syntax of this language, we need to explain why the use of a formal language for building theories of dynamics is desirable. And, we need to suggest why a new language is preferable to the ones that we already know.

Everyday Language

By far the most common language of stating theories about social dynamics is the same one we use in everyday discourse, with some slight tailoring for the purpose (i.e., creating "jargon" to define particular types of things and relations among them). We might, for example, state a theory about a particular form of social dynamics as follows: The more time that actors spend in direct face-to-face interaction, the more they will come to perceive that they share many things in common with one another. As they come to perceive themselves as more similar to one another, they come to form increasing feelings of liking or attraction to one another; as feelings of attraction increase, the actors will strive to prolong the interaction.[5]

This statement is clearly a theory about social dynamics, and a very important one at that. There are actors (individual persons), each is characterized by levels of continuous variables (call them, say, propensity to initiate interaction, degree of perceived similarity to the other, and strength of liking or attraction for the other), and the model specifies causal relations operating over time among the variables. The statement of the theory has a number of appealing features: The terms used have meanings we understand without special effort, the relations are simple and straightforward, and the empirical referents of the statements are easily discerned, thereby making empirical examples readily accessible that are consistent with (or contradictory to) the general statement.

A closer look at the theory, though, reveals some problems. These difficulties are typical consequences of formulating theoretical models in everyday language. First, there is a tendency to overgeneralize when stating theories in this fashion. The formulation of the theory above does not tell us the conditions under which the proposed relationships hold, nor does it specify conditions limiting or modifying the relationships in question. Second, the theory statement fails to enlighten us on a number of points: Are the relationships linear? (That is, does each increase or decrease in perceived similarity generate the same increase or decrease in liking, or are there thresholds?) What are the time-shapes of the relationships? (Does the propensity to interact respond immediately to changes in liking, or are there lags and delays?) Do the relationships run in one direction (Does increased similarity cause increased liking, but not vice versa?) or in both directions? Are similarity, liking, and interaction levels "self-referencing"? (Do changes in the degree of liking depend on the degree of liking that already exists? Does liking increase, decrease, or remain the same in the absence of change in similarity and interaction?)

What these questions really boil down to is this: Theoretical statements in everyday language tend to fail to precisely specify the relations among concepts. Of course, one could ask how precise the theorist is obligated to be. The position taken here is that a statement of a theory must be specific enough to enable us to create a class of models that have important commonalities of dynamic behavior and to be specific enough to eliminate from consideration classes of models that do not produce the same basic patterns of behavior.

The statement of the theory above is not sufficiently specific by this criterion because it allows for "interpretation" at so many points that it is consistent with models that produce a wide variety of fundamentally different dynamic behaviors. In its simplest possible interpretation, the theory is consistent with models that produce accelerating exponential increases or declines in similarity, liking, and interaction over time. However, with very slight modifications that are not ruled out by the theory (as we stated it), increases at different rates for different variables, increases and decreases at decreasing as well as increasing rates, or even (more arguably) some forms of simple cyclical behavior, can be produced by models with legitimate claims to parentage in the theoretical statement. It is our position that such a theoretical statement is not sufficient because of the high degree of indeterminancy in predicted behavior.

The use of everyday language to state theories does not always result in formulations that are insufficiently specified. Much more careful and fuller explication of this theory could remove much of the ambiguity. Everyday language, however, is an awkward tool for such specifications— and particularly for specifying the parts of the theory that are explicitly dynamic.

Everyday languages are evolved to suit certain needs and limitations. Consequently, they tend to have two related characteristics that limit their utility for unambiguous statements of theories: They are (1) richly evocative and (2) highly abbreviated. The terms of everyday language are capable of meaning very different things depending on the contexts in which they appear, and can be understood (in part) as signals or stimuli that set off extremely complex ideas and cognitions when sent between two individuals sharing the same culture. These characteristics are very useful in managing everyday social life, but are not ideal for the statement of theory (though, of course, every statement of theory ultimately has reference to the culture and language of the persons creating and consuming it). The variety of possible meanings of terms and relations among terms in everyday language is very great, and, in many cases allows for the creation of numerous markedly different mental models consistent with the same statement. Everyday language also tends to be highly abbreviated, relying on context and shared culture to "fill in the blanks" so that interaction can continue. In stating theory, such linguistic tendencies result in a failure to specify limits, conditions, forms of relationships among variables, and time-shapes of relationships.

Mathematical Language

At the opposite extreme from everyday language is mathematics. As a language of scientific discourse, mathematics has several advantages over everyday language. All of the information to be conveyed by a statement in mathematical language must be made explicit. Each of the variables in a statement is a pure abstract symbol, and all of the relations among variables are expressed by operators and functions. The vocabulary in the language of mathematics is highly restricted, and each term has a defined and shared meaning. And, importantly, the more complex meanings created by stringing symbols and operations together bear determinate relationships to the parts that compose them. Specialized sublanguages having these desirable characteristics have been evolved that apply well to making statements about continuous state/continuous time dynamics, most notably differential equations and the calculus. With these specialized languages, complex and powerful operations of deduction from systems of statements about dynamic relations can be made.[6]

The use of mathematical language to state social science theories is very common. Such applications are most apparent in theoretical economics and psycho-physics, but are also quite common in almost all of the subdisciplines in the social sciences. The use of differential equations (and their equilibrium form of "structural equations" and their log-linear analogues) are commonplace in political science, sociology, history, and psychology.

There are, however, a number of disadvantages to the use of most existing mathematical languages for stating social science theories, and particularly theories about processes and change. First, it must be admitted, most social scientists are not very well trained in the uses of mathematical language. While mathematics can provide powerful tools for making statements about dynamics, it is of little practical utility if those who wish to make such statements cannot do so coherently and if their statements are unintelligible to those who hear them.

As serious a limitation as this is in practice, there are also two more general reasons for concern about using mathematics as the language of discourse about cultural, political, and economic dynamics. One of these problems is technical, the other stylistic.

The phenomena about which social scientists wish to create theories are quite varied. Some of the social systems are relatively simple, and the theories formalizing the dynamics of them can be correspondingly simple. Other phenomena are exceedingly complex and call for quite complex theories to adequately formalize the laws of their dynamics.

Put very simply, most mathematical languages for stating theories of dynamics are more powerful than we need for simple problems, and not sufficiently powerful for complex ones. Many of the most elegant applications of mathematical language in the social sciences are viewed by some as arid formalisms of trivial problems. They are considered so restricted and oversimple as to be of little general utility. Theories of two-person games and triadic interaction, as well as deductive theory about collective behavior are indeed powerful and explicit, but are often accused of being either good theories about trivial phenomena or being bad theories about nontrivial phenomena. On the other hand, mathematical formulations of complex problems often exceed the capacities of their creators and consumers to understand and explicate them. The introduction of conditional relationships, nonlinear relationships, and complex patterns of coupling among even small numbers of variables can rapidly exceed our capacity to solve such systems, or to comprehend the meaning of the solution if one is found.

In addition to these "technical" limitations on the utility of formal mathematics, there are "stylistic" problems. It is sometimes argued that "natural" or everyday language is the appropriate language for studying cultural phenomena, as in the the humanities. In contrast, mathematics is the language of sciences dealing with material aspects of the world. The problem arises in finding a language of discourse that is fully compatible with both the material and cultural aspects of social action. That is, the language that we use for theory building in the social sciences must not only enable us to talk about "things," but also about "the meaning of things." There is no inherent reason, of course, why everyday language and mathematics cannot be used to deal with both material and cultural phenomena. But neither provides specialized vocabulary or easy syntax for establishing the connections necessary for social science theory.

Semimathematical Languages

Because of the limitations of mathematical languages for stating theories of dynamics—practical, technical, and stylistic—social scientists have created a number of "intermediate" languages that lie between everyday and mathematical languages. These languages seek to retain much of the rigor of definition and deductive power available from mathematical forms, while at the same time they resemble everyday language. One such language, DYNAMO, will be used in this volume.

These "semimathematical" or "intermediate" languages have a number of distinct advantages for social science theory building. On the one hand, they have highly restrictive (but still quite powerful) vocabularies and syntax. As such, they remove ambiguity from statements about the elements of the theory and require complete specification of the exact forms and limits of the relations among the elements. Theoretical models stated in formal languages may be foolish, internally inconsistent, and bear no relation to events in the real world. They cannot, however, be ambiguous and open to various interpretations. The semimathematical languages that have been explicitly formulated for the purposes of stating continuous state dynamic models of social behavior—such as DYNAMO—have rules of syntax that require the theorist to formulate theories in particular ways. These strict rules of definition and syntax, far from restricting the range of possible theories, actually aid the theorist by requiring that certain questions be answered (and hence the alternatives considered) at each stage in formalization of the theory.

As a direct result of the more restrictive vocabulary and grammar of the languages, theories using semimathematical languages tend to be far more tightly structured and explicit than natural language theories. Yet, the most common "semimathematical" languages generally have a more flexible structure than "pure" mathematical ones. For many of the problems about which social scientists want to theorize, this is an advantage, although there is often a substantial price in deductive power to be paid for this greater flexibility of expression of the semimathematical languages.

To propose that we use specialized formal languages for building theories about social dynamics is somewhat radical. Not all will agree that everyday or natural languages are insufficient to specify dynamic relations. Others will not agree with the proposition that "pure" mathematics cannot capture the richness of those phenomena about which we wish to theorize.

The plausibility of these conclusions resides in their illustration. And so, in the remainder of this volume we will develop a series of models of progressively more complex social dynamics within the grammar and syntax of a "semimathematical" language (DYNAMO) that is closely tied to the "general systems" and "systems dynamics" traditions of theorizing about social action. This language is an attempt to bridge mathematics (systems of simultaneous linear and nonlinear difference and differential equations) and theorizing about economic, political, and cultural dynamics from a "systems theory" perspective.

All languages, be they "everyday" or highly formal and specialized, reflect particular ways of seeing the world. The theories and models, and the approaches to theorizing and modeling in the remainder of this volume, are "cultural artifacts" of a particular way of viewing the world: the "systems" perspective.

"Systems" Approaches to Dynamics

In the broadest sense of the term, a "system" is nothing more than an ordering or relating of a set of parts into a whole. A "system" is composed of both the "things" ("elements" or "parts") and the relations among them. Theories are one example of systems in that they consist of parts (concepts) that are ordered by relations (propositions, equations, or other connecting statements) into a larger whole. The things about which theorists theorize can also be seen as "systems" in this broad sense: The mental organization, knowledges and cognitive structures of social actors, patterns of social relations, and basic social forms like community, class, nation, and world "system" are all "systems" of differing compositions and complexity.

In this volume we will be using the vocabulary of "systems" (in this broad sense of "things" and "relations among things") and insights borrowed from the methods of "systems analysis." "Systems analysis" is most commonly thought of as a method for understanding and working with electromechanical devices (such as computers) or highly rationalized human intellectual creations (such as computer programs or the patterns of social relations in formal organizations). As a logical approach to constructing and analyzing theories, however, "systems" concepts and language can be applied to any pattern of relations, and need not be restricted to the study of mechanical or "rational" systems.

The methods of theory building applied by systems analysis are really no different from those routinely taught in courses in theory construction. The first step is to "define the boundaries of the system" to be theorized about. That is, we first must decide on the limits of the phenomenon to be described and provide its definition. The second step is to "define the elements of the state space, and partition the state space into subsystems." That is, we must identify the variables that describe the phenomenon and group them into subsets that make sense for our purposes. Third, we "describe the connectivity of the state space elements, and the forms of relations among the states of the system." That is, we identify which variables are direct causes of change in which others, and describe the limits and functional forms of these causal relations. Finally, we "define the dynamic aspects of the relations among state space elements." That is, we describe how fast each of the causal connections operates, and the "time shape" of the relations among the variables.

The reason that we burden the reader with some new vocabulary (i.e., systems, subsystems, connectivity, state spaces, etc.) to describe already familiar aspects of the theory-building task is that the use of these systems analysis concepts help us to think more abstractly about what we do when we build theories. Particularly, they are very helpful in leading us to see our theories as systems that share properties with other systems of similar structure but different substantive content.

Perhaps the chief virtue of using the concepts of systems analysis to describe the tasks of theory building is that the usage points out the similarities in the enterprises of members of different disciplines, of "micro" and "macro" theorists, and of practitioners from differing paradigmatic perspectives. Certainly social scientists have very different concerns and approaches: A Marxian political economist seeking to theorize about capital flows among nation states in the world system would seem to have little in common with a psychophysical psychologist studying the structure of individual memory. But if we think about the tasks of these practitioners as the building of theoretical systems, their activities are not really so different. In both cases the analysts could be said to be concerned with building theories that describe dynamics: rates of capital flows and rate of information flows. Both problems involve quite large state spaces: the national economies of states in the world system and memory locations in a network or schema. Both problems are systems of relatively high "connectivity": Most nations trade with most other nations, and most elements of memory schemas are quite directly accessible to most others.

This is not an idle exercise in semantics to point out the similarity between these two quite different social science enterprises when seen from the "systems" perspective. That the two problems are so similar suggests that very similar methods can be used for building and analyzing theories about the dynamics of capital flows and the dynamics of memory and recall. These methods, of course, are the subject of the remainder of this volume. The similarity of the two problems also suggests that theorists working in very different substantive areas can obtain guidance and insights about their own problems of theory building by comparing the structure of their own theorizing as a system to other theories as systems, even where the substantive content may be very different. The use of systems concepts, then, can aid in improving communication across and within social science disciplines.

Theoretical activity in most of the social sciences is divided by paradigmatic emphases, as well as by substantive specialization. The

Marxian political economist in our example above differs from the cognitive psychologist not only in the aspect of human behavior that he or she seeks to explain, but also in a series of assumptions about the nature of the important kinds of variables to consider and the ways in which these variables are connected.

Systems thinking and systems analysis are likely to be associated in the minds of many social scientists with a particular set of theoretical problems (i.e., the maintenance of order), particular kinds of dynamics (i.e., equilibrium-seeking negative feedback), and particular policy positions (i.e., "conservative," or possibly "liberal," but rarely "radical"). And indeed, there is a strong historical connection between the use of "systems" language and preferences in theoretical activity in most of the social sciences. But the connection is not a necessary one. Systems thinking is equally consistent with the analysis of contradiction, disorder, and change, as it is with the analysis of harmony, order, and stability.

A large part of the theoretical activity in most of the social sciences (especially anthropology, sociology, history, political science, and economics) can be classified as arising from one of three major traditions: structural-functionalism, conflict analysis, or Marxism.[7] Structural-functional analysis has historically been most closely connected with the use of systems thinking because of the use of systems concepts by theorists in this tradition, and the emphasis of such work on the dynamic feedback mechanisms by which actors and environments are "adjusted" to one another. Conflict analysis has largely avoided the use of systems conceptualization (perhaps because of its association with structural-functionalism), but is quite consistent with systems thinking. Conflict analysis highlights the processes of change in patterns of social relations arising out of the interactions of actors with differing goals and resources. While conflict theorists tend to emphasize disorder and change rather than stability and order, their ideas are completely consistent with systems thinking: Dynamic, goal-oriented interactions among multiple actors are easily conceptualized as systems and can productively be analyzed as such. The historical antipathy between systems theorists and Marxists in most social science disciplines is most peculiar, for Marxist approaches to theorizing are more "systems" oriented than the thinking of most other schools. Marxist analysis emphasizes the inherent tendencies of most systems of social relations to develop strains (dialectical contradictions) that result in their destruction and replacement with new systems. The processes by which systems destroy themselves are just as easy to analyze by systems methods as are the processes that cause systems to maintain or elaborate their structures.

What social scientists do when they theorize is remarkable in its diversity of substance and approach. The concepts of systems theory and the methods of systems analysis provide some useful bridges across disciplines and perspectives and hence are very useful for discussing the building of formal theories of dynamics. Systems terminology helps the theorist to "take a step back" from the substantive issues of the phenomenon they are theorizing and to see the theory itself as a type of system. Once this mental leap has been made, very useful insights can be obtained by applying general principles of systems dynamics to the theorizing of particular phenomena and by borrowing ideas from contexts that are substantively quite different but structurally quite similar to the theorist's concerns. Systems terminology, then, serves as a useful device for describing and organizing the theory building process and for increasing communication across the social science disciplines.

System Complexity, Systems Dynamics, and the Organization of the Book

Our advocacy of the utility of "systems" concepts and "systems analysis" methods for building and analyzing theories of social dynamics should not be taken as an advocacy of "general systems theory." General systems theory is a body of theory about abstract systems—in the broad sense of the term that we are using here. It is an attempt to state general laws about the statics and dynamics of "wholes" composed of "parts" and "relations among" those parts. In its most extreme form, advocacy of the general systems paradigm suggests the possibility of building a "unified" science consisting of general laws that govern the behavior of all phenomena—from systems of subatomic particles to the world ecological-social system. Within the social sciences similar proposals have been made, suggesting that the theories of economists, political scientists, anthropologists, sociologists, psychologists, and others (e.g., management, education, social work, and other "applied social sciences") can be integrated into a single "social systems" framework.[8]

The claim of general systems theory to be able to integrate social science theorizing has been attractive in the abstract (as, of course, are the similar claims of Marxism, structural-functionalism and other "paradigms"), but have not realized in practice. Despite this, many of the central ideas of "general systems" theory do provide useful ways of thinking about problems in each of the social sciences; these same ideas provide powerful tools for seeing similarities (and differences) in the theoretical approaches to problems of dynamics across the social sciences.

We have organized the work in this volume according to one of the central concepts of systems theory in an order of increasing "complexity" of the kinds of theoretical systems discussed. In the first part (Chapters 2 to 5) we will be concerned with learning the vocabulary and syntax of "systems" approaches to problems of dynamics, with learning the basics of a semimathematical language for formalizing dynamic models (DYNAMO), and with strategies for research on dynamic theories utilizing computer simulation. Once we have these tools in hand, we turn to a progression of increasingly complex theoretical models.

Many very important theories about dynamics in each of the social science disciplines are very simple systems. That is, they are composed of small numbers of parts (variables), and relatively simple relations among these parts (usually expressed as sets of propositions or equations). An economist may wish to formalize a system that describes the rate of change in the level of economic production as a function of changes in the supplies of the factors of production; an anthropologist might wish to describe the growth and decline of the population of a village as a function of changing natural and human environmental constraints; a psychologist may theorize about change over the life cycle in individual's "intelligence" or "cognitive development"; a sociologist may wish to describe the rates of fertility in a cohort over time. These "systems" (and, of course, many others) have very similar formal structures qua systems, and may well display similar dynamic behavior. We will examine the structure and dynamic behavior of such "simple" systems in the abstract (Chapter 6), and by example (Chapter 7).

Many additional phenomena from the various social science disciplines can be usefully thought of as slightly more complicated systems composed of several variables connected into "chains." The flows of money in the economy, the patterns of sending and receiving messages in social networks, the movements of individuals through stages of the life cycle, and many other similar problems in all of the social science disciplines have very similar structures and dynamics qua theoretical systems of this type. Some of the varieties of systems representable as simple "chains" are discussed in the abstract (Chapter 8), and by way of several examples (Chapter 9).

Part II (Chapters 6 to 9) provides all of the tools necessary for building and understanding truly complex theories of social dynamics. In the last portion of the volume (Chapters 10 to 13) we will develop some more complicated theories by linking the simpler systems examined in the second section together, and examine their structures and dynamics. The models in this section are developed as solutions to particular theoretical problems (arms races, stress-coping-social support dynamics, and macropolitical-economic dynamics). These models, however, are also generally useful as they illustrate how complex systems are built up out of the coupling together of simple ones—a lesson applicable to the development of all complicated dynamic systems.

One need not accept the claims of general systems theory or of unified social science to utilize the methods of theory building and theoretical research that we advocate in this volume. Implicit in our organization of the materials, however, is the idea that what social scientist do when they theorize about dynamics involves essentially the same set of activities and conceptions (in a formal sense) across all of the social sciences. Without accepting the claims of general systems theory, we do accept the utility of viewing political, economic, and cultural dynamics as dynamic systems. Going one step further, we also implicitly accept the utility of thinking about the theories themselves as systems that can be understood as abstract models and applied across the varied substantive areas of the social sciences.

The particulars of the diagraming conventions and computer language (DYNAMO) that we will use in this volume are derived from one particular school of applied systems analysis—the "systems dynamics" approach of Jay W. Forrester, his students, and colleagues.[9] The approach of "systems dynamics" to constructing formal models of social dynamics is peculiar in some ways, but uniquely well suited to the ways that social scientists go about dealing with thinking about dynamics. As with the use of concepts from "general systems" theory to organize the discussion, however, one need not accept the particulars of "systems dynamics" in order to benefit from the use of the language and tools of this approach. What is of tremendous utility for social scientists about the use of the language and concepts of "systems dynamics" is the structure, rigor, and clarity that comes from thinking about theoretical problems in social dynamics using a semiformal language well suited to our needs.

Conclusions

There are three major arguments in this chapter. First, we suggest that it is useful to distinguish between theorizing about statics and the dynamics of economic, political, and cultural phenomena. A very large portion of social science theory is concerned with static comparisons or with the properties of systems in their ideal-typical or equilibrium states. There is nothing wrong with this. But many theories are directly concerned with process and change rather than structure and stability.

And even theories of comparative statics must have some implicit basis in dynamics. Many of the intellectual tools that we have developed for the analysis of comparative statics are rather blunt instruments for analyzing and formulating theories about change. There is a need ,then, for more theorizing that is explicitly concerned with dynamics and uses tools best suited to dynamic analysis.

Our second argument is that "formal" specialized languages are desirable for creating and analyzing theory in general and theories of dynamics in particular. Everyday language tools for building dynamic theories tend to be too evocative and flexible; mathematical formulations of theory tend to be too restrictive and inflexible. In place of these more common tools, we advocate the use of specialized "semimathematical" languages specifically designed to describe complex mathematical processes (simultaneous linear and nonlinear difference and differential equations) in language that resembles—but imposes restrictions on—everyday language.

Third, we have suggested that many of the concepts of "systems" theory and the language and general conceptual approach of "systems analysis" provides a common ground on which theorists of various stripes can formulate and discuss theories of social dynamics. Without accepting the "general systems theory" world view, or the specifics of the "systems dynamics" tradition within this perspective, we will use these ideas as organizing principles for this volume. As we hope to demonstrate, there is a great deal to be gained from applying systems thinking to the problem of systematic theory building across all of the social sciences.

Notes

1. Such propositions can be made much more elaborate by including mulitple Xs and Ys, by describing the relationship in detail, and by adding limits propositions, all without modifying the nature of the statement as one of static covariation.

2. For an excellent discussion of principles of classification and their connection to causal theories in the life and social sciences, see McKelvey, 1982.

3. There is a considerable epistemological debate, particularly in historical analysis, about whether nonreplicable observations can be used as the observational basis for the formation of covering laws. Obviously, it is the position of the author that observations over time from a single realization are just as valid a basis for generalization as are observations across multiple cases.

4. Epistemological debates surrounding the role of language in explanation and the possiblities of the application of scientific method to cultural phenomena are extremely interesting and important, but go beyond the scope of this volume, which largely presupposes a positivist approach.

5. This particular formulation can be traced to Homans (1961), but is by no means a fair representation of his work.

6. For some interesting discussions of the strengths and weaknesses of mathematical applications in social science theory, see particularly Abelson, 1967, Arrow (1956), Ando et al. (1963), Berger et al. (1962), Hamblin (1971), Kemeny and Snell (1962), Kruskal (1970), Land (1971), Lave and March (1975), Lazarsfeld (1954), and Rapoport (1959).

7. There are, of course, any number of ways of classifying and characterizing paradigmatic approaches in the social sciences. The current classification is used only for purposes of illustrating the general applicability of systems thinking, and makes no claim to be a particularly useful way of talking about the diversity of social science approaches.

8.· For broad overviews of "general systems theory" and its applications to "unified science" and "unified social science," see particularly Berrien (1968), von Bertalanffy (1968), Klir (1971), and Kuhn (1963, 1975).

9. A more complete description of the "systems dynamics" perspective and major works in the tradition are presented in the next chapter.

2

Constructing Dynamic Models of Social Systems: Systems Concepts

In this chapter we will discuss some of the basic concepts of systems thinking and examine how these concepts can be used in formalizing theories about continuous-state/continuous-time dynamics. The first step is to get a grasp on the general idea of a *system,* and the related notions of *subsystem, coupling,* and *complexity.* This first step is an important one because of the confusion that can arise when the ideas of abstract systems are applied to the study of human behavior.

Part of the confusion arises from the fact that the notion of systems has been used at three different levels of analysis in the social sciences. One application has been to the study of the observable behavior of individuals (as in sociometry and early small-groups and social-network analysis). At this level theories and models concern specific observable individuals who have a particular pattern of relations (the network) which, taken together, constitutes a system. A second use of the concept of systems and the tools of systems analysis has been in the analysis of relations among aggregates, and among social actors that are larger than individual persons. At this level we find formal theories of the behavior of governments, formal organizations, populations of consumers, and the like. The phenomena that are being theorized about are still quite concrete, but consist of the behavior of aggregates of individuals, or the behavior of social actors composed of many individuals and the relationships among them. There is a third way in which systems thinking has been widely used in social science thinking (particularly in sociology, anthropology, and political science). At this third level of analysis, systems are composed of abstract concepts and *general variables.* At this level of analysis we find statements about such things as the system of relations between ethnic diversity and political polycentrism, or between the latent pattern maintenance and goal attainment functions of social systems. That is, the elements of the system are not concrete, but rather are highly abstract variables and concepts.

The applications of systems thinking at these quite diverse levels of analysis are not contradictory, but they stress the necessity of being quite clear about what one means when one uses the term *system*. By rigorously applying concepts from systems analysis, and by using formal languages to state theories, it is possible to identify the nature of systems to be theorized with considerable precision. We must, however, begin with a very broad and imprecise definition.

At the most abstract level, *systems* are simply wholes composed of related things.[1] The behavior of each of the "things" (be they atoms, people, business firms, nation states, or abstract variables) in a *system* is conditioned directly and indirectly by the behavior of each of the other things. The appearance and behavior of the "whole" system is the product of both the nature of the things and of the relations among them. In theorizing about the dynamics of such structures, we need a vocabulary to describe the "things" and to describe the "relations" among them—particularly dynamic causal relations. We will devote the two major sections of this chapter to these issues. The discussion of "things" calls forth the concepts of system boundaries, states and state spaces; the analysis of dynamic relations among things requires the language of *connectivity* and *control*.

Systems Elements and Systems Boundaries

One analyst may describe the network of interlocks among directors of corporations as a "system" and theorize about the movement of information in such a network. The network in this case is clearly a type of system, as we defined the term. It has parts (the corporate directors) who stand in relations to one another (either being members of the same boards or not). Taken as a whole, the actors and their interconnectedness form a system with distinctive static and dynamic properties (e.g., centrality, connectedness, etc.). A good deal of the theory of small groups, social networks, and social exchange consists of propositions about the statics and dynamics of such systems.[2] In this case the elements of the system (the "things") are concrete individuals, and the "relations among the things" are relatively simply characterized as the presence/absence (or the strength of) a relation between each pair of individuals.

A second analyst might have an interest in the relationship between governmental policy and mass political support. Such a problem might be approached by treating the government as a unitary actor, and by dividing the population into two aggregates: supporters and opponents. The relations among these three "things" or elements might be quite complex: The level of support and opposition might change (with delay, and possibly in nonlinear fashion) in response to shifts in government policy; government policy, in turn, may shift (with delay, and possibly in a nonlinear fashion) in response to perceived shifts in mass support. The "elements" of the system in this example are quite concrete (the government, the population of supporters, the population of opponents), but are composed of aggregates (supporters and opponents) and social actors (the government, which might be thought of as a system of individuals and relations in itself for other purposes). The relations among the elements of such a system might be a good deal more complicated than in our small groups or network system, but can be specified as a set of precise rules that describe how changes in the behavior of one element of the system (e.g., shifts in government policy) affect the levels of other elements of the system (e.g., the numbers of supporters and opponents).[3]

A third analyst may wish to talk about the "system" of relations among the abstract properties of a bureaucratic organization. (S)he might define the "elements" of the system as the degree of "centralization," the degree of "formalization," the degree of "complexity," and the level of "conflict." The "relations among the parts" of the system may be stated in a set of propositions of the type: "as the degree of centralization increases by one unit (on an arbitrary metric scale), the degree of formalization increases by three-tenths of a unit, but does so with the time shape of a first-order exponential delay of five time units." (More on "delays" later.) Here the elements of the system are general variables (centralization, formalization, complexity, etc.). The relations among these system elements are stated as abstract hypotheses about statistical regularities in the relationships between one property and another.[4]

It may seem at first that these examples of types of systems theories are fundamentally different from one another. It is certainly true that they represent quite different disciplinary interests and quite different approaches to conceptualizing, as well as different levels of analysis. Despite the seeming dissimilarity, the examples are really rather alike from a "general systems" point of view. All three systems are relatively complex in that there are numerous elements and these elements are connected in rather complicated ways.

Theorists disagree over the "right" way to define the units of analysis appropriate for theorizing. We take no position on this particular issue, other than to suspect that there is substantial virtue in rigorous theoretical research on both concrete and abstract systems, and on systems at the "micro" and "macro" levels. The critical point is that from a systems perspective there is little practical difference between theories and models that describe patterns of relations among actors and those that describe patterns of relations among aggregates and "social actors" and those that describe relations among abstract general variables. In principle at least, the notion of a system allows the possibility of models of social action that include both multiple actors and multiple traits nested hierarchically so as to cross levels of analysis in the same theory. For example, a system might consist of a number of productive organizations (each composed of divisions, work units and individuals) interacting to form an economy, which, in turn, is in interactions with other economies. Each of these entities (individuals, work units, divisions, organizations, and economies) might be thought of as having multiple properties that affect its interaction with other actors.[5]

The capacity of a system to include both variables and actors, and to allow virtually any form of relations among variables and actors, accords a great deal of flexibility in constructing theory about social action. The available flexibility, however, should not be used as an excuse for sloppiness. The first task in any systems-based theory construction is to define with great precision its *state space*. To properly specify and formalize a model, it is an absolutely necessary first step to decide what the "things" to be theorized about are. Very simply, the list of "things" in the theory constitute the state space and define the boundaries of the system.[6] Where the theorist decides to draw the boundaries of the system is, of course, highly consequential. In the field of formal organizations, for example, many early models of the relations among organizational properties have been termed "closed systems" models because of their inclusion of only variables describing the structure of the focal organization itself. These "closed" systems models are counterposed to "open" systems models that also include characteristics of the organization's environment.[7] The dispute here is over where the boundaries of the system are best drawn: Is only the organization to be included, or is the environment part of the system as well?

General systems theory and systems analysis methodologies offer little assistance in resolving such questions. In principle it is desirable to include all of the factors (be they actors or variables) that have effects on the phenomena of interest. That is, one makes the system a "closed" one by including everything within the theory. This injunction for greater inclusion from a formal systems analysis point of view makes a great deal of sense in principle, but not in practice. Only rarely do social scientists theorize about systems of action that are fully closed. In verbal specifications of theories, it is very common to find a number of telling phrases: "under certain conditions," "within limits," and "all other things being equal." These statements recognize that the theory in question has not attained closure and that consequently there are limits on the generalizability and applicability of the model. In statistical formalizations one can find equivalent (though often more hidden) statements about the lack of closure. The assumptions of randomly distributed residuals, uncorrelated residuals, and proper specification of multiequation structural equation models, for example, are intended to attain system closure. They are equivalent to saying that this specification of the model either includes all of the relevant variables, or if it does not, the parts that have been left out do not affect our understanding of the relationships among the variables that have been included.

In defining boundaries for social science theorizing, deciding what the system boundaries are is a pragmatic and paradigmatic question, not a technical one. Full "closure" of a theory is rarely or never possible. The drawing of system boundaries, then, remains one of the most difficult tasks of theory building, requiring creative insight and artistry.

Despite its arbitrary nature, the precise definition of the boundaries of a system and the listing of the elements (individuals, aggregates, and variables) of the state space is an essential first step to all successful formalizations. Systematic application of two systems concepts can often be very useful in dealing with this problem: the notions of *subsystems* and *connectivity*.

Subsystems

Like "system," the term "subsystem" can only be broadly and generally defined. If a system is the whole of a set of parts and relations among parts, a subsystem is a partition of that whole. It is usually most helpful to define subsystems in such a way as to partition a complex system into a series of smaller and simpler ones with less dense ties between than within partitions. If we were examining the network of treaty ties among nations in the world system, for example, we might well see the "system" as composed of two "subsystems" (one centered on the United States and the other on the USSR), with many ties within each subsystem, and few ties between the subsystems. If one were analyzing patterns of father-son intergenerational social mobility, it might prove useful to partition the patterns of relations into two subaggregates of "movers" and "stayers." If one were defining the historical process of class conflict and revolution, it might be most helpful to divide the "system" of action into subsystems of economic, political, and cultural/ideological production.

Most conceptual schemes in all of the social sciences have a great deal in common in how they go about partitioning systems into subsystems. This is not to say that the kinds of systems that different theoretical traditions examine are very similar, nor that they go about defining the state spaces or relations in similar ways. The commonalities among various approaches, however, do allow the formulation of some general rules that can be of considerable use in attempting to define the boundaries and partitions of a system of action.

Social scientist's models can generally be partitioned into sets of variables characterizing actors that exist within general fields or environments. In most cases, the variables in question are nested within actors, and actors are nested within a general field or environment in a relatively simple hierarchy.[8] In some cases, the models attain true multilevel complexity in which the relations among and within actors are characterized by multivariate relations, with several levels of analysis existing in the same model (e.g., individuals within groups within organizations within societies).

It is often most helpful in beginning the construction of a theory to start with the concrete actors, if there is more than one. One of the most fundamental ways that most social science theories partition systems into subsystems is by their use of actors (though not in theories that deal with relations among properties of abstracted whole systems).[9] Many sociological theories, for example, contain a single actor, such as a composite or generalized individual, organization, or society. Other theories are about two, three, or small groups of actors. Relatively few deal with any substantial numbers of actors. With the exception of some "network" approaches, sociologists who wish to theorize about large numbers of individuals tend to theorize about single aggregates or patterns of action (e.g., "the complex organization") rather than the "individuals" (be they groups, persons, classes, or whatever) that make up the pattern. Many other disciplines have a stronger taste for concreteness, and are likely to build theories about systems composed of multiple actors (each with distinctive traits) in interaction, such as families in a village or firms in a market. In any case, it is often a good first step in identifying the elements of the system to identify actors as subsystems.

The next step is to define the characteristics of each "actor" (be it an individual, a dyad, a group, a network, an organization, nation-state, etc.). The traits or variables describing each actor can often be further partitioned into subsystems of closely connected variables. In models of single whole societies, it is quite common to partition the variables into a series of subsystems: demographic, religious, political, economic, military, and so forth. In models with several actors, each actor might be described by numerous traits that denote processes within the individual giving rise to traits that affect the interaction between individuals. Here the systems are partitioned first by actors, and then by variables. In most cases, the partitioning of variables into subsystems is not an absolute matter. Variables that are closely dependent upon one another and have direct causal relations are more usefully grouped together; variables that are theorized to be connected only tenuously or through the connections along long causal chains can be partitioned into different subsystems.

In most social science theories the actions and interactions of individuals are seen as occurring within "fields" or "environments." Environmental factors are, by definition, outside of the spaces or subsystems of actors. Such environmental factors can be either constants (i.e., exogenous, or not affected by the actors) or variables that have causal relations with actors and other variables). These "emergent" or system properties are not part of the subsystems bounded within particular actors, but are nevertheless important parts of the system as a whole.

Suppose, for a moment, that we were interested in constructing a theory about the economic interaction between two national economies. The system can be partitioned first into two subsystems on the basis of actors. The actors (the national economies) can be described in terms of a number of variables (firms, capital, raw materials, labor supply, etc.), as could the interaction between the two nations (composed of flows of the factors of production, money, and commodities).

In such a model, there are a number of implicit "constants" that do not enter the model—for example, the territory occupied by each nation might be assumed to remain fixed, so there would be no need to define this fact with variables in the "environmental" subsystem of the model. Yet the two nations might well be exposed to vagaries of weather patterns that have differential impacts on the performance of their economic systems, and hence affect the trade relation between them. The weather pattern, however operationalized, would be a necessary element of the "environmental" subsystem of each actor.

There are also a number of properties here that are characteristics of the system as a whole, but not directly part of the state spaces bounded by either nation (though these properties have effects on both actors). The "supply" and "demand" for factors of production and commodities, for example, and the transaction costs of internation transfers are characteristics of the whole system (and hence a necessary part of the theory), but are not specifically part of the state space of either economy.

While these guidelines from general systems thinking are helpful, there are no fixed rules for the definition of system boundaries and the partitioning of systems into subsystems. It is very useful, however, to approach these questions in a structured fashion. Each theoretical and research tradition carries with it a very substantial conceptual baggage that can provide much of what is needed to define the systems and subsystems. In fact, much of the value of comparative statics theories and typologies lie in their identifying the boundaries and partitions of the property-space covered by theoretical models.

Implicitly or explicitly, a major role of "conceptualization" and "definition" is to identify boundaries and subsystem partitions by providing answers to the questions Who are the actors in the system? What traits describe each actor? Can these be divided into subsets? And what are the conditions outside of each actor that influence the action?

Relations Among Things: Connectivity

The first step in thinking about a problem from the systems perspective is identifying the "things" or elements that fall within the boundaries of the system. The second step is dividing them into partitions or subsystems. The next step, following from the definition of systems as "relations among things," is to identify which of the elements are connected to which others. Systems theory and particularly the derived applied field of systems analysis have a variety of useful ways of describing the relations among elements of systems. Many of these ways of describing the coupling among elements in the theoretical model are intended to reference processes operating over time; and this makes them useful for constructing theories about social dynamics.

Imagine that we have done the first step of creating a list of the elements of our theoretical model for a particular problem. We now sit with a list of actors and variables in front of us. The next step is to make a set of explicit hypotheses about which elements of our list are directly (that is, without any intervening steps) connected to other elements on the list. This is often best done using diagrams or matricies.[10] Two elements may be considered directly connected if a change in one element produces a change in the other without producing changes in other elements in the process. A change in one element may, of course, also produce changes in other elements as a result of the "first order" change, and may also have indirect as well as direct connections with some other element. These effects, however, are automatically specified when the full "first order" connectivity of the elements is created, and hence are not a source of immediate concern in constructing the theory.

The notion of "connectivity" in a set of theoretical elements is not unique to the systems approach. In fact, analogous concepts exist in all of the major languages commonly used by social scientists to formalize multivariate relations. In path-analytic terms, two elements are connected (at the first order) if there is a "direct effect" of one on the other.[11] In flow-graph terms, the elements are connected if a signal originating at one point reaches the other point without passing through any connecting paths.[12] In the language of directed graphs, two elements are connected if they share an "edge."[13] In the language of differential equations and "systems dynamics," two elements are connected at the first order if one element enters into an expression determining the rate of change in the other.[14]

The creation of a list of the elements of a theory and a complete specification of the connectivity of the elements is a good practice for any theory building exercise. The resulting artifact, be it a diagram, matrix, a collection of bivariate propositions, or some other form of representation of the "skeleton" can be of substantial interest in itself. When a theory is represented as a set of elements connected at the first order, it constitutes a "graph" or "network" and can be described as having certain properties. Theoretical models, as well as social networks and graphs, can thus be compared in terms of their formal properties of "density," "centrality," and so on. A good understanding of the nature of the theory itself as a structure is often helpful later in the process of analyzing models derived from it, because we can identify its most important variables and relations.

Relations Among Things: Control

Where the concepts of systems theory and systems analysis are of particular utility is in describing in greater detail the ways that elements are connected. Many of the applications of systems theory are in the area of machine processes, and the logic of describing production processes can often be generalized to other phenomena. It is often useful (though not necessary) to distinguish between direct connections among material things and linkages based on information. Linkages among material quantities can be termed *chains*. Connections among informational elements or between informational and material elements constitute the "control structures" of systems and are characterized as *loops* and *feedback*.

Most social scientist's models involve relatively few material elements and chains, but often very large numbers of informational elements and complex control structures. The material elements and chains, however, are often the central focus of the theory and are a good place to start in mapping connectivity. After the basic chains or production processes are mapped, then attention can be turned to the informational or control structures that monitor and control these chains. An example might help to clarify some of these distinctions and to illustrate the strategy for mapping connections among elements in a theory.

Suppose that we were interested in building a model of the age structure of a population in order to project the probable size of the aged population over time. As we will see in later chapters, this simple demographic example is a prototype of systems that occur with great frequency in all of the social sciences. At any one point in time, we can divide the population into groups (say, young, middle aged, and aged), with individuals moving from one category to the next one after a fixed waiting time. In this way of thinking about population dynamics, there are three material "elements" or "things" in the model: the number of the young, the number of the middle aged, and the number of the aged. (There is actually another level as well, a "sink," or "absorbing state," called "deceased.") These states—the young, the middle aged, and the old—are connected by a "chain": the same material quantity—an individual—moves from one state to another. We can draw a simple diagram describing the connectivity of these "material" quantities.

Our "simple" example, however, is not quite so simple as it seems. To discuss the dynamics of population we must specify the mechanisms and timing of the transitions from one state to another (e.g., from young to middle aged). To do this we need to specify the rate at which transitions occur. That is, we must describe the structure that controls the rates of flow between the states in the chain.

What governs or controls change in the number of young persons, the number of middle-aged persons, and the number of aged persons in our simple model? Young people are created by birth and disappear through either death or transition to the "middle aged" category (assuming no immigration or emigration). The rate at which births occur is determined by a large number of variables, including the current number of middle-aged people. That is, a variable that is later in the chain (the number of middle-aged people) is a cause of a variable that occurs earlier in the chain (the number of young). This is an example of "control" by "feedback." The number of young people who exist at any point in time is also determined by the rate of deaths among them and by the rate at which they make transitions to the "middle aged" category. The number

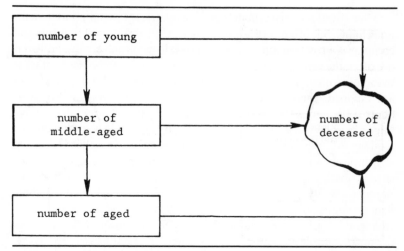

Figure 2.1: A simple chain of material states.

of deaths and the number of transitions to middle age are controlled by many factors, including the current number of young people. That is, the number of deaths among the young is a function both of external factors and the size of the population at risk. The current number of young people is a cause or part of the "control" loop governing the rate of change in the number of young people. If we continued our consideration of the dynamics of this simple chain we would see that there is a good deal more to the "control structure" of this simple model, as is shown in Figure 2.2.

The more elaborate structure of Figure 2.2, in contrast to Figure 2.1, illustrates the second step in the process of thinking about the connectivity among the elements of a theoretical model. The linkages in Figure 2.1 are the place to start in specifying the connectivity among the elements of theoretical models. These connections are of the most fundamental type, involving the actual movement of measurable quantities from one status to another. Many of the theories constructed by social scientists involve only a single chain of this type, and sometimes the chain consists of only a single element. We will examine models of this type at some length in the second section of this volume. Most other models of concern to social scientists include a relatively small number of chains that are interconnected by (often quite complicated) control mechanisms. We will examine some models of this type in the third section.

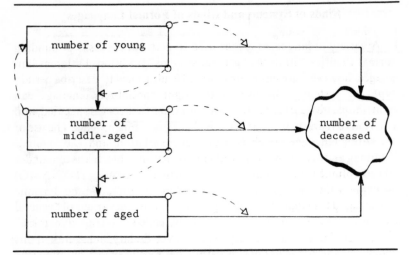

Figure 2.2: A simple chain with control structure.

The second kind of linkages among elements, the "control" or "information" systems as illustrated in Figure 2.2, is where the real action lies in most theories. Connections of this type do not involve the actual physical transition of a quantity from one state to another, but rather express effects on the rates at which flows or transitions occur. In the language of systems, "information" is "taken off" by "monitoring" and acts as input to "decisions" that govern the rates at which variables change or transitions occur. In the more common language of discourse in theory construction, connections of the control system type shown in Figure 2.2 are the "causal parameters" that describe what variables in the model have effects on the rates of change in other variables. Mapping this form of connectivity is, therefore, central to the task of building a theory.

The first step in using "systems" thinking to specify connectivity should be to find the "chains" of states that represent actual physical movements of things. The second step is to identify the causal connections among the elements of the model, so that the "informational" and "control" mechanisms can be mapped. As with the consideration of the elements of the theory, mapping the connections among the elements is made much easier by the use of formal languages designed for this purpose.

Kinds of Systems and Kinds of Formal Languages

A variety of languages can be used to perform the tasks of building formal theories within the "general systems" tradition. Different languages, however, are easier or more difficult to use to describe certain types of systems. The use of the right specialized language can contribute substantially to the ease with which a theory is specified, and can lead to many new insights in the theory building process. The use of the wrong language can obscure theoretical relations and lead to mind-numbing and arid formalisms rather than new insights. In the remainder of this volume we are going to use one particular language (DYNAMO) to express theories about continuous-state continuous-time dynamic processes. This language is closely connected to one variant of "general systems" thinking about social relations called "systems dynamics." Before we turn to the necessary details of vocabulary and syntax of this language, and to the use of simulation methods in theory building (the topics of the next three chapters), we should be a bit clearer about the strengths and weaknesses of this language.

Systems Dynamics and DYNAMO

One of the most widely used languages for formalization of systems theories of continuous-state continuous-time dynamics in the social sciences was developed by Jay W. Forrester and his colleagues at MIT. The "systems dynamics" approach to thinking about problems of this type was developed by these scholars in direct connection with a computer language called DYNAMO. DYNAMO has been used in the social and physical sciences to construct simulation models to study a wide array of substantive problems.[15] The computer language is available for both mainframe and micro systems, and can be implemented under most major operating systems.[16] All of the applications in this volume were prepared on DOS type personal computers, operating under the UCSD Pascal system.

The "systems dynamics" approach to thinking about continuous-state continuous-time dynamics provides one very powerful way of applying the "general systems" concepts that we have been discussing above to particular social science problems. It is not, however, necessary that one accept all of the peculiarities of the conceptual baggage of "systems dynamics" in order to apply systems thinking or the DYNAMO language. In the next chapter we will examine in some detail both the strengths and the weaknesses of the systems dynamics approach, along with the basics of DYNAMO.

The main ideas of the systems dynamics method are embodied in the DYNAMO language, which acts as a "translator" between the everyday language used by the theorist and the mathematics of nonlinear difference and differential equations that are calculated by the computer. Computers, by and large, are quite unable to understand everyday language (though the problem is being worked on); social science theorists, by and large, are quite unable to understand simultaneous nonlinear differential equation systems (and this is, perhaps, a problem that we should be working on). The role of DYNAMO is to allow the theorist to state ideas about social dynamics in a language that is close to everyday use (though it is different enough that we need to spend some time on its vocabulary and syntax) and to convert these statements into mathematical systems that can be simulated by the computer and understood by experimentation. With a little practice and persistence, the DYNAMO language can be used to state almost any well-specified theory about social dynamics. The chapters in the second and third parts of this volume provide a number of examples that can act as starting points for others.

When Not to Use DYNAMO

The systems dynamics method of thinking about dynamic systems and the DYNAMO language have been and can be very widely applied to social science problems. This particular approach to thinking about theory building and this particular language, however, are not the right choice for all classes of problems of interest to social science theorists.

Social science theorists are rightly concerned with the study of statics as well as dynamics. There are a number of specialized languages that are more useful for the study of statics than DYNAMO. Where the concern is primarily with discrete-state statics (as, for example, in the study of the structure of networks), a powerful array of specialized concepts, language, and tools have been developed for formal representation based on graph theory, smallest space analysis and the like. There are also well-developed languages for the analysis of continuous-state statics that should be used in preference to DYNAMO for problems of that type. The most powerful and familiar of such formalisms for dealing with continuous-state statics are "structural equations," and their implementation into "path analysis." More powerful extensions of these languages—particularly "flow graphs"—based on linear programing, electrical and hydraulic engineering have also been advocated for complex feedback systems.

There are also well-developed alternative languages for the formalization and analysis of dynamic systems that may be of greater utility than DYNAMO in some circumstances. Where the phenomenon to be understood is most easily thought of in discrete state/discrete time terms, queuing theory and event analysis provide tools. Applications of "game theory" thinking and language are perhaps the most familiar examples of such systems in the social sciences. Several computer simulation languages (e.g., SIMULA) are much easier to adapt to problems of this type than is DYNAMO. Where the focus is on phenomena most usefully conceived of as having discrete states but with continuous time dynamics, event-history methods based on Markov processes can provide a very powerful complement to simulation analysis using DYNAMO. Several other simulation languages designed for the modeling of "mixed" categorical and continuous systems (e.g., GASP, SLAM) may also be usefully applied.

There are also alternatives to DYNAMO for the analysis of continuous-state, continuous-time dynamics. By far the most common language for formalizing theories of continuous-state, continuous-time dynamics (i.e., systems in which continuously occurring change in some variables have effects on the rates of change in other variables) is differential equations. Differential equations and the calculus provide very powerful tools for concisely describing and making deductions from statements about rates of change in continuous variables. As briefly discussed in the previous chapter, there are some limitations on the types of systems to which differential equation mathematics can be usefully applied. There are also several competing alternative simulation languages for continuous-state, continuous-time or mixed discrete and continuous state systems, including CSSL and GASP/SLAM. These languages are equally powerful, but are less grounded in general systems theory (which may be regarded by some as an advantage, by others as a disadvantage).

Conclusions

Many of the basic ideas of general systems theory and systems analysis provide useful ways of approaching the task of building theories about social dynamics. In this chapter we have examined the notion of systems and examined some ways of identifying and partitioning the state spaces of systems and mapping the connectivity and forms of dynamic relationships among state space elements.

With these somewhat lengthy, but necessary, basic ideas that help to organize thinking about dynamic systems in hand, we can turn our attention to the mechanics of building theories of social dynamics in the systems dynamics tradition using DYNAMO.

Notes

1. The concept of "system" has been widely discussed in the social and physical sciences. Some general introductions to systems thinking and systems concepts across a variety of disciplines are provided by Ashby (1958, 1962), Bertalanffy (1968), Buckley (1967, 1968), essays in Demerath and Peterson (eds., 1967), Emery (ed., 1969), Grinker (1965), Hall (1962), Hare (1967), Klir (1971), Kremyansky (1960), Kuhn (1963, 1975), Lange (1965), Luenberger (1979), Mesarovic (1961, 1964, 1968), Sommerhoff (1969), and Weiner (1948).

2. To get a flavor of the breadth and variety of systems types of theorizing about microdynamics in the social sciences, the reader might look up Barnes (1972), Berger et al. (1966), Bonini (1963), Brams (1975), Caplow (1968), Cohen (1962), Coleman (1972), Davis and Leinhardt (1972), Neumann and Morgenstern (1947), Rapoport (1960, 1966), Shubik (ed., 1964), White (1963), and Whitten and Wolfe (1973).

3. Applications of systems thinking to aggregates and "social actors" composed of networks of individuals are very common. A flavor of the diversity of problems and approaches can be had from Boulding (1978), Bremer (1977), Buckley (ed., 1968), Cole et al. (1973), Cyert and March (1963), Dutton and Starbuck (1971), Guetzkow et al. (eds., 1972), Meadows et al. (1974), Patten (ed., 1971), Perrow (1984), and White (1963, 1965).

4. Some examples of the more abstracted use of "systems" concepts and tools in various social sciences can be seen in Bayless (1966), Bellman (1961), Burns et al. (1985), Burns and Buckley (1976), Deutsch (1963), Easton (1958, 1965), Emery and Trist (1960), Kennedy (1962), and Parsons (1937, 1957, 1966). The particular example used here is derived from Hage (1972).

5. Complex hierarchical and elaborately partitioned systems of both actors and variables are discussed in particular by Pattee (1973) and Baumgartner et al. (1976). Two particular multilevel models are quite interesting in the current context. One, by Kochen and Deutsch (1980) deals with the statics of formal organization; the other is a dynamic model of the world system by Mesarovic and Pestel (1974).

6. The question of closing systems by including all relevant elements is discussed at some length by Forrester (1968). Foster et al. (1957) offer some provocative comments on the question of indeterminacy in systems resulting from lack of closure.

7. There are a number of interesting discussion of the boundary problem. In the sociology of formal organizations, for example, the question of "What is an organization?" is frequently and variously addressed. Interesting discussions are offered by Hage (1980) and Perrow (1979) on this particular version of the more general boundary question.

8. The notion of multilevel processes is one of the most exciting areas of development in general systems theory. Some of the most interesting social science essays on this subject can be found in Baumgartner et al. (1976) and Burns et al. (1985).

9. Models of theories that involve only relations among abstract properties of a system or "general variables" are the exception to the rule of partitioning state spaces first by actors. Such models have only a single actor: the system.

10. An excellent illustration of the application of matrix methods for analyzing connectedness is contained in Brunner and Brewer (1971).

11. Excellent introductions to structural equations and path analysis are now quite numerous. Still, two of the originals are among the best: Blalock (1971) and Duncan (1975).

12. See, for an introduction to flowgraph analysis in the social sciences, Heise (1975). A more general and mathematical treatment can be found in Lorens 1964.

13. Many of the basic methods of directed graphs and network analysis are described in Barnes (1972), Berge (1962), Busacker and Saaty (1965), and Knoke and Kuklinski (1984).

14. See, for discussions of the idea of connectivity within the systems dynamics tradition: Forrester (1968), Pugh (1980), Roberts et al. (1983), and Richardson and Pugh (1981).

15. A partial list of work utilizing systems dynamics methods and the DYNAMO language shows the wide array of substantive problems that the language can be used to address: Alfeld and Graham (1976), Cole et al. (eds., 1973), Coyle (1977), J. W. Forrester (1961, 1968, 1969, 1973), N. B. Forrester (1973), Hamilton et al. (1969), Jarmain (1963), Levin et al. (1975), Levin et al. (1976), Lyneis (1980), Mass (1975), Mass (ed., 1974), Meadows (1970), Meadows et al. (1974), Meadows and Meadows (eds., 1973), Meadows et al. (1973), Randers (1980), Richardson and Pugh (1981), Roberts (1978), Roberts et al. (1983), Schroeder et al. (eds., 1975), and Weymar (1968).

16. Information on DYNAMO software is available from Addison-Wesley Publishers of Reading, Massachusetts (who carry some PC versions), and from Pugh-Roberts Associates of Cambridge, Massachusetts (who carry a full line of mainframe and micro applications).

3

The Systems Dynamics Approach

The State Space

The *state space* of any system is simply the list of variables and their ranges describing the boundaries of the system.[1] The term *state* is used synonymously with the term *variable,* defining some characteristic of the phenomenon which takes a range of values. System states, like other variables, may be discrete (that is, "qualitative") or continuous (that is, "quantitative"). For example, the state space of a model describing political relations between two nations might contain the qualitative state "war," which is thought of as being either present or absent; an alternative formulation of the same problem might see the state space as containing a quantitative variable "level of aggression" that varies continuously from none to total war. In studying the dynamics of interaction among a small group of actors (individual persons, business firms, clans, etc.) one might conceive of the problem of the structure of network connections among the actors as one of qualitative states (i.e., each pair of actors are or are not "tied" to one another) or quantitative (i.e., the strength of the tie between each pair of actors varies in intensity from zero to some upper limit).

The system dynamics approach generally, and the DYNAMO language in particular, has a bias in favor of quantitative states. Because of the nature of the language it is easier to talk about continuously varying quantities than discrete states. Other languages for modeling continuous time dynamics are more balanced in this regard, but have other features that can create awkwardness of use.[2]

The systems dynamics tradition is somewhat unusual among systems approaches for the way that it conceptualizes and describes state spaces. All quantities describing the status of the system in question are regarded as being either "material" or "informational," with separate vocabularies and syntaxes being applied to the two categories.[3] Other approaches within the systems tradition do not draw this sharp distinction.[4] While the distinction between material and informational states is not necessary in the DYNAMO language, the structure of the language predisposes one to think in these terms.

"Material" and "informational" states are distinguished by writers in the systems dynamics tradition because it is felt that the principles governing the dynamics of physical quantities are fundamentally different from the dynamics of informational quantities.[5] Material quantities are regarded as "conserved" in that they persist over time and must occupy some state at all times. The most obvious examples of such things are physical objects such as people, money, and machines. These objects may occupy only one status at a time (e.g., each person is either young, middle aged, aged, or deceased). Another, less elegant way of putting it, is that material quantities are "used up" by being "used." For example, once the transition from youth to middle age has been made, individuals who fall in the middle aged category do not fall in the youth category (however much they may wish to).

"Information" states, in contrast, are regarded by systems dynamics as being fundamentally "nonconserved." That is, "information" is not "used up" by being "used." If I know something and tell you, we both know. This is a "nonconserved" dynamic. Material objects (such as money) may used by actors as "signals" to convey information, but are nonetheless conserved quantities. If I have a dollar and I give it to you, I no longer have it. This is a material or "conserved" dynamic. The distinction between kinds of states in the system dynamics tradition is both conceptual and mathematical. Quantities that persist—"material" states—are described by the mathematics of integration and the calculus, whereas quantities that are nonconserved—"information" states—are described by the algebra of differences.[6]

The distinction between material and informational states in the system dynamics approach is both attractive and troubling. At a philosophical level, critics both within and without the systems tradition reject the distinction as a false dichotomy. Information theorists, for example, insist on the treatment of all "states" as informational; the new physics is struggling with the seemingly no longer valid distinction between material and informational. At the mathematical level as well, there has been criticism of the distinction between "conserved" and "nonconserved" states. One consequence of rigidly maintaining the distinction is to lead to models that contain both differential and difference equations and hence draw on both calculus and algebra to describe state space dynamics. As the more mathematically inclined correctly point out, the distinction is unnecessary and inelegant from a mathematical point of view, and restricts the applicability of the tools of direct solution to systems dynamics models.[7]

The systems dynamics approach distinction between material and informational states can also be defended against these criticisms, at least on pragmatic grounds. While both the philosophical and mathematical critiques have a good deal of validity, the particular distinction between conserved and nonconserved quantities can be of considerable utility in social science construction.

At the philosophical and conceptual level, the distinction between material things that are persistent and "conserved" on one hand and "informational" things that are nonconserved on the other accords well with the way that most social scientists conceptualize social behavior. In thinking about social dynamics, most theorists tend to distinguish between acts and the meanings attached to acts. "Action" and "interaction" by themselves are most often seen as having a physical (behavioral) character that is logically separable from the meaning attached to them; action and interaction become "*social* action" and "*social* interaction" when they take on meanings as symbols for other actors. By distinguishing sharply between material and informational states, the systems dynamics approach and the DYNAMO language tend to structure the analyst's thinking about dynamics along those same lines most commonly used by sociologists, anthropologists, political scientists, and historians.

The mixed difference and differential mathematics peculiar to systems dynamics models restrict their analyzability by direct solution. At this point, there is a clear disjuncture of approach between that of mathematically inclined practitioners (especially in political science, economics, and sociology) and the intent of modelers in the systems dynamics tradition. Mathematical modelers dealing with continuous state/continuous time dynamics have shown a strong preference for models expressed as simultaneous linear differential equations. This preference is based on the use of direct solution as the method of choice for analysis of, and deductions from, the formalized theories. The systems dynamics approach is predicated on experimentation and simulation, rather than direct solution, as the primary method by which theorists can understand and make deductions from their theories. Simulation and experimentation are less powerful methods of understanding and analyzing a theory and its consequences than direct solution; however, greater flexibility of expression is obtained, and as a consequence far more complex phenomena and theories can be expressed. The mixed mathematics capabilities of the systems dynamics approach does not prevent the formulation of strict differential or strict difference equation models. It does lead one in the direction of flexible expression and away from mathematical analyzability.

The distinction between material states and informational states in the systems dynamics approach and the DYNAMO language is, therefore, consequential and reflects certain biases. By and large, these biases may be appealing to theorists interested in constructing formal theories of social dynamics. The distinctions between "conserved" and "nonconserved" quantities or between "material" and "informational" things seems to accord well with the distinctions between behaviors and meanings common in social science discourse. The greater ease of expression possible utilizing mixed mathematics and abandoning direct solution as a method of deduction is also appealing because it allows for the expression of quite complex relationships and for analysis by simulation, experimentation, and discovery, rather than by direct deduction and solution.

Material States: "Levels"

The most basic elements of theories expressed in the system dynamics language of DYNAMO are material states, called *levels*. In approaching the construction of a dynamic model, the identification of the levels of the system is the place to start. For example, in the simple model we examined above as Figure 2.1 and Figure 2.2, the levels of the system were the number of young, middle aged, aged, and deceased persons. These levels are continuous variables that are "conservative" and accumulate over time at rates governed by causal variables.[8]

In the diagraming conventions of the DYNAMO language, "levels" are represented as rectangles, with arrows flowing into and/or out of them.[9] The imagery is from fluid dynamics, and is intended to suggest a tank or storage location for quantities that flow into and out of the state, as in the flow of water into and/or out of a tank. There is no necessity in adopting the particular conventions of the DYNAMO language to represent the states and connections among them in a theory about dynamics. We will use these symbols throughout the volume, however. The more general languages of flow diagrams and circuit diagrams could also be used effectively to represent dynamics, but do not have quite the same evocative quality as the DYNAMO symbols, and are not as closely tied to the DYNAMO language.[10] At various times in this volume we will use both DYNAMO diagrams and simpler (but less specific) "circles and arrows" diagrams of connectivity, as suits the needs of the presentation. All theory building exercises usually begin with the simpler form of diagrams that show only the elements and connectivity among them; DYNAMO diagraming conventions are a useful tool in the step of translating such diagrams into equation form.

"Levels" are used in the DYNAMO language with a very specific syntax. The content and structure of the "sentences" are important in helping to structure thinking about dynamics. The statement below is a fairly typical "level equation" describing the "material state" of the number of persons in a population (POP.K). It illustrates all of the important features of the the systems dynamics language for describing the dynamics of such states.

L   POP.K = POP.J+DT(BIRTHS.JK+IMMIG.JK–DEATH.JK–EMIG.JK)

This somewhat intimidating-looking expression can be readily translated into plain English: The number of persons at time point "K" (POP.K) is equal to the number of persons at the previous time point "J" (POP.J), plus the integration or accumulation over time (DT) of a quantity. The quantity, in this case, includes the rate of births during the time interval between J and K (BIRTHS.JK), the rate of immigration (IMMIG.JK), the rate of deaths (DEATH.JK), and the rate of emigration (EMIG.JK). The "L" in at the beginning of the line is used to identify the "equation type," and is used by the DYNAMO simulation routines to control the order in which calculations are performed. There are a number of things to note about the way that this sentence is constructed.

First, note that the dynamic relation is conservative in the sense discussed previously. Population at a later point in time is equal to population at the earlier point in time, except as modified by births, deaths, immigration and emigration.[11]

Second, note that the "dependent variable" on the left side of the equation has a single time script: It describes the status of the variable at some particular instant in time (that is, "K"). Because this is the case, the level or status of the variable in the state space always refers to a quantity of things—such as numbers of people, percentages of national product, or degree of attitudinal support. It is a good practice, in thinking about the states of a system, to clearly define the "units" of all such variables as part of the process of defining terms.

Third, in contrast to the single time script of the "dependent" variable, each of the quantities in the expression to be integrated (that is, births, deaths, immigration, and emigration) carry two time referents: "JK." These quantities are called "rates" (more on them later), and are expressed in units per unit time. That is, for example, BIRTHS.JK in the level equation above are measured in numbers of events occurring between time point J and time point K. The "causal" factors determining population (that is, the independent variables in the equation, if one prefers), then, are explicitly dynamic quantities. They express the rates at which certain processes are occurring with respect to time.

The final important thing to note about the syntax of statements about "material states" is that there are numerous elements on the righthand side of the equation. Alternatively, one might say that there are several simultaneous causal processes producing change in the system state. In this particular case, two processes produce increments in the population (the rate of births and the rate of immigration), and two produce decrements (the rate of deaths and of emigration). Each of these processes is explicated in greater detail in "rate" and supporting equations that we will consider shortly.

The syntax of the level statement with its multiple possible causal processes is a good stimulus to clear thinking about the dynamics of states. The structure of the statement itself leads one to ask what causes the level to go up or down, and do each of these causal processes have the same or separate determinants? The syntax should lead one to consider whether the causes for increases and decreases are the same. In the case of population dynamics, of course, they are not; many social processes, however, may be reversible in the sense of having the same causes for both increases and decreases in level over time.

The syntax of the level statement also urges one to think in multivariate terms by allowing the easy expression of multiple simultaneously operating causal processes. This is the "normal" way of thinking about problems in multivariate statistical models, but is not always the language of verbal theory. Verbal formulations tend to be highly simplified (and perhaps oversimplified) ways of stating theories as bivariate "propositions"; the systems dynamics level equation leads one to automatically consider the simultaneous operation of multiple causal processes. The syntax of the level statement makes quite explicit what most social scientists mean when they refer to changes in the levels of particular variables over time as resulting from the simultaneous operation of many factors or the "conjuncture" of historical forces.

Occasionally it is useful to think about a level that has only things "flowing into" it, or only "flowing out" of it. In the simple population dynamic that we examined as Figure 2.1 and 2.2, for example, the level "deceased" is such a quantity. Individuals flow into this level, but they do not exit (at least for the purposes of most social science models). In the language of systems, states that have only processes incrementing them over time are called *absorbing states,* while states that have only processes decrementing them over time are called *sources.* In the peculiar jargon of the language of the system dynamics tradition, these special kinds of levels are termed *sources* and *sinks* and are represented in diagrams with a special symbol resembling an amoeba.

While it is perfectly possible to formulate a dynamic model without giving special consideration to the question of where material quantities ultimately come from and where they finally go, the existence of the special symbols and concepts of sources and sinks can lead one to ask important questions that help to clarify and specify theories. Too often we do not realize that we are theorizing about a part of a process in our theories, not the whole phenomena from source to sink. These devices, of course, also lead to asking silly questions that result in trivial answers, as in the simple population model example.

Most of the dynamic processes addressed by social scientists tend to involve relatively simple chains of levels governed by quite complex control systems. The notions of sources and sinks are helpful in improving theory specification about such processes in two ways. First, they lead one to consider, for each state in the theory, what the previous link in the causal chain was, and what the next link in the causal chain may be. This can often lead to elaboration of the model in interesting and valuable ways. Second, the specification of the sources and sinks of "conserved" processes provides one way of understanding the boundaries of the phenomenon analyzed by the theory. We may choose, for some purposes, to regard the source of a material state as exogenous. In representing this as a diagram or level equation, the exogenous variable becomes a "source." Designation of a level as a source indicates that we are not going to specify its causes as part of the theory (i.e., it is "exogeneous"). Similarly, designation of a given level as a sink indicates that we regard it as having no consequences for other variables in the theory. Both types of statements are thus clear ways of identifying some of the "limits" of the theory we are developing. As with all statements of limits, the choice of which states are sources and sinks is a pragmatic one, defining the boundaries of the phenomenon for the purposes of the construction of the theory.

Specification of the material levels or states of a system is the first very necessary step in fully formalizing a dynamic system. Once we understand the boundaries and limits of the material or conserved quantities, the next step is to describe the informational levels and connections among them that complete the definition of the state space of the theory.

Information States: "Auxiliaries"

A large proportion of the state space of most models involves descriptions of the current levels of "information" or "nonconserved" quantities. For example, the perceptions of acts, cognitions about them, formulation of decisions, and mapping of strategy can all be considered "informational." Economic actors make decisions on the basis of prices, political actors seek to gauge "public opinion," individuals form attitudes on the basis of observing behaviors. All of these processes involve "levels" of information. More generally, all of the elements of the "control" processes that govern the dynamics of change in levels or material chains are represented in systems analysis generally (and system dynamics particularly) as informational.

In our simple model of population dynamics (Figure 2.2) for example, the "informational" or "control structure" is the portion of model that shows how the rates of "flow" between the "levels" (i.e., young, middle aged, aged, deceased) are controlled by information flows.

Because of the special importance assigned to "information" in systems theory, a somewhat different vocabulary and syntax has been developed by systems dynamicists than that normally used for "material" states. In the diagraming conventions of DYNAMO, informational states are represented as circles, with "flows" of information denoted by dashed lines. To serve as a starting point for discussion, part of our original population dynamics model (Figure 2.2) has been elaborated with these symbols in Figure 3.1.

The informational level "number at risk" in this very simple example is a direct function of the material level "number of young." The dotted line connecting the "number of young" and the "number at risk," however, does not represent the actual movement of people from one state to another. Rather, the flows of information are "nonconservative," and the dashed line indicates only the "take off" or "monitoring" of information about the material state "young," not the actual movement of persons. Similarly, the connections between the informational state "number at risk" and the flows between the states of young and middle aged, or the states of young and deceased, do not represent movement or change in physical things. The "number at risk" is a piece of information that is used in the determination of the rates of transition between states, but the information is not "used up" by being used. Hence, this "flow" as well is represented with a broken line and the little circle representing an information "take off" or "monitoring."

There are also, in Figure 3.1, two "information states" represented by the special symbols of circles with an intersecting line segment. These "information states" are "constants"—quantities that are used in explicating the control system, but which are not, in themselves, determined by other variables in the theory. These quantities are the

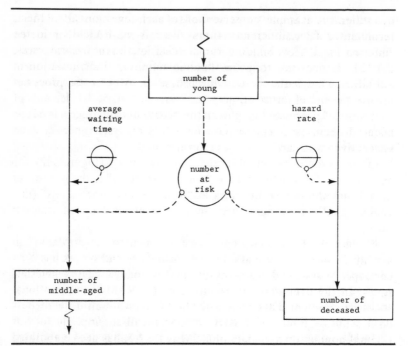

Figure 3.1: The roles of auxiliaries and constants.

informational equivalents of the "sources" and "sinks" of the conserved parts of the state space. Of course, in our simple model, a next step of elaboration might well be to turn one of the "constants"—the hazard rate—into a "variable," or information state that is a function of other variables.

The information states, or "auxiliaries," of most models describing social dynamics can be numerous and connected in complicated ways. Suppose, for example, that we were modeling the interaction between two nations engaged in an arms race. (We will develop this particular model at some length in a later chapter.) Each nation bases its behavior on its own goals, preferences, and capacities, but also on its perceptions of actions being taken by the other. In the simplest case, these perceptions might be entirely accurate and nonproblematic monitoring of the level of armaments held by the opponent. This kind of relationship would be expressed in the sentence (equation) in DYNAMO:

A   PARMS.K = ARMS.K

That is, the level of arms perceived (PARMS.K) at time K is equal to the actual number of arms at time K (ARMS.K). Note two things about this statement: It is not "conservative" (at each time point, PARMS is recalculated from other quantities; there is no PARMS.J in the equation for PARM.K). And the creation of the information state PARMS.K does not result in the destruction or transformation of ARMS.K. That is, the creation of information by perception does not use up the object perceived.

It might well be that the informational monitoring process is not so simple as the auxiliary equation above proposes. Lets look at an alternative specification of the process that creates the informational level "perceived arms" or PARMS:

A   PARMS.K = DELAY3(ARMSI.JK,2)
X   +CONST(ARMS.K+NORMRN(FEAR,10))

Because of its length, it was necessary to carry this statement beyond a single "logical record," and the statement is continued on a second (X-type) record. This formulation suggests a much more complex process of how information about the level of an opponent's arms is perceived. Roughly, this statement can be translated as follows: The level of arms that we perceive our opponent to have at time K (PARMS.K) is the sum of two complex quantities. The first is a delayed perception (in this case, a third-order exponential delay with an average length of two time periods: DELAY3(ARMSI.JK,2)) of the rate at which our opponent has been adding to his arms stock over the preceding time period (ARMSI.JK). The second quantity is some fixed multiplier (CONST) of our opponent's current level of arms (ARMS.K) plus an amount of normally distributed noise (NORMRN). The amount of this noise, or error in perception, has a mean of some constant quantity (FEAR), and a standard deviation of 10 units.

This particular specification is probably not a very useful one for describing the cognitive processes that actually occur in arms races. It does, however, illustrate some important points. By distinguishing clearly between "material" flows on one hand, and the "information" that is monitored and transformed to "control" these flows, a great deal of structure is forced on the theory constructor. In this simple example we are led to the important insight that arms races are governed by perceptions of threat that may be imperfect reflections of the material conditions. And we are required to be quite specific about where information comes from, how it is transformed, and where it goes to create the control system that governs the flows and transformations of the material states of the system.

The syntax of statements about the determinants of informational levels ("auxiliary" statements) is very flexible.[12] Virtually any kind of terms may be used, and they may be combined in virtually every possible fashion, including special functions involving time and nonlinear relations. Informational levels can be created out of information "monitored" from material states, other informational states, rates of change, and constant terms. In our example above, a variety of constants (FEAR), levels (ARMS.K), and rates of change in levels (ARMSI.JK) are all used to create the perceived level of arms. None of these quantities on the right-hand side, however, are "used up" or transformed in the process.

The "independent variables" in the auxiliary equation can be combined in a variety of ways. Often simple linear relations are plausible specifications (addition, subtraction, multiplication, division), but often nonlinear combinations (such as thresholds), or combinations involving noise, delay, and distortion are necessary to mimic the informational processes of social actors. A variety of shorthand tools for some of the most common types of complex relations are provided in the vocabulary of the language itself (see Chapter 4), and others can be created (user-defined macros). The much greater flexibility of the language when dealing with information than with material things reflects the prior assumption that information dynamics are fundamentally different from material dynamics.

The state space of any pattern of social dynamics, then, can be defined using the "level" and "auxiliary" equations of the DYNAMO language. The particular syntax of these forms of statements about the elements of the state space reflect some peculiarities of the conceptual approach of a particular theoretical school—that of "systems dynamics." These peculiarities of the language for describing the state space of a theory are, in most cases, helpful and consistent with the way that most theorists think about social dynamics. The language, however, is also quite flexible (though not infinitely so), so that questions of what are "levels" and "auxiliaries," as well as what is meant by terms such as "sources," "sinks," and "constants" are open to the pragmatic definition of the theory constructor.

Once the elements of the state space, both material and informational, have been described, the next step in the process of theory building is to describe the processes that determine the rates of change in elements of the state space. That is, we must next specify how the causal connections work across states and time.

Rates of Change

The "levels" of a system define the status of its material states at a point in time, but do not speak directly to the issue of the dynamics of the system. "Level" equations make reference to rates of change (the "JK" terms), but do not explain these rates. "Auxiliary" equations, on the other hand, describe both the informational elements of the state space and the over-time relations among these elements. After the state space of a theory has been defined with the tools discussed above, attention must be turned to the dynamics of the conserved states: That is, what causes the state of the system to change from one time point to the next. In the system dynamics approach, the hypotheses about the causes of change are embodied in separate statements, called "rates," with their own special syntax.[13]

Recall for a moment our earlier example of a level equation describing a very simple model of population dynamics:

L   POP.K = POP.J+DT(BIRTHS.JK+IMMIG.JK−DEATHS.JK−EMIG.JK)

Again, this statement says that the size of the population at instant K is equal to the size of the population at some prior time point, J, plus the integration (or accumulation, if you prefer) of births, deaths, immigrations, and emigrations that occur at certain rates per unit time across the interval between J and K. Births, deaths, immigrations, and emigrations are thought of as occurring continuously across the time interval between J and K.

The purpose of rate equations is to describe the "causes" of these rates, that is, to specify the effects of causal factors on the rate at which the level (in this case, population) is changing. Causal effects operate on the rates of change, which are decomposed into a series of separate processes: births, deaths, immigrations, and emigrations. The level of the population, then, is really just a momentary snapshot of the accumulated consequences of causal processes (rates) that are occurring continuously in time.

Systems dynamics models, like models formulated more directly into differential equations, are really speaking to the causes of rates of change in the states of the system. A system dynamics flow diagram of our simple population model will help at this point both to reiterate the notion of dynamic models as revolving around rates of change and to introduce diagraming conventions.

The symbol for a "rate" in the systems dynamics flowgraph conventions is "milk-can" shaped and is intended to invoke an image of a

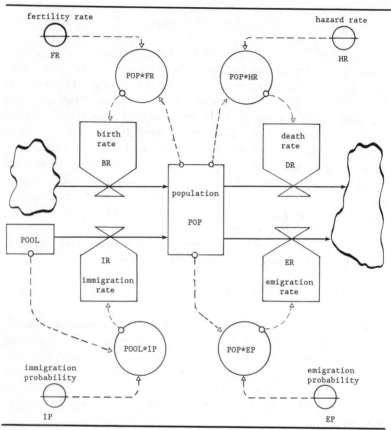

Figure 3.2: Rates in a simple population model.

gateway or valve controlling the "flow" into or out of a level. All flows into and out of levels must contain such valves to define the rate at which increments or decrements to the level in question occur. In our current model, population change is a result of four forces that either add to or subtract from the level of the population and which have different determinants. If any of the flows in question (that is, any of the rates) had the same causes, they could be combined into a single-rate statement, though the theorist might wish to keep separate statements for each theoretically important factor for ease of explication. Again, mathematical elegance is not the chief goal of formal theory in the DYNAMO approach.

The diagram is very useful in showing what factors are hypothesized to contribute to the rate of change in population by their effects on births, deaths, immigration and emigration. In our simple model, we show the simplest possible specification: Each rate (BR, DR, IR, ER) is determined by the current level of population (that is, the system is, in one sense "self-referencing") and by a constant. The diagram, however, only shows which terms are connected to which rates of change and is usually not sufficiently for complete specification. The statement of the determinants of rates of change in equation form is used to make these specifications. For the model in Figure 3.2, the "rate" equations are shown below.

```
R     BR.KL = POP.K*FR
R     DR.KL = POP.K*HR
R     IR.KL = POOL.K*IP
R     ER.KL = POP.K*EP
```

The first statement says, rather obviously, that the number of births occurring (BR.KL) between time point K and time point L (K and L are used, rather than J and K, to control the order in which calculations are done when simulations are performed) is equal to the number of persons in the population times a constant (FR). The fertility rate (FR) in this case is the probability that a given person will give birth in the interval between K and L. The other rate equations (for DR, IR, and ER) are similar, but use different constants: a "hazard rate" (probability of death over the interval from K to L); an "immigration probability" (the probability that a given member of the pool of possible immigrants actually immigrates between time points K and L); and, an "emigration probability" (the probability that a member of the focal population will emigrate in the time period between K and L).

"Rate" equations are largely unrestricted in form, and they can grow to be quite complex. One can imagine, for the current simple population model, that one might wish to replace the constants (FR, DR, IR, and ER) with more elaborate expressions. The fertility rate, for example, might be made a variable by making it a function (described in an "auxiliary" equation) of the average age of the population, levels of economic performance, values about desirable family size, etc. These quantities, in turn, might be specified to be functions of other levels, auxiliaries, and rates. In principle, all of this complexity would properly be a part of the "rate equation" or sentence. In practice, since the determinants of rates are often hypothesized to be extremely complex and involve many other variables, "auxiliary" type equations are used to express the portions of the rate. This can sometimes lead to confusion, as "auxiliaries" are used in the DYNAMO language to describe both "levels" of "information" and to perform the auxiliary calculations that enter the right-hand side of rate equations.[14]

The "rate" equations are the focal point for hypotheses about the dynamics of systems. In systems dynamics models (and differential equation models generally), the status of the system at any point in time (that is, the state space) is the result of continuously ongoing causal processes (that is, the rates). Hypotheses about the determinants of variation in the rates of change in dynamic models are, consequently, where the real "causal" theorizing occurs.

The syntax of the DYNAMO language is of assistance in the effort to think clearly about the causes of change in social phenomena. For each "level" in the system, one or more "rates" must be defined. By considering the specific "flows" that increment and/or decrement the level, the problem of specifying the causes of change can often be divided into several simpler (but simultaneously operating) processes. For each of these causal processes (i.e., rates), the language requires that we identify the factors that explain the rate in question. That is, the specification of the rate equation requires that we think clearly about what other levels, rates, auxiliaries, and constants determine the rate. This is equivalent to identifying the "independent variables" that have dynamic causal impacts. Lastly, the language requires that we write a specific hypothesis about how these factors "fit together" to produce change in the rates.

Because the language of rates and auxiliaries is very flexible, virtually any form of relation among independent variables and the "rate" can be specified. It is often best to work backwards by first asking what determines the rate and then what determines these factors, and so on until the "chain" of expressions is complete.

For example, let's look at the birth rate in the example that we've been considering. The birth rate itself is determined by a very simple expression: The number of births between two points in time is equal to the population "at risk" times the probability of an event—that is, the fertility "rate" or probability. The size of the population at any point in time is not problematic; it is accounted for by the level equation. This part of the "chain" is complete, as it connects directly to an already fully specified part of the model (the level of population). The causes of the fertility rate, however, could be further elaborated. We might wish to formulate a theory of fertility probability, perhaps based on the age structure of the population and the economic wealth of the population. This would require us to calculate these quantities, or to supply them as constants (that is, to specify the age structure and wealth levels as the "left-hand" side of either auxiliary or constants types of equations).

Again the theorist faces a forced choice: To treat age structure and economic wealth as exogenous, or to provide expressions that specify their causes.

This method of working backwards in the elaboration of the determinants of rates creates models that are fully self-referencing (that is, "closed systems") or have specific points at which simplifying assumptions have been made. In Figure 3.2, for example, we have as much as stated that our "theory" of population dynamics will not deal with the causes of fertility, mortality, immigration, and emigration probabilities; instead these factors are treated as constants. Several things are accomplished by this method. First, of course, we become quite clear about the boundaries of our theory. Wherever constants enter the chains that describe the causes of rates of change, limiting assumptions are being made. Secondly, the method of working backwards helps us to take apart what are often very complex causal processes into a series of simpler, sequential processes. It is not uncommon to have as many as 10 or 20 "auxiliary" and "constant" types of statements to specify the process that determines a particular rate. Mathematically, this is extremely inelegant; but the clarity of thinking and clarity of expression gained in describing the (often complicated) processes that cause change is usually worth the price.

Conclusions

The systems dynamics approach to formalizing theories about dynamics is one of several traditions within "systems theory" and "systems analysis." The conceptual approach of system dynamics and much of the method of constructing theory from this perspective is embodied in a particular formal language called DYNAMO. In this chapter we have examined generally how the "systems" analysis tradition thinks about social dynamics and, more particularly, have examined the basic elements of the "systems dynamics" approach.

The "systems dynamics" school of theorizing about dynamics has provided one such "higher" language for constructing theories about continuous state continuous time dynamics: DYNAMO. This particular language for describing state spaces and the dynamic connections among the elements of state spaces has a number of conceptual peculiarities, unique vocabulary, and uncommon syntax. The structure of this particular language, however, is unusually useful for formalizing social scientists' theories.

Systems dynamics distinguishes between "conserved" and "nonconserved" elements of the state space of a theory, and provides different vocabulary and syntax for describing these types of elements (e.g., "levels" and "auxiliaries"). This rather unusual distinction reflects both a conceptual and mathematical approach. The language can be used with or without its notions of differences between "material" and "informational" states, and can be used with either differential mathematics or difference mathematics, or both. The distinctions among types of states, however, is often an aid to thinking about social science problems where behaviors and meanings are regarded as separate, but connected phenomena. The use of both differential and difference types of expressions allow for great flexibility of expression, a desirable feature to most theorists.

The systems dynamics language also has a somewhat peculiar approach to dealing with the formalization of theory about the dynamic connections among states. Where differential equations are written in unified form, expressing the impacts of independent variables on the rates of change in dependent variables, the DYNAMO approach takes such expressions apart into (often large numbers of) "level," "rate," and "auxiliary" equations. These equations are mathematically inelegant, but allow the theorist to reason through the causal chains that determine the rates of change in states. While the statements are not compact, each component expression tends to express a rather simple (and hence, comprehensible) part of the overall causal relation, and the connections among the parts of the causal statements can be easily traced.

The DYNAMO language, like all other specialized languages for accomplishing particular expressive tasks, provides some shorthand tools for accomplishing complicated and often repeated operations. In formalizing theories about the dynamic relations among the elements of complex state spaces we don't need 110 names for different kinds of snow, but our task is considerably simplified if we have some shorthand ways of describing dynamic connections. The tool kit provides some of the most useful such "words".

Notes

1. More complete discutions of the idea of a "state space" may be found in Brunner and Brewer (1971), Chorafas (1965), Hall (1962), and Weiner (1948).

2. Mixed discrete and continuous state languages such as SLAM, GASP, and SMOOTH tend to be rather complicated, difficult to learn to use, and require substantial computer power. Other continuous state languages such as CSSL are elegant and efficient, but closely tied to the mathematics of differential equations. Languages intended primarily for discrete state models (e.g., SIMULA)

generally cannot be applied where there are any continuous states in the model. For some interesting discussions of the strengths and weaknesses of particular languages, see particularly Robinson (1972) and Buxton (1968). These discussions, while excellent, are considerably dated, as new languages appear quite frequently.

3. Many system dynamics approaches differentiate kinds of elements of the state space still further. Information is often divided into "data" and "orders"; material flows are often differentiated into "personnel," "money," "raw materials" and "capital." These categories are not as "primitive" as the information/material distinction, but are particularly useful for modeling management problems. See particularly Goodman (1974), Pugh (1980), and Roberts et al. (1983).

4. "Semiotics" and "information theory" tend to reduce all elements of the state space to cultural representations, or information. Many researchers in artificial intelligence, machine systems, and general system theory draw no fundamental distinction between types of state space elements— regarding each as a function or assembly process. See particularly Gilbert (1966) on information theory approaches.

5. Perhaps the best arguments in favor of this approach come from the founder of the systems dynamics school; see Forrester (1961, 1968).

6. In fact, the DYNAMO language is highly flexible, and need not be used in accordance with the philosophical strictures of the "systems dynamics" school. Conserved quantities may be treated with either algebra or calculus, as may nonconserved quantities. The common practice of distinguishing types of things and types of mathematics, however, is a generally useful thinking tool.

7. For a particularly insightful discussion of the peculiarities of the systems dynamics approach, see Day (1974). Pritsker (1974) provides an illustration of translation between DYNAMO and the more explicitly mathematical language GASP. Robinson (1972) also compares several languages approaches to the same problem.

8. There are a number of excellent introductory treatments of the details of the DYNAMO language and its implementation in simulation analysis. It is not our intent to duplicate these primers and users manuals in this volume. Those readers who wish to become proficient in the DYNAMO language will have to study the following sources: Goodman (1974), Pugh (1980), Pugh-Roberts Associates (1982), Roberts et al. (1983).

9. On the flow-diagraming conventions of DYNAMO, see the sources listed in the previous note, particularly Goodman (1974).

10. See, for example, work on path diagrams (a particular variant of linear systems) in Duncan (1975) and Blalock (1961, 1971). The more general diagraming conventions of "flow diagrams" (for continuous state systems) are examined in Heise 1975, Lorens (1964), and Stinchcombe (intuitively, at least, 1968). Methods for diagraming and "solving" discrete state systems by means of directed graphs are dealt with in a large number of sources, including Barnes (1972), Berge (1962), Busacker and Saaty (1975), Flament (1963), Harary (1969), Harary et al. (1965), Hoivik and Gleditsch (1975), and Huggins and Entwisle (1968).

11. "Level" equations need not necessarily involve integration of rates, though most continuous and conserved quantities are usefully regarded in this fashion. Nor do level equations have to involve conservation. That is, it is not necessary that the previous level of the system enter into the calculation of the current level of the system.

12. Auxillary statements in DYNAMO may use virtually any functional form to describe relations among quantities and over time. Certain common functions, such as discrete lags, are more difficult than others to create in the language. For much greater detail, see the sources cited in note 8, above.

13. Differential equation models can be thought of as being composed of statements of the form: $dY/dt = f(M,N,P)$. Level equations perform the task of integrating Y, while the rate and auxiliary equations are used to specify the functional forms of the effects of M, N, and P.

14. This peculiarity represents a conceptual flaw in the DYNAMO language. The "states" and "rates" of material quantities are clearly distinguished by the use of separate equation types; the "states" and "rates" of informational quantities are both represented by the single "auxiliary" equation type.

4

The Toolbox: Special Functions
for Dynamic Models

In the process of formulating dynamic models of social systems, certain kinds of relations occur with great frequency. The DYNAMO language has created convenient shorthand versions of a number of such formalisms that speed the process of theory specification. While it is not our purpose here to provide a user's guide to the DYNAMO language, it will be helpful if we briefly introduce some of the most commonly used tools in expressing dynamic relations.[1] This quick overview will both help the reader to understand the models used for illustration in later chapters, and give a sense of the kinds of relations that frequently used in discussing dynamics. Again, the "semimathematical" nature of these functions acts as a bridge between everyday language and mathematics for the theorist—making formalization a more or less normal part of the task of theorizing about the causes of change in social structures.

Describing Relations Among State-Space Elements

A key task in the formalization of any theory is the specification of the forms of the relationships among the elements of the state space. In the early stages of constructing a theory it is sufficient to list the elements of the state space (that is, the "concepts" or "variables") and to map the connectivity of the space—that is, which states are and are not direct causes of change in other states. To say that two variables are connected, or even that one is a cause of the other, however, is hardly sufficient. In order to understand how a variable changes over time, and potentially make predictions about its time course, we must know how variables affect it, not simply that they do.

We have, in fact, a variety of very useful tools for describing the relationships among state space elements. The relations among many state space elements can be rather conveniently expressed using simple mathematical terms: addition, subtraction, division, multiplication, and exponentiation. A large variety of linear and nonlinear relations among quantitative (continuous) states can be captured with such terms. In addition to normal mathematical functions, the DYNAMO language accept trigonometric functions. Thus, for example, one might wish to create a "test pattern" to examine the responsiveness of a model using a sine wave of a certain amplitude and period.

In addition to the normal armament of mathematical and trigonometric functions, the DYNAMO language allows one to "draw" pictures of relationships between continuous variables (and "time," of course is a continuous variable) using a TABLE function. The table function accepts as arguments sets of points (X,Y) that describe any continuous relation, and perform interpolation between the points. It is particularly useful for describing relationships among quantitative variables that are fundamentally nonlinear (e.g., having more than one "bend"), or which have upper or lower limits (as in the case of an S-shaped curve).

For example, an S-shaped relationship between the variable X and time could be expressed like this in DYNAMO:

A   X.K = TABLE(XTAB,TIME,0,10,1)
T   XTAB = 0/.5/1.5/3.0/4.0/5.0/6.0/7.0/8.5/9.5/10

The first statement says that the value of X is to be defined by a table called XTAB, in which the horizontal dimension is TIME. TIME ranges from 0 to 10, and a value of X will be supplied for each unit increment of TIME. The second statement provides the values of X that correspond to the values of TIME from 0 to 10, respectively.

One reason why many social scientists do not "formalize" their theories is a hesitancy to use mathematical forms to express relations among state variables. Many kinds of relations among states in models of sociological models, however, are fundamentally "qualitative" or logical relations—rather than "quantitative" or mathematical relations. The DYNAMO language (and most others designed for "mixed" or discrete state modeling) provides a useful set of shorthand functions for describing qualitative relations, in addition to the mathematical functions for describing quantitative relations.

The MIN and MAX functions select either the smaller or the larger of a pair of values—providing one mechanism for expressing conditional and limited relationships. For example, the statement:

A   Y.K = MAX(0,MIN(X.K,100))

first selects the smaller of the current value of X or 100, and then selects the larger of this result or 0 to be the current value of Y. That is, the function sets Y equal to X, except that Y cannot be smaller than 0 nor larger than 100.

The more general form of logical functions is also provided by the CLIP function, which is a simple "if, then, else" type of test (a specialized form the SWITCH statement, tests for arguments being equal to zero). For example, the statement:

A   Y.K = CLIP(FUNCT1,FUNCT2,THRESH.K,100)

sets the current of value of Y equal to FUNCT1 (which could be a constant, a variable, a conditional statement, or whatever) if the value of THRESH.K is greater than or equal to 100; it sets the current value of Y.K to FUNCT2 if THRESH.K is less than 100.

The clip function is a very useful tool for modeling relationships that change, depending on the values of other processes. In our model of the elements of Marx's theory of capitalism, for example (see Chapter 13), a simple logical test is used to determine whether the strength of the working class exceeds that of the capitalist class. If the workers are stronger, a number of the fundamental relationships in the model "switch": The state is now regarded as controlled by workers, capitalists are eliminated, and profit and exploitation of surplus value are reduced to zero.

It is possible then to use logical functions both to describe the relations among qualitative variables, and to include qualitative change as well as quantitative change in the dynamic theory. This capacity gives much greater flexibility than the language of statistical models which, by and large, are required to have time-invariant coefficients.[2]

A major advantage of such "semimathematical" languages as DYNAMO for formalizing theory lies in the ease and precision with which they allow the statement of hypotheses about the relations among variables. The availability of both logical (qualitative) and mathematical (quantitative) functions make the task of expressing even very complicated ideas about relations among variables rather straightforward. The language requires theory builders be more precise than they might have been had they used everyday language to discuss how variables are connected. This can only be an improvement. Formalized statements about how elements of a state space are connected may be illogical, and they may be inconsistent with empirical evidence, but they are not indeterminate. One of the joys and frustrations of everyday language for describing relations among states is that such statements can be so imprecise as to allow virtually any empirical result to be judged to be consistent (or inconsistent) with the theory.

Semimathematical languages such as DYNAMO provide considerable ease and flexibility in specifying relations. Complex expressions are simplified by breaking them down into sequences of simpler relations: Levels are determined by multiple "rates," each of which is determined by multiple "auxiliaries," each of which, in turn, is determined by other levels, rates, and auxiliaries until, at some point, the circle is closed. The languages allow both qualitative (if-then-else, and/or) relations and quantitative relations (either linear or nonlinear), as well as providing the possibility of creating specialized jargon to express particular forms of relations.[3] The resulting statements about how variables "go together" do not read as well as English—but are far less ambiguous. The statements also tend to be far more intelligible than parallel statements in the language of sets, formal logic, algebra, or differential equations.

Special Functions for Dynamic Analysis: Delays

In formalizing theories about explicitly dynamic relations among variables there is a need for additional specialized vocabulary. The particular nature of theory about dynamics is that we are greatly concerned with processes that occur over time. It follows that we need a vocabulary for describing connections among variables that directly address the "time-shape" of the effect of causal variables on response variables.

The most fundamental "time function" necessary for specifying theories about dynamic relations has already been discussed. It is so well hidden in the basic vocabulary and syntax of DYNAMO and similar languages that the theorist (rightly) has to give them little thought. This "special dynamic function" is integration with respect to time, and is an automatic part of the use of "level" and "rate" equations. "Integration with respect to time" can be thought of as the simplest form of over-time relation. It says, for example, that the amount of change in some (dependent) variable Y over a period of time (e.g., between "J" and "K") is the summing up or accumulation of signals received from some (causal) variable X over the time interval. These "signals" are sent at "rates" that are dependent upon other things (auxiliaries). The "integrating function" that is a part of the syntax of "levels" and "rates," then, is expressing a particular form of relation among states that occurs over time: the continuous accumulation of causal impacts that occur at rates specified by other variables.

In most semimathematical languages for describing dynamic relations, another special function for dealing with the time-shape of effects is provided: the "lag." A "lag" suggests that the "signal" or causal force emitted by a variable at one point in time has an instantaneous effect on the receiving variable after a fixed interval of time has passed. Thus, it might be convenient to specify a dynamic relation between two states as follows: The number of persons who are 25 years old on Nov. 12, 1976 is equal to the number who where 24 years old on Nov. 12, 1975, lagged by one year (assuming no deaths, etc.). Because of its strong bias toward continuous time functions (as opposed to the discrete time function of a lag), the DYNAMO language does not directly and easily provide for the specification of "lags."[4]

The "continuous integration" and "lag" time functions can be thought of as two rather distinctive "time-shapes" of responses to stimuli. In integration, a change in the independent or stimulus variable is responded to in a cumulative and linear fashion until the full impact has been realized; in a lagged response, the dependent variable does not change at all for a specified period, then reaches its full realization instantly. These time shapes are illustrated in the Figure 4.1.

There is no necessity that the time-shapes of the relationships among variables be restricted to these two simple forms. Indeed, some of the most interesting aspects of the over-time behavior of states in models of social action and interaction are consequences of the time-shapes of responses to stimuli. As in modeling static relations a linear approximation is often "good enough" to capture the essentials of a more complex pattern, continuous integration is often "good enough" in dynamic models for rough and ready theory exploration.

The DYNAMO language provides shorthand functions for two other common time shapes: first- and third-order exponential delays. A first-order delay shows immediate response to a stimulus, with exponential decline thereafter. A third-order delay displays an initial "lag" period of little response, followed by a rapid increase and a slow decline.[5] These time shapes are shown in Figure 4.2:

Four particular functions are provided in the DYNAMO language for first- and third-order delays of material and informational quantities: DELAY1, DELAY3, SMOOTH, and DLINF3. Material delays conserve the quantity "in transit" in a delay if the length of the delay changes; informational delays do not conserve the quantities in the delay. This is of consequence only if the average length of the delay is specified to be a variable (for example, the length of the delay in information reaching the top of an organization changes proportional to the number of levels in the organization).

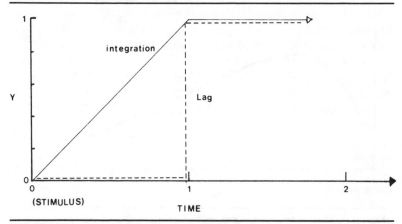

Figure 4.1: Integrating and lag response to unit impulse.

Delays can be used in describing relations among material or informational quantities, and have a quite simple syntax, for example the statement:

A   Y.K = DELAY3(X.K,5)

says that the value of Y at time K is responsive to the value of X by a time shape of a third-order exponential delay (that is, S-shaped), with an average delay time of five units. Thus, both the form and the magnitude of the delay are specified in a single statement.

In practice, the distinction between material and informational delays is seldom of great consequence; the choice of the time-shape of response (that is, first, third, infinite, or some other order) can be extremely consequential. Theorists have rarely given attention to the question of the time-shape of the relations among variables because they have been primarily concerned with static or equilibrium analysis. Again, the DYNAMO language helps, requiring that the theory builder ask him/herself specifying questions about the nature of the dynamic relations among the states in the theory: Given that a change in X causes a change in Y, how is this stimulus realized in a response over time? How long does it take for the full effects of each change in X to be realized in responses in Y (that is, what is the period of the delay)? Does Y begin responding immediately and then approach its full realization asymptotically (as in a first-order delay)? Is the response initially low, but increasing at a decreasing rate thereafter (as in a second-order delay)? Is initial response low, but then accelerating and finally decelerating (as in

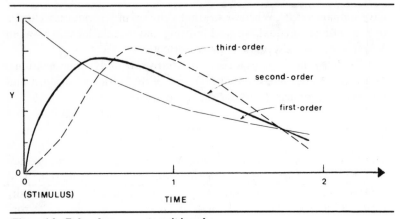

Figure 4.2: **Delayed responses to unit impulse.**

a third-order delay)? Is there no response at all for a fixed period, and then an instantaneous adjustment (as in a lag or high-order exponential delay)?

In theorizing about dynamics, we must specify not only the functional form of relations among variables (i.e., linear additive, if-then, or whatever) but also the time-shape of the relationship. There are many possible time shapes that can be specified and analyzed using mathematical formalisms, but the vocabularies of time relations in mathematics are very difficult. On the other hand, the everyday language of the theorist is often insufficiently specific in describing the time-shapes of responses. Vagueness will not do, for, as we shall see in later chapters, the time-shapes of responses have very important impacts on over-time behavior. The language of "delays" in DYNAMO is one useful shorthand for specifying the most common forms of time relations.

Ghosts Within the Machine: Noise

Formalizations of theories utilizing statistical terminology (e.g., the general linear model) routinely include "residual" or "error" terms as independent variables. In assessing how well such models can account for observations, we frequently find that the residual term is by far the largest of the variance components. In constructing models of dynamic relations with semimathematical languages, it is also useful to consider the role played by "noise," "error," and "residual sources" The DYNAMO language (and other similar languages) provide shorthand tools for this purpose. Theories that are stated in logical deductive terms have similar caveats. When we say that a change in X produces a change in Y, all else being equal, we are admitting that the relationship between X and Y will not always be realized perfectly.

Like delay, noise plays a very important role in dynamic relations. This role is somewhat different than that of the "residual" in static and nonrecursive models. Consider the static model:

$$Y = a + bX + e$$

This "sentence" says that the score on Y at a given point in time is equal to some constant amount (a), plus some amount that is a function (b) of the score on X at the same time point, plus some random error (usually with an expected value of zero, and a normal distribution). The "error" component here is conceptually simple: It represents a separate source of variations in the scores across realizations (observations) of Y.

Things change a bit when we consider a dynamic (in this case lagged and conserved) relation:

$$Y_{t+1} = a + b_i (Y_t) + b_2 (X_t) + e$$

That is, the score on Y at the second time point is a linear additive function of a constant, the score at the previous point in time (conservation), the score on an independent variable (X) at the previous point in time, and "error." Now, at each point in time the actual value of the state Y is composed of all of these components. As a result, the score on Y at each later time point is a function of past "errors" as well as past scores on Y and X. If "errors" are truly random with a mean value of zero, this is not a problem for understanding why Y changes the way it does over time. But the particular value of Y at each point in time is somewhat indeterminate due to both current and past errors. That is, "errors" remain in the system over time and may cause the time-track of Y to differ from what we would have expected had there been no error.[6]

If we made our simple statistical model fully recursive (that is, with X causing changes in Y and Y causing changes in X), the role that error plays is still more complex. In that case (and we won't burden you with the equations), the random-error component of each variable at each point in time is "multiplied" through the system, so that scores on both X and Y at later points in time are a function of earlier scores on X and Y and earlier errors in X and Y.

Most of the systems that we will be considering in the later chapters of this volume represent patterns of dynamic relations among states that are at least as complex as this last case of statistical models. The role that noise and error play in systems with nonlinear and feedback relations is often very difficult to deduce directly. Consequently, the normal strategy for dealing with error is to ignore it in the early stages of model formulation, and then add it to the model in a controlled and systematic manner to understand its consequences (more on such simulation approaches to analyzing complex theories below). The DYNAMO language (as do most others) makes this a relatively simple process by providing two functions that generate pseudorandom noise. The NOISE function is a simple white noise generator (that is, it produces random numbers); the NORMRN function generates normally distributed random numbers with a mean and standard deviation selected by the analyst. With some cleverness, other noise patterns can be created if they are needed. For example, one might specify:

L   Y.K = (PARM1*Y.J)+(PARM2*X.J)+NORMRN(0,10)

That is, the level of Y at time K is equal to the autoregressive effect (PARM1) of its value at the previous point in time, plus the lagged effect (PARM2) of the value of X at the previous time, plus an error component of normally distributed noise having a mean of 0 and a standard deviation of 10 units.

Ghosts Without the Machine: Test Functions

The purpose of constructing formal theories of dynamic processes is to gain an understanding of the dynamic consequences of the relations among the elements of the state space. In models involving large state spaces, with high connectivity and nonlinear, delayed, noisy, and feedback relations among the states, the dynamic behavior of the theory can be very difficult to deduce directly. In such complex cases, understanding and analysis of the theory can best be accomplished by simulation. We will deal with this approach at length in the next chapter.

The last group of shorthand functions provided by most semimathematical languages for formalizing continuous state continuous time dynamics are "test patterns" used (primarily) in simulating the over-time consequences of the theory. In understanding by simulating, the basic procedure is to subject the formal model of the state space and relations among state space elements to "shocks," and to observe the consequences. DYNAMO provides some useful tools for creating such shocks.

It is frequently useful to subject models to shocks that are composed of "white noise," random noise, constants, or simple mathematical functions such as sine waves. We have already considered the vocabulary necessary to create these tests. In addition, three other test patterns are particularly useful: PULSEs, STEPs, and RAMPs.

PULSEs consist of instantaneous shocks of specified magnitude and timing, and are useful for assessing the "transient response" of models (more on transient response in the next chapter). For example, the statement:

A   TEST.K = PULSE(10/DT,5,15)

creates a test signal of a total magnitude of 10 units (it is necessary to divide the desired magnitude of the shock by the size of the integration interval "DT" to take the fineness of the integration into account; alternatively one could leave the first parameter as a raw number, which would set the value of the "peak" of the shock, but not its total magnitude, which would vary with the size of DT). This shock occurs for the first time at TIME = 5 and occurs every 15 time units thereafter.

We can often learn a good bit about the behavior of our theory by subjecting it to sudden discrete changes in exogenous stimuli by use of STEP functions, or to stimuli that are continuously increasing or decreasing over time, by use of RAMP functions.

The statement

A   TEST.K = STEP(10,5)

for example, creates a test signal that has a value of 0 (by default) until time point 5, and 10 units thereafter. The statement:

A   TEST.K = RAMP(5,10)

creates a test signal that is 0 (by default) for the first 10 time points and increases by 5 units for each unit of time thereafter.

Virtually any pattern of stimuli can be generated by clever use of the PULSE, STEP, and RAMP functions. In addition to using such signals for sensitivity experiments, such shocks can be important parts of models in other ways. Exogenous shock patterns can be used to model changes in exogenous stimuli (the model in Chapter 10 does this), and can be used to schedule the occurrence of exogenous events or unusual changes in relations among endogenous variables that are time dependent.

Conclusions

The purpose of this brief chapter has been to introduce some of the vocabulary that can be of assistance in formalizing and assessing dynamic relations. We have discussed a set of mathematical and logical functions that are generally useful for describing relations among state space elements. These functions are quite familiar. We have also described a number of specialized functions that are less familiar, and particularly useful for describing the forms of the "time shapes" of relations among state space elements.

One major and very important group of functions are DELAYs, which can be used to describe how long it takes a change in one state to be realized in a response in another state, and the form that the response takes with respect to time. Responses can be constant with respect to time (by use of the integration function DT), may begin sharply and then decline in intensity (for example, first-order exponential delays), may begin slowly and then accelerate (as in third-order exponential delays), or may be characterized by discrete lags (very high-order delays, or "boxcars"). Theorists have rarely given much attention to the length of time that it takes for causal processes to occur, or to the time shapes of the processes. In dynamic models with feedback, however, these aspects of the relations among variables can be extremely important. Delays allow one fairly easy way of specifying some of the most common patterns.

The other group of time functions that we have examined here are most commonly used in testing models by subjecting them to shocks. PULSEs, RAMPs, and STEPs are particularly useful for generating test patterns for this purpose, though they can also be used to describe (rather unusual) forms of relationships among variables. We have been deliberately a bit vague about how these test functions are used in the process of formulating and testing models of dynamic theories. As we consider the general methodology of utilizing computer assisted simulation in theory building, in the next chapter, their use will become much clearer.

Notes

1. There are a number of excellent sources that are very helpful in learning the basics of the computer language DYNAMO. To work effectively with DYNAMO, readers will also have to become more familiar with the specifics of the program and its use. The most useful introductions are given by Goodman (1974), Pugh (1980), Pugh-Roberts Associates (1982), and Roberts et al. (1983).

2. The DYNAMO language, while it has many useful functions, particularly for describing nonlinear and over-time relations, is rather inelegant with regard to discrete lags and certain logical functions. Particularly annoying are the absence of the "AND" and "OR" functions and the rather peculiar form of the "IF-THEN-ELSE" operation.

3. The macro facility available in most versions of DYNAMO allows the user to create specialized functions of any complexity that can be called upon as specialized "jargon" in model construction.

4. Such a function, however, can be created by use of a macro. In some versions of DYNAMO a specialized "boxcar" or "pipeline" delay can be used to capture discrete delays with some effectiveness. DYNAMO is not particularly friendly to discrete time functions, which are extremely important in large classes of dynamic models; see, for example, Takacs (1962).

5. Integration can also be thought of as a "zero-order" delay; discrete lags can also be thought of as infinite-order delays.

6. Dealing with the complexities of such over-time error processes and their consequences for the statistical estimation of parameters is the "bread and butter" of econometrics. Any of a very large number of econometrics texts can provide an excellent introduction to error processes and their effects on parameter estimation.

5

Complexity and Analyzability: Understanding Dynamics by Simulation

At a number of places in the preceding chapters the term "complexity" has been used to refer to social phenomena and to the theories that we would construct about them. Patterns of social action and interaction that involve change over time are inherently more "complex" than patterns that do not change, or are considered at only a single point in time. The theories that are used to understand and make generalizations about dynamic patterns consequently tend to be more "complex" than theories of systems in equilibrium or theories that describe patterns of covariation across systems at a single point in time.

The complexity of phenomena, and the complexity of the theories that we create to understand the phenomena, have consequences for how we can go about understanding the full implications of our efforts at theorizing. Some theories are fully comprehensible by logical deduction (using either "common sense" or more formal means.[1] Many others (particularly when stated in mathematical forms such as linear differential equations or structural equations) can be quite fully understood by direct solution.[2] Many of the theories that are constructed to describe the dynamics of social action and interaction, however, are too "complex" to be understood by these means. One of the main reasons for formalization of theories about dynamics utilizing semimathematical languages is to enable us to apply an alternative tool for analyzing and understanding our theories-simulation.

In this chapter we will first take a somewhat more rigorous look at the notion of the "complexity" of a theory and examine why this raises problems of analyzability. We will then look at how simulation methods can be used to analyze and make deductions from complex theories. This discussion has two parts. First we will briefly examine the logic of "understanding by simulating," then we will discuss strategic approaches to simulation analysis.

Complexity and Analyzability

The term "complexity" has a rather clear meaning within systems analysis.[3] Now that we are in command of the basic systems language of "state spaces," "connectivity," and various functional and time relations among states, we can provide a definition that is sufficient for our purposes. A system may be said to be more complex than another if it contains more elements in its state space than the other; it may be said to be more complex if the states in its state space may take on more values than the other (e.g., continuous state systems are more "complex" than discrete state systems); it may be said to be more complex than another if the elements in its state space are more extensively interconnected than those of the other; and, a system is more complex to the order of the functional forms connecting the states to one another (i.e., a relationship described by a complex polynomial is more "complex" than one described by a simple linear equation). Finally, a system is more complex than another if the time-shapes of the relations among the states are of higher order (e.g., a system connected by relationships involving third-order delays is more "complex" than one involving simple continuous integration).

The logic behind all of the dimensions that lead to increased "complexity" in the definition above is this: A system is complex to the degree that we must have more information in order to be certain about (that is, to make accurate predictions about) its behavior. Simple systems are capable of only a limited variety of possible behaviors; hence it is rather easy to predict their response to any given stimulus. More complex systems are far less "analyzable" because they are capable of producing a larger variety of responses to stimuli. This range of possible behaviors is frequently termed the "degrees of freedom" of the system, analogously to the statistical use of the term: Less information is necessary to make accurate predictions about the dynamics of simple systems than complex ones.

Formal theories about social action and interaction can be regarded as systems (in this case, systems composed of symbols and relations among symbols) of varying complexity, just as can the social phenomena they mimic. Theories are simpler if they have smaller state spaces (fewer concepts), are conceptualized qualitatively rather than quantitatively, have relatively few "laws" governing the connections among concepts (e.g., a "causal chain" is "simpler" than a "path model"). Theories are simpler if they posit relations among terms that are easily characterized (e.g., "if-then" or $Y = a + bX$) rather than more difficult to describe (e.g., "if X is a and not b, then Y is c, or $\ln(Y) = \sin(X)$). And theories are simpler if they describe relations that occur over time in simple fashions (e.g., statements about covariation at a time point are "simpler" than statements about the effects of prior changes in one variable on subsequent changes in another).

We need no special intellectual tools to comprehend the meaning of, and make deductions from, simple theories. Syllogisms with only a few terms or single linear equations are "obvious" in their meanings and implications.[4] Slightly more complex theories are still amenable to direct analysis if we can learn to use certain tools. Quite complex lines of qualitative relations can be parsed using the rules of formal logic; most linear and some nonlinear simultaneous equation multivariate models can be directly solved with calculus and persistence.

Truly complex theories, however, often exceed our capacity to comprehend them. The effects of changing one variable may be almost impossible to trace if that variable is interconnected in complicated and dynamic ways with large numbers of others that are themselves connected. In many cases the available mathematical and logical tools are simply insufficient to give determinant answers to questions about the consequences of changes in variables and the overall behavioral tendencies of the theory under various conditions.

Because theories about dynamics must specify relations in time, as well in functional form, they tend toward complexity. It is in circumstances of this kind of complexity that simulation methods are often used in the physical and social sciences to understand and work out the implications of theories.

Understanding by Experimentation:
The Logic of Simulation

A "simulation" is usually defined as a construct that has the appearance or form, but not the substance of some real object.[5] In a certain sense, all theories about social action and interaction are simulations—theories are artifacts designed to mimic (albeit in highly selected and abstracted ways) characteristics of real social action.

Both social and physical scientists routinely employ simulations in the study of complex dynamic relations.[6] Meteorologists create artifacts (usually computerized models) designed to mimic the interactions of temperature, pressure, humidity, and other factors over space and time. Ecologists describe the rise and fall of populations of various species in changing environments over time. Political scientists create models that mimic swings in voter sentiment; economists seek to mimic trends in investment, consumption, interest rates, and the like. In all of these cases it is the simulation (the theory or model) itself that is the focus of attention. In a certain sense, the scientists are studying the simulation as a way of attempting to understand the reality that it (supposedly) represents.

It is misleading to think of "simulation analysis" as a single thing. In fact, there are three distinctive and separate activities that are all often called "simulation": making projections, validating theories, and analyzing theories. When the economist makes a prediction about the course of interest rates over the next quarter by projecting forward from current values of a dynamic model of the economy, (s)he is "simulating." This type of use of dynamic theory involves the application of a theory that has already been constructed and validated, and is not our focus in this volume. When political scientists create a dynamic theory of trends in voter sentiment, substitute known values and parameters from a real case, and make "postdictions" about election outcomes they are "simulating."[7] In this case the object of the exercise is to assess the validity of the theory that gave rise to the simulation model. This use of simulation for validating models is also outside our interest in this volume.[8]

The third use of simulation, and probably the least well-understood use, is for analyzing and constructing theories themselves. This is the application of simulation method that most concerns us here. Social science theories that involve extremely large state spaces with complex functional and time connectivity among the elements can rapidly exceed the capacity of the analyst to comprehend the implications of the theory. This is particularly true for theories involving dynamics where nonlinear and feedback relations exist. To explicate such theories, explore their implications, and make deductions from them, simulation methods are often the only available alternative. The use of simulation methods for this purpose is different from the questions of application and validation of the theory. In this application, simulation is used to answer such questions as: Does a pattern of small group interaction embodied in the formal theory have tendencies toward equilibrium, or not (or more properly, for what ranges of values of state space elements and relations among them does the theory display equilibrating behavior)? Which political parties have the largest impact on the overall behavior pattern of coalition formation in a model of legislative dynamics? Which exchanges among the business firms in a model of a local economy are the most critical ones in producing the over-time behavioral tendencies of the model?

Where the purpose of the application of simulation methods is to understand the theory itself, the logic of the inquiry is a familiar one. We are attempting to build an understanding of an artifact by experimentally subjecting it to known stimuli and observing the consequences. With carefully designed programs of experimentation it is often possible to obtain quite sound "approximate solutions" to the behavioral tendencies of even the most complex and nonlinear of theoretical systems.

In thinking about very simple theories such as $Y_{t+1} = bX_t$, we can "simulate" the dynamics without any special aids. That is, we can ask and answer without difficulty such questions about the dynamics of this theory as: How does Y behave over time if X is a constant? What is the responsiveness of Y to changes in X? Under what circumstances does Y reach a steady state? In asking and answering these questions, we are simulating the theory. That is, we are subjecting the theory (in this case a simple linear equation with a lag of one time unit) to a series of mental experiments. We "plug in" values for X (e.g., X is a constant, X varies randomly, and so on) and calculate the implications for the time track of Y. We can also, of course, "understand" the implications of this theory by direct solution of the mathematics: A steady state in Y is attained, according to this theory, only where X is a constant, the response of Y to X (at lag of one time unit) is precisely B, and the value of Y at any time point can be calculated if we know the value of X at the prior time point.

If our theory was somewhat more complex, involving, say, a system of several simultaneous linear differential equations, the implications would be more difficult to work out in one's head and we might have to resort to some calculations. We might proceed by altering the values of each of the variables one at a time and observing the consequences for other variables. A small system of simultaneous linear differential equations can also be "understood" by direct solution: The equilibria of such equation systems can be directly calculated (if they exist), and the values of partial derivatives are informative about the questions of the relative importance of variables. Despite the different technology, we are still striving to understand our theory and work out its implications by simulating it, just as we were when all the necessary calculations could be done in one's head.

When the theory that we are trying to get a grasp on is still more complex, as when there are multiple actors with multiple states coupled together in nonlinear fashion, we can use simulation methods to understand its implications. As in the simpler cases above, the logic is straightforward. We systematically vary the values of state space elements and the relations among them and observe the consequences for the behavior of the model over time. In complicated models, of course, we may never be able to achieve a full comprehension of the system's behavior because the variety of possible system states and relations becomes very large very quickly. We can, however, derive approximate solutions.

Simulation, then, is simply a method of understanding by experimenting with an artifact. Theories about the dynamics of social action and interaction are "artifacts," and one method for understanding them is to experiment with them or simulate them. "Complex" theories, particularly ones involving statements about relations that operate over time, can often be understood only by such experimentation, since they exceed our capacity to comprehend their meanings by "common sense" or direct solution.

By their very complexity, however, theories about the continuous-time continuous-state dynamics of social action also suggest an infinite range of possible "experiments." What does one really need to know in order to "understand" a theory of this type? And how can we design "critical experiments" with our theories to reach this understanding?

Simulation Strategies for Analyzing Complex Theories

Social science theories formulated as continuous-state continuous-time dynamic models can very easily become so complex that the optimal strategy for working with them is computer-assisted simulation. Indeed, one major reason for the formalization of such theories into "semimathematical" languages is to allow computers to do the tedious and mechanical calculations necessary to understand the full implications of our theoretical models. The mechanics of using computers to perform simulation experiments are, for our purposes, rather uninteresting. What is of interest for our purposes is the question What should we ask the computer to calculate? That is, what questions do we want to ask in order to analyze our theory and how can we design the necessary critical experiments (in this case, the "experiments" being simulations of the model on the computer)?

One kind of question that we might want to explore by simulation consists of "what if . . . " speculations. What if, for example, there were no middle-aged people at a certain point in time in the simple population model we discussed in Chapter Two? What would the time-trace for total population size look like under this circumstance, as opposed to a circumstance in which the middle-aged population was initially set at some "normal" level? What if half of the male population were destroyed by a war at a certain point in time; what would the long run consequences be?

These kinds of experiments to explore the implications of theories about dynamics can be very informative. Indeed, one can test a theory and sometimes make reasonable decisions about competing specifications for it on the basis of such experiments. We might, for example, have in mind two alternative specifications of how actors in competition with one other respond to one another's behavior. While holding everything else constant, we can explore the over-time behavior of the interaction between the competing parties under the alternative specifications of how the process works (that is, examining some of the consequences of specifying a different form of relations among state space elements). Let us suppose that our experiment with the first specification of how actors interact yields a pattern of exponential escalation of conflict between the actors, while our second specification yields a pattern of a waning exponential decline in conflict levels. We have not, by this experiment assessed the empirical validity of either of the theories; we have, however, learned that one or the other is a better specification of what we really meant to say about this aspect of our theory.

"What if . . . " kinds of experiments with theories can be very valuable and can be used to make informed decisions about alternative specification of the theory. Such experiments, however, tend to be rather unsystematic. It is also important to subject any dynamic theory to systematic experimentation. In addition to examining specific "realizations" of the theory to explore specific questions, there are three kinds of "general" questions that should be explored: equilibrium tendencies, sensitivity, and transient response. Each of these general questions can be addressed by particular programs of experimentation with the theory.

Equilibrium

One of the most important things to explore about a theory is the type of behavior over time that it implies. There are two different but closely related questions here: questions of the equilibrium behavior (that is, loosely, the "long-run" tendencies) and questions about the transient response, (loosely, the "short-run" behavioral tendencies).

There has been an unfortunate tendency in the social sciences for theorists to confuse the notion of the "equilibrium behavior" of systems with assertions that (a) social systems do indeed have stable equilibria, (b) that observed social patterns, particularly ones that don't seem to be changing very much at the moment, are "in equilibrium," and (c) that such equilibria represent "desirable" adaptations."[9] Each of these assertions may or may not be true with regard to a particular pattern of social action. Examining the equilibrium behavior of a theory of social dynamics does not imply the acceptance of any of these assertions.

Exploring the equilibrium tendencies of a system is equivalent to asking what the time traces and final levels of the elements of the state space are under a particular set of fixed (and unchanging) initial conditions. For example, we might wish to know what the final level for the size of the total population is, given a particular age structure, fertility pattern and mortality pattern. If births exceed deaths, of course, population does not reach a "stable equilibrium." We are asking a particular kind of "what if . . . " question in equilibrium analysis: What if the initial status of the state space were fixed, the parameters of the model held constant (that is, the relations among the elements of the state space), and no external or exogenous shocks occurred.

For any particular specification of the levels of the elements of the state space and relations among the elements, we are usually interested in two things about the "equilibrium tendencies": whether the system does, in fact, approach a steady state (that is, a condition where the levels of the variables do not change with respect to time); and what the "time-traces" of the variables look like over time (that is, do they approach their limits, if any, linearly, by some monotonic function, or do they oscillate or behave in some unstable fashion). Where models do reach a stable equilibrium, we may also be interested in the actual level of the state variables at equilibrium as well. Where models do not reach a stable equilibrium, we may with to assess these levels at some fixed point of time.

The methodology for determining "equilibrium" results by means of computer aided simulation is obvious and simple. The initial values of the state space element are set at the desired levels, all sources of "exogenous" shock or change in the model are eliminated, and the results of the operation of the model are calculated for as long a period of time as is necessary. That is, the model is simulated until the values of the state space elements stop changing at some desired level of accuracy, or until the failure to attain a steady state becomes obvious.

Usually we are interested in still more general questions than whether stable equilibrium is attained, at what level, and by what time path for a particular set of initial conditions. The really interesting questions about the equilibrium tendencies of a theory are not limited to a particular "realization," but rather are the following: Under what conditions is stability attained? Under what conditions are the time paths of variables "smooth"? Many fairly simple models, and particularly models with linear relations among state space elements have "general equilibria." That is, they display very much the same time-traces and final conditions of stability regardless of the particular levels of the variables at the initial time point. Models with nonlinear connections and feedbacks, however, do not always produce the same kinds of over-time behavior when they begin at different initial levels.

To answer these more general questions, the theorist must design and execute a set of experiments with his or her model. In principle, each element of the state space must be systematically varied through its entire range while holding all other variables constant, then while varying each other variable in a systematic fashion, then each pair of other variables, etc. In each case, the model is run to its stable result (or to a fixed time point, if it does not display stability). In principle, if all of the resulting information could be comprehended, a general solution about the equilibrium limits of the theory would be obtained. That is, we would know under what conditions the theory predicted what kinds of stable or unstable realizations.

In practice, such a program of systematic experimentation is usually both impractical and unnecessary. For models of any complexity, the number of alternative sets of initial conditions is ridiculously large. It is not worth the time and trouble to generate all of the possible results and it is doubtful that we could summarize them in any meaningful way if we could generate them. A better strategy is to think first, and design a more intelligent program of experimentation. There are several useful guidelines. (1) Most variables vary in fairly narrow ranges, and we probably have little interest in the implications of the theory for conditions that are not likely to ever be observed. (2) If we consider that variables in the state space tend to covary, many of the possible combinations of initial conditions can also be regarded as less useful, even if they fall within the plausible ranges for each variable. (3) While the overall behavior of the model may be quite complex and nonobvious, portions of the model may be very simple and straightforward. There is no need to go excessive lengths to explore obvious relationships (but be careful, not all that appears obvious in complex models, is). (4) Finally, we can restrict our attention still further by focusing on variables that are more central to the theory. Elements of the state space that are more closely coupled with more other elements of the space are likely to be more consequential in determining the equilibrium behavior of the system; elements of the state space that are connected to only a small number of other elements are likely to be less consequential.

By thinking first, then, the exploration of the equilibrium conditions of a theory can be considerably simplified. By focusing on the most "central" (in the network sense of the term) elements of the state space, by bypassing obvious relationships, and by limiting the ranges of initial conditions considered, a pretty good picture of the general long-run behavior implications of the theory can be had. This solution to the problem of assessing the equilibrium tendencies of complex models generates decidedly "approximate" solutions and understandings. In complex theories, however, approximate understanding of the implications of the theory may well be all that is possible. In many circumstances, particularly in the early phases of constructing and examining alternative theories of social dynamics, approximate understanding of the equilibrium bounds of the theory is all that is necessary.

Sensitivity

Exploration of the conditions under which a theory implies stability or continuing change in the long run is a special case of "sensitivity" analysis. More generally, "sensitivity" analysis is an attempt to assess which variables or relationships are the most consequential for determining the over-time behavior of the system. Returning very briefly to our simple population model in the earlier chapters we might ask whether adding an additional young person to the population or adding an additional old person to the population has greater consequences for the total size of the population in the future (the answer, fairly obviously, is that adding a young person does, because of the implications for the birth rate). Alternatively, we might wish to compare alternative assumptions about the parameters of the system. For example, we might want to know whether a 5% increase in birth rate or a 5% decrease in the death rate has greater implications for the size of the population in the future. In each case we are asking which variable is "more important," or how "sensitive" the over-time behavior of the system is to change in particular quantities or relationships.

As in seeking to understand the long-run or equilibrium implications of our theory, sensitivity analysis calls for an intelligently planned set of simulation experiments. Again, in principle each variable or relationship or interest should be systematically varied throughout its range while holding all the other variables and relationships in the system constant at each of their possible levels. The consequences of each change in the variable or parameter of interest for all other system states at some future time point could thus be systematically assessed. Again in practice such an exercise is, if not impossible, usually wholly unnecessary.

The same principles of design hold for a set of experiments with the sensitivities of variables and parameters as hold with exploration of questions about equilibrium. Variables and relationships that are most "central" to the theory deserve more attention than those that are less connected. There is little point in exploring the sensitivity of the model to implausible levels of states or implausible combinations of state levels. Many relationships may be quite simple, even if the theory as a whole is not, and hence need less attention. Variables that have very limited interactions with others in their consequences, for example, are much easier to understand than those involved in complex feedback relations (a corollary of the centrality principle).

Good judgment is necessary in deciding how much effort should be devoted to assessing the sensitivity of the whole theory to change in particular variables and relationships. Usually a good sense of the "relative importance" of variables can be had by examining the connectivity of a theory, and confirmed by relatively simple simulation experiments. Once key relationships or variables have been located, more detailed experiments can be conducted by varying the variable or relationship in question systematically across its useful range at selected levels of other variables.

As in the case of the analysis of the equilibrium bounds and behavior of the theory, the analysis of sensitivity by simulation experiments generates "approximate solutions." Such solutions may be the only possible ones for very complex theories. In most cases the approximations to understanding of sensitivity by simulation are "good enough" for purposes of developing theories and for comparing alternative theories.

Transient Response

Equilibrium analysis and sensitivity analysis of a system are efforts to answer the general questions: What are the long-run behavioral tendencies of the dynamics specified in the theory? and Which variables and relationships are the most consequential for determining the over-time behavior of the system? The answers to these basic questions tell us a good deal about the general plausibility of a theory of social dynamics. In both equilibrium and sensitivity analysis, however, our attention tends to focus on the "long-run" or "final" consequences of the network of assumptions that is the theory. While these are very important things to understand about the theory, we may also be interested in the behavior of system in the "short-run," and in the analysis of immediate rather than ultimate consequences of changes in variables.

Transient response analysis examines what happens when the system is subjected to stimuli. Its primary purpose is to trace the cycle of consequences resulting from a change in one part of a complexly connected system, and thereby to gain an understanding of the forces underlying the behavior of real systems in which many stimuli are constantly "shocking" the system.

The nature of the experiments that are conducted to examine the transient responsiveness of models follow from this intent. First the model is allowed to run to its steady state for some particular set of initial conditions; if no such steady state exists, some "baseline" realization of the system is used as the starting point instead. At this point the variable or parameter of interest is subjected to a stimulus with known characteristics (usually a PULSE, or a STEP, in DYNAMO terminology), and the pattern of change in the other variables in the system is traced as the response occurs along the pathways connecting the variables of the system.

Returning one last time to the simple population model of the earlier chapters, we might conduct a transient response analysis in the following way. First, to establish a baseline a certain set of initial conditions of the state variables and a certain set of initial conditions and a certain set of parameters (i.e., birth rates, death rates, etc.) could be specified, and the particular realization of the model calculated. The population model is one that does not attain a steady state across plausible levels of most variables, so transient response analysis is done on a "baseline" realization. Next, we might "schedule" a "war" to increase the death rate tenfold for a one-year period after some period of time, and rerun the model, making no other changes. We could then compare the results of the two realizations to attempt to understand the time shape of the system's response to changes in the death rate. In the population model this kind of transient shock reduces total population at all future points in time and creates oscillations in the time path of the model as well.

The analysis of transient response is an important step in under-standing most dynamic theories. Where elements in the state-space have complex over-time relations (delay and feedback), transient response testing provides the major device for understanding the process of change implied by the specification. Sometimes the theorist will find unanticipated consequences of their assumptions in exploring transient responses. In designing a program to assess the transient response characteristics implied by his or her theory, the analyst must again use good judgment and the principles of design that have been discussed with regard to equilibrium and sensitivity analysis. The range of alternative experiments that could be done to understand the processes of change in any dynamic theory of even moderate complexity is very great. Again, however, good judgment and careful experimental design can often yield very good "approximations" to understanding with relatively little effort.

Conclusions

Theories of the kinds of dynamics of interest to social scientists can rapidly become complex enough to require special aids and tools for their understanding, as well as for their construction. In this chapter we have examined how complexity in dynamic theories arises, and examined one strategy—simulation—for understanding and analyzing complex theory.

Complexity in theories arises from the number of elements of the state space, the range of values that can be taken by state space elements, the degree of connectivity of the state space, and nonlinearity in the functional and time-shapes of relations among state space elements. Many, though by no means all, theories of the continuous state continuous time dynamics in the social sciences are of sufficient complexity that they exceed our capacities to understand their full implications "intuitively" or by means of general (e.g., mathematical or logical deductive) solutions.

Simulation of realizations of such theories can often provide approximate solutions that are sufficient for our purposes. One major reason for the formalization of theories about dynamics is to enable the use of computers to calculate the results of large numbers of simulation "experiments" with theories.

In addition to experiments with theories that explore particular realizations (i.e., particular sets of values of variables and forms of relationships among them), strategies of "research on theory" can be designed to create approximate general understandings of complex theories. Most particularly, programs of systematic simulation experiments can be designed to understand the "equilibrium," "sensitivity," and "transient response" implications of theories. Fully determinant answers to questions about long-run and short-run behavior implied by the theory, and about the relative importance of particular assumptions are not possible with simulation methods. In most cases, however, careful and thorough application of principles of experimental design can yield a program of experimentation that provides information sufficient to our needs.

Notes

1. On methods for the formal analysis of theoretical systems by the application of logical rules, see particularly Dubin (1969), Hage (1972), Hearn (1958), Reynolds (1971), Stinchcombe (1968), and Willer (1967).

2. For some exemplary discussions of direct solution methods for analysis in social science applications, see Abelson (1967), Blau (1970), Blalock (1969), Caplow (1968), Cohen (1962), Coleman (1964a, 1964b, 1966, 1972, 1973), Davis (1967, 1972), Fararo (1972), Hamblin et al. (1973), Hummon (1971), Kassarda (1974), Kemeny and Snell (1962), Land (1970, 1975), Leik and Meeker (1975), Rapoport (1960, 1966); and Rapoport and Chammah (1965). Some outstanding examples of the approach in other kinds of systems analysis can be found in Braun (1975), Hall (1962), Luenberger (1979), and Takacs (1962).

3. There are a large number of excellent works in both the "general systems" tradition and in the disciplinary social sciences that devote extensive discussion to the meaning and implications of systems complexity. My list of favorites includes Ashby (1952, 1958), Baumgartner et al. (1976), Burns et al. (1985), Boulding (1970), Brunner and Brewer (1971), the essays in Foerster and Zopf (eds., 1962), Perrow (1984), Kochen and Deutsch (1980), Lange (1965), Mesarovic and Macko (1969), Pattee (1973), Schank and Colby (eds., 1973), Simon (1965, 1981), Sommerhoff (1969), Weaver (1948), and Weiner (1948).

4. Actually, this must not be entirely true. A fair amount of training is necessary for the proper application of even "simple" deduction or for comprehending the "simple" linear equation.

5. Perhaps the most interesting discussion of the nature of simulation models are contained in the essays of Abelson (1968) and Simon (1969, 1981).

6. For discussions of the application of simulation methods in various social science disciplines, see particularly Abelson (1968), Alker and Brunner (1969), Bloomfield and Padelford (1959), Brody (1963), Coe (1964), Cohen and Cyert (1965), Cole et al. (1973), the essays in Dutton and Starbuck (1971), Federico and Figliozzi (1981), Guetzkow et al. (eds., 1972), Guetzkow and Valdez (eds., 1981), Laponce and Smoker (eds., 1972), Levin (1962), Malone (1975), Marshall (1967), McPhee et al. (1971), Meier et al. (1969), Orcutt et al. (1961), Patten (1971), and Schmidt and Taylor (1970).

7. For an excellent example of this type of validation exercise in political science, see Brunner and Brewer (1971).

8. The topic of empirical validation of dynamic theories by simulation methods is widely discussed in a number of disciplines, ranging from applied statistics to management and economics. The interested reader can get an introduction to this literature by looking at Chorafas (1965), Coleman (1964), Deutsch et al. (1977), Dutton and Starbuck (1971), Emshoff and Sisson (1970), Federico and Figliozzi (1981), Hermann (1967), Martin (1968), Mihram (1972), Mize and Cox (1968), and Naylor et al. (1965).

9. The debate in sociology has been particularly bitter as "systems" approaches have been confounded with politically conservative policy positions and structural-functional theorizing. The debate sheds a good deal more heat than light, but for the interested reader a good introduction is provided by the essays in Demerath and Peterson (eds., 1967) and an article by van den Berghe (1963).

Part II

The Dynamics of Simple Systems

If we applied the definition of "complexity" that we developed in the previous chapter to the formal theories of social dynamics that have most concerned social scientists, we would classify these models as quite "simple." Most dynamic theorizing in the social sciences focus on the behavior of systems with relatively few states, low connectedness, and relatively simple functional and time relations. Perhaps the largest group of processes that have received attention involve only a single "dependent" state. Many others involve chains of a few states that are coupled together in very simple ways, very few involve extensive feedback or other complexities in their relationships among variables over time.

Simple systems, we must hasten to point out, are not trivial. Indeed, the "simple" systems that we will examine here have dynamics that are of extreme importance. The dynamics of growth, diffusion, contagion, population movement, and mobility are all quite effectively modeled (at least in "baseline" form) as consequences of quite simple dynamic systems. These dynamic processes are central to our understanding of economic, political, and socio-cultural phenomena. Simple models are widely applied with great profit in all of the disciplinary social sciences.

One goal of the chapters in this section is to reexamine these processes (all of which are treated extensively in the statistical and mathematical literatures as well) within the framework of dynamic "systems" developed in the previous section. These exercises will clarify the nature of the systems approach and its formal language, improve our understanding of some of the most common dynamic theories in the social sciences by translation into this language, and suggest ways in which a wide array of theoretical problems might be attacked as "simple systems."

There are two other reasons for spending a good bit of time with "simple" systems, in addition to the central role that such systems have as theories in themselves. Both of these reasons have to do with how we can go about constructing and understanding theories of systems of greater complexity.

"Simple" systems are the component parts of complex ones. To construct theories of complex social dynamics, or to analyze theories of

97

high complexity, it is necessary to have a firm grasp on the behavior of their component parts. To choose a simple example, one cannot understand the dynamics of the transmission of a message in a social network without having a grasp of how the individuals composing the network receive, process, and send information. The dynamic behavior of the network (a more complex "system" composed of "subsystems"— the actors plus the relations among them) is not reducible to the characteristics of the individuals in the system; but the behavior of the network is not intelligible without understanding the characteristics of the individual actors. All of the elements of even the most complex systems are, in themselves, quite simple, and we will examine these elements in the chapters in this section. Understanding the dynamics of these simple systems is a necessary, but not sufficient, condition for constructing and understanding theories about the dynamics of more complex systems.

In addition to being "building blocks" for more complex models, we can make a good deal of theoretical progress by tinkering with simple models and making them "slightly" more complex. Using the language of system dynamics and the method of analysis by simulation, we need not be as restrictive in our assumptions about the dynamics of simple systems as we would be if we were using statistical or mathematical models.

Statistically formulated statements of theories most often assume that the populations they describe are homogeneous (i.e., all individuals in a given population are equally probable to be subjected to a stimulus in a period of time and all individuals have the same probability distribution of responses to stimuli). It is sometimes useful to elaborate such models by creating multiple populations. In models of movements between occupational statuses, for example, one early approach to dealing with the poor fit of simple Markov processes was to divide the population into "movers" and "stayers." We will take a look at how relaxing homogeneity assumptions can provide greater insights in simple dynamic processes.

Theories of the dynamics of simple systems have also often assumed that the functional relations among variables are linear (or log-linear, in some cases), and that the processes are time homogeneous (i.e., they involve smooth integration, rather than lag and delay). Such assumptions are necessary for the successful application of statistical and mathematical methods to the verification and analysis of the theory, but are not necessary if the "approximate" solutions available by simulation are sufficient. We will also consider some of the ways that more relaxed assumptions about the forms of relations among variables and over time can lead to greater insights about the dynamics of simple processes.

Baselines

Before we make our theories about the dynamics of "simple" systems "slightly" more complex by adding nonlinearity, more complex time relations, or population heterogeneity, the "baseline" models should be thoroughly understood. In many cases, the highly simplified "baseline" models of diffusion, growth, and other similar processes do remarkably well in accounting for the essence of the dynamics, and additional complexity may not be worth the effort.[1] Even if increasing the complexity of such theories does contribute to improving our understanding, we must compare them to simpler baselines to determine "how much" better the more complex theory is. Thus even if the intent of the theorist is, ultimately, to create a complex model, it is best to start simple.

Increasing Complexity of "Simple" Systems

The simplest of all continuous time, continuous state models is quite easy to envision. It involves a single state, a single rate, and a simple signal, as in Figure II.1.

This model says that the level of Y accumulates from a source at the rate B. The speed of this process is governed by a random process. What makes this model so "simple" is that it involves only a single "level," and the process describing the rate of change in this level (i.e., the "rate") is a single and simple signal (random "white noise," in this case). The behavioral possibilities of the model in Figure II.1 are not very interesting. We will, however, spend a few minutes with it later because of its importance as a "baseline."

In increasing the complexity of this model to the point where it can usefully represent social dynamics, we can move in either of two directions. In practice, we usually move in both, but is useful to keep a conceptual distinction: (1) the number of states and flows among them can be increased, or (2) the complexity of the control structures governing these flows can be increased. That is, in different terms, we can consider either "more variables" or "more complex relationships" among them.

Consider the modification of Figure II.1 shown in Figure II.2.

In Figure II.2, the theory has become more complex by the addition of more independent variables and more complex relations between the independent variables and the single material state (Y). Roughly translated, the theory in Figure II.2 could be stated as follows. The level

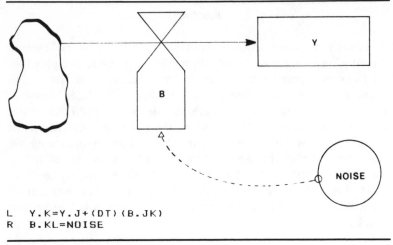

$$L \quad Y.K = Y.J + (DT)(B.JK)$$
$$R \quad B.KL = NOISE$$

Figure II.1:   Simple baseline model.

of Y changes over time at rates (B) proportional to the discrepancy (D) between a goal (G) and the current state of the system (Y). However, the response involves delay of an average duration of one period and having the shape of a third-order exponential (DELAY3,1). The discrepancy between the goal and the current state of the system might be calculated as a simple difference (D = G – Y). Goals, however, might be set as a function of a level of motivation (MM) and the current level of the system (Y), in some complex way. For example, the goal at any point in time is some fraction (determined by MM) of the current status of the system.

In this case, the "control" system displays considerable complexity. Indeed, the control structure could be said to represent a structure that is "self-referencing" and "goal directed"—that is, the rate of change in Y depends on the level of Y, and the action taken (B) is a function of a comparison of the current state of the system to some goal, and the goal is itself variable according to the state of the system.

This kind of elaboration of a simple system is of considerable importance in the study of human behavior. While many dynamic processes may be modeled with quite "simple" or "dumb" control structures, other forms of social behavior may require that we regard the control systems as being "smarter." Smarter control structures make reference to the self, are aware of the physical and informational environments, and formulate action strategies in very complex ways. As we proceed through the development of models in this section, one way

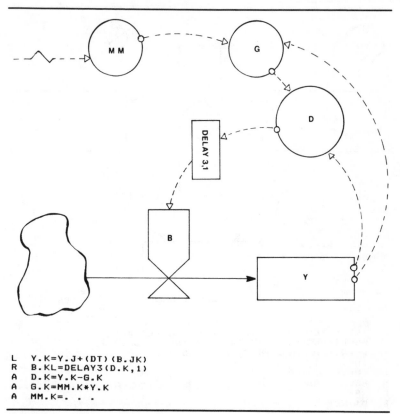

```
L    Y.K=Y.J+(DT)(B.JK)
R    B.KL=DELAY3(D.K,1)
A    D.K=Y.K-G.K
A    G.K=MM.K*Y.K
A    MM.K=.  .  .
```

Figure II.2: More elaborate control.

in which we will elaborate "simple" dynamics is to make them "smarter."

The elaboration of our simple baseline that is shown as Figure II.3 represents another direction of movement toward greater complexity.

This model has three "dependent" variables (the number of persons who are WELL, the number who are ILL, and the number who are DEAD). Transitions occur back and forth between WELL and ILL at rates governed by constants (the INFection rate and the RECovery rate); transitions occur between WELL and DEAD at a constant rate (DA, DAN) and between ILL and DEAD at constant rates (DD, DDN). Models of this type, that describe movements of "things" among multiple "statuses" are common in all of the social sciences—differing only in the definitions of "things" and definitions of "statuses."

The theory in Figure II.3 is more complex than the one in Figure II.1 primarily because it includes more elements in its state space. The

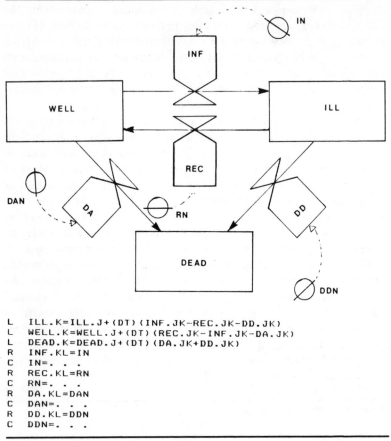

```
L    ILL.K=ILL.J+(DT)(INF.JK-REC.JK-DD.JK)
L    WELL.K=WELL.J+(DT)(REC.JK-INF.JK-DA.JK)
L    DEAD.K=DEAD.J+(DT)(DA.JK+DD.JK)
R    INF.KL=IN
C    IN=. . .
R    REC.KL=RN
C    RN=. . .
R    DA.KL=DAN
C    DAN=. . .
R    DD.KL=DDN
C    DDN=. . .
```

Figure II.3:   More elaborate state space.

connections among the states remain quite simple (indeed, unrealistically so). While maintaining quite simple forms of relationships among the elements of the state space, the state space is expanded to include multiple simultaneous equations or processes.

Outline of Part II

In the four chapters that follow, we have two major goals. First, we will become comfortable with the basic "building blocks" of more complex systems, and develop an understanding of their dynamic behavior. Second, we will examine some of the most widely used "simple" dynamic systems models in the social sciences using the DYNAMO language and simulation methods. As we do both of these things, we will be developing skills in systems thinking, translation from everyday to formal language, and a sense of how simulation experiments can be used to enrich the insights of "theoretical research" on the wide range of social science problems that can be characterized as "simple" systems.

The first two chapters (6 and 7) deal with systems that are relatively simple in terms of their state spaces, but increasingly complex in their "rates" or control systems. We will first discuss the basic ideas of "dumb" and "smart" control structures, and the related ideas of "feedforward" and "feedback." We will look at the construction of simple systems with increasingly complex control structures, and examine their typical dynamic behaviors. After these basic principles are in hand, we will illustrate the utility of such simple models by developing a theories of growth, decline, diffusion, and contagion.

The following two chapters (8 and 9) concern elaboration of models with relatively simple control structures into more complex systems by the addition of states. We will first discuss the architecture of "chains," and look at the wide applicability of such models for subject matter of interest to social scientists. To illustrate the dynamics of "chain" models, we will then develop models of three kinds of processes of great interest and generality: age structures of populations, models of vacancy chains and models of multistate mobility and transition processes.

Note

1. The role of "baseline" models in theory building is extensively discussed in an article and rejoinder by Mayhew (1984), and a sympathetic critique by Turner and Hanneman (1984).

6

Single-State Systems:
The Complexity of Control

The basic building block of all systems dynamics models is a single-state variable (the "level") and the expression describing the causes of over-time variation in the state (the "rate"). A surprisingly large number of social science theories are concerned with the dynamics of systems that are composed of very few states and, in many cases have only a single "dependent variable." Such theories, however, are not necessarily simple, as they often specify quite complex hypotheses about the causes of variation in rates of change.

One theorist might, for example, be concerned with the dynamics of attitudinal intensity (as in the study of the strength of support for political candidates). The intensity of belief might be conceived of as a continuous (and conserved) state that changes over time at rates determined by the timing and intensity of propaganda, the subject's perceptions of the attitudes of members of their reference groups, and other factors. In this case, the system has essentially a single dependent state (attitudinal intensity), but this state may change over time at rates that are governed by quite complicated combinations of exogenous variables.

Another theorist might be concerned with the analysis of characteristics of aggregates, such as the number of organizations of a certain type existing in a given geographical space over time. In this case too, the theory is concerned with dynamics that are "simple" in one sense: There is a single dependent variable (the number of organizations). But, hypotheses that might be specified concerning the causes of increases in the organizational population (that is, the rate of organizational formation) and the causes of decreases in the organizational population (that is, the rate of failure) might be extremely complex.

There are many problems in each of the social sciences that may be usefully conceptualized as systems involving few states but complex rates. As the examples above illustrate, these problems are "simple" in the systems sense of the word, but hardly trivial. The dynamic behavior of "simple" systems is also not so easy to comprehend as one might expect. Depending on the complexity of the relationships expressed in the equations for the rates of change, and on the time paths of the exogenous variables, virtually any form of over-time behavior can be displayed by even the "simplest" of systems.

Systems analysis and systems theory provide an extremely powerful set of tools for describing and examining the complexity of the expressions for rates of change: "control structures." The expressions describing the causes of rates of change in states can be thought of as "mechanisms" controlling the speed at which processes that increase or decrease the level are occurring. These mechanisms can themselves be quite simple or quite complicated, and we can think about them in this way.[1] Some of the mechanisms governing change in patterns of social action and interaction may be quite "dumb" or simple, involving little more than responses to external stimuli. Other patterns of social action and interaction may be thought of as processes controlled by "self-referencing" mechanisms of "feedback" and "feedforward". Still more complicated control structures involve referencing goals, or even setting goals as part of the processes controlling action. As the complexity of the control structures that govern rates of change in a single-state increase, the range of possible behavioral responses increase as well. Systems with very simple control structures are capable of only a limited range of over-time behaviors, systems with complex control structures are capable of much more complex patterns.

In the remainder of this chapter we will examine "control structures" of increasing complexity, and look at some of the behavioral tendencies of single-state systems governed by such control structures. As will quickly become apparent, most theories of the dynamics of social action and interaction tend to use quite simple specifications of control structures. In most cases this is entirely appropriate, as many very important problems from all social science disciplines can be very effectively modeled as being relatively "dumb." An exposure to the range of possible control structures of greater complexity, however, should stimulate interest in the utility of more complicated specifications.

Types of Control Systems

In thinking about the ways in which the dynamic behavior of a variable might be generated or controlled, it is useful to keep in mind our earlier definition of complexity. The same ideas can be applied in discussing the complexity of the "control structures" of theories, as well as in discussing whole systems. A more complex control system is one that makes reference to more pieces of information about the system, utilizes more of this information simultaneously (i.e. the control system has high connectivity), and combines information according to functional and time forms of high order.[2]

It is possible to envision a continuum of control system types from less to more complex. At the simple end, the "control structure" governing the rate of change in some variable Y might consist of a single qualitative relation: If X, then Y. Rather nearer the other end or the possible spectrum of control system complexity are homeostatic mechanisms like thermostats: the "control system" here monitors the room temperature, compares its "perception" of the temperature to a "goal," and increases the rate of heating if the actual temperature is less than the goal.

For constructing theories about human social action and interaction, it is most useful to divide control systems into classes according to the complexity of the connections among pieces of information, rather than the number of pieces of information involved. The "simplest" control structures are describe patterns of action that are of a "stimulus-response" or "dumb" type. A DYNAMO diagram showing the basic structure of such a control structure is shown in Figure 6.1.

Control mechanisms of this simplest type receive stimuli from the environment (X1 and X2), which may be noise, constants, or functions of other variables, and produce automatic responses of increase (B1) or decrease (B2) with respect to time. A good deal of highly socialized human behavior can be effectively understood as involving only such simple mechanisms. Such dynamic models are often used, as well, to approximate more complex processes—as in the case of simple linear equations in exogeneous variables describing the behavior of aggregates.

A slightly "smarter" form of control system involves "self-referencing." Stimulus-response type control structures produce fixed responses to stimuli, regardless of the state of the system. Self-referencing systems' responses to stimuli depend on external stimuli and the current state of the system. The diagram in Figure 6.2 shows a prototype of a simple "self-referencing" control systems with feedback and feedforward.

Consider, as an example of such a "self-referencing" control system, the number of departments and hierarchical levels in a bureaucracy. One theory might hold that the "differentiation" (that is, the numbers of vertical and horizontally specialized units) of the organization increases

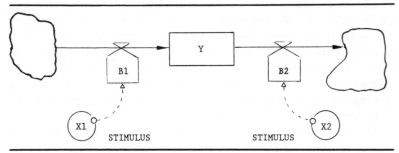

Figure 6.1: Stimulus-response control.

in direct proportion to the "carrying capacity" of the environment. This is a "stimulus-response" type of control. An alternative theory might suggest that the rate of addition of new units to a bureaucracy depends not only on the carrying capacity of the environment, but also on the existing level of differentiation: In the same environment with slack carrying capacity, it might be argued, organizations that are highly differentiated will increase their differentiation more rapidly than those that are less differentiated. In this example, the response to an environmental stimulus (slack carrying capacity in the environment) depends on the current state of the systems (how differentiated the organization already is). The behavior of the system might be said to be "self-referencing."[3]

Such simple mechanisms though, are often not sufficient to represent the control structures of many dynamic social processes. Many patterns of human social action and interaction are more usefully thought of as oriented toward the attainment of goals. Control systems in which information about goals as well as the state of the exogenous variables and the system itself are taken into account are, in some sense, "smart" systems. In goal-seeking control structures, the response of the system to a stimulus is contingent on the relationship between the current state of the system and some "desired" or goal state. A prototypical example of a goal-seeking control system structure is shown in Figure 6.3.

To return to our organizational differentiation example, suppose that the profitability of the organization depended on the "fit" between the carrying capacity of the environment and the differentiation of the organization. In a theory involving "goal-oriented" control, the organization's behavior in the face of an environment that has slack might be theorized to follow this process: The organization has a goal of increasing profit, and in each period of time the rate of addition (or elimination) of organizational units depends upon the level of current

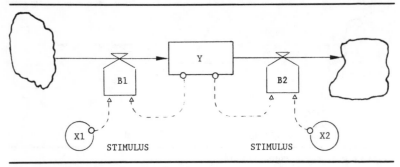

Figure 6.2: Self-referencing control.

profits. If profits are positive, organizational units are added; if profits are negative, organizational units are eliminated. In this control system, the rate of change in the number of organizational units is contingent upon a comparison between the current state of the system and a goal state. Rather than simply responding, or responding in a way that is conditioned by the current state of the system, the response is generated here by a much more complex process of comparisons to goals.

The next step up in the increasing complexity of control mechanisms should be rather easy to anticipate. Beyond "goal-seeking" mechanisms, we can readily imagine that much human social action and interaction can be usefully thought of as being governed by "goal-setting" or "adaptive" control. Such processes involve not only comparisons of the state of the system to goals, but also dynamic modification of the goals. A prototype of such a control structure is shown as Figure 6.4.

We can modify our theory of organizational behavior to make it "intelligent" (in the sense of goal setting) rather than simply rather "smart" (in the sense of goal referencing). Suppose that our organization's leadership monitors the environment and uses this information to set profit goals. The rate of addition or elimination of organizational units depend, as in the previous model, on the ratio of profits to profit goals. However, as the environment changes the goal for profitability is modified, and the organization is responding to environmental change both behaviorally and in the processes that set the goals that govern behavioral responses.

One could go on to consider even more intelligent mechanisms of control, but such mechanisms are beyond the scope of the current work—and are very rarely utilized in contemporary social science theorizing about the dynamics of systems. In fact, most theories of social action, in properly striving for parsimony, specify quite simple control

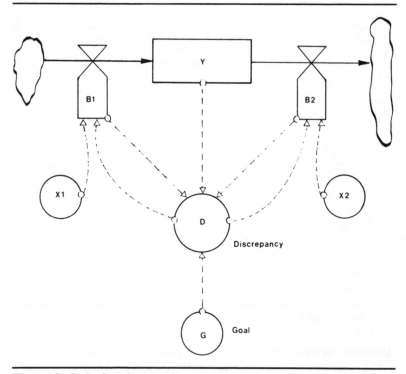

Figure 6.3: Goal-referencing control.

structures. In the third section, we will have some opportunity to look at more complicated forms.

Often the mechanisms that govern the dynamics of social action and interaction are quite complex, but can be approximated by simpler and hence more analyzable models. These "simple" control mechanisms themselves are capable of very complicated-appearing responses to stimuli, and are a good place to start in building theories of social dynamics.

The Dynamics of "Dumb" Control Structures

The dynamics of a very wide range of forms of social action can be very effectively described and analyzed as systems with quite simple control structures. Whether we are talking about an individual person, some other social actor, or the average tendency of a homogeneous aggregate of actors, many forms of social dynamics seem to be quite

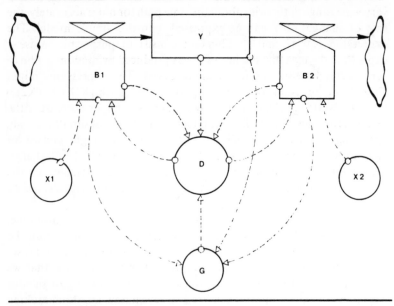

Figure 6.4: Adaptive control.

interpretable as governed by "stimulus-response" types of control.

Because theories using such control structures are so common, and because such structures are the bases for more complex ones, it is useful to spend a bit of time becoming comfortable with the kinds of over-time behavior that these control systems can produce.

In Figure 6.1, in the section above, we presented a diagram of a simple stimulus-response control system. In this example, the single dependent system state is incremented over time and decremented over time at certain rates. In the DYNAMO language, this can be expressed as:

```
L     Y.K = Y.J+(DT)(RI.JK−RD.JK)
R     RI.KL = f1
R     RD.KL = f2
```

where Y is the "level" of the state variable, and "RI and RD are arbitrary names used to refer to the "rate of increase" and "rate of decrease" in Y. The terms f1 and f2 are any logical or mathematical expressions involving any number of exogenous variables (that is, Y does not appear in f1 or f2, else the system would be "self-referencing").

With sufficient cleverness, any pattern of over-time behavior of Y can be produced by varying the expressions for f1 and f2. And, indeed, a very wide range of theories about the time path (or more accurately, the rate of change) of Y can be expressed with this simple model. The expressions for f1 and/or f2 might consist of pure white noise—expressing the idea that change in Y was produced by random action (a very useful baseline model in many cases). The expressions might consist of expressions of the familiar form: $f1 = a + b_1(X1) + b_2(X2) + b_3(X3) + NOISE()$. That is, the rate of increase and/or decrease is the result of the linear addition of the effects of a number of simultaneously operating exogeneous variables. The expressions might consist of equations of the increasingly familiar form: $f2 = ae^{b1(X1)+b2(X2)}$; that is, the log-linear or multiplicative interaction of several variables. Or the expressions could consist of sets of logical tests and hierarchically nested relations.

In order to get a good sense of how "dumb" systems behave over time, however, it is useful first to explore their response to simple stimuli. To do this we will perform three sets of simulation experiments. First we will subject our very simple integrating system (i.e., the one that we described in the DYNAMO equations above) to a variety of signals. This experiment is important in itself to reveal how the static-looking expressions produce imply dynamic behavior. The second and third experiments will look at the less common and obvious dynamics of simple integrating systems that have "delayed" effects: that is, time forms of relations that are not linear.[4]

Experiment: Simple Integration

Let us begin with the most obvious of all dynamic formulations. In our first experiment we have a dependent variable (Y) that is incremented (we could, of course, run these processes in reverse, decrementing the level) over time at rates (RI) that are functions of (a) a constant, (b) white noise, (c) normally distributed noise, (d) a steadily increasing stimulus (RAMP), (e) a change from one level of stimulus to another (STEP), and (f) a set of timed PULSEs. Simulations showing each of these stimuli, and the over-time level of the response state Y are shown in Figure 6.5.

In the first panel of the figure, the response variable (shown with the asterisk) is subjected to a constant input (the input signal is shown with the plus sign). It is hardly surprising, but nonetheless is quite important, that in "conserved" states the incoming signal continuously accumulates, generating a pattern of linear growth. Any slope can be produced by altering the sign and magnitude of the constant input. If, for example, the effect of the independent variable on the rate of change in Y were

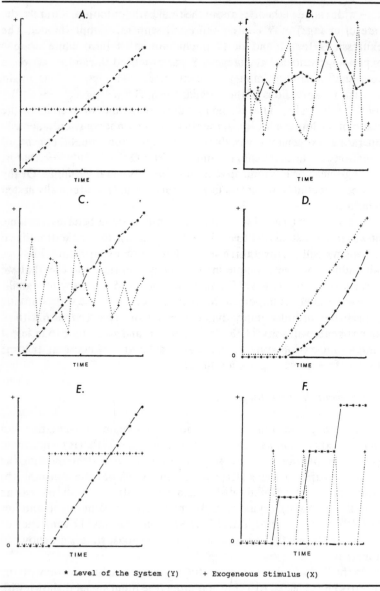

* Level of the System (Y)   + Exogeneous Stimulus (X)

Figure 6.5: Stimulus-response experiments.

negative, the response of Y would be linear, but with negative slope with respect to time. Differing slopes (but always linear shapes) of the response could also be produced by the action of multiple constants on

Y. A process that was described by the following equation, for example, would produce an absolutely flat time response, despite the complex equation (so long as each X is a constant of unit value or the Xs change in exactly compensating fashions with respect to time):

$$Y.K = Y.J + DT(.5 + .3(X1) + .2(X2) - 1.0 (X3))$$

It is worth noting at this point, as we shall again and again, that a given time path of response variable can be produced by a very wide variety of alternative underlying mechanisms. A pattern of constant change, for example, may reflect the action of one constant, a combination of many constants, compensating changes among multiple causes, or the action of a feedback control mechanism. The data do not speak for themselves. It is up to the theorist to offer convincing reasons for supposing that one underlying mechanism or another is producing a given response pattern.

In panel b of the figure white noise is used as the stimulus to our simple control system. The integration of white noise should, in the long run, have an expected value of zero. As the time trace shows, however, it is possible for a purely random process to display what appears to be consistent trends for some periods of time. This process is called "drift." The important point to note about the responses of simple integrating control systems to white noise is that integration dampens the "jagged" over-time behavior of the "independent variable" into a smoother-appearing response and that this response may display substantial short run orderliness, despite the purely random causal process.

In the third panel (c), our "dumb" control system has been subjected to a stimulus that is normally distributed with an expected value of a positive constant. The stimulus in panel c combines the constant trend of panel a with the "noise" of panel b. The response of the system is also the sum of the previous two patterns: linear trend in response to the constant part of the stimulus, and random variation around the trend as a result of the noise component. Where the rate of change in the stimulus is a constant, then, integration produces a linear trend in the response; where the stimulus is random, integration produces a dampened response with an expected value of zero.

When the independent or causal variables are themselves displaying trends (unlike the cases of noise or constant input), how does a simple integrating system respond? In panel d the stimulus is set to a constant of zero for a period of time and then increases at a constant rate (that is, the independent variable begins a linear upward trend). Since our response variable accumulates or integrates these increasingly large values of the stimulus, a pattern of exponential growth is produced. Many systems with more complex control structures (i.e., feedback) also produce exponential over-time behavior. The importance of the experiment in panel d is that it demonstrates that a simple system can also produce exponential responses when stimulus variables display trends. This fact again suggests that it may be dangerous to "reason backwards" from an observed behavior pattern to a hypothesis about the process that produced it.

In panel e of the figure another experiment with a trending independent variable is shown (a step function). For the first several time periods the stimulus is constant at zero, then shifts to a constant positive number. In both periods, the response is linear (because the stimulus is a constant), but the slope of the response changes when the stimulus takes on a positive value. Finally, in panel f we experiment with the "transient response" of our "dumb" control structure. The system is subjected to shocks (pulses) that occur at regular intervals. Each of these signals is absorbed by the response state, which changes in a stepwise fashion as it does so.

The over-time behavior of a single dependent state governed by a "dumb" or simple stimulus-response control structure is not difficult to anticipate with a few moments' thought. Despite this simplicity, there are several important basic lessons in this exercise. Where the causal effect of one variable (the stimulus) on the other is a constant, the response variable displays linear trend with respect to time. Constant causal pressures then produce trends, not absence of change in dependent states. Where causal variables are trending linearly, accumulating systems display exponential trending. Episodic "shocks" are accumulated as well by systems governed by such simple control structures. If the shocks are purely random, they may produce short-term "drift" in the level of the system; if they contain a "bias" (as in the case of panels c and f), trend, as well as drift, can be produced by seemingly random causal stimuli.

In a more general sense, it is most important to realize that systems governed by very simple control structures can produce quite complex responses if the stimuli to which they are subjected are complex. We have also only considered the simplest possible "ideal types" of stimulus-response systems. Often a single state may be affected by a large number of independent variables at the same time. The combined force of a number of constants, trends, noises, and shocks can produce extremely complex response patterns. These possible "realizations" of very simple "dumb" systems become even more complicated if we make more realistic assumptions about the time-shapes of the relationships between stimuli and responses.

Experiment: Simple Integration with First-Order Delay

There are many cases in which it is unrealistic to assume that the response to a stimulus is instantaneous and constant. A "first-order" exponential delay assumes that the initial response to a stimulus is strong, but that the response continues to occur at exponentially declining rates thereafter. When a series of stimuli are received, first-order "exponential delays" are equivalent to weighting the most recent signal most heavily in formulating a response, but also using information about the previous signal (assigning it less weight than the current one) and the signal before that (again assigning less weight to it) and so on.[5]

First-order delays can occur in social systems in many ways. Suppose that the management of an organization orders the production of 100 widgets. Because of resistance and friction between workers and management, however, the production line will only produce 80% of the unfilled orders from management in each time period. If there are no new orders, 80 widgets will be produced in the first period after the order is given and 16 in the second period after the order is given (that is 80% or the remaining 20 widgets that were ordered but not yet delivered). By the beginning of the third time period after the order is given, 96 widgets have been produced and 80% of the remaining four are consequently done in the third period. The original order of 100 widgets will eventually be produced (actually not, as the process only approaches full realization, and never actually gets there), but may do so after a considerable time. The "friction," "inertia," and "resistance" of responses to stimuli in social systems can often be effectively modeled as exponential delays of various average lengths.

In the top panel of Figure 6.6 the transient response of our "dumb" system to a PULSE (that is, one time shock) is shown under different assumptions about the degree of friction and resistance (that is, the average length or half-life of the DELAY1 function). The figure shows the response of the system to first-order delays of 1, 2, 5, and 9 time periods. The responses shown are all of the same shape, but differ in how long they take to be fully realized. The delay of "average length" of two units reaches 50% of its final value at time point five—two time units after the shock (which occurred at time-point three); the delay of "average length" of five units reaches 50% of its final value after 5 time units, etc.

Real social systems, of course, do not sit still while each stimulus is translated with friction and delay into a response. Rather, continuous streams of stimuli are occurring. In the bottom panel of Figure 6.6 we show a very simple experiment to illustrate what happens when multiple

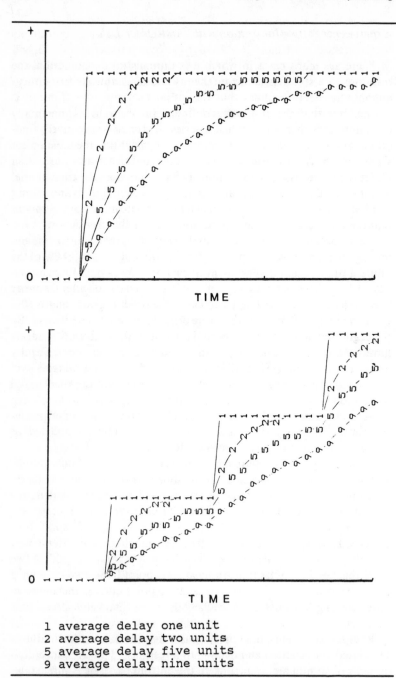

Figure 6.6: First-order delay.

stimuli are occurring in "dumb" systems with delay. In the experiments shown in the bottom panel, a set of pulses occur at time points 3, 13, and 23. Control structures with first-order exponential delays of average lengths of one, two, five, and nine time periods are shown responding to this stimulus.

There are two interesting aspects of the results in the bottom panel of the figure. The "delays" produce responses to the stimuli that are progressively "smoother" as the average length of the delay increases. This is a fundamental and important characteristic of all delays, with major implications for modeling the dynamics of social action: To the extent that relations among things operating over time involve resistance and friction, "dependent" variables tend to be seen as sluggish and smoothed reflections of the stimuli that generated them.

The second important aspect of the behavior of the simple stimulus-response mechanism in the bottom panel of the figure is somewhat more subtle. The delays of very short average length (that is, the curves one and two) succeed in "catching up" between the stimuli—which occur only every 10 time periods. The delays of greater average length (the curves five and nine) have not completely closed the gap between the original stimulus and their final response by the time that the new stimulus occurs. As a consequence, the responses of states with lengthy delays always lag behind the ongoing stimulus and never "catch up" (actually the short delays never catch up either, but the gaps are so small as to be, usually, of little importance). When the delays in a system are relatively long compared to the frequency of stimuli—and they usually are, as stimuli occur continuously—dynamic systems are never observed "in equilibrium." The status of the state space at any point in time in a system with friction and delay is a reflection of stimuli in past periods, as well as of immediately preceding stimuli. Where social action involves delay and friction, then, responses are not only "smoothed" reactions to stimuli, but are responses to past as well as to current stimuli.

Experiment: Simple Integration with Third-Order Delay

Simple "friction" resulting in the smoothing of responses to stimuli is very common in social systems. In many cases, however, the delay in responding to stimuli takes the form of a "higher order" function of time. The DYNAMO language provides as a convenient tool the third-order delay as a built-in function, and the time shape of this curve is sufficiently complex to capture a very interesting and important class of responses: those with "latency." In Figure 6.7 we show the results of the same sets of experiments that we discussed at some length in the

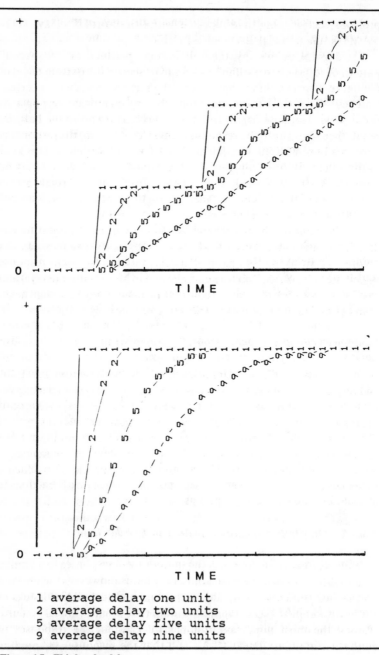

Figure 6.7: Third-order delay.

previous section, this time repeated with "third-order" delays (DY-NAMO's functions DELAY3 or DLINF3).

Third-order delays, by their definition, produce an "S-shaped" pattern of response to a stimulus—as can be seen in the bottom panel of the figure. One can think about such delays as responses with a certain "latency." That is, it takes some time for any significant response to occur. Once response begins to occur, it accelerates up to the halfway point, then slows until the response is completed (again, the response is never really completed, but this rarely is of any importance). This kind of time-shape is more complex than the first-order delay, and may be more realistic for modeling the dynamics of many forms of social action in which the "resistance" or "inertia" is not constant, but is rather stronger at first and declines later.

The top panel of the figure repeats the experiment of subjecting our "dumb" control structure with delay to a series of timed shocks. As before, the important lessons are that delay tends to "smooth" response (albeit the "smoothing" is more complicated in higher-order delays) and that, in the presence of delays of substantial magnitude, the system never "catches up" in its responses to the string of incoming stimuli.

Summary: The Behavior of "Dumb" Control Structures

In this section we have examined some of the possible configurations and responses of the simplest of dynamic systems. The results themselves are somewhat complex, and it is probably helpful if we repeat some of the main points before turning to more complicated structures.

Systems with control structures that are of the simplest type, "stimulus-response," as opposed to the more complex "self-referencing," "smart," and "adaptive" types, are nonetheless capable of producing extremely complicated behavior patterns. The range of possible behavior of such systems is limited only by the complexity of the stimuli that it is subjected to and by the form of its response (i.e., whether the response involves simple integration or some nonlinear "delay" pattern of response).

We have examined the responsiveness of a simple system to a variety of abstract and ideal typical kinds of stimuli (constants, white and normal noise, pulses, steps, and ramps) that are the building blocks of the more complex and compound stimuli that occur in social systems. Among the most important results here are that the responses to constant stimuli are linear trends and that the responses to trending stimuli are exponential.

We have also taken a brief look at what happens when the time shape of responses to stimuli take somewhat more complex forms in "dumb systems." (The consequences are not the same in systems with more complex control structures.) Two types of "delays" (or "resistances" or "frictions") in responses were examined, corresponding to simple resistance and response with latency. The general lessons here are that such delays in response "dampen" and "smooth" the response of the system to stimuli, and that in the presence of such "delayed" responses systems never fully "catch up" in their responses to changes in their environments.

The Dynamics of Self-Referencing Systems

In the previous section we considered the behavior of systems that simply responded in a mechanical "stimulus-response" fashion to environmental changes. A large number of important phenomena can be be effectively represented by systems with such simple control structures, and virtually any pattern of observed trends over time can be reproduced by such models. Theories about the dynamics of social action, however, often suggest that actors or variables do not simply respond to external stimuli. Conceptions of the "control" systems governing the dynamics of action that allow actors to make reference to their own current status ("self-referencing"), as well as to external stimuli, are the next step up in the complexity of control structures.

Stimulus-response control structures take into account only changes in the environment and accumulate the past history of these events to generate the current status of the system. "Self-referencing" control structures take into account not only external events, but also the current status of the system in determining rates of change. That is, the current state of the system is one cause of change in the system. In the language of systems analysis, such control structures are characterized by "loops" of "feedback" and/or "feedforward," as is illustrated in the idealized diagram in Figure 6.2, shown earlier.

The dynamics of self-referencing systems, or systems with feedback, are quite different from those of the simpler stimulus-response type. We will spend a bit of time examining these dynamics in the abstract, just as we did with stimulus-response systems, because the "loops" in such systems are a basic building block of more complicated control structures. Once we have a feeling for the behavior of systems with simple "feedback" loops, the behavior of more complex "goal-seeking" and "adaptive" systems becomes quite easy to anticipate.

One way to understand why the dynamic behavior of self-referencing systems is inherently different from dumb systems is to examine the equations that describe the two types. The formal structure of the simplest dumb system can be stated as:

L $Y.K = Y.J + (DT) (RI.JK)$
R $RI.KL = f(X)$

That is, the level of the variable Y at a later time is equal to its level at the previous time plus the effects of some function of exogenous variables X. The basic form of a simple self-referencing system can be stated as:

L $Y.K = Y.J + (DT) (RI.JK)$
R $RI.KL = f(X) + g(Y)$

That is, the rate of change in the dependent variable is a consequence of both exogenous factors (X), and the variable itself (Y).

What kind of an effect the dependent variable has on itself over time (i.e., the $g(Y)$ term), is up to the theorist to specify. In most models, this function is a simple constant. This is equivalent to hypothesizing that the rate of change is proportional to the level of the system. If the function is a negative number, increases in Y create decrements in the rate of change. This is what is known as "negative feedback." If the function is a positive constant, the rate of change in Y increases as Y increases, and "positive feedback" exists.

Let's suppose, for example, that we are interested in the dynamics of vocabulary development in individuals. One theorist might propose that the number of new words learned in each period of time is a function of the level of social interaction with adults (regarded as an exogenous X) and a positive function of the existing level of vocabulary. That is, the more vocabulary that exists, the more adult conversation is understood, resulting in more rapid learning of new words. This hypothesis is one of a positive feedback of the level of vocabulary on the rate of change in vocabulary development. Alternatively, one might hypothesize that the rate of change in vocabulary development is a function of interaction with adults, but a negative function of the existing level. That is, interaction gives rise to new vocabulary learning, but as learned vocabulary increases the number of unknown words declines and learning of new words slows. This theory proposes that there is negative feedback between the level of the state (number of words known) and the rate of change in vocabulary (new words learned per unit of time).

Systems governed by positive loops tend to display accelerating time trends. Since the current level of the system serves as a stimulus for further change, positive feedback tends to "amplify" whatever tendencies exist in the system. Systems governed by negative loops have the exact opposite tendency. As the level of the system becomes higher, the rate of change becomes more negative, creating a tendency to "dampen" the impacts of stimuli.

The behavior of real systems with feedback structures can, as with dumb systems, be very complex. If the time paths of the stimuli (exogenous variables) are complicated, and if there are numerous independent variables and feedback loops having impacts of the same dependent variable, the time path of the dependent variable can have any shape. The complicated behavior of real systems, however, is made up of combinations of several basic response patterns. We can get a better grasp of the behavior of feedback systems by looking at some of these "ideal typical" scenarios with simulation experiments.

Experiment: Positive Feedback

In a set of experiments, let's subject a single state system governed by positive feedback to several kinds of exogenous stimuli. In each of these cases, the system is set initially at 0, and the positive feedback loop operates to increment the rate of change by 10% of the current level of the system. The system is first subjected to a constant stimulus, then to a randomly varying pattern, to a trending independent variable, and lastly to episodic shocks (i.e., X is a STEP, NOISE, RAMP, and PULSE). The separate components of the rate of change are shown in three of the panels, with the impacts of the exogenous variable represented by +'s and the impacts of the positive feedback represented by the #'s.

In the first panel we see that the response of a positive feedback system to a constant input is exponential. The explosive growth of the system is generated by the effects of the feedback loop (the #), which creates increasing change as the level of the system increases. When the input stimulus is quite noisy, as it is in the experiment shown in the second panel of the figure, exponential growth also occurs, and for the same reason. The underlying process generating the pattern, however, is far from clear in this experiment—typical of data in which the signal-to-noise ratio is low (here the ratio is, on the average, about .2). In the third scenario, our system is subjected to a linearly trending independent variable (the +'s), and generates "super exponential" growth (that is, the rate of change itself increases at an increasing rate) again as a consequence of self-referencing. In the last experiment of the series, two

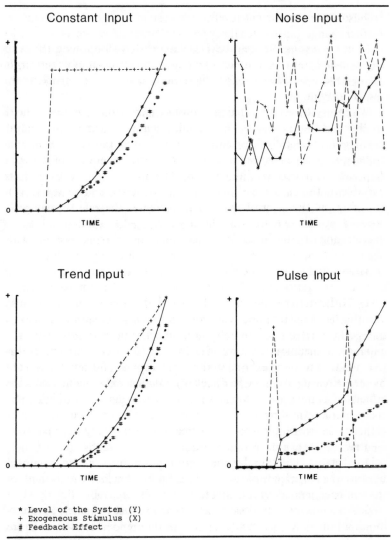

    * Level of the System (Y)
    + Exogeneous Stimulus (X)
    # Feedback Effect

Figure 6.8: Positive feedback.

exogenous shocks occur, with no external stimuli between these events. The response of the system is again exponential, but the steepness of the exponential changes increases with each shock (because each shock increases the level of the system, hence increasing the power of the feedback).

Experiment: Negative Feedback

To get a feeling for the differences in the dynamic consequences of negative and positive feedback, we repeat the same set of experiments with a negative feedback loop. The result of this set of experiments are shown in Figure 6.9.

When a system is subjected to a constant exogenous stimulus without feedback, it responds with linear trend; when the system is governed by positive feedback, its response is accelerating growth; when it is governed by negative feedback, as in the first panel of Figure 6.9, it responds with decelerating growth. The impact of the exogenous variables in this case (the +'s) would create a linear trend in the level (*). However, as the level of the system increases the rate of change is reduced by the operation of the negative feedback (#), resulting in deceleration. In the presence of constant input then, systems with negative feedback control structures tend toward a steady state.

The second experiment with negative feedback control subjects the system to random stimuli. As with positive feedback in a noisy system, it is very difficult to perceive any pattern in the time-shape of the response variable here. In fact there is no trend, as the negative feedback acts to dampen the effects of the exogenous shocks. In the third figure the exogenous variable is trending linearly, and the system, being conservative, tends to respond exponentially. This response, however, is limited by the increasing negative feedback (#). Our last experiment shows the effects of shocks on systems governed by negative feedback. The complex pattern of response here is generated by the accumulation of rather large exogenous shocks (+) creating increasingly large negative feedbacks (#) that are self-dampening as the system tends to return to its original state. The general tendency of the system over time is upward because the magnitude of the shocks is far greater than the strength of the feedback mechanisms acting to limit their impacts.

Self-referencing or feedback systems can produce extremely complex-looking behavior. Their fundamental dynamic tendencies, however, are quite apparent from our discussion and experiments. If the rate of change of a system is a positive function of the level of the system (positive feedback), the control structure tends to create accelerating change that drives the system away from its original condition. If the rate of change in the system is a negative function of the level of the system (negative feedback), then the control structure tends to produce decelerating change that drives the system toward its original state.

These insights about the basic dynamics of self-referencing systems

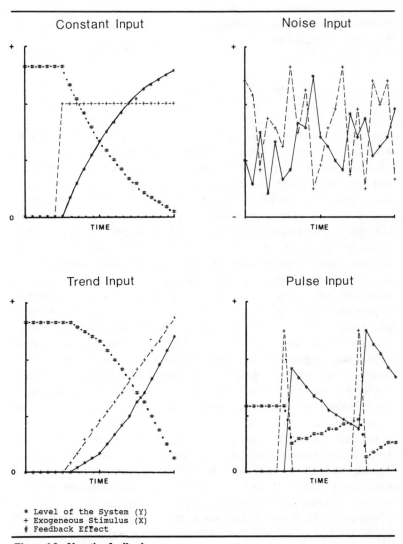

Constant Input

Noise Input

Trend Input

Pulse Input

* Level of the System (Y)
+ Exogeneous Stimulus (X)
# Feedback Effect

Figure 6.9: Negative feedback.

are quite familiar,[6] but this familiarity should not lead us to ignore their importance. The underlying dynamic tendencies of self-referencing systems are quite different from those of systems with "dumb" control structures that respond only to external stimuli. Unlike "dumb" systems, self-referencing systems can produce self-generating and self-limiting behavior and hence are frequently a more powerful analogy for theorizing about processes of social action and interaction than systems with less complex control structures.

Smart Systems: The Dynamics of Goal-Referencing Control

Many patterns of social action and interaction are regarded by theorists as being governed by processes that are more complex than stimulus-response and self-referencing feedback. It is often helpful to think of social actors as making reference to goals, as well as to exogenous factors and their own current status, in formulating acts.

The decision of an organization to change its formal structure, for example, is probably best thought of as an act formulated with reference to exogenous stimuli, the current state of the organizational structure, and some goal. Organizations, as "intendedly rational" actors, change their structure in an attempt to attain goals—greater profitability, better insulation from competition, conformity with the value preferences of important constituencies, or other factors. The streams of signifying acts performed by persons in face-to-face interaction can be thought of as the consequence of goal-referencing feedback as well. Individuals in such situations perceive the behavior of others (that is, makes reference to the environment), are aware of their own behavior, and have "goals" for the interaction. These goals may be instrumental, expressive, or both. The stream of acts is governed by the combination of information about the environment and the actor and by the goals.

Control systems that take goals into account, as well as information about the environment and current status of the system, could be called "smart," at least in comparison to stimulus-response and simple self-referencing systems. In terms of their formal structure, however, smart systems are simply feedback systems with a slightly more complex structure, as can be seen by comparing the diagrams of the prototype in Figure 6.3 with those in Figures 6.1 and 6.2. This similarity of formal structure is matched by a similarity of fundamental dynamic behavior of systems governed by simple self-referencing and goal-referencing control structures. Self-referencing systems tend to amplify (where the feedback is positive) or dampen (where the feedback is negative) stimuli received from the environment. Goal-referencing systems behave in the same fashion, but the effects of the feedback loop are proportional to the discrepancy between the current state of the system and some goal, rather than directly proportional to the current level of the system. Goal-referencing systems have a tendency to approach or diverge from certain goal levels, in contrast to the tendency of simple self-referencing systems to approach or diverge from their current levels.

To illustrate this behavior, let's construct a simple goal referencing system and examine its response to stimuli. Such a system is shown in the DYNAMO equations:

L   Y.K = Y.J+(DT)(RI.JK)
R   RI.KL = ENVIRON.K+FEEDBACK.K
A   ENVIRON.K = f(X)
A   FEEDBACK.K = PARM*DISCREP.K
A   DISCREP.K = Y.K–GOAL
C   GOAL = constant

The first statement specifies that the dependent variable (Y) changes at rates RI. The second statement says that RI has two component parts, one a consequence of ENVIRONment, and the other a consequence of FEEDBACK. The third statement defines the environmental impact on rates of change in Y as an arbitrary function (f) of some variable or variables X. The fourth statement specifies that the rate of change in Y is proportional (either positively or negatively, and with some intensity) to a "DISCREPancy." The meaning of this discrepancy is defined in the next statement as the simple difference between a GOAL (a "desired" level of Y) and the current status of Y. Then in the last statement the GOAL is set as a constant.

Experiment: Smart Feedback

To specify this theory into a particular model, we need to make some further assumptions. The magic number in this system is the quantity "PARM" that defines the effect of the discrepancy between goal and current status on future changes in status. For our simple example we will assume that PARM is negative. That is, our system contains negative feedback and attempts to close the gap between the goal and the current status of the system. For our simple example we will also assume that PARM is a number between zero and unity (in fact, we assume PARM = – .25). If PARM were zero, the discrepancy would have no effect on the rate of change; if PARM were unity, the discrepancy would be completely eliminated in each period of time. A value between zero and unity here is equivalent to assuming that the system responds to, but does not completely eliminate, the discrepancy in each period of time.

Some alternative sets of assumptions could also be made, though they do not seem to correspond readily to most kinds of dynamic systems that we ordinarily seek to understand. The feedback parameter could be set as a positive rather than a negative number. This positive feedback is equivalent to saying that the system seeks to diverge from the "goal" state. The feedback process could operate with an intensity of greater than unity as well. This alternative assumption would cause the system to "overshoot" or "overreact" to the discrepancy, creating either an oscillatory pattern around the goal (if the control process were a negative loop), or a pattern of "super-exponential" divergence from the goal state (if the loop were positive). Since these alternative scenarios are relatively rare in modeling real systems, we will bypass them and turn to examining the responsiveness of our "smart" system to constant, random, trending, and periodic environmental stimuli. The results are shown as Figure 6.10.

In the first panel of the figure we see a "smart" system striving to attain the goal of a level of 50 in the presence of a constant environmental stimulus of 5 units per unit of time. Since the system began at a level of zero, the initial discrepancy between the goal and the current status of the system is large. The feedback process (#) operates to increase the level of the system at rates that decrease as the discrepancy is narrowed. In the presence of the constant environmental stimulus (+) that begins at the third time point, however, the system "overshoots" its goal of 50 units. As this occurs, the effect of the feedback (#) becomes negative, attempting (unsuccessfully in this case, because the feedback has insufficient intensity relative to the continuing environmental pressure) to drive the level of the system back down to the goal level. As is fairly clear from the diagram, this particular process does approach a stable equilibrium, but the equilibrium level is not equal to the goal level.

In the second panel of the figure, our smart system is subjected to random stimuli from the environment. As before, the feedback process (#) initially operates strongly to raise the system from its initial level of 0 toward the goal state of 50. As the level approaches the goal, the discrepancy becomes less and the effect of the feedback approaches 0, except for its operation to smooth away the disruptive effects of the random shocks being received from the environment (+). In this case, since the effects of the environment have neither a positive nor a negative effect (on the average), the equilibrium level of the process is equal to the goal state, though the goal is never exactly attained.

In our third test of the behavior of this system the environment sends a strong upwardly trending stimulus beginning at the third time point.

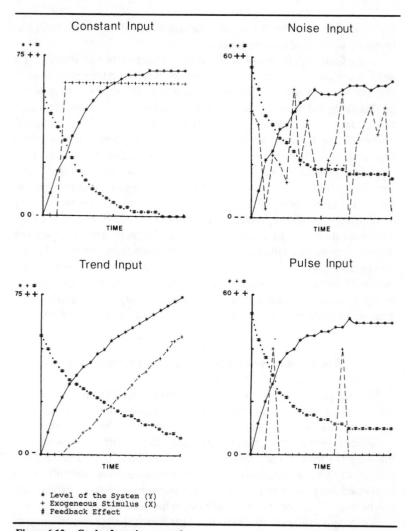

Constant Input

Noise Input

Trend Input

Pulse Input

* Level of the System (Y)
+ Exogeneous Stimulus (X)
# Feedback Effect

Figure 6.10: Goal-referencing control.

As in our first test, this environmental stimulus is too strong for the feedback process to fully control, and the level of the system (which reaches its goal of 50 by the ninth time point) continues to grow. The rate of increase in the system as a consequence of the steadily increasing environmental stimulus (+) is substantially reduced by the feedback process (#) and becomes increasingly negative as the system grows further and further away from the goal state. This particular process never reaches a steady state, despite the negative feedback loop, because the rate of increase in the environmental stimulus is greater than the intensity of the feedback process.

In the final experiment we have subjected the system to shocks (of a peak magnitude of 10 units) at the third and thirteenth time points. As in the second experiment with a series of random shocks, disruption of the goal-seeking behavior of the feedback loop (#) is only temporary, and the system approaches equilibrium at the goal level of 50 units. Although the figure is a bit too crude to demonstrate the point, the negative feedback loop exponentially smooths each of the disruptions.

The fundamental dynamic tendencies of systems with goal-referencing control systems are very similar to those of simple self-referencing systems. Indeed, both kinds of control structures are special cases of feedback systems, and produce similar-looking behavior in most cases. The notion that rates of change in variables may depend upon the discrepancy between the current state of the system and some goal state, however, is a powerful tool for thinking about the dynamics of social action. In some ways, however, systems that are "smart" in the sense of being goal referencing are still not smart enough to provide good analogs to many patterns of human social action and interaction.

The Dynamics of Goal-Setting Control Structures

Beyond goal-referencing control structures are still more complex ones in which the goals themselves are responsive to environmental and system status factors. Control systems of this level of complexity are sometimes termed "intelligent" or "adaptive" feedback systems. In building theories about human behavior, social scientists often have models of this complexity in mind. Such theories have normally been expressed only in everyday language, however, as their statistical and mathematical versions do not have desirable properties.[7]

A moment's thought suggests that "intelligent" or "adaptive" control is a very helpful imagery for describing many patterns of social action and interaction. Suppose, for example, that we have two actors playing a competitive game. Each actor may have the fixed goal of winning, but must formulate narrower strategic goals that change as a function of the unfolding interaction. At some points the actor may (if the rules of the game allow such complexities) attempt to maximize the accumulation of resources by making defensive moves; at other points the actor may attempt to attack. The strategic goals change over time as a consequence of the actor's own status, the behavior of the opponent, and the ways that these factors are related to the general goal of winning. More generally, many forms of human social action may be seen as governed by control structures that have several levels of goals that are more or less responsive to change over time originating from various sources.

In a formal systems analysis sense, goal-setting or adaptive control structures are simple elaborations of the goal-referencing structures that we have examined above. The difference between the structure of our prototypical goal-referencing system (Figure 6.3) and our prototypical goal-setting system (Figure 6.4) is straightforward. In both control structures the self-referencing or feedback effect is governed by a comparison of the existing state of the system and a desired or goal state. In the simpler goal-referencing system, the goals are regarded as fixed. In the goal-setting control structure, the goals are regarded as variables, and change over time as a consequence of other factors.

There are a number of interesting possibilities raised by making the goals of the system variable rather than fixed. The goals of the system may vary as a function of exogenous factors. For example, an adolescent male's desired (goal level) of "toughness" may change over time as a function of the expectations of the groups with whom he interacts. Of course, this process could be made even more complex by supposing that differential association is affected by toughness. The goals of the system may also change as a function of the same environmental influences that affect rates of change directly. For example, external threat to a society may have effects on internal cohesiveness both by directly affecting the rate of change in cohesion (as the public in general become frightened), but also by affecting the desired level of population morale and nationalism held by political elites, causing them to invoke public rituals to increase cohesiveness still further.

In addition to the possibility of making goals contingent on the environment, goals may also be directly contingent on the state of the system itself. In Figure 6.4, for example, we show goals as being affected by both the rates and the level of the system, as well as by environmental factors. Some goals may be contingent on the level of the process already attained. It might be hypothesized, for example, that the desired or goal level of occupational prestige attainment is a function of the level already attained: each person, regardless of his or her level of prestige, might be hypothesized to have a goal of 5% more prestige. Hence, as attainment rises (falls), the goal rises (falls). The goals of the system may also vary according to rates of change. If sales are decreasing, for example, goals for investment may be reduced by business management. In this case it is not the level of production or consumption that is having an effect on the goals for investment, but rather the rate of change.

The logically simple extension from goal-referencing systems to systems that set goals dynamically seems a small step, and in the abstract it is. However, the one additional "degree of freedom" is very consequential for both stating and analyzing the dynamics of social action. Systems, be they human or artificial, that change their goals as a consequence of contingencies arising from environments are a powerful analogy for understanding more complex patterns of social action and interaction that are only poorly approximated by systems with fixed goals. Many social science theories of dynamic processes utilize such imagery, but its implications have rarely been formalized.

Because of their flexibility and adaptability, we cannot present any single set of experiments to demonstrate the fundamental dynamic tendencies of models with adaptive feedback control. The answer to the question of how such systems *generally* behave is, quite properly, "it all depends." What it depends on, however, is not some hidden mystery. As simple extensions of goal-referencing feedback, the dynamics of adaptive models display tendencies either to equilibration or to destabilization, depending on whether the feedback is positive or negative. In adaptive control models, however, the criterion that the system is attempting to reach or avoid through feedback keeps changing as a consequence of the current state of the system and exogenous factors. The shot pattern produced by the adaptive system depends on whether it is trying to hit or to miss the target, and on the fact that the target is moving.

Feedback Control and Delay

We argued earlier that social dynamics often involve complicated forms of relationships with respect to time, as well as among variables. In examining the behavior of systems governed by stimulus-response types of control, we explored several basic time-forms (DELAYs), and discovered that such delay can have the consequences of "smoothing" trends and preventing the full realization of the consequences of stimuli. We also suggested that the effects of delays in systems with more complex control structures were different. It's now time to talk a bit about this issue.

All systems that involve feedback loops (i.e., self-referencing, goal-referencing, and goal-setting systems) are particularly sensitive to the time shapes of relationships. In all such self-referencing systems, the rates of change depend on the current state of the system in ways that are increasingly intricate as the control structures become more complicated. If there is delay in the loop connecting the current level of the system to the rate of change, the feedback is operating with reference to a level that no longer, in fact, exists. As a result, the time trace of the system may be considerably different in the presence of delay than in the presence of instantaneous feedback, often overshooting or undershooting. Since feedback systems are self-referencing, distortions introduced by delays are themselves multiplied through the system, resulting in further disruption.

We have all had experiences with the effects of delay in systems controlled by feedback loops. Suppose that you are taking a shower, and you find that the water is not hot enough for your liking, so you turn the control knob to increase the flow of hot water. After what seems to be a reasonable interval, you notice no effect, so you turn the knob further. Suddenly the water is warm enough, and then too warm, so that you turn it down again. Again, nothing seems to happen, so you turn it down further. What has happened here is an overcompensation by the goal-referencing feedback structure (you), to a delayed response of the system (the water heater, pipes, valves, and all that). The main point here is that there has been an overcompensation as a result of delay in the system. We usually, of course, don't do as badly as just suggested. The lack of realism of this simple example, in fact, suggests a more complex model. Often the control structure is aware of the delays and hence either no overcompensation or a much-dampened compensation occurs.

Delays obviously occur in human-human, as well as human-machine interactions. Let's suppose that an individual is undergoing some stressful life event that is substantially reducing the individual's social performance (an example that we will treat in some detail in a later chapter). The individual is aware, with relatively little delay, of experiencing stress, and will seek to compensate. Our stressed person is also connected to a network of other persons who, upon perceiving that (s)he is undergoing stress, will attempt to be supportive. It takes far longer for members of the social network to become aware of our focal person's distress than it does for the person to become self-aware, however, and this can have interesting (and sometimes quite unfortunate) consequences. Where the stresses are relatively minor, and the individual is able to fully compensate for them without outside help, the delayed response of the network gives rise to a (sometimes annoying) helpfulness from the network after the crisis is already past. Where the crisis is so severe as to overwhelm the capacity of the focal individual to cope with it, help may come too late. In either case, the process of smooth interaction between person and environment and between person and social support network may be disrupted both by the crisis and by the delayed (and hence less than optimal) response to it. Such dynamics, most readers will agree, can be extremely consequential in human affairs.

To get a firmer grasp on the consequences of delay in feedback systems, let's construct an ideal-typical system and examine its responsiveness. We take as our starting point the goal-referencing negative feedback system we considered two sections ago, reproduced here.

L $Y.K = Y.J+(DT)(RI.JK)$
R $RI.KL = ENVIRON.K+FEEDBACK.K$
A $ENVIRON.K = f(X)$
A $FEEDBACK.K = (PARM)(DISCREP.K)$
A $DISCREP.K = Y.K-GOAL$
C $GOAL = 50$
C $PARM = -.75$

One way in which delay occurs in human systems is that there is a slowness in perceiving the state of the system and changes in the state of the system. That is, humans are often slow to pick up the full magnitude of changes in their environment. We might model this phenomenon by modifying the equation describing the discrepancy in the above model to read:

A $DISCREP.K = DELAY1(Y.K,3)-GOAL$

Delays might also be hypothesized to occur in responding to the state of the discrepancy, as well as in perceiving the state of the system. Let's suppose, for the purposes of illustration, that the system responds to the perceived discrepancy with latency (third order, or S-shaped delay), also having an average length of three time periods. Hence:

R $RI.KL = ENVIRON.K+DELAY3(FEEDBACK.K,3)$

To get a sense for the effects of each delay and for the compounded effect of them both, we can design a series of simulation experiments. In the first experiment we create a "baseline" run by setting the system in equilibrium (that is, giving it a starting value equal to its goal value of 50 units). The system is a negative feedback one with an intensity of $-.75$ (PARM). After the third time unit we disrupt the system with an exogenous shock (the DYNAMO program for this set of experiments is appended). The results of this baseline are shown as the first panel in Figure 6.11.

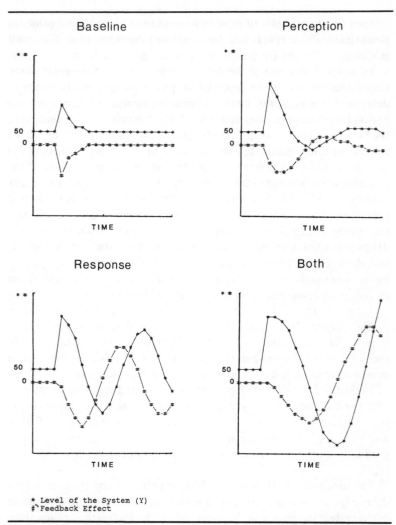

Baseline   Perception

Response   Both

* Level of the System (Y)
\# Feedback Effect

Figure 6.11: Feedback with delay.

The full value of the initial shock (which would have been to raise the system level (*) to 52.5 in a system without feedback) is dampened by the immediate negative feedback (\#), so that it reaches a maximum of about 51.5. The negative feedback loop acts quickly to return the system to its initial level. After five time units have passed, the full effects of the initial shock have been almost completely removed, and the time-trace of the system level is essentially flat.

In the next panel of the figure we have added a delay of perception (of three time units average length), and repeated the experiment. The result is notably different from that of the same negative feedback system without delay. Because of the delay in perceiving the full extent of the shock, the initial negative feedback response is less in the system with delay, and, consequently the shock is more fully realized in the first time period (the system reaches about 52.25 at its maximum, as opposed to the 51.5 of the system without feedback). As the process continues, more interesting things occur. The control structure is always lagging behind the real status of the system (notice that the peaks and valleys of the feedback curve are two to three units later than the corresponding peaks in the system levels). As a result, the control structure takes the wrong corrective action, causing the system to overshoot its goal. In this case the system level not only returns to the goal state of 50, but actually drops below that level before recovering. Similarly, the feedback loop is initially negative (to compensate for the positive shock to the system), but assumes positive values (at about time points 10 to 15) to correct for its earlier overcompensation. A cycle of oscillating response is set off in this experiment as a direct result of delay in perception of the true state of the system. Note that the cycles of response show progressive dampening in this case. That is, the peaks and valleys become closer to the goal state the longer the system operates. While the system overcompensates, it does, eventually, approach equilibrium.

In the third panel of the figure we have repeated the experiment with only the delay of response but no delay of perception. Not surprisingly, the result is similar to that of the delay in perception. That is, oscillation and overcompensation are introduced to the system, and the cycles gradually dampen over time as the system approaches its goal state of 50.

The time trace of the response-delay experiment and the perception-delay experiments, however, are not identical. Both the initial response of the system to shock and the amplitude of the cycles (though not their period) are much greater in the response-delay experiment. Recall that the time shapes of the delay in perception and in response were specified to be different (that is, a first-order delay of perception and a third-order delay of response). Because the third-order delay responds more slowly at first than the first-order delay, the impact of the shock on the system is greater. Because this latency of response persists, the speed with which the system adjusts to its overcompensating mistakes is also slower, so cycles of overadjustment are more severe in the presence of this form of delay. The comparison of the second and third panels of the figure should suggest that the theorist's specification of the time shape of the relations among variables in dynamic systems is just as important as their choice about the form of the functional relations. Differing forms of time relations produce different time shapes in feedback systems, just as they do in stimulus-response systems.

Finally, let's see what happens when *both* delays of perception and delays of response operate simultaneously. These results are shown in the fourth panel of the figure. The consequences are striking, and important for thinking about human systems that often contain multiple sources of delay.

First, note that the system reaches a (slightly) higher level immediately after the initial shock in this experiment than in any of the others. The system is slow to perceive the full magnitude of the exogenous shock, as it was in the second panel; to this is added a slow response to the misperceived gap, as in the third panel. Consequently, the immediate response to the exogenous shock is additively dampened by the two delays.

Second, note that the period of the oscillations in the experiment with two delays (of average length of three each) is much greater (roughly double) than in the experiments with a single delay. Multiple delays in feedback loops interact multiplicatively to increase response times. From this fact follows the third important thing to notice about the results of the last experiment.

The system in the last panel of the figure is not approaching equilibrium over time. Note that the successive peaks and valleys of both the system level and the feedback process are further and further away from the goal level. As a direct consequence of the delay, a negative feedback system that would otherwise tend toward stable equilibrium now tends toward disequilibrium. In this case (though not generally for systems with multiple delays) the total delay is sufficient that the feedback loop tends to deepen each crisis, accentuating movements away from equilibrium.

Lest this seem a trivial and contrived example, it has been argued that federal monetary policy has, on occasion, suffered from the same type of dynamic. Efforts to slow inflation, because of lags in perceiving the rate of change in the economy and because of lags in implementing policy, may end up restricting money supply at the wrong time, leading to even more severe recessions than would have otherwise occurred.

The central points of this experiment are that the consequences of delay in feedback systems are fundamentally different from the consequences of delay in simple stimulus-response systems. Because action is self-referencing in feedback systems, misperception, latency, and other forms of lagged response tend to lead to distortions and overadjustments. This is because the effects of delays and distortions are multiplied through the system over time, just as all other signals are, by feedback loops. The consequences of delays for the dynamic tendencies of complex systems can in some cases be rather difficult to anticipate. If delays are of sufficient magnitude or of certain periods relative to the dynamic relations among variables, systems that would otherwise appear to tend toward equilibrium may not, and systems that may appear to have self-destructive tendencies may never realize them.

Conclusions

In this chapter we have examined the dynamics of a variety of abstract systems, ranging from very simple to slightly more complex. In particular, we have discussed a hierarchy of types of control structures of systems that can serve as an aid to thinking about, and building formal theories of social action.

The least complex systems considered here are those whose over-time behavior is due solely to responses to exogenous variables—what we have termed "stimulus-response" or "dumb" control structures. Conserved systems governed by stimulus-response control structures have distinctive dynamic tendencies that differ from those of systems governed by more elaborate control structures. Because of the operation of conservation, such systems respond to constant inputs with linear change, to trend input with exponential change, and to shock with stepwise change. "Delay" or nonlinearity in the time shapes of relationships in such systems result in varying degrees and forms of smoothed or dampened response to environmental changes. If the delays are of substantial magnitude, the system may never attain full realization of the impacts of environmental variables.

We also examined the dynamic behavior of systems governed by several more complex forms of control structures. The behavior of social actors may sometimes be more effectively captured if we regard the actors as self-referencing, goal-referencing, or even goal-setting, in addition to environment-referencing. The fundamental dynamic behavior of systems governed by structures of these types are fundamentally different from those of stimulus-response systems.

All more-complex control structures involve feedback. We have distinguished here between feedback that makes reference only to the current state of the system (self-referencing), feedback that makes reference to goal states as well as the current state of the system (goal-referencing), and feedback that modifies goals as well makes reference to them in controlling rates of change (goal-setting or adaptive systems).

The presence of feedback in the control structure of systems implies the multiplication and interaction of causal factors, as opposed to the simple addition of stimulus-response systems. That is, each change that occurs in a feedback system is also a cause of further change in the system.

Each loop (that is, feedback structure) can have a tendency to move the system toward a goal or away from a goal (the goal states themselves, of course, may be changing in the more complicated variants of feedback systems). The over-time behavior of feedback systems is fundamentally determined by the tendencies of these loops to move toward goal states (negative feedback), or to diverge from them (positive feedback). The behavior of a system governed by multiple feedbacks of both positive and negative characters as well as responses to environmental stimuli may be too complex to understand intuitively, but is decomposable into the interaction of the fundamental tendencies of the simple response and feedback response that make up the control structure.

Nonlinear causal relations and incomplete realizations—delays— also have different effects in systems governed by feedback than they do in stimulus-response systems. In feedback systems, delay in perception of change or delay in response to change can have nonintuitive effects. In negative (goal-seeking) systems, delay causes "overcorrection" and sets off cycles of oscillatory behavior. Usually such disruption slows the realization of movement toward equilibrium inherent in negative feedback loops; if the delay is sufficient in intensity, however, a tendency toward ever-deepening cycles can be generated.

We have, quite deliberately, kept the discussion of the dynamics of control structures at a very abstract level. It is quite important to understand the range of alternative types of control structures in the abstract because they are very useful "ideal types" that can be used by theorists in specifying the dynamics of patterns of social action of particular interest. It is quite important to understand the fundamental dynamic tendencies of these abstract systems to improve our understanding of the behavior of "real" systems, whether naturally occurring or artificial. As we shall see in the next chapter, interesting patterns of social action can be analyzed and theories about them built up from the application of these abstract tools with little difficulty.

Notes

1. The notion of "control" structures is central to all systems analysis and cybernetic thinking. The reader may be interested in examining some of the classic works in this tradition to get a sense of how

"systems" approaches use the notion of control as the basis for the classification of systems. See particularly Ashby (1958, 1962), Bayless (1966), Bellman (1961), Berrien (1968), Bertalanffy (1968), Cannon (1939), Foerster and Zopf (1962), Kremyanskiy (1960), Maruyama (1968), von Neumann (1951), Schank and Colby (1973), Schutzenberger (1954), Simon (1957, 1969, 1981), Sommerhoff (1969), and Weiner (1948).

2. There is no single consensual classification of types of control systems. The schema presented in this chapter is peculiar to the author, but is at least broadly consistent with the approaches of most writers in systems theory and cybernetics.

3. Theory and research on the development of single organizations and populations of organizations in management and sociology has advanced a number of interesting dynamic theories that emphasize relatively simple control structures. Some focus more on self-referencing growth, others more on exogeneous sources. For examples, see Anderson and Warkov (1961), Blau (1970), Cadwallader (1959), Campbell (1962, 1965), Cyert et al. (1971), Cyert and March (1963), Emery and Trist (1965), Haire (1959), Hummon (1971), Land (1975), and Simon (1947).

4. We have not provided the DYNAMO code for these simple experiments in appendicies (as we will do from time to time). The core of the models are as shown in the text.

5. The integrating, discrete, and continuous delay processes discussed here in terms of simulation methods are also dealt with statistically (Box-Jenkins, ARIMA, and Spectral models), and mathematically (stochastic processes and Fourier series). With regard to the latter, see Bartholomew (1973) and Doreian and Hummon (1976).

6. There are many excellent texts on the dynamics of feedback systems. Perhaps the most accessible to social scientists are those of Forrester (1968), Roberts et al. (1983), and Richardson and Pugh (1981).

7. Such models involve nonconstant coefficients, and are only now making their appearance in the statistical literatures in the various social sciences.

APPENDIX 6.1. Feedback and Delay Models

```
*              DELAY AND FEEDBACK EXAMPLES
NOTE
NOTE ALL FOUR SYSTEMS HAVE STRONG NEGATIVE FEEDBACK
NOTE SUCH THAT .75 OF THE DIFFERENCE BETWEEN THE CURRENT
NOTE STATE OF THE SYSTEMS AND THEIR GOAL STATES IS CLOSED
NOTE IN EACH TIME PERIOD. EACH MODEL IS INITIALIZED AT
NOTE EQUILIBRIUM AND THEN SHOCKED TO TEST TRANSIENT RESPONSE
NOTE
NOTE MODEL ONE IS SIMPLE NEGATIVE FEEDBACK
L              Y1.K=Y1.J+(DT)(RI1.JK)
N              Y1 = 50
R              RI1.KL = ENV.K+FEED1.K
A              FEED1.K = (-.75)(Y1.K–GOAL)
NOTE MODEL TWO HAS A FIRST ORDER DELAY OF 3 UNITS LENGTH
L              Y2.K = Y2.J+(DT)(RI2.JK)
N              Y2 = 50
R              RI2.KL = ENV.K+FEED2.K
A              FEED2.K = (-.75)(DELAY1((Y2.K-GOAL),3))
NOTE MODEL THREE HAS A THIRD-ORDER DELAY OF 3 UNITS LENGTH
L              Y3.K = Y3.J+(DT)(RI3.JK)
N              Y3 = 50
R              RI3.KL =ENV.K+FEED3.K
```

```
A           FEED3.K = DELAY3(((-.75)(Y3.K-GOAL)),3)
NOTE MODEL FOUR APPLIES A THIRD-ORDER DELAY OF 3 UNITS
NOTE LENGTH TO A SIGNAL THAT HAS A FIRST-ORDER DELAY OF 3
NOTE UNITS
L           Y4.K = Y4.J+(DT)(RI4.JK)
N           Y4 = 50
R           RI4.KL = ENV.K+FEED4.K
A           FEED4.K = DELAY3((-.75)(DELAY1((Y4.K-GOAL),3)),3)
NOTE THE ENVIRONMENTAL STIMULUS TO ALL FOUR MODELS IS
NOTE SET AS A PULSE OF MAGNITUDE 25 AT TIME 3
A           ENV.K = PULSE(25,3,50)
NOTE THE GOAL STATE FOR ALL FOUR MODELS IS SET TO BE EQUAL
NOTE TO THE INITIAL LEVEL OF 50 UNITS
C           GOAL = 50
NOTE OUTPUT SPECIFICATIONS
SPEC DT =.1/LENGTH =20/PRTPER = 1/PLTPER = 1
NOTE INTEGRATION INTERVAL IS SET TO 1/10 TIME UNIT.
NOTE SMALLER INTEGRATION INTERVALS ARE NECESSARY
NOTE TO ATTAIN ACCURACY IN SYSTEMS WITH DELAYS
NOTE THE SIMULATION IS TO RUN FOR 20 TIME UNITS
NOTE TABULAR AND PLOT OUTPUT IS TO BE PRODUCED FOR
NOTE EACH TIME POINT
PRINT Y1/Y2/Y3/Y4
NOTE PRINT VALUES FOR THE OUTPUT SERIES
PLOT Y1 = *(46,56)/FEED1 = #(-2,4)
NOTE PLOT Y1 USING THE * SYMBOL ON A Y AXIS WITH 46 AND 56
NOTE AS MINIMA AND MAXIMA. ON THE SAME PLOT, PLOT FEED1
NOTE WITH THE SYMBOL # WITH -2 AND 4 AS MINIMA AND MAXIMA
PLOT Y2 = *(46,56)/FEED2 = #(-2,4)
NOTE PRODUCE A SIMILAR PLOT FOR MODEL TWO
PLOT Y3 = *(46,56)/FEED3 = #(-2,4)
PLOT Y4 = *(46,56)/FEED4 = #(-2,4)
RUN
```

7

Simple Processes: One-Way Transitions, Growth, and Diffusion

Many of the dynamic processes that have been of greatest continuing interest to social scientists are relatively simple single-state systems that produce monotonic trends. Psychologists and social psychologists have sought to understand the process of cognitive development; economists and historians have theorized about the processes of economic growth and development; political scientists have focused attention on "political development" and the growth of the state; anthropologists and sociologists have devoted considerable attention to the processes generating increasing complexity of social organization. While the particulars of these research traditions are quite different, they have many commonalities when viewed from a systems perspective as theoretical problems. In each of these cases our primary attention turns to the behavior of a single "dependent" variable, and we seek to understand the forces that lead to its rate of change over time. In most of the models of interest, this change tends to be in one direction: toward increasing development, complexity, or whatever. Of course processes of decline, decay, entropy, and extinction could be modeled as the inverse of growth and development.

Because such systems are so important in all of the social sciences, it is quite important that we grasp their dynamics from the current perspective before we move on to more "complex" problems. In this chapter we will develop a series of related models of such "one-way" processes using the substantive example of the diffusion of some trait in a closed population. This particular problem has received considerable attention in and of itself because of its wide application (e.g., the spread of rumors, diseases, religious conversions, etc.). We have chosen it, however, because the several basic models of diffusion processes provide prototypes for a very wide range of problems. The several models that we will explore are all quite "simple" in terms of their state-spaces, but differ in the complexity of the control structures that drive and limit change in the "dependent" state. They provide a good illustration of the principles of "complexity of control" that we discussed in the previous chapter, and help us to understand the dynamics of more complex systems—which are made up of these simpler parts.

The Problem: Diffusion in Populations

The spread of ideas, beliefs, and behaviors in human populations is one of the fundamental processes of social change. Social scientists have been intrigued by the puzzles of why some ideas and practices become more widespread than others and why some spread "like wildfire," while others diffuse very slowly. Diffusion has been studied in the adoption of agricultural practices medical technology, the spread of rumors, and a wide variety of other specific contexts.[1] In all of these cases, the central concern is explicitly dynamic: Why is it that the rate of change in the level of adoption or belief in a population is higher or lower? What is the time-shape of the process? How far does the process proceed before it stops?

Because diffusion processes are so important, they have received a good deal of attention from theorists, as well as from analysts concerned with specific substantive problems. There are extensive literatures that utilize statistical and mathematical approaches to formalize and analyze theories about the dynamics of diffusion. The dynamic models that we will develop here are parallel to these statistical and mathematical approaches.[2]

Models of diffusion processes are but one example of a wider class of models of growth and development. Diffusion models take as their dependent variable the probability that a transition occurs from a source (e.g., unaware of a rumor) to an absorbing state (e.g., aware of the rumor). The "realization" of the underlying stochastic process that generates such transitions is the proportion of the population that makes a change in a period of time. There is no reason, however, for us to restrict our attention to systems that deal with qualitative change. Quantitative variables as well (like levels of cognitive, economic, political, or organizational development) can be treated with models like those that we will discuss below.

Developing the Baseline Model

In a fixed population, let us suppose that actors can fall in one of two categories: Either they don't know of a proposed innovation or they do.

Alternatively, one could think about dividing the population into groups that have adopted or not adopted an innovation, or that do and don't display any trait of interest. At any point in time, some proportion of the population are "knowers," and this proportion changes over time as some of those who don't know become knowers. Those who "know," however, never become "nonknowers"; the process is unidirectional.

The "material states" or levels in this case are two aggregates: those who "don't know" and those who do. These are conserved quantities (a given actor must either know or not know, but not both), connected by a single flow rate from not knowing to knowing. The flow in this case goes in only one direction, as those who don't know become aware (we leave aside, for the moment at least, the elaboration of the model to include people who "forget"). Since the flows are in one direction only, the state "knower" is an "absorbing state," and there is a single transition rate. The chain of material states for this model, then, would be diagrammed as in the first panel of Figure 7.1. A single "level equation" defining the number of knowers can represent this aspect of the process. We also want to keep track of the number who don't know as a separate or "auxiliary" quantity for reasons that we will explain shortly. Thus:

L   K.K = K.J+(DT)(RI.JK)
A   POP.K = K.K+DK.K

The level equation here says that the number of knowers at the later point in time (K.K) is equal to the number at the prior point in time (K.J) plus the integration or accumulation (DT) of the rate of increase or transition (RI) from not knowing to knowing over the time interval between J and K. Now we need to make hypotheses about the causes of change in the number who know or the rate of transition. This is where the model begins to become interesting.

Stimulus-Response Control

Although we can clearly do better, let's start theorizing by thinking about the system in question as one characterized by dumb or simple stimulus-response control. In such a system, the rate of change is a function of only exogenous factors: constants, noise, and the action of independent variables. One very common baseline diffusion model is to suppose that there is a single exogenous source of stimuli that operates at a constant rate over time. In this case, the model would have the very simple form:

R   RI.KL = EXOG.K

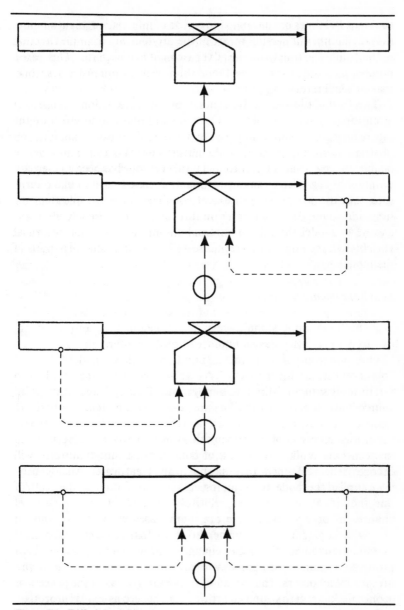

Figure 7.1: Diffusion models.

A   EXOG.K = Constant

Suppose, for example, we were interested in customer awareness of a new product advertised on television. If we ran the advertisement at a constant 100 times per day over the period of interest, we might suppose that the number of persons aware of the product was a simple function of the number of times that the advertisement had been run. There are a number of problems with this theory of how diffusion processes work, that we shall return to presently.

This formulation of the dynamics of one-way transitions focuses our attention on the nature of the exogenous stimulus and its effect on the rate of change. This effect might be hypothesized to be constant function of stimulation (e.g., each time the advertisement is run, x number of people become aware of the product until everyone has been converted), or might be regarded as having (probably decreasing) marginal returns such that the second advertisement convinces fewer people than the first, and so on. As elaborations on this very basic approach, we might choose to model the rate of external stimuli as a function of causal variables, or include delayed response of the system to stimuli as parts of the model.

Self-Referencing Control

As useful as simple stimulus-response models of diffusion (or growth, or survival) are, they have a number of obvious shortcomings.

One major problem is the assumption in these models that the "observations are independent." As we've formulated the problem so far, the only source of stimulus is exogenous. That is, there is only "point source" diffusion in that the knowers don't become tellers. There are many cases of diffusion where such a presumption might be reasonable (or at least a reasonable approximation), as in the case of advertising in mass media. While advertisers, of course, hope that "knowers" will become "tellers" of others, they may not to any great degree. Analogously, if we applied the model to the biological survival of humans, the death of one individual probably has relatively little effect on the survival chances of others.[3] But, there are many cases where those who do "know" become sources for further diffusion. In the case of the spread of disease, for example, the rate of change in the number of persons ill is a positive function of the number who are already ill, because those who are sick infect others. The spread of rumors in groups or the process of economic "takeoff to sustained growth" can be seen as similar processes.

From the systems analysis perspective, this kind of a theory is quite different from the stimulus-response model. The current theory supposes that the process of diffusion is a self-referencing one: The rate of change depends upon the current state of the system (that is, the number who become aware in a period of time depends on the number who already know). The process has become self-referencing, and now can be diagramed as in the second panel of Figure 7.1. Exogenous sources of stimulus may or may not be included, as we see fit, and the "rate equations" take the following form:

R   RI.KL = EXOG.K+f(K.K)

The key question here is "f." That is, in what way does the rate of change in knowing (RI.KL) depend on the number who already know (K.K)? One obvious thought is that each "knower" becomes a "teller" at a constant rate (or, in a more stochastic variation, each knower has an expected value and variance in telling). In this case, the function "f" becomes a constant (or distribution) number of tellings per "knower" per unit time.

Another very common variation on this model proposes that those who become knowers early in the diffusion process are more enthusiastic tellers than those who come later. In this case, the value of the function "f" is itself a function of the level of the process, declining as some rate as K.K increases. For example, each knower at the early stages of the diffusion may tell five new people per unit of time; those who become converted later may be less enthusiastic, telling only one or two new people per unit of time. In the DYNAMO language, we might represent such hypotheses with a table expression to draw a picture of the hypothesized relation, or use some mathematical function. For example:

R   RI.KL = TELLING.K
A   TELLING.K = TABLE(VIGOR,K.K,0,100,20)
T   VIGOR = 5/4/3/2/1/0

The first statement sets the rate of change in those knowing (RI) to a quantity called "telling." This is simply a convenience to help keep the logical steps clear. The second statement is a calculation involving the table function. It says that the value of the term TELLING at any time point K is defined by a table called VIGOR (an arbitrary name) that defines values corresponding to the variable K.K between 0 and 100 in increments of 20. The last statement identifies the values corresponding to K = 0, K = 20, K = 40, K = 60, K = 80, and K = 100 as 5, 4, 3, 2, 1, and 0, respectively. That is, as K.K increases from 0 to 100, the rate of telling declines from five tellings per unit time to no tellings per unit time. The function defined here is arbitrary, and one might wish to use an ogive, gamma, Weibull or other parametric form.

A third frequent variation on the same theme is to hypothesize that each new knower is initially enthusiastic and tells others at a high rate, but gradually becomes less enthusiastic. That is, tellers become "exhausted." The rate of telling in this case is a negative function not of the level of the process, but rather of the rate of increase in the process. That is, when a large number of people become knowers in a period of time, the rate of telling increases even more rapidly. When conversions are few, there are few enthusiasts, and the rate of telling declines. Processes of this type can be represented by setting the rate of telling to be a "delay" of past rates. The hypothesis of initial enthusiasm followed by rapid decline could be effectively captured with a first-order delay; an alternative hypothesis might suggest that new converts are initially hesitant, but then increase telling for a time before losing enthusiasm. This latter process could be captured by making current rates of conversion a function of a third-order delay of past rates.

Each of these variations has received some attention in theoretical and empirical literatures on growth, survival, and diffusion, and may be more or less applicable to a particular case. The important commonality across these variations is that the rate of increase (or survival rate, or transition rate) is dependent in some way upon the current level of the process itself. In short, these theories of diffusion, growth, survival, and other such one-way transitions are self-referencing and controlled by feedback.

Goal-Referencing Control

The various theories that we have examined so far deal with the ways in which growth and diffusion depend on external stimuli and the ways that they are self-generating. But we have missed something important. All of the processes that we have discussed so far can be used to explain why growth or diffusion occur, but have little to say about why it stops or is limited. To capture this aspect of the processes we must add negative feedback.

Whatever the source of the stimuli, be they from the environment or from actors who already know, not all "tellings" result in conversions from "not knowing" to "knowing." Since "knowing" is a final or absorbing state, when stimuli are directed at those who already know, they have no effect, and hence have no consequence for rates of change. In closed populations or where there are resource constraints, growth and diffusion processes are inherently limited by the supply of available unconverted resources (be they raw materials of some sort, people, or whatever).

As an elaboration of this basic idea, we might suppose that all of the people in the population are not equally "at risk" of making a transition, even if they are exposed to stimuli. Some may be completely resistant to change. For example, people who do not have television sets will never make purchases of products that are advertised only on television. This kind of "population heterogeneity" is similar to the "mover-stayer" problem in social mobility analysis, and has often been dealt with in models of one-way transitions by supposing that there are a group in the population who cannot be reached, so that the diffusion dynamics operate with an "upper bound," or ceiling that is less than the whole population. In this case, this upper bound of "mobilizable" population serves as a "goal" state affecting the rate of transition.[4]

Alternative sets of assumptions about the distribution of "mobilizability" or resistance to exogenous or self-generating stimuli are quite frequently used in "survival" analysis. Among the most common of these sets of assumptions is that of a "liability of newness" in survival chances or, stated inversely for purposes of diffusion rather than survival analysis, decreasing marginal returns to stimuli.[5] Roughly, this assumption suggests that the odds that a given stimuli will reach a given member of the population are distributed as some form of negative exponential. A relatively large proportion of the population is quite easy to convert, but smaller additional proportions are increasingly difficult to reach. In statistical models of such processes, various distributions are often used to represent the distributions of such odds of "resistance" to transition.

Thinking about this aspect of the problem from the systems perspective, we would say that there is a connection between the rate of change and the system state representing the population of those who have not undergone transitions, as is shown in the third panel of Figure 7.1. The number of unmobilized or unconverted in the population acts as a constraint or goal state that is referenced in determining rates of transition. To capture this aspect of the problem, our rate equations must now have this general form:

R   RI.KL = EXOG.K+g(DK.K)

Where DK.K is the difference between the total population and the number who already know.

The question for the theorist in this model becomes In what way does the rate of increase in the population of knowers depend on the number who don't already know? That is, what is "g"? DK.K represents the pool of those available for conversion from not knowing to knowing, and its impact on rates of change has been conceptualized in several alternative ways.

The most obvious way in which the rate of transition depends on the number of actors who have not yet made transitions is as an absolute upper bound. That is, the rate of transition cannot, logically, exceed the number of actors "at risk." Thus, even if our model predicted that there were 100 stimuli to change ("tellings") generated by either exogenous sources or by actors who already had made the transition, if there were only 10 actors available who had not already been converted, 90 of the tellings would, necessarily, fail to result in conversions. This limitation could be represented with the simple statement:

R   RI.KL = MIN(TELLING.K,DK.K)

That is, the rate of transition (RI) is equal to either the rate of telling (as we discussed it in several alternative formulations above), or the number of remaining actors at risk (those who "don't know" or DK), whichever is the smaller.

This first formulation of the negative feedback or limiting effects of the size of the population at risk assumes, implicitly, that a given telling or stimulus to make a transition will reach an actor at risk if one is available. This may be a reasonable model in cases where it is easy for "tellers" to easily distinguish between those who have already made transitions and those who have not, so that stimuli are directed only at the unconverted. In many cases, though, this seems rather unrealistic.

We might find an alternative assumption more reasonable for some transition processes: that stimuli are distributed at random, and, consequently the probability that a given stimulus will reach an actor that has not yet made a transition is simply equal to the proportion of the population that have not yet changed. The number of conversions or transitions, then, is equal to the number of tellings or stimuli multiplied by the odds that a given telling reaches an actor still "at risk." That is,

A   PR.K = DK.K/POP
R   RI.KL = (TELLING.K)*(PR.K)

Here the rate of transition (RI) is limited by the proportion of the population who are at risk (PR), regardless of what process is generating the stimuli. This statement implicitly incorporates the insight of the previous one; where there are no unconverted available, the probability of success (PR) becomes zero, and consequently the rate of transition is zero.

All of the models thus far assume, again implicitly, that all of the actors who have not already made transitions are equally likely to, should they be exposed to a stimulus. In some cases this is a reasonable assumption, but more often it is not. Actors are likely to differ from one another (i.e., they are "heterogeneous") in a large number of ways that affect the probability that they will undergo a transition if they are exposed to stimuli. Physicians presumably differ in their propensity to experiment with new technologies, some being more willing to try new treatments, some being more conservative. Some peasants are more likely to take chances on a new variety of seed recommended by a government agricultural agent than others.

A variety of assumptions might be made about the ways in which individual differences among those who have not made transitions affect the rate of transition. The most common such models of "population heterogeneity" in transition probabilities assume that resistance is distributed according to one of several statistical models. Alternative models suggest that (1) most individuals have low resistance, and progressively fewer and fewer have higher resistances, or (2) resistance is "normally" distributed, with relatively few individuals having low resistance, most having some, and again relatively few having high levels of resistance.

These alternative assumptions about the distribution of resistance to change in the population can be embodied in our model by assuming that those easiest to convert are earliest to make transitions. Consequently, the resistance to conversion increases nonlinearly (either monotonically or nonmonotonically, depending on how one believes resistance to be distributed) as the size of the unconverted population declines. Rather than using the simple multiplier of the previous set of equations, a mathematical or table function is used to define the probability (PR) that a given stimulus results in a conversion:

A PR.K = f(DK.K/POP)
R RI.KL = TELLING.K*PR.K

where f is a mathematical function like a logarithm, or an arbitrary function (like a TABLE statement) reflecting the dependence of the probability of a successful telling on the proportion of the population who are at risk.

One could, of course, go further in developing baseline models, and we will suggest some additional possibilities after a time. The basic forms of "dumb," "self-referencing," and "goal-referencing" control models, though, are of great generality and importance. It is worth spending some time with them and understanding their dynamic behavior.

Dynamics of the Baseline Model

Over time patterns of monotonic growth (or decline) can be produced by theories that are quite different from one another. In their simplest forms, however, the stimulus-response, self-referencing, and goal-referencing control structure models have different characteristic dynamic behaviors. Before considering some slightly more elaborate variations, let's perform simulation experiments to get a firm grasp on the shapes of the over-time growth paths implied by the models discussed in the previous section.

We will consider four alternative formulations of the problem. On one hand, the stimuli to change may be either exogenous or endogenous. In the case of diffusion processes, this is equivalent to having the "telling" come either from external sources (e.g., mass media), or from "knowers" becoming "tellers" (as in rumor processes). On the other hand, limitations on the extent and rate of change (goal-referencing negative feedback) can be either a simple function of the available resources, or can be seen as increasing as resource limits are approached. In the case of diffusion, these alternative assumptions are equivalent to supposing that "tellings" are directed only at those who do not know (until there are no more), or that "tellings" are distributed at random, and are hence successful in direct proportion to the percentage of the population that do not already know.

Combining the two alternative ideas about the causes of growth and the two alternative ideas about the way that growth is limited produces four possible models, each with a characteristic dynamic behavior. In Figure 7.2, plots of the time traces of simulations of models of these four types are shown (the DYNAMO program to produce the four scenarios is appended).

The first trace line in the figure is produced by a model that embodies the hypotheses that change is driven by exogenous factors (at a constant rate of five "tellings" per unit of time), and that all tellings reach and convert nonknowers until the supply of such actors is exhausted. The growth path is quite predictable from these assumptions: Increases in the number of actors who know are linear until no more are available for conversion, at which point the rate of change becomes zero.

The second trace line supposes that there is no exogenous stimulus to change, that one individual initially "knows," and that each individual who "knows" tells, on the average, .75 other actors per unit of time. As in the first example, "telling" is directed only at those who don't already know and continues until there are no more such actors. The over-time behavior of this process is fundamentally different from the first, as it produces exponential rather than simple accumulating growth. This, of

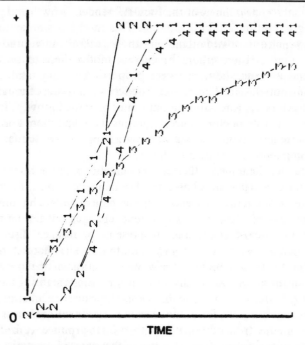

1. constant telling
2. knowers become tellers
3. constant telling with proportional success
4. knowers become tellers with proportional success

Figure 7.2: Basic models of diffusion.

course, is a direct consequence of the self-referencing positive feedback loop: Knowers become tellers. In the first time period there is one "knower," in the second time period 1.75, in the third 1.75 plus 1.75(.75) etc. The process here is one of contagion in its most rampant form.

In the third scenario we combine the idea of exogenously driven growth with the notion that the rate of success of these tellings is proportional to the number of actors who don't already know. That is, in the early stages of the process virtually every "telling" results in a conversion to knowing; in later stages, most telling is redundant. The consequence of this change in the theory is quite notable. The growth trace is no longer linear to an upper bound (as in the first model), but is now a "waning exponential" in which the rate of change is inversely proportional to the distance from the "goal state" (i.e., complete elimination of nonknowers).

In the final scenario the notions of self-referencing growth and goal-referencing limitation are both present. This model is similar to the second, in which one individual initially knows, and all individuals who know tell others. However, in the current model these tellings are random and are successful in direct proportion to the size of the nonknowing population. This model produces what is often thought of as the classical or typical diffusion pattern of S-shaped growth. In the early stages, the rate of change accelerates as more and more knowers also become tellers. In the later stages growth slows as a consequence of the increasing redundancy of the tellings.

For different phenomena, the four models shown in the figure may provide more or less plausible baselines. The important point about this exercise follows from the differences among these models. The simplest of dynamic models (those of monotonic change) have inherently different realizations depending on the presence or absence of self and goal-referencing positive and negative feedback. The theorist must, therefore, give careful thought to the ways in which a particular case of growth, transition, survival, or diffusion may be self-generating and/or self-limiting. Careful prior thought about the causes of change and limits on change is doubly important because, as we shall see below, it is possible for models from quite different theories to produce realizations that appear quite similar. Here, as in most other cases of dynamics, it is often quite dangerous to reason backwards from the data to the theory.

Variations: Exhaustion and Heterogeneity

The basic models of diffusion processes can be elaborated in a number of ways to make more realistic and interesting theories. Two of the most common of these variations are: (1) to make different assumptions about the propensities of knowers to become tellers and (2) to make different assumptions about the distribution of resistance to change in the population. With little difficulty, the basic models can be elaborated to explore these variations.

Exhaustion

In the self-referencing models that we have considered so far (i.e., models in which all "knowers" become "tellers"), we have assumed that all of the individuals in the population are the same in their propensity to become tellers, and that they "tell" at a constant rate. In many circumstances both of these assumptions might be questionable. One might offer the alternative hypotheses that those who are converted early in the process of diffusion are more enthusiastic than those who are converted later, and hence are likely to "tell" at higher rates. One might also suppose that the rate of telling by those who know varies with time: Perhaps converts are initially more likely to try to convert others, but their enthusiasm for telling declines after a time. Let's take a closer look at the consequences of this latter idea—that tellers become "exhausted."

The notion that knowers become "exhausted" can be captured by use of the DELAY functions in DYNAMO. By setting the rate of new tellings proportional to "delayed" changes in the number of knowers, alternative time-shapes of telling can be represented. In Figure 7.3 three alternative scenarios are presented that make different suppositions about the rate at which knowers become tellers.

The leftmost trace in the figure (#) corresponds to the hypothesis that knowers become tellers immediately, and continue telling at constant rates until the population of available nonknowers is used up. The second trace-line (*) is generated by a model that utilizes a first-order exponential delay. This time-shape corresponds to tellers having high levels of enthusiasm initially, but then declining exponentially in their rates of telling. The third trace-line in the figure (+), utilizes the third-order or S-shaped delay function. This shape corresponds to a hypothesis that new converts are initially hesitant to become tellers but then become tellers with high intensity before becoming exhausted.

The most obvious difference among the three realizations shown in Figure 7.3 is the speed with which the diffusion process is completed. With no exhaustion in telling, of course, the process operates much more rapidly than with either of the other two hypotheses. The model that supposes initial enthusiasm (the first-order delay) operates more rapidly than that which supposes initial hesitancy on the part of new knowers (the third-order delay) because of the multiplication of all changes through the self-referencing positive feedback of the system.

Beyond the difference in the speed of the process, it is very difficult to tell the three scenarios of Figure 7.3 from one another. All three have the same exponential growth pattern, and appear (in this scale of plotting at least) to have identical smooth traces. The important lesson in this observation is that rather different theories can often produce results that are nearly indistinguishable at the empirical level.[6] The three trace lines in Figure 7.3 could differ because the basic rates of telling differ, because some or all have delays of different average lengths, and/or because of different time-shapes of the exhaustion of telling. The distinctions among these theories may be rather marked, as might the effects of policy interventions based on belief in the efficacy of alternative models.

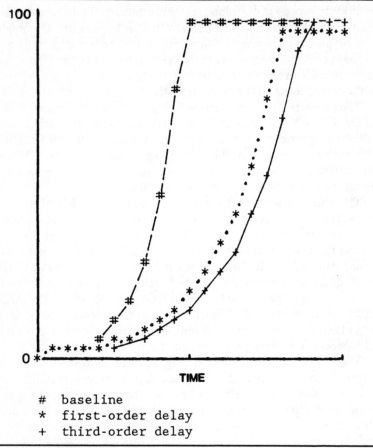

Figure 7.3: Exhaustion of telling.

Heterogeneity

In the theories that we have modeled thus far we have made assumptions about the distribution of propensities of individuals to make transitions that may be unrealistic. We have hypothesized either that all tellings result in conversions, or that the probability that a telling results in a conversion is a linear function of the distribution of the population between those who know and those who don't know. In many cases it might be more realistic to assume that the propensities to change are not homogeneous across the individuals in a population.

Rather than assuming that individuals will automatically undergo a transition if they receive a stimulus (and have not already been converted), we might suppose that individuals differ in their resistances. The most common models embodying this idea of heterogeneity assume that the underlying distribution of resistance to change is described by either a negative exponential or cumulative normal (S-shaped) distribution. In the former case, most individuals have low resistance to change, and will undergo transitions if stimulated, but progressively fewer and fewer have higher and higher resistance. In the latter case, most individuals are seen as having moderate levels of resistance to change, while relatively few are very likely and very unlikely to change if simulated.

We can explore the consequences of these alternative hypotheses by modifying our basic model slightly. As a baseline, we will assume that the population is homogeneous in the probability that a telling will result in a conversion, and that telling is distributed at random from all knowers. This is the same as the fourth of the baseline models discussed previously. As a first alternative hypothesis about the distribution of resistance, we will suppose that most people are relatively easy to convert (i.e., that resistance is distributed as a negative exponential). This alternative hypothesis is embodied in our model by using a table function to map such a relationship between the number of persons in the population who don't know, and the probability that a telling will result in a conversion. That is, as the proportion of the population who have not been converted declines, the probability of further conversions also declines. As a second alternative hypothesis, we will assume that the probability that a telling fails to result in a conversion is a cumulative normal (S-shaped) function of the proportion of the population who have not already been converted. That is, the probability of conversion as a consequence of telling is initially low, increases up to the mean, then declines again as more and more of the population are converted. This hypothesis is also modeled by using a table function to map the relationship between the proportion of the population who have not already been converted and the probability that a telling will result in a conversion (the DYNAMO code for these models is appended). The results of simulations of the three alternative assumptions about the distribution of resistance are shown as Figure 7.4.

The most important thing to notice about the results of these experiments with alternative hypotheses about the distribution of resistance to change is that the shapes of the curves differ. The baseline model (*) of population homogeneity describes a smooth and symmetric S-shaped curve over the time period, a consequence of similar shapes of the effects of the positive and negative feedback forces. The other two

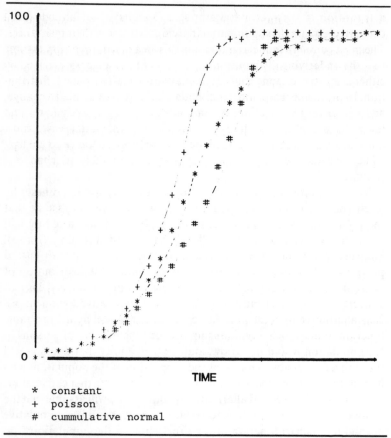

Figure 7.4: Heterogeneity.

models do not produce symmetric patterns.

If we assume that a large part of the population has little resistance to change, we would expect the early stages of the diffusion process to be more rapid than under the assumption of homogeneity. And, indeed, this is the case, as shown by the trace line (+) of the exponential model. Since some of the population has quite high resistance to change under the assumption of the exponential model, however, the final stages of the diffusion are slower than under the assumptions of the baseline model. One might describe the consequences of assuming a negative exponential distribution of resistance, then, as skewing the whole diffusion process to the "left." Although we do not perform the calculations here, the inverse assumption of a positive exponential distribution of resistances (that is, most have high resistance) is to produce a "skew" to the "right."

The assumption that resistance is normally distributed, rather than constant across members of the population produces a more complicated pattern (the #s in Figure 7.4). Since there are relatively few actors who are easy to convert under this hypothesis, the diffusion process is slower initially than in the baseline example (though it is difficult to see this in the figure due to the small number of converts in the early stages of either process). As the large "middle mass" of actors are reached and converted, however, the process becomes more rapid than in the baseline (compare the slopes of the *s and the #s in the middle of the diagram). Finally, as we reach the advanced stage of the process in which only those with high levels of resistance to change remain, the process again moves more slowly than in the baseline example.

The alternative hypotheses about the distribution of resistance in the population produce results that are importantly different: The shape of the realizations differs, not just the speeds of the processes. Again, however, the theories might be said to be more different than the empirical realizations. While the three sets of assumptions that have been made about the distribution of resistance in the population are very different, the resulting diffusion curves are sufficiently similar that exploratory data analysis might not distinguish them.

An Elaboration: Contagion

A wide range of phenomena can be usefully conceptualized as one-way transition processes or monotonic growths or declines. An even wider array of interesting social dynamics can be captured with quite minor modifications of the models that we have considered thus far. To get a flavor of the possibilities, let's consider one more elaboration on the basic diffusion model that enables it to describe the process of contagion. While the model here is created specifically with reference to infectious disease, the spread of rumors, fads, and crazes might also be analyzed with modifications of this model.

In the processes that we have been considering so far, the "event history" of individuals consists of two states: For a time individuals are "nonknowers," then they make a transition to the absorbing state of "knowing." Nonfatal infectious diseases have a slightly more elaborate historical process: First one is well, then ill, and then recovered (assuming that the disease did not produce death). In the case of a fad or fashion cycle, individuals are at first unconverted, become active believers for a time, then "drop out." Some may, however, enter an alternative absorbing state of "permanent convert." If we allow only a single absorbing state (i.e., the disease is not fatal, or everyone eventually gives up on the fad), a simple chain of three states describes the "material flows" of such a process, as in Figure 7.5.

Since movements among the states go in only one direction, two rates (an infection rate and a recovery rate) are sufficient to capture the dynamics of the situation. Infectious diseases are spread by direct contact between persons who are currently ill and those who have not yet been infected. Consequently, the rate of infection references both of these states, creating the same dynamic of self-generating and self-limiting growth that we explored previously. In the current model, however, there is a difference. Not all persons who have ever been ill act as sources for further spread of the disease. After a period of time being ill, individuals recover and no longer act as sources for further infection. The recovery rate (number of persons recovering per unit time) is determined by the number who are currently ill (and hence "at risk" of recovering) and a constant reflecting the average time it takes for recovery to occur.

The diagram of this process points out the central role played by the number of persons currently ill in this model. The number of people who are currently ill has effects on both the rate of recovery and on the rate infection and hence is the key to the model. How many people are ill at any given time of course depends on the balance of the intensities of the infection and recovery processes. These, in turn, are critically dependent upon the assumptions embodied in the "contact rate" between ill and susceptible persons, and on the recovery time constant. The effect of the contact rate is obvious: The more that sick persons come into contact with susceptible ones, the larger the power of the exponential growth tendency of the model. The effect of the recovery time constant is also fairly obvious: The longer that persons are ill, the more rapid will be the contagion (holding constant the contact rate). Because these two loops both reference the number of persons who are ill, the rate at which the diffusion occurs is dependent on the interaction of these two terms. If the contact rate were zero, for example, it would not matter what the recovery time was; similarly, though less immediately apparent, if recovery times are sufficiently short there will be no spread of the disease (because no people are ill long enough to come into contact with susceptible while they remain infectious).

The time patterns produced by such a model are shown in the simulation in Figure 7.6 (the DYNAMO program is, again, appended).

In this model the basic features of our two-state diffusion processes

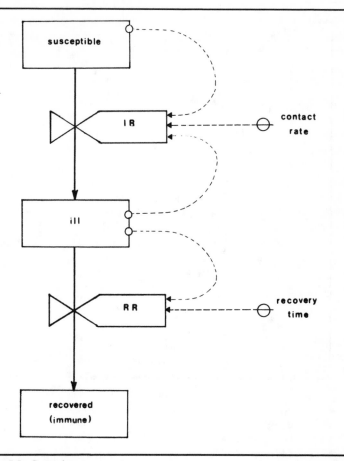

Figure 7.5: Contagion.

are preserved. The number of persons at risk (i.e., susceptible) follows an S-shaped downward path, and the number of recovered follows the now familiar upward S-shaped trajectory. The two curves, however, are not mirror images of each other: The growth of the immune population occurs only after the delay of the average length of the illness period. In this model then, the new state of "ill" is acting as a "delay," similar to the delays introduced in the models previously discussed where we assumed that tellers became "exhausted".[7]

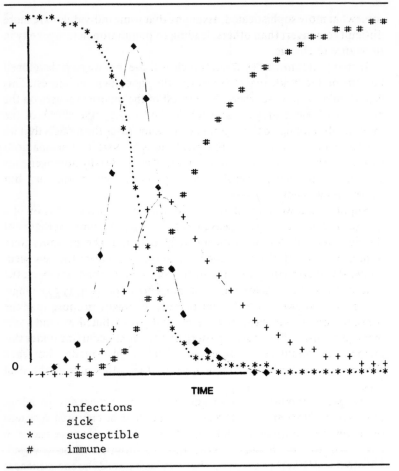

◆	infections
+	sick
*	susceptible
#	immune

Figure 7.6: Influenza model.

Directions for Development

Modeled heterogeneity

All of the models of diffusion and contagion that we have discussed in this chapter have made quite simple assumptions about the propensities of individuals to undergo or to resist transitions. In many of the models we have assumed that all of the individuals in the population are homogeneous in this regard and that which individuals make transitions is due to purely random processes. In other models we have been somewhat more sophisticated, assuming that some individuals are more difficult to convert than others, leading to population heterogeneity in resistance to change.

In many circumstances, models such as those that we have developed here are perfectly adequate to represent the phenomena of interest. This is particularly the case where the interest of the theorist focuses on the behavior of the aggregate as a whole, and not on the status of the individuals making up that aggregate. In some cases the models that we have developed here are good representations because it is reasonable to treat all of the individuals in the population as essentially homogeneous with regard to their propensities to respond to a given stimulus. But sometimes it is not.

Suppose that we were interested in the problem of the diffusion of a new seed variety among the peasants of a village. The simplest theory of the dynamics of this situation might assume that the peasants were homogeneous with regard to their propensities to adopt the new seed. Under this theory, the pattern of diffusion would depend simply on the time shape of the stimulus and the homogeneous propensity to change. Becoming somewhat more sophisticated, we might propose that the peasants are not identical, but are normally distributed around some mean propensity. The general pattern of diffusions occurring under this assumption would be the same as in the simpler model, but each particular diffusion history might appear rather different from the ideal type.

But peasants are not homogeneous in their propensity to adopt innovations. Nor can the differences among them be captured very well by assuming a normal distribution of propensities. Poor peasants in particular, who might benefit most from the adoption of the new seed, are often least likely to adopt it. They can least afford the consequences if the new technology does not live up to expectations. Models of the diffusion process that do not take this important form of "population heterogeneity" into account are not likely to be very adequate representations of the dynamics of diffusion of agricultural innovations.

There are several approaches to dealing with the complexity raised by heterogeneity in the population. In some cases the effect of the heterogeneity can be directly modeled as a simple function. This is the approach that we used when we supposed that the distribution of resistance to change was a negative exponential or cumulative normal function. In the case of the diffusion of agricultural innovation we might proceed by supposing that resistances to change were distributed in the population of interest as a simple function of the distribution of wealth in the population. In this way, information about the effects of "independent variables" (such as the distribution of wealth) can be added to the basic diffusion model.

The heterogeneity in the population may be qualitative, as well as quantitative. Let us suppose that not only wealth, but also ethnicity or religious beliefs affect the propensity to adopt new innovations. To capture these effects it might be necessary to divide the population into separate subpopulations and view the diffusion as a series of parallel processes occurring simultaneously within the several groups.

There are obviously limits on how far one might wish to go in modeling population heterogeneity. At some point, and for some purposes, a completely different approach to systematic theorizing and analysis of diffusion might be far more appropriate than the types of models that we have discussed in this chapter. In many cases for studying diffusion dynamics particularly, discrete-state and social-network models may provide better tools. Discrete-state modeling languages allow one to associate variable characteristics with each actor in the population and hence create models that describe situations in which the population in completely heterogeneous with regard to characteristics that affect probabilities of transitions. Each peasant, to continue our illustration, might be characterized by his or her religion, ethnicity, age, income, and other characteristics. Such models are particularly useful if the interest of the investigator is at the level of individual rather than aggregate behavior, and, of course, where high levels of relevant heterogeneity force such a choice for realism.

Social network models of phenomena like diffusion take the insights of general discrete-state models and push them much further. In social-network models, the probabilities of transitions for individuals depend not only upon the characteristics of the individuals, but also on the network of relations among individuals. For example, the probability that an particular actor will be subjected to a stimulus in a particular period of time can be seen as dependent on how many other individuals the actor has contact with (where the stimulus is spread by self-referencing growth). In the aggregate, of course, such "connectedness" is captured by assumptions about the average contact rates. Where individuals are heterogeneous, however, such average rates of connectedness are of little help in predicting dynamics. In network models, individual resistance to change may also be seen as a consequence of social position, as well as individual characteristics. In network models, individuals may reference others as well as themselves in making decisions about whether to adopt or not to adopt an innovation. Again, the network approach may be more appealing than the continuous-state approach where interest focuses on individual transition probabilities, or when heterogeneity in distribution of network positions is so high as to require it.

Continuous States and Aggregates.

All of the examples of one-way transition processes in this chapter have been drawn from the study of diffusion and other very similar processes. Consequently, the discussion has been in terms of system states that are aggregates of actors or proportions of populations of actors. Because we have been using these particular examples, much of the discussion has used terminology that implies discrete states and qualitative transitions; for example, individuals make transitions from being nonknowers to being knowers.

It is important to emphasize that the theories and models that have been developed here deal with continuous states. Many of the models that have been used to describe diffusion and contagion processes might serve equally well as baselines for thinking about change in such things as individual's attitudes, levels of economic production, and other "continuous" variables. For example, the dynamics of the intensity of a person's confidence in a group leader could be approached as a simple growth process. The rate of change in confidence might be seen to depend on exogenous events (e.g., the leader's perceived performance), be partially self generating (perhaps by selective perception and ego defensive attribution), and partially self-limiting (perhaps as a consequence of the upper limits on the total emotional intensity possible for a given individual). Similarly, the process of economic production could be approached as a simple "transition" model in which raw materials make transitions to finished goods which make further transitions, with delay, to become waste.

Theories that see emotional intensity and economic production as relatively simple chains of transitions governed by exogenous, self-referencing, and goal-referencing feedback may or may not be useful ways of thinking about the dynamics of these phenomena. And the ways that we think about the dynamics of diffusion and contagion as involving "contact rates," "tellings," "immunity," "resistance to change," and so on do not apply to theorizing about the dynamics of belief or material production. Our point is simply that the models developed in previous sections with specific reference to diffusion have similar structures as systems to models of other continuous state dynamics. Economic production is not the same thing as the spread of a rumor, but it is possible to theorize about the dynamics of the two processes using systems that have very similar structures, and hence similar forms of possible dynamic behavior.

Conclusions

Many dynamic processes of interest to theorists can be usefully thought of as relatively simple one-way transitions or processes. Such macrosocial phenomena as diffusion, contagion, growth, and decline can all be captured by models with relatively few "states." Microlevel parallels involving one-way transitions among "qualitative" states or monotonic change in "quantitative" states are also easy to imagine. We have by no means exhausted the range of possible applications with the examples in this chapter. We have, however, provided an introduction to some of the most commonly occurring types of systems models of this type.

Our discussion has been in terms of the increasing complexity of models with few states as they move from having "simple" control structures to having more "complex" ones. "Simple" systems that respond only to external stimuli can produce a very wide variety of behavior, depending on the nature of the stimulus, and on the complexity of the response. It is useful to think of almost all simple systems representations of the dynamics of social action as being "open" in the sense that they respond to exogenous stimuli. Theorizing about what external factors affect rates of transition and growth is always a useful first step in approaching problems such as those that we have dealt with here.

In many ways, though, the more interesting aspects of social dynamics are produced by more complicated aspects of control structures that are self-referencing and goal-referencing. Models of diffusion are particularly useful as illustrations because the ways in which self-referencing and goal-referencing control is occurring are quite apparent. As we suggested in the previous chapter, models with these more complex forms of control structures have more complicated characteristic dynamics and are capable of far more varied behavior. Such more complex control structures are quite common in social phenomena, and the theorist should search for them when thinking about problems of this type.

Two additional lessons should be taken from the examples in this chapter: (1) the same phenomenon can be usefully conceptualized and analyzed in a variety of ways depending on the purpose of the investigation, and (2) quite different theories can produce outcomes that as so similar that they are very difficult to distinguish.

As an illustration of the first point, consider the discussions of how to deal with population heterogeneity in diffusion models. For some purposes such heterogeneity can be simply ignored or treated as noise, as in trying to understand the effects of exogenous factors on differences among similar (but each heterogeneous) populations. For other purposes, it may be preferable to deal with heterogeneity by means of assumptions about population distributions and by introducing independent variables into the model to deal with the most important forms. In still other cases a completely different form of modeling using discrete language might be called for to best represent theories in which the differences among actors, rather than their average similarities, are critical.

As an illustration of the second point, that different theories can produce similar results, recall our basic models and extensions. S-shaped "diffusion"curves can be produced by a variety of quite different processes. They may be the result of relatively complicated positive and negative feedback operating simultaneously on a homogeneous population, as we have developed in our models here. S-shaped curves, though, could also be produced by nonhomogeneous distributions of propensities of knowers to become tellers, or for actors to resist conversion. In the absence of an otherwise plausible theory, it is often impossible to distinguish such alternatives from looking at the time-traces that they produce. That quite different causal processes can produce very similar-looking outcomes should be a cause of concern to the theorist concerned with dynamics. It is not enough to be able to reproduce plausible behavior using models from one's theory; and, it is often very dangerous to place great weight in building a theory on reasoning backward from the realizations of dynamic processes to hypotheses about the processes themselves.

Notes

1. For some examples of the use of diffusion models in vaious social science applications, see Brown and Philliber (1977), Boulding (1956), Burmeister and Dobell (1970), Bush and Mosteller (1955), Chow (1967), Coleman et al. (1966), Davies (1969), Dixon (1980), Dodson and Muller (1978), Dunn (1971), Eyestone (1977), Gray (1973), Griliches (1957) (a classic), Hummon (1971), Katz and Hamilton (1963), Kelly and Kranzberg (eds., 1978), Oster (1982), Pitcher et al. (1978), Rapoport (1978), Rogers (1983), and Teece (1980).

2. Mathematical and statistical approaches to unidirectional transition models are very highly developed. Among the many excellent introductions to this literature are Bailey (1957), Bartholomew (1973), Coleman (1964a, 1968, 1981), Doreian and Hummon (1976), Hamblin et al. (1973), Kemeny and Snell (1962), Leik and Meeker (1975), Nielsen and Rosenfeld (1981), Mahajan and Peterson (1985), Meade (1984), and Monin et al. (1976).

3. Survival distribution analysis and event history analysis are variations on the same kinds of models that we are considering in this chapter, though such models can also deal with many more complex dynamics as well. See particularly Tuma and Hannan (1984) and Allison (1984).

4. On the partitioning of the population into those "at risk" and those "not at risk" ("movers and stayers") in social mobility analysis, see particularly Hout (1983), Leik and Meeker (1975), Spilerman (1972a, 1972b), Singer and Spilerman (1974), and White (1965).

5. Alternative assumptions about the distribution of mobilizability give rise to the various

parametric survival models. Arbitrary heterogenity with respect to time but proportional effects for individuals can also be assumed in statistical models by use of partial likelihood methods. See particularly Allison (1984) and Tuma and Hannan (1984).

     6. If our observations were subject to sampling or measurement error (as they usually are), the problem of "inducing" the proper form for the underlying process from its realization becomes even more troublesome.

     7. Indeed, an alternative formulation of this model could treat the number who have recovered as a simple "boxcar" delay of the number infected.

APPENDIX 7.1. Basic Diffusion Curve Models

```
* DIFFUSION, GROWTH, DECLINE PROCESSES
NOTE
NOTE FOUR MODELS ARE SHOWN WITH DIFFERING CONTROL
NOTE          STRUCTURES
NOTE
NOTE ********************************************************
NOTE MODEL ONE: LINEAR GROWTH TO A CEILING
NOTE LET "K" BE THE NUMBER OF PERSONS KNOWING,
NOTE LET "DK" BE THE NUMBER NOT KNOWING. POP = K + DK
L          K1.K = K1.J+(DT)(RI1.JK)
N          K1 =5
R          RI1.KL = CLIP(EXOG.K,0,DK1.K,0)
NOTE RATE OF INCREASE IS EQUAL TO EXOG IF DK1 IS GT ZERO
NOTE RATE OF INCREASE IS EQUAL TO ZERO IF DK1 IS ZERO
A          DK1.K = POP-K1.K
C          POP = 100
A          EXOG = CONST
C          CONST = 10
NOTE THE STIMULUS IS A CONSTANT 10 UNITS PER UNIT TIME
NOTE
NOTE ********************************************************
NOTE MODEL TWO: SELF-REFERENCING GROWTH TO A LIMIT
NOTE
NOTE One person knows initially, and all knowers become
NOTE tellers with an intensity of three-quarters tellings
NOTE to non-knowers per unit time.
NOTE
L          K2.K = K2.J+(DT)(RI2.JK)
N          K2 = 1
A          TELL1.K = (K2.K*.75)
R          RI2.KL = CLIP(TELL1.K,0,DK2.K,0)
A          DK2.K = POP-K2.K
NOTE
NOTE ************************************************************
NOTE MODEL THREE: CONSTANT STIMULUS, PROPORTIONAL RESPONSE
NOTE
NOTE In this model, telling occurs at a constant rate of 10
NOTE tellings per unit time. Success in telling (PS)
```

```
NOTE is proportional to the population not knowing.
L           K3.K = K3.J+(DT)(RI3.JK)
N           K3 = 5
A           TELL3.K = EXOG.K
A           PS3.K = DK3.K/POP
R           RI3.KL = (PS3.K)(TELL3.K)
A           DK3.K = POP-K3.K
NOTE
NOTE ********************************************************
NOTE MODEL FOUR: PROPORTIONAL STIMULUS AND PROPORTIONAL
NOTE RESPONSE (I.E., MODEL 2 AND 3 COMBINED)
NOTE
L           K4.K = K4.J+(DT)(RI4.KL)
N           K4 = 1
A           DK4.K = POP-K4.K
A           TELL4.K = K4.K*.75
A           PS4.K = DK4.K/POP
R           RI4.KL = (PS4.K)(TELL4.K)
NOTE
NOTE ********************************************************
NOTE OUTPUT SPECIFICATIONS
NOTE
SPEC        DT = .25/LENGTH = 15/PLTPER = 1
PLOT        K1 = 1, K2 = 2, K3 = 3, K4 = 4(0,100)
RUN
```

APPENDIX 7.2. Self-Referencing Growth Variations

```
* SELF-REFERENCING GROWTH VARIATIONS
NOTE
NOTE PROGRAMS USED TO GENERATE FIGURE 7.3
NOTE
NOTE ********************************************************
NOTE MODEL ONE:         Knowers become tellers at a rate of
NOTE                    one-half telling per unit time, but do so
NOTE                    with a first-order delay of average length
NOTE                    of three time units. All tellings are
NOTE                    successful if there are any DKs available
L           K1.K = K1.J+(DT)(RI1.JK)
N           K1 = 1
A           TELL1.K = (.5)(DELAY1(K1.K,3))
A           PS1.K = CLIP(1,0,DK1.K,0)
C           POP = 100
A           DK1.K = POP-K1.K
R           RI1.KL = TELL1.K*PS1.K
NOTE
NOTE ********************************************************
NOTE MODEL TWO:         As in model one, but now knowers become
```

```
NOTE                        tellers with a third-order delay instead
NOTE                        of a first-order delay.
L           K2.K = K2.J+(DT)(RI2.JK)
N           K2 = 1
A           TELL2.K = (.5)(DELAY3(K2.K,3))
A           PS2.K = CLIP(1,0,DK2.K,0)
A           DK2.K = POP-K2.K
R           RI2.KL = TELL2.K*PS2.K
NOTE
NOTE ********************************************************
NOTE MODEL THREE:    As a baseline, the same model is created,
NOTE                 but with no delays in knowers becoming
NOTE                 tellers.
L           K3.K = K3.J+(DT)(RI3.JK)
N           K3 = 1
A           TELL3.K = (.5)(K3.K)
A           PS3.K = CLIP(1,0,DK3.K,0)
A           DK3 = POP-K3.K
R           RI3.KL = TELL3.K*PS3.K
NOTE
NOTE OUTPUT SPECIFICATIONS
SPEC        DT = .1/LENGTH = 20/PLTPER = 1
PLOT        K1 = *, K2 = +, K3 = #(0,140)
RUN
```

APPENDIX 7.3. Diffusion and Population Heterogeneity

```
* DIFFUSION WITH POPULATION HETEROGENEITY
NOTE THREE MODELS OF DIFFUSION FOR FIGURE 7.4. MODELS ASSUME
NOTE FLAT (LINEAR) DISTRIBUTION OF RESPONSIVENESS TO STIMULI
NOTE POISSON-DISTRIBUTED RESPONSIVENESS, AND CUMULATIVE
NOTE NORMALLY DISTRIBUTED RESPONSIVENESS
NOTE
NOTE ********************************************************
NOTE MODEL 1:        Assumes that the population is homogeneous,
NOTE                 i.e., all members of the population have equal
NOTE                 probability of responding to a stimulus
L           K1.K = K1.J+(DT)(RI1.JK)
N           K1 = 1
A           TELL1.K = TPARM*K1.K
C           TPARM = .5
A           PS1.K = DK.K/POP
C           POP = 100
A           DK1.K = POP-K1.K
R           RI1.KL = (TELL1.K)(PS1.K)
NOTE
```

```
NOTE MODEL 2:          In this model, it is assumed that most of
NOTE                   the population has low resistance, with
NOTE                   smaller and smaller proportions having
NOTE                   greater resistance, leading to a 'Poisson'
NOTE                   distribution of resistances.
L          K2.K = K2.J+(DT)(RI2.JK)
N          K2 = 1
A          TELL2.K = (TPARM)(K2.K)
A          DK2.K = POP–K2.K
A          PS2.K = TABLE(POIS,DK2,K,0,100,10)
T          POIS = 0/.25/.45/.575/.675/.75/.825/.875/.925/.975/1.0
R          RI2.KL = (TELL2.K)(PS2.K)
NOTE
NOTE *******************************************************
NOTE MODEL 3:          In this model, we use the normal distribution
NOTE                   i.e., relatively few people have either very
NOTE                   low or very high resistance, most falling
NOTE                   around a mean.
L          K3.K = K3.J+(DT)(RI3.JK)
N          K3 = 1
A          TELL3.K = (TPARM)(K3.K)
A          DK3.K = POP–K3.K
A          PS3.K = TABLE(CNORM,DK3.K,0,100,10)
T          CNORM = 0/.25/.38/.45/.475/.50/.525/.55/.62/.75/1
R          RI3.KL = (TELL3.K)(PS3.K)
NOTE
NOTE *******************************************************
NOTE OUTPUT SPECIFICATIONS
NOTE
SPEC       DT = .1/LENGTH = 20/PLTPER = 1
PLOT       K1 = *, K2 = +, K3 = #(0,100)
RUN
```

APPENDIX 7.4. Influenza Epidemic Model*

```
* INFLUENZA MODEL
NOTE From Pugh-Roberts associates (1982) with modification by the author
NOTE
NOTE Total Population
N          TOTAL = SUSC+SICK+IMM
NOTE
NOTE Susceptible Population
L          SUSC.K = SUSC.J+(DT)(–INFEC.JK)
N          SUSC = SUSCI
C          SUSCI = 999
NOTE
NOTE Sick Population
```

```
L           SICK.K = SICK.J+(DT)(INFEC.JK–RECOV.JK)
N           SICK = SICKI
C           SICKI = 1
NOTE
NOTE Immune Population
L           IMM.K = IMM.J+(DT)(RECOV.JK)
N           IMM = IMMI
C           IMMI = 0
NOTE
NOTE Infection Rate
R           INFEC.KL = PRCON*CONTAC.K
C           PRCON = .2
A           CONTAC.K = AVCON*(SUSC.K/TOTAL)*SICK.K
C           AVCON = 5
NOTE
NOTE Recovery Rate
R           RECOV.KL = SICK.K/RECOVT
C           RECOVT = 5
NOTE
NOTE ****************************************************
NOTE OUTPUT SPECIFICATIONS
SPEC        DT = .25/PLTPER = 1/LENGTH = 30
PLOT        SUSC = X, SICK = S, IMM = Y, INFEC = I
PLOT        INFEC = I, RECOV = R
RUN
```

8

Simple Multistate Systems: Chain Models

The single-state models that we introduced in Chapter 7 are just a starting point for a broader class of models involving simple "chains" of closely coupled states. Even the simplest such models involving only two states and unidirectional transitions are useful for representing many important forms of social dynamics. And, if these models are made slightly more complex by adding additional states and allowing flows to move in both directions among states, an even wider variety of common social processes can be represented and analyzed.

The kinds of processes that we will consider in this chapter and the next are quite straightforward extensions of the simple "transitions" models. They are more complex only because the chains of closely coupled states involve more statuses and more possible transitions. For example, a simple two-state chain of the type considered in the previous chapter might be used to theorize about transitions between working and retirement (a process that largely, though not always, goes in only one direction between two statuses). If we sought to construct more general theories of the work-career, however, we would have to consider a wider variety of statuses, and possible bidirectional movements: Individuals move among the statuses employed full time, employed part time, unemployed, and retired. While they can occupy only one status at a time (which makes the whole model a single chain of conserved states), they may move in both directions among the statuses; that is, individuals make transitions from unemployed to employed and back again, change from unemployed to part-time work, from part time to full time and back again, and so on. While this process is undeniably more complex than the simple one-way transition, it is clearly a similar type of theoretical problem.[1]

Processes that can be described by chains of closely coupled states, like the sequence of moves in the work career, are the central theoretical problems in many areas of social sciences. Some obvious applications are in building theories of the movements of persons among social statuses: the life-cycles of individual's movements through the economic market place, through levels in hierarchies such as professions or organizations, through family statuses, and from involvement to noninvolvement in voluntary organizations and social movements. But multistate transition processes are not restricted to individual persons; economic, political, educational, and religious organizations are born and die, change form, move from one ecological niche to another, merge, and separate.

Changes in the statuses of individuals, groups, organizations, and larger patterns of social organization are not the only kinds of "conserved flows" that are of interest. The movements of goods through a manufacturing or distribution process can be seen as a conserved flow, and may be of interest in itself, or as a part of a more complex model.[2] The movement of units of income and wealth among income and wealth holders, or networks of exchanges of any discrete and conserved commodities (e.g., honorific positions or network ties, if these are fixed and conserved) are also processes of multistate transitions.[3]

Like the simple one-way transition processes we examined previously, multiway, multistate transition processes are a "family" or "class" of related models, with near-infinite possible variations. Because of their generality we cannot set out general rules that will describe all of the possible dynamic behaviors of such models. Complex chains, however, are composed of simple chains coupled together in various ways, and can be partially understood by examining their structure in light of what we already know about the general behavior of simpler processes. Because of the tremendous variety of "chain" models it is useful to think about the variations in their structures as a way of approaching the understanding of their behaviors. We will spend this brief chapter on this issue before turning to some exemplary applications in the next chapter. This will help us to gain a sense of the range of possible applications and to try to grasp the ways that such systems behave.

Varieties of Chain Models

We can classify variations in the forms of chain models using the same concepts that are useful for discussing the complexity of theories in general. That is, theories are more complex than others to the extent that they involve more states (that is, have larger state spaces), to the extent that these states are connected to one another, and to the degree that the control structures governing action are themselves complex, involving many variables and forms of relations among variables and over time that require many rather than few parameters to specify.

From this general definition it follows that chains that have more states are more complex (hence having greater "degrees of freedom" of alternative possible behavior and being less easily analyzed) than those that have fewer states. Chains in which more states are more closely coupled to one another (that is, have higher connectivity) are less determinant and more flexible than those with less connectivity. Chains in which flows are governed by self-referencing, goal-referencing, and adaptive feedback display greater degrees of freedom than those governed by stimulus-response control structures. Where the control structures involve complicated interactions of many variables and are nonlinear in variables or with respect to time, behavioral possibilities of chains are greater and analyzability less.

These general-systems principles applied to varieties of chain models are of some utility in understanding the range of possibilities for modeling theories and for comparing them in terms of their structures and complexity. The principles are probably too abstract and general, however, to fire the imagination. In order to illustrate the general principles, but more importantly to get a better sense of the range and kinds of problems that are usefully conceptualized as multistate chains, let's examine in more detail some of the variations on the theme of increasing complexity within the family of such models.

More States in the Chain

The first models that we examined involved a single dependent variable or state and (implicitly) a source or sink. Such models are quite common, and very useful for many problems, as we saw in the previous chapter. It is often the case that we have no immediate interest in where the quantity in a level comes from or where it goes when it leaves a level.

One might, for example, build a theory of the level of the material standard of living of a society that does not explicitly take natural resource constraints (natural resources being the "source" of material wealth), or waste disposal constraints (waste being the "sink" for material wealth) into account. Within limited ranges, at least, such a model with a single level is plausible and useful. Similarly, if we were interested in the dynamics of attitudes or beliefs, our interest focuses almost exclusively on the current "level" of the process, and we usually pay no attention to where the attitude or belief comes from (in the sense of a movement of "psychic energy" from one use to another) or where it goes when the attitude or belief is reduced or disappears. One could readily expand the list of examples of important applications of models with one active state. In all theories of this type there is a single level of interest, and the sources and sinks associated with the level play no causal role in the dynamics of the system.

Models of transitions, diffusion, bounded growth and decline, and analogous processes involve two (or sometimes more) simultaneous dependent states. In diffusion models, for example, it is common to divide the population into two groups, those who "know" of a message or have adopted an innovation and those who "don't know." It might at first seem that there is really only one level here—for if a person does not fall into one category, they must fall into the other, so that there is only one "degree of freedom." In most such theories, however, the number of knowers and the number of nonknowers play different causal roles in the theory, and hence must be considered as separate states. In our diffusion-process theories, the number of knowers has an effect on the rate of change when knowers become tellers. The number of nonknowers plays a causal role in determining the rate of change by affecting the probability that a given telling reaches a person who is still at risk of making the transition from not knowing to knowing. Where the levels of the variables enter the theory as causal factors, the process needs to be considered as a multistate process (even if some of the states are "absorbing states"), rather than as a single state with implicit sources and sinks.

One might wish to reconceptualize a theory of levels of material well-being as a three-state chain, rather than as a single state with implicit sources and sinks, in light of this discussion. Rather than thinking of the level of wealth as coming from an unspecified and unlimited source and disappearing into an unspecified and unlimited sink, a more complex theory might treat natural resources as a causal factor affecting the rate of transition from natural resources to material wealth. In this case, the level of natural resources must be treated explicitly as a state in the model. Similarly, if we supposed that the level of waste had effects on the rates of wealth creation or of wealth use, it could not be treated as a simple implicit sink. Thus, a slightly more complicated conceptualization of the problem of material wealth leads to a model with the structure of several levels linked in a simple chain (natural resources flow into material wealth flows into waste), rather than a single state model with implicit sources and sinks.

From this simple illustration, it can easily be seen how chain models with larger numbers of states develop. We might choose, for example, to create a still more complex model of material wealth by dividing resources into different kinds, identifying different production processes, different resulting products with differing survival or depreciation rates, and multiple kinds of waste. Input-output matricies, and large scale econometric models follow this line of development, often including hundreds or even thousands of different connected states to model the flows of materials through production and consumption processes.[4]

Sociologists often use models of individual's "event histories" that are quite elaborate in their numbers of closely coupled states. The movements of individuals among economic statuses, for example, could be treated with more or fewer levels. For some purposes it might be adequate to see the problem as one of flows from prelabor market status to on the labor market to postlabor market. But for other purposes more detail might be necessary. One might include educational statuses as levels in models of the work career, occupational, industrial, and sectorial distinctions of job types, and other "levels" such as unemployment, and voluntary withdrawal from the labor market. While such a model could easily include hundreds or even thousands of such statuses, its fundamental character is quite straightforward; each individual (or dollar, or resource unit, or quanta of attitudinal intensity, or whatever) may occupy one and only one of the states at a time, and must occupy one of the states at all times.

For many social processes, one could create models of chains of connected states that involved very large number of levels. But most problems can also be simplified by reducing finer distinctions to coarser ones. The optimal level of complexity of this type is ultimately determined by the needs for descriptive adequacy and theoretical articulation. There is no single and final answer to this problem, but there are some general rules for deciding how much complexity, by way of additional state variables, to introduce.

Simplicity is much to be desired over complexity in deciding how many levels to use in conceptualizing chain processes. The dynamics of chain models, as simple as they are, can become quite complicated and difficult to understand if nonlinearities in the relations of either variables or time are present. Reducing the number of states in the chain to a minimum may aid the analyst both in understanding these dynamics and in communicating the results coherently to others.

Simpler models are also to be preferred over more complex ones on the grounds of parsimonious explanation. While models with more levels may appear more elegant or provide fuller descriptions of social processes, they do not necessarily represent more powerful explanations. States that play no independent causal role in determining the dynamics of systems can, and sometimes should, be eliminated from models. In the language of path analysis, for a parallel example, we do not include variables that have no unique effects on dependent variables, and may eliminate as redundant variables that have only indirect effects on others. Similarly, in the analysis of flowgraphs, "loop reduction" is commonly practiced to gather together several effects along pathways into simpler, more compact statements, where such reductions do not confound separate processes.[5] One can, however, go too far. The complex expressions resulting from completely valid reductions of systems with many states to more abstract ones with fewer states may be difficult to comprehend, and gather together factors that the theorist would rather retain as descriptively separate.

There is yet another reason for preferring chain models with fewer states over those with more states that has little to do with either the descriptive or explanatory adequacy of the models. Models with more states are simply more work to create and to analyze. If there is little to be gained in terms of describing a process more realistically or in understanding its causal texture by making the chains more elaborate, it is inefficient to spend human and machine resources in formulating and simulating more complicated models. Simulation methods for understanding theories are often quite intensive in both human and machine time; models with many additional states that contribute little to explanation or representation can be quite costly without much return.

The elaboration of theories of transitions or flows into more complex expressions often occurs by the addition of more states to the "chain." Models with single "dependent" states can effectively represent many important processes. Such models have contributed much to our understanding of social dynamics, but it is also quite reasonable to extend the modeling effort to consider, in a single integrated framework, processes that involve the movements of people, data, and things among large numbers of states.

More Connectivity Among the States

The dynamic processes that we considered in Chapter 7 were "simple" chains in a second way. In addition to having only two (or at most three) states, these states were connected in the simplest possible way: Transitions or flows occurred in only one direction, and (where there were three states, as in the model of an epidemic) in a single fixed sequence, for example from well to ill to recovered, but never from well to recovered without passing through the state of being ill. These "chains" might be termed unidirectional, and (relative to the logically possible alternatives for such systems) having low connectivity, with only one possible sequence of moves or flows. Systems of this type have structures like those of the top panel of Figure 8.1.

As the examples of diffusion processes demonstrated, even the simplest of chain models are adequate for constructing and testing theories about important social processes. Obviously, though, many other social dynamics cannot be very well approximated with such models. Bidirectionality is very common in social dynamics. Individuals move from being unemployed to employed and from employed to unemployed. People migrate from the country to the city, but many also return to the country from the city. Money flows from owners to workers in the form of wages, but returns to owners in the form of purchases of goods.

Combining the notion of bidirectional flows with the simplest form of multistate models (the single sequence), a variety of relatively complicated processes can be captured. A dynamic process with the structure of the figure in the second panel of Figure 8.1, for example, might be used to represent the process of career movements in a large organization. This model proposes four possible statuses: entry level management, line management, staff management, and executive. All movements originate at the entry level in this model, and movements out of the entry level are allowed only into line management. Line managers may become staff managers, but may not directly become executives, who are selected from among staff managers. Staff managers may rise to executive positions, but they can also fall back into the line management—creating a bidirectional flow among middle-level managers. This model of the mobility dynamics within organizations is, of course, still quite primitive, but serves to illustrate the point. The number of possible sequences of flows or movements in this model is much greater than in the simple chain. The levels of each of the states and the rates of transition among the states at any point in time in this model can display far more complicated over-time behavior than the simple unidirectional flow models.

Many social processes do not display simple and fixed sequences of possible moves or flows like the first two diagrams in Figure 8.1. In many cases it is possible for flows to occur from a single "origin" to many alternative "destinations"; and, for flows from many different "origins" to flow into a single "destination." One obvious example of such processes is that of career-status mobility. The mobility matrix of transitions from first job to final job, so common in studies of status attainment, is a representation of such a process. In such a matrix, flows occur over the careers of individuals in all possible directions. If we considered a status hierarchy with only three levels (for simplicity), the

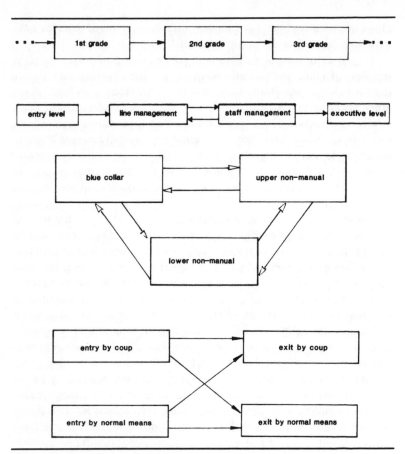

Figure 8.1: Elaborated connectedness.

processes involved could be represented by a chain model like that in the third panel of Figure 8.1. In this model, moves are possible back and forth between each pair of states, giving rise to an unlimited number of possible careers. This model has the maximum possible connectivity for three states.

Complex transition processes not involving bidirectionality can also be seen as generalizations of the simple chain model. In the last panel of Figure 8.1, for example, a simple model of a multistate survival process is shown. In this model there are two origin states (regimes come to power either by legal-normative means or by military coup) and two "destinations" (regimes leave power either by legal normative means or by coup).[6] Flows, by definition, do not occur between the two origin states or between the two destinations, nor are flows bidirectional. Regimes that enter by coup, however, may exit by either coup or legal-normative means; as may regimes that came to power by legal-normative means. Interest here focus on the rates of transition—that is, the probability that a movement will occur in a period of time from a given origin to a given destination. This model is a simpler one than the full mobility matrix (though it has been simplified by the way that the problem has been defined; just as the mobility matrix problem can be simplified by not allowing bidirectional movements—as in "father-son" models). Because the connectivity of the system is considerably less, the number of possible sequences and number of rates of transition that are occurring are less. It is, nonetheless, a very useful device for theorizing about survival or transition processes that have multiple "hazards" (for example, the risk of exiting power by normal means and the risk of exiting power by coup) that apply differentially to different populations (for example, those regimes that came to power by coup versus those that came to power by normal means).

The notion of modeling "event histories" of transitions among statuses can be extended to virtually any degree of complexity, depending on the descriptive and theoretical objectives. The mobility matrix, with its complete connectivity, and the two-state absorbing process of regime survival with more limited and unidirectional flows, are only two of the more interesting possibilities. Each of the social-science disciplines have many major substantive problems that can be viewed usefully as models with relatively few states but extensive connectivity. A few more possibilities, drawn from the author's "home" discipline of sociology may suggest, by analogy, some further possibilities.

Individual's economic careers and the structuring of labor markets are central topics in contemporary studies of organizations, work, and both micro and macro class stratification research. The representation of quite complex opportunity structures and rates of movements across positions in these structures are quite straightforward extensions of the chains that we have examined above. An example of an elementary map for such a model is shown in Figure 8.2, and could profitably be elaborated still further. Such chains could easily be used to represent and experiment with the effects of "internal versus external labor markets," "sectorial segmentation," the "social distribution of employment and unemployment" and other phenomena of interest. Realistic models of processes of these types are impressive in their bulk, but relatively simple in their basic structure as chains of connected states where most states display bidirectional movements.

Some of the issues of interest to researchers and theorists in the

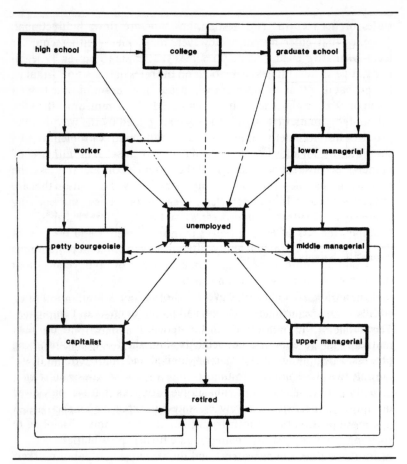

Figure 8.2: Class-career flows.

"social networks" tradition can also be cast as questions of the dynamics of chains of various degrees of connectivity.[7] Rates of exchange, sending and receiving of social ties, the diffusion of information, and other processes can be conceived as chains in which the actors are seen as levels or states, and the relationships of connectivity, exchange, or whatever among them are seen as flows. A simple schematic of one possible network is shown as Figure 8.3, purely as an illustration of the possibilities. Approached in this way, some of the classic questions of sociometry—and their revised versions in "social networks"—can be examined by means of formal models and simulation. "Structures" of higher or lower degrees of connectivity, of any size (up to the limits of

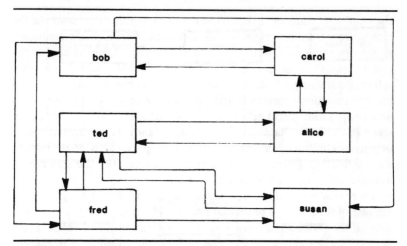

Figure 8.3: Network connectedness.

the software and hardware available), and of any configuration (e.g., wheels, stars, branching trees, etc.) can be represented and simulated. The "systems" of interest in social network applications are thus representable as chain models of flows (relations) among states (actors) in many cases; many of the questions of interest to network analysts, such as the implications of the degree and form of connectivity in a network are, when seen in this light, exactly the same issues as those of the implications of increasing the "complexity" of systems by increasing their "connectivity."

More Complex Control

The dynamic behavior of chain systems depends not only on the number of states and their connectivity but also on the control structures that govern the rates of flow among the states. These control structures can be thought of as varying in complexity by the same definition of "complexity" as do the state spaces of models. Two theories with the same number of states and degree of connectivity among the states may still differ greatly in the range of behavior they produce if they differ in the complexity of their control structures.

The simplest of chain-model control structures of any interest are processes governed by constant rates or by control structures referencing either the origin state or the destination state. For example, a model embodying the logic of a Markov process suggests that the probability of a transition from an origin to a destination is a constant. Consequently, the number of transitions that occur in a period of time (for example, the rate of flow from an origin to a destination) is equal to the transition probability times the number of cases "at risk" (for example, in the origin status). This process is a simple "feed-forward" one that references the origin state. Similarly, but at a somewhat higher level of control structure complexity the rate of movement between an origin and a destination might be seen as a constant function of the destination state. In a vacancy chain model, for example, the rate of movement from origin to destination is governed by the discrepancy between the level of the destination state and a goal state (for example, the number of unfilled positions at the destination status).

There is no necessity, of course, that the control structures governing the rate of flow along a particular link in a chain model make reference only to the states at the origin and/or destination. In our elementary sketch of class-career flows (Figure 8.2), for example, the rate of movements from midmanagerial positions to petty bourgeoisie might very well be conditioned on the level of unemployment—as many such moves are thought to be voluntary and are more likely to be undertaken in "good times" than in bad.

By extension, we can see that some chains may have quite complex control structures that may even approach attempts at full-information monitoring and control. The production processes of continuous-flow manufacturing can be seen as (usually) relatively simple chains of states coupled by control structures that take into account information about all other states in the system (or attempt to).[8] Other highly rationalized planning processes, such as personnel, money, and information flows in bureaucracies may have the same flavor of relatively simple chains governed by control structures that attempt full information monitoring and rationalization. The "complexity" of a chain depends not only on the numbers of states and their degree of direct connectedness but primarily on the complexity of the information and control system. Many systems representable as chains may be of relatively low complexity in terms of the numbers of states and flows among them, but be of considerable complexity in terms of the control structures governing those flows.

Additional Complexities of Control

The behavioral tendencies of relatively complex chain models depend most importantly on the considerations of the number of states and their connectedness by means of direct flows and by information flows (i.e., their control structures). In attempting to mimic the behavior of real social action systems, however, even further complexity is usually called for. Real systems usually involve considerable delay in the movement of both material and informational quantities; signals are often "noisy" or distorted; the production of a behavior by signals is probabilistic rather than certain; and, there may be thresholds, resistances, ceilings, and other nonlinearities in the flows of both the material and informational quantities in chains.

Delay, distortion, and nonlinearity of flows of both material and informational quantities interact with the structure of chains and their control structures to produce even greater behavioral possibilities. By their very nature as connected "systems," the effects of noise, delay, and nonlinearity multiply through the system over time. Errors in perception in one part of a behavioral chain may result in inappropriate responses in connected parts of the system that result in complete destabilization. Small distortions of information or of material flows may prove to be the "straw that breaks the camel's back" in systems where responses are nonlinear, resulting in "disaster" or in overresponse that further destabilizes systems. Perhaps more commonly in many systems of social action, responses to signals in chains are partial and delayed in such ways that there is very little response to even rather great stimulus, or strong stimuli produce outcomes other than those intended. Increasing pressure for higher production, for example, may yield less production and higher turnover, requiring new hiring of untrained personnel that lowers productivity still further. The important point in these examples is that noise, nonlinearity, and delay in "chains" multiply through the system over time due to the interconnectedness of the system, producing (potentially) very complex behavioral responses to rather simple stimuli.

Conclusions

In this short chapter we have explored some of the ways that the very simple systems considered previously can be expanded to represent more complicated processes. Our primary concern has been with increasing the complexity of the basic model by the addition of more states. Rather than thinking about social action as a series of singular changes from one state to another, the models we have considered in the current chapter allow for multiple outcomes from multiple origins, movements of people, information, and material quantities back and forth between states all occurring simultaneously. While it is often analytically useful to think about social dynamics in terms of single dependent variables or single states as in the previous chapters, there is also a good bit to be gained by creating more elaborate dynamic theories as sets of interconnected effects or transitions.

Models of single chains of states can be made more complex in a variety of ways that serve to increase the range of phenomena that they describe and increase the "degrees of freedom" in the behavior that they can display. In this chapter, we have categorized these possibilities as increasing the number of states, increasing the connectivity of the states, and increasing the complexity of control systems governing rates of change. In identifying chain models that display these forms of increased system complexity, it has been our intent to show that many of the core theoretical models in various areas of social science research can be represented by such models.

To illustrate the utility of the strategy of formulating theories of the dynamics of action in such structures, and to show how such formulations can raise further questions for theoretical research, it is now time to build and examine the behavior of a few such (slightly) elaborated chain models.

Notes

1. Work in statistical and mathematical approaches to multistate transition models has grown very rapidly in the social sciences in the past several years, after a lengthy period in which only single-state models were considered. For some introductions to mathematical and statistical approaches to models with multiple qualitative outcomes, readers may wish to examine Coleman (1981), Tuma and Hannan (1984), and Allison (1984).

2. Jay W. Forrester's (1961) classic DYNAMO model of a business firm is an excellent example of a very powerful model developed from a few simple chains.

3. The movements of discrete quantities among discrete states (usually actors) is clearly one of the kinds of processes that we are considering in this chapter. Say, for example, the moves of armies across territories. Such models could be developed within DYNAMO, but the language is relatively inefficient for such purposes, and more event-oriented languages would be more appropriate.

4. For an interesting comparison of economic growth models that is sensitive to the conceptual distinctions we are using in this volume, see Meadows and Robinson (1985).

5. On the problems attendant upon inclusion or exclusion of "redundant" variables in structural equation models, any multivariate statistics text in the social sciences can be consulted. Heise (1975) discusses the logic and techniques of loop reduction methods in flow diagram analysis.

6. For an example of the application of statistical methods to the regime transition problem, see an example reported in Tuma and Hannan (1984, Ch. 10).

7. Though languages other than DYNAMO may be preferable for building models of such phenomena.

8. See particularly Perrow (1984) on the complexity of control structures.

9

Multistate Systems:
The Behavior of Simple Chains

Making simple 'chain' models more elaborate by adding more states, allowing greater connectivity among the states, and building 'smarter' rules governing flows allows us to model theories of quite complicated social processes. In the current chapter we will develop models of three commonly studied processes that illustrate some of the possibilities for models of this type: a model of population movements, a model of promotions in a hierarchical organization, and a model of movements among the social statuses in a "mobility" matrix.[1] The applicability of these models, however, goes well beyond the particular substantive contexts in which we will develop them. The kinds of processes that can be usefully conceptualized as simple chains are extremely numerous and central to all of the social science disciplines.

Population-age structures are generated by a very obvious process. Individuals are born and move in one direction through a series of states (age categories) with fixed "delays" or "waiting times" until they reach an "absorbing state." Such a system has many states, but relatively low connectivity, and relatively simple rules governing most transition rates. Many social processes have similar structures. Individual's changes in status within groups, tribes, formal organizations, and professions, for example, display such unidirectional change and more or less fixed waiting times. And virtually all models of any complexity in any of the social sciences must contain one or more "demographic" subsystems to account for the movements of people, data, or things over time.

Promotion regimes in hierarchical organizations (at least as idealized in most formal models) are similar to population-age structures but involve more complex rules governing transition rates. Generally, promotion rates are thought to depend on vacancies—so that such models are characterized by control by "goal oriented" (i.e. the elimination of vacancies) feedback. "Demand-driven" changes—such as vacancy chains of occupational positions—are important parts of the dynamics of most social structures. The "queuing" and delay of information, material goods, and people in all sorts of systems with fixed numbers of positions are found in applications in all of the social sciences.

Transition processes with multiple origins and multiple destinations, such as those analyzed with the "mobility matrix," are another variation on the theme. Such processes tend to be represented as governed by rather simple rules (e.g. Markov or semi-Markov processes), but involve movements among many closely connected states. Less restrictive models, like the "mobility matrix," that model movements between multiple-origin states and multiple destinations are extremely general in their applications: Individuals change religious affiliations, nations become parts of (or disengage from) alliances, and firms move across market niches, to suggest some of the possible applications of such models.

The three models considered here by no means exhaust the possible variations on simple chains. They do serve as useful starting points for further elaboration for the development of similar models for other such social processes, and to illustrate the behavioral possibilities of what are still relatively simple systems.

Population Age Structures

Among the most important social processes are those that generate age structures within populations. The distribution of populations by age is an important conditioning factor that limits other forms of social action as well as directly affecting the reproduction of the population itself. Age structures are often studied in and of themselves, as in demography, or as "subsystems" of other models, as in studies of economic development. Not only are age structures studied at the level of nation-states, but they are also very important in understanding the behavior of large-scale and small-scale social organizations such as bureaucracies or families.

There is broad consensus about the most useful ways to represent age structures and on the basic nature of the processes that govern their dynamics. Though by no means are all of the factors that affect the relevant rates (for example, "birth" and "death") fully understood.[2] Since our purpose here is largely to illustrate the general dynamic behavioral characteristics of systems composed of long but simple chains, we will focus on a highly idealized but familiar type of demographic process: the age structure of the general population. Models with finer descriptive character (e.g., differentiating gender groups, or narrow age categories) or for differing contexts (e.g., the age structure or distribution of "time in grade" of employees within an organization) can be seen as slight variations on the same theme.

Developing the Baseline Model

For simplicity, we will divide the population into six age categories: ages 0-1, 1-4, 5-14, 15-44, 45-64, and 65+. This particular classification is used because it corresponds to convention and best reflects some of the major nonlinearities in fertility and mortality rates. The particular groupings chosen are for convenience in capturing particular effects (and for reducing the tedium and computer cost of treating each year of age as a separate level). For example, the rather fine distinctions at the earlier ages are necessary to reflect the dramatic differences of mortality rates between infants (ages 0-1) and young children (ages 1-4); the age group 15-44 is convenient for use in modeling the birth rate. As always, the levels or states of a system are defined pragmatically and with an eye to the causal connections of the model.

The connectivity among these states is rather obvious, and is shown in Figure 9.1. The model is driven from a "source" by transitions that occur at a rate (the birth rate, BR), and by two kinds of transitions that occur for each of the levels in the model (save the last): Individuals make transitions from their current age category to the next one in the sequence (R12, R23, R34, R45), or to the "sink" (DR1, DR2, DR3, DR4, DR5). The basic structure of this chain is a quite common one of a single "normal" sequence of moves originating at the same status for all individuals, and having multiple exit points.

The control structures, or "rates" in this model are likewise quite straightforward. Each transition in the process (except the very first one of birth) is governed by a self-referencing "feed forward" at constant rates. For example, the number of persons moving from the "state" of infancy to the "state" of early childhood (R12) depends on the number of infants "at risk" (SS1) and a probability of such a transition (P3). In our baseline model we assume that this probability of survival is constant across all persons in the category. The probability that an infant makes a transition to the sink rather than to early childhood is also a function of the number at risk and a constant probability. Since a transition of one or the other sort must occur within one year, these two "transition probabilities" (PARM2 and PARM3) must sum to unity. There is a single (positive) "feedback" loop in the model that connects

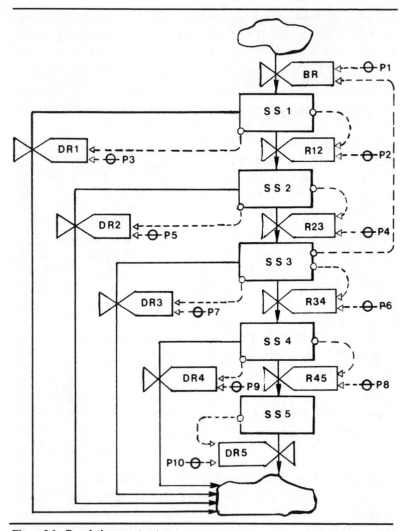

Figure 9.1: Population age structure.

the birth rate (BR) to the size of the population in the age category between 15 and 44 (SS3) and a "risk" probability (PARM1) of a birth that applies to this age group. This part of the process can be represented in DYNAMO code as:

```
L    P01.K = P01.J+DT(BR.JK–ISR.JK–IDR.JK)
R    ISR.KL = P01.K*PARM1
```

```
R     IDR.KL = P01.K*PARM2
R     BR.KL = P1544*FERT
C     FERT = PARM3
```

where PARM1 and PARM2 sum to unity and represent the probability of survival and death, respectively, among persons ages 0-1. The birth rate (BR) is represented as a constant function (FERT, for "fertility") of the number of persons in the age category of 15 to 44.

Each of the other levels in the model is similarly defined, having as a source the transitions out of the preceding level in the sequence, and having as outflows either "survivals" or "deaths." Because we have aggregated the age categories to save space and time, it has been necessary to impose the assumption that the age-specific mortality rates are homogeneous within each category and that there are equal numbers of persons in each of the specific ages within categories (the baseline model is provided as Appendix 9.1). These assumptions do introduce some inaccuracy into the model, particularly in studying responses to transient shocks. They do not, however, distort the general behavioral tendencies of the chain that are our major concern.[3]

Behavior of the Baseline Model

Because the connections in the simple demographic chain are so straightforward, the general dynamic tendencies of the model are well understood. Nonetheless, the first step toward understanding more complex problems is to get a firm grasp on the baseline condition. Let us then conduct a set of experiments to get comfortable with the dynamic implications of the rather simple theory we have specified so far. To do this, we need to provide starting values for the age structure of the population, for the fertility rate, and for age specific mortalities. To make things interesting, we have selected values that represent the situation of the United States in about 1980.[4]

While any number of useful baselines might be thought of for answering various "what if" questions about population age structure in the United States, let us focus first on the long-term or "equilibrium" tendencies of the situation prevailing at about 1980. If we substitute the observed fertility rates, age specific mortality rates, and sizes of population groups into our model and allow it to run for a long time (in our example, 200 years), we can observe the equilibrium tendencies of the basic model. The time traces of this simulation are shown in Figure 9.2 and the numeric results are given in Table 9.1.

The scenario that we have modeled in Figure 9.2 and Table 9.1 is

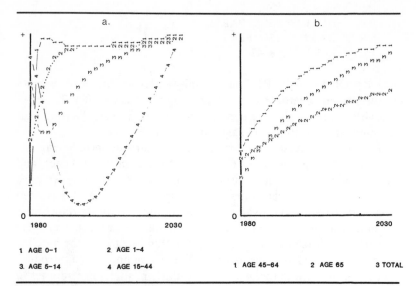

Figure 9.2: Age structure baseline model.

clearly "unrealistic" in a number of ways. We have made no attempt to deal with the effects of immigration or emigration here for simplicity's sake (though such effects are likely to be very important in reality). More immediately relevant, our "baseline" assumes that fertility and mortality rates remain fixed over the entire period. Clearly this will not be the case, but we need to first grasp the behavioral tendencies of the model when as many factors are "held constant," before we can really understand the consequences of change.

There are several things of interest in these results. First and foremost is that the "normal" or "long-run" or "equilibrium" tendency of the conditions prevailing in 1980 is to produce continued growth of the population, but at quite slow rates. Second, as must be the case when no change in fertility or mortality rates is allowed, the age structure of the population eventually reaches stability. It is important to note, however, that this "eventually" is quite a long time. Changes in the relative sizes of the younger population groups occur relatively quickly, taking about 50 years to complete most of their change. The adjustment of the size of the population over age 65, however, takes a bit longer to stabilize (as it is the receiver of all changes in other groups, with a lag). Third, the "equilibrium" age structure of the population implied by the conditions (age, specific mortality, and fertility) that existed at 1980 is quite different from the age structure of the population that existed at 1980.

TABLE 9.1
Population Age Structure Baseline (U.S., 1980)

Year	0-1	1-4	5-14	15-44	45-64	65+	Total
	Population in Millions and Percentage of Population						
1980	3.3	13.1	34.9	105.2	44.5	25.6	226.6
	(1.4)	(5.8)	(15.4)	(46.4)	(19.6)	(11.3)	
2030	3.6	14.2	35.5	105.3	67.8	54.6	280.9
	(1.3)	(5.1)	(12.6)	(37.5)	(24.1)	(19.4)	
2080	3.6	14.4	35.9	106.7	70.5	60.8	291.9
	(1.3)	(4.9)	(12.3)	(36.5)	(24.1)	(20.8)	
2180	3.7	14.7	36.9	109.5	72.5	63.1	300.5
	(1.3)	(4.9)	(12.3)	(36.4)	(24.1)	(21.0)	

Most striking is the projected increase in the proportion of the population over age 65, which nearly doubles from 11 to 21%.

So long as mortality and fertility rates are fixed at 1980 levels (and ignoring immigration and emigration), there is a tendency for the American population to continue to increase in size at a slow rate. This is a natural consequence of the "positive feedback" loop between the size of the fertile population and the number of births. This tendency is actually toward exponential growth in population size, though the slope is so slight that our plots look essentially linear with respect to time. More critically, there is a very strong tendency inherent in the model at 1980 toward rapid and extensive change in the age structure of the population. The total size of the population is projected to increase by roughly a third over the next 200 years; the number of persons over age 65 is projected to increase by 150%.

A Delicate Balance:
Sensitivity to Fertility Change

In our baseline example, we assumed that the fertility rate remained constant at its 1980 level of 3.42 births per 100 persons ages 15-44 per year. With existing age specific mortality rates, we saw that this birth rate was above "zero population growth." The next step in assessing the behavior of this model might be to explore the sensitivity of the results to our assumption about the fertility rate.[5] We can easily do so by conducting two experiments: First we will decrease the fertility rate from 3.42 to 3.00 and observe the long-run effects on the trend in total population and in the age structure; then we will increase the fertility rate from 3.42 to 3.8. These are relatively mild manipulations, involving

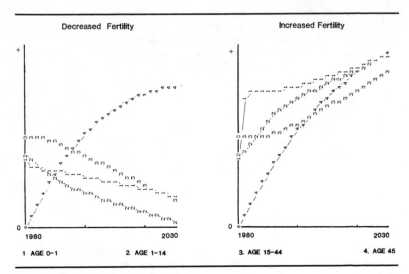

Figure 9.3: Age structure fertility experiment.

increases or decreases of about 10% in fertility. The results of these two experiments are shown in Figure 9.3 and Table 9.2.

The results of these experiments are rather dramatic, and suggest the delicate balances that are necessary to maintain stability in population structures. A roughly ten percent decrease in the fertility rate is sufficient to lead to a long-term pattern of decline in total population size (after the consequences of current disequilibria are fully realized), coupled with steady increases in the average age of the population. A rough ten percent increase in fertility, in contrast, is sufficient to lead to rapid growth in total population and a marked shift toward a younger age structure.

The Consequences of Differential Mortality

In addition to fertility, the other forces shaping the age structure of the population are the age-specific mortality rates. To gain a sensitivity to the impact of these factors, let us conduct another set of experiments.

Suppose, on one hand, that we focused all of our research and treatment efforts on the reduction of mortality among infants, and succeeded in reducing the rate of deaths in the first year by 25% from its 1980 level. Or, alternatively, suppose that we focused all of our resources and energies on the prolongation of life, and succeeded in reducing the mortality rate among persons of sixty-five or more by a similar proportion. What would the consequences be for the total size of the

TABLE 9.2
Population Age Structures
Under Alternative Fertility Rates

Year	0-1	1-4	5-14	15-44	45-64	65+	Total
Scenario I: Baseline (U.S., 1980)							
1980	3.3	13.1	34.9	105.2	44.5	25.6	226.6
	(1.4)	(5.8)	(15.4)	(46.4)	(19.6)	(11.3)	(100)
2030	3.6	14.2	35.5	105.3	67.8	54.6	280.9
	(1.3)	(5.1)	(12.6)	(37.5)	(24.1)	(19.4)	(100)
2080	3.6	14.4	35.9	106.7	70.5	60.8	291.9
	(1.3)	(4.9)	(12.3)	(36.5)	(24.1)	(20.8)	(100)
Scenario II: Decreased Fertility							
1980	3.3	13.1	34.9	105.2	44.5	25.6	226.6
	(1.4)	(5.8)	(15.4)	(46.4)	(19.6)	(11.3)	(100)
2030	2.8	11.3	29.1	94.4	63.7	52.7	254.1
	(1.1)	(4.5)	(11.5)	(37.1)	(25.1)	(20.7)	(100)
2080	2.5	10.0	25.6	83.0	58.0	52.4	231.5
	(1.1)	(4.3)	(11.1)	(35.9)	(25.1)	(22.6)	(100)
Scenario III: Increased Fertility							
1980	3.3	13.1	34.9	105.2	44.5	25.6	226.6
	(1.4)	(5.8)	(15.4)	(46.4)	(19.6)	(11.3)	(100)
2030	4.4	17.1	41.8	115.7	71.7	56.3	307.0
	(1.4)	(5.6)	(13.6)	(37.7)	(23.3)	(18.3)	(100)
2080	5.0	19.6	47.8	132.3	83.5	69.2	357.4
	(1.4)	(5.5)	(13.4)	(37.0)	(23.4)	(19.4)	(100)

population and its age structure? In Figure 9.4 and Table 9.3 the results of these experiments are displayed.

The results may seem, at first, a bit surprising. A substantial increase in the survival rate in the first year of life has little effect on either the total size of the population or on its age structure (compare the middle panel of Table 9.3 to the top panel). On the other hand, a substantial increase in the survival chances of the aged population leads to both rather rapid increases in total population and to a dramatic shift toward an older population.

This result is surprising because, in the abstract, changes in infant mortality might be expected to have greater long run effects—because they "multiply" through the system by increasing the size of the fertile population sometime later. Increasing the survival rates of the aged, in contrast, has only its first-round impacts, and is not multiplied by feedback. There is, however, no mystery here. The multiplicative impact

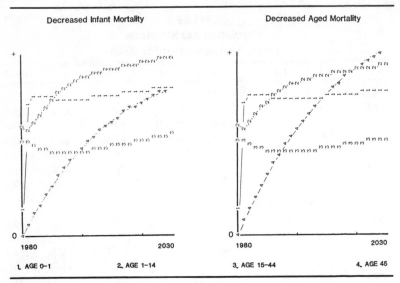

Figure 9.4: Age structure mortality experiment

of changes in the infant mortality rate are, in fact, present in these results; in a population with such a low birth rate, however, the numerical impact of even a quite dramatic change in infant survival chances is small. Because the aged population is much larger than the infant population, and because the reduction in mortality simulated applies continuously across many years of age (from age 65 onward, as opposed to the single year in the first scenario), the numerical impact is much larger.

There is an object lesson in this example. It is that changes that are more structurally important do not necessarily have observable results that are more dramatic than changes that are less structurally important in all realizations of a model. In systems terms, a modification of infant mortality is much more significant than a modification of mortality among the aged because it precedes the feedback loop from the size of the fertile population to the birth rate, and hence is multiplied by the feedback. Changing mortality among the aged has only its direct first-order effects that merely accumulate. Because of the sizes of the populations to which these effects apply in any realistic model, however, the latter change is of much greater numerical consequence.

Summary

The age-structure model is a very simple and straightforward elaboration of the simple chain system. The dynamic behavior of the

TABLE 9.3
Population Age Structures
Under Alternative Mortality Rates

Year	0-1	1-4	5-14	15-44	45-64	65+	Total
Scenario I: Baseline (U.S., 1980)							
1980	3.3	13.1	34.9	105.2	44.5	25.6	226.6
	(1.4)	(5.8)	(15.4)	(46.4)	(19.6)	(11.3)	(100)
2030	3.6	14.2	35.5	105.3	67.8	54.6	280.9
	(1.3)	(5.1)	(12.6)	(37.5)	(24.1)	(19.4)	(100)
2080	3.6	14.4	35.9	106.7	70.5	60.8	291.9
	(1.3)	(4.9)	(12.3)	(36.5)	(24.1)	(20.8)	(100)
Scenario II: Decreased Infant Mortality							
1980	3.3	13.1	34.9	105.2	44.5	25.6	226.6
	(1.4)	(5.8)	(15.4)	(46.4)	(19.6)	(11.3)	(100)
2030	3.6	14.3	35.7	105.6	67.9	54.6	281.7
	(1.3)	(5.7)	(12.7)	(37.5)	(24.1)	(19.4)	(100)
2080	3.7	14.5	36.3	107.4	70.8	61.0	293.7
	(1.2)	(4.9)	(12.3)	(36.6)	(24.1)	(20.8)	(100)
Scenario III: Decreased Aged Mortality							
1980	3.3	13.1	34.9	105.2	44.5	25.6	226.6
	(1.4)	(5.8)	(15.4)	(46.4)	(19.6)	(11.3)	(100)
2030	3.6	14.2	35.5	105.3	67.8	68.5	294.8
	(1.2)	(4.8)	(12.0)	(35.7)	(23.0)	(23.2)	(100)
2080	3.6	14.4	35.9	106.7	70.5	79.9	311.0
	(1.2)	(4.6)	(11.6)	(34.3)	(22.7)	(25.7)	(100)

system is, in the abstract, quite easy to understand from its structure as a simple chain with primarily "feed forward" linkages creating delay, and a single positive feedback loop. The forward linkages produce simple linear trends that occur at rates dependent upon the relative sizes of the transition probabilities (age-specific mortality rates). The model, however, also displays a good deal of sensitivity to changes in the birth rate that produces long-run tendencies away from stable equilibrium. This sensitivity and "instability" of population is a natural consequence of the simplicity of the system structure. While the model has many levels and rates, it has only one feedback loop, and this loop is a positive one (for example, the larger the size of the fertile population, the larger the number of births). Just as in the very simplest of positive feedback systems, population is inherently unstable and seeks either to collapse or explode. The speed and shape of the realization of this tendency is much more complex than the simple feedback systems we considered in earlier chapters, owing to the delays and differential rates of transitions among the many states. The basic dynamic tendencies of the system, however, are determined by the nature of the control structure, and not by the elaboration of the model into a more complex chain.

Vacancy Chains

The control structures governing the dynamics of population age structures are, in the terms that we have been using, a combination of "dumb" and self-referencing feedback. That is, the rates of change in age groups depend only on their current size and on constants (transition probabilities). The system is also quite simple in its connectivity in that only "one-way" transitions occur, and each state is connected only to one origin and two destinations.

In recent years economists, sociologists, and human resource managers have focused a good deal of attention on another demographic phenomenon that appears to be analyzable as a system with a very similar structure to general population movements: rates of promotion within hierarchies.[6] The primary tool used for analysis is a slightly smarter feedback system called the "vacancy chain." These models are not only of considerable interest in themselves as representation of dynamics of personnel movements; they also provide a useful contrast to our age structure models. And as with the simple demographic model, vacancy chains can be widely applied in other contexts.

In the population age-structure system, dynamics are governed primarily by "feed-forward." That is, the rates of transition of individuals from origins to destinations depend on the numbers in the origin state and transition probabilities. In a sense, this is a model in which "push" or "supply" is central. In contrast, most models of mobility processes in organizations are based on "pull" or "demand" factors; the number of persons who are promoted from one level to the next higher one is seen as a consequence of number of persons in the destination status (or, more correctly, the number of vacancies at the destination status). As the number of persons in the destination status departs from some goal, vacancies are created which pull individuals from lower to higher levels. When a vacancy occurs in a high level, demand is created at all lower levels; hence overall mobility rates depend on where vacancies occur and the relative sizes of the strata in the hierarchy.

Developing the Baseline Model

The levels and the degree and forms of connectivity in a model of a vacancy chain are very similar to those of the age-structure model. In our simple hierarchical or sequential system, we will imagine that there are three ranked subpopulations (we will call them "entry level," "mid level" and "executive"). All individuals enter the organization at the lowest level, and cannot be promoted to executive status without passing through the middle levels. In our simplest model, all individuals are seen as remaining in the organization until they attain executive status, from which they ultimately retire. While these assumptions are obviously far too simple, they will serve for the moment. A diagram of the basic model is shown as Figure 9.5.

The primary and important difference between the system shown in Figure 9.5 and the earlier age-structure model (see Figure 9.1) is the nature of the control system. In the current model, rates of transition—the hiring rate(HR), the promotion rate from entry to mid level (PR1), and the promotion rate from mid level to executive (PR2)—are governed by a comparison of the number of persons at the destination level to some goal state (the desired level). This comparison results in the perception of a vacancy (ELVAC, MLVAC, and EXVAC), which, in turn drives promotion rates. The DYNAMO program for this model is similar to the population model, and is provided in Appendix 9.2.

Behavior of the Baseline Model

The behavioral tendencies of the vacancy chain model should be quite easy to anticipate. The system is governed by goal-directed feedback, and hence tends toward a stable equilibrium in the number of persons at each level and in the rates of transitions among levels. Since we have not provided for misperception or delay in the baseline specification of the model, adjustment of the executive level to retirements occurs completely within one time period; adjustment of the middle level to a retirement at the executive level takes two time periods; and adjustment of the entry level to an executive retirement takes three periods as the vacancy "trickles down." The overall rates of mobility, then, depend entirely on retirements from the executive level. The probability that an executive retirement results in promotion for an individual at a lower level depends on the number of persons in the lower level—that is, on the shape of the pyramid. Where the numbers of persons in the levels are similar, a retirement improves everyone's chances of promotion equally. Where there are many more people at lower levels than at higher ones, retirements at the top improve the prospects of middle-level persons more than those of entry-level persons.

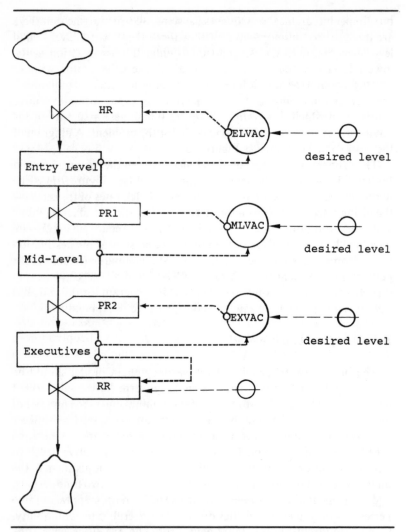

Figure 9.5: Vacancy chain.

The basic vacancy chain, then, has a structure much like that of the population age-structure model we examined above. But because its dynamics are governed by goal-oriented feedback rather than by self-referencing and dumb feedforward its behavioral tendencies are quite different. Where the population model has a tendency toward unconstrained growth or decline, the vacancy chain has a strong tendency toward stability. In the population model, dynamics are driven by supply (births); in the vacancy chain, dynamics are driven by demand (retirements). Let's explore some of the implications of these dynamics.

Growth, Structural Change, and Mobility

Research on structure of mobility in organizations has focused on the effects of size and technology (or, more properly, the division of labor resulting from a given technology). From our baseline model it is easy to understand why these two factors are critical in understanding mobility rates and patterns in demand-driven simple sequence models. Increases in the size of an organization (if the new vacancies are filled by hiring into entry-level positions and the relative sizes of the strata are preserved) improve the prospects of all organizational members and result in higher general rates of mobility. Reductions in size, if they are accomplished by increasing the rate of executive retirement (which they seldom are, in real world cases) also improve mobility chances.

Changes in the division of labor within an organization are also important in determining the structure of opportunity, but do not have exactly the same kinds of effects as changes in organizational size. Whereas general increases or decreases in size affect people in each strata proportionately, changes in the relative numbers of persons in levels of the hierarchy have disproportionate effects on mobility chances. Shifts in the shape of the pyramid toward a taller and thinner hierarchy (that is, one in which the "grade ratios" are closer to unity) result in a period of rapid promotion but limited hiring as new vacancies are filled at the top. Shifts in the opposite direction, toward an organization with larger numbers of persons at lower levels, conversely, improves hiring chances, but slows rates of mobility within the organization.

By way of illustration of these principles we can perform simulation experiments on our simple hierarchy. In our first experiment we will explore the implications of changes in organizational size. After setting the system in equilibrium (with 600 entry-level persons, 300 middle-level persons, and 100 executives), we will increase the goal states for total size of the organization by 100 persons per time period for 10 time periods, then decrease it for 10 time periods. In keeping with the assumption of constant grade ratios, these changes will be distributed proportionately across the grades. For our second experiment, we will alter the shape of the pyramid, first increasing the relative sizes of the higher levels at the expense of the lower level for 10 time periods, then reversing the process.

Experiment: Growth and Decline

The basic results of the simulation experiment with growth (from time 1 to time 10) and decline (from time 10 to time 20), are shown in Figure 9.6. In the first panel the number of personnel at each of the three levels is shown; in the second, the rates of transition (hiring, promotion, retirement) are presented.

The number of personnel at each level of the hierarchy, quite predictably, increases and decreases with changes in demand. The responses also show a certain degree of smoothing because of the delay inherent in positions "trickling down." And responses to decline are less than responses to growth because of the constraint that all "reductions in force" be accomplished by retirements at the senior level in this model. Since the senior level is relatively small (10% of the population) and since personnel retire at fixed rates, there is a limitation on the responsiveness of this model to decline.

The costs and benefits of growth and decline are not equally distributed across the hierarchical levels in the simple vacancy chain. In the period of rapid growth, hiring and promotion expand, increasing the mobility chances at all levels (see the second panel of Figure 9.6). As the size of the executive stratum expands, the chances that a middle-level manager will be promoted in a given period of time increase from about 6% to slightly over 8% by the fifth time period. Chances for promotion into the executive, however, stagnate and begin to decline as early as the fifth time period, despite continuing increases in the numbers promoted. Similarly, the chances that a given entry level person will be promoted to middle-level status roughly double in the first several time periods of growth (from about 4% to about 8%), but then decline toward their new equilibrium level, despite continuing increases in the numbers of personnel being promoted.

The consequences of decline in the simple hierarchy are even more dramatically unequal than responses to growth (time points 10 to 20 in Figure 9.6). Because some vacancies continue to occur at the executive level due to retirements, the impact of shrinking demand on the mobility chances of middle-level personnel is somewhat buffered. The number of retirements, however, does not create enough demand to absorb all of the surplus middle-level personnel. Consequently, while the chance of promotion from middle level to executive status declines very rapidly, promotion to the middle level and hiring cease altogether.

Changes in size, then, have differential impacts on mobility chances of personnel in the several strata under the constraint that vacancies are created only by retirement and proportional increases in stratum size.[7]

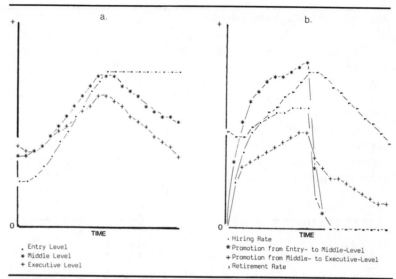

a.

. Entry Level
* Middle Level
+ Executive Level

b.

. Hiring Rate
* Promotion from Entry- to Middle-Level
+ Promotion from Middle- to Executive-Level
, Retirement Rate

Figure 9.6: Growth and decline experiment.

While rapid growth improves the mobility chances of individuals at both the entry and middle levels in the current model, the negative consequences of rapid decline fall more heavily on the lower strata.

Experiments: The Shape of the Hierarchy

In a second experiment we manipulate the structure of the pyramid, while holding constant the total number of personnel. In the first 10 periods we induce a shift toward a "narrow and tall" hierarchy, that is, one with more equally sized strata. Over the second 10 periods we shift the shape of the organization's pyramid back to its original shape. The results of this manipulation are shown in Figure 9.7, with the numbers in each strata shown in the first panel and the rates of transition in the second panel.

The changes in strata size are accomplished rather smoothly, with slight delays due to the time taken in positions "trickling down." Unlike the previous example, however, the system is able to absorb the changes induced without stress. That is, at no time are there substantial gaps between the goal state of the system and the actual levels, as witnessed by the trace lines in the first panel of Figure 9.7 returning to their original levels by the twentieth time period. This result is in contrast to the size experiment, where substantial gaps exist, and the system does not reach its goal by the end of the experiment. This result is, of course, a

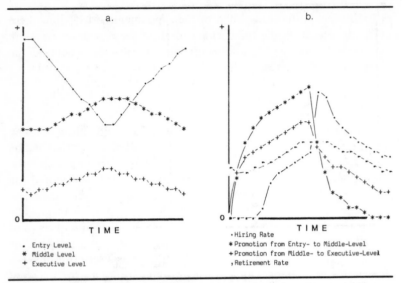

TIME

- Entry Level
* Middle Level
+ Executive Level

· Hiring Rate
* Promotion from Entry- to Middle-Level
+ Promotion from Middle- to Executive-Level
, Retirement Rate

Figure 9.7: Structural change experiment.

consequence of the way that the experiment was designed. During the first 10 time periods increases in the size of the middle and upper strata were induced—creating little stress, as such vacancies are rapidly filled by promotion and hiring. In the second half of the experiment, where the sizes of the two upper strata are being reduced, retirements (which are proportional to the number of persons in the upper stratum in this experiment) occur at rates sufficient to accomplish the reductions in force at the upper levels without large departures from organizational goals. Had the rates of retirement been less, the rate of decline in the size goals for the upper strata higher, some stress would have been created. Had we run the experiment in the opposite direction, first decreasing the desired size of the upper strata and then increasing it, some stress would also have been induced.

Changes in the structure of the pyramid have differential impacts on the mobility chances of personnel at different levels (see panel b of Figure 9.7). As in the previous experiment, the consequences of change for the mobility chances of individuals at the middle levels are somewhat buffered by the presence of continuing vacancies above (due to retirement), while hiring and promotion to middle levels are more affected by structural changes. The number of upper-level personnel increases over the first half of the time period, and this buffers the impacts of later structural change because the retirement rates depend on the numbers in the upper strata. The shapes of the curves of numbers of transitions in the second half of the experiment clearly show these buffering effects. While the declines in all of the transition rates are exponential in the face of routinizing change, the declines are steeper the further down the hierarchy that one goes.

Summary

While our vacancy chain models are obviously unrealistic in many regards, they are suggestive of the complexity of behavior that can be produced by quite simple structures. Perhaps most important, the vacancy chain models suggest that changes induced by size and the division of labor can be complex and unequal—depending on the shape of the hierarchy and the rules governing the creation of vacancies. The experiments suggest that, in systems of this type, the consequences of growth and decline are not mirror images of one another: The consequences of increasing the number of upper-level positions and decreasing the number of upper-level positions are not mirror images of one another, and the degrees of organizational stress and the expansion or constriction of individual mobility chances induced by changes in size and structure can be quite complex even in quite simple systems.

Some Directions for Extensions

The vacancy chain model developed and briefly examined here is the simplest possible version. It is quite adequate for understanding the much greater complexity of possible behavior of simple chains governed by feedback, relative to those governed by simple feedforward. The model, however, is rather too simple to be a good representation of mobility processes in real hierarchies (though some very restricted cases, such as movements of lawyers in law firms or professors in academic departments can be captured to a degree).

There are a number of simple changes that might make it more useful as a research tool. We will mention only a few of the more important possibilities in passing.

First, the number of levels in the hierarchy might be modified—and even made a function of other variables. Organizations with different numbers of levels (say GS1 to GS18, for example) can be captured by simple extensions of the current three levels. If we wished to examine mobility processes over time in real organizations, it might be necessary to provide some external or internal mechanism that causes the numbers of levels to increase or decrease dynamically.

Second, individual's chances of promotion are dependent upon their duration in their current state. The elaboration of the simple hierarchy to include cohort groups within each hierarchical level would make it possible to capture this aspect of individual mobility more accurately than in the current model. It would be possible in this way to include both organizational factors (for example, the total number of vacancies) and individual factors (for example, the effect of time in state on the probability that an individual is selected to fill a vacancy) in the model of the mobility structure.

A third line of development of the current model would modify the connectivity among states rather than simply the number of states. We presently provide that the only way that individuals leave the organization is by way of retirement from the most senior level. Clearly this is unrealistic for most organizations. More commonly, individuals may leave the organization from any level, and some may never achieve the highest level prior to leaving—even if they remain in the organization for a very long time. The vacancies created, and hence mobility patterns, would be dramatically modified from the current model if individuals could be fired from each level, or perhaps left the organization at increasing rates voluntarily if they remained too long in a level without promotion.

Fourth, we have also supposed that an organization can be represented as a single hierarchy, that promotions occur only one step at a time, and that all vacancies are filled from within. Clearly the connectedness of states in most real organizations is far more complex. Organizations differ, through opportunity or policy, in the extent to which they are likely to fill vacancies at various levels from within or without. Obviously, such differences can have dramatic impacts on the distribution of opportunity. Most organizations are better characterized as a series of parallel "ladders" of opportunity (with the ladders being of different heights) rather than a single hierarchy. Some ladders, say within the sales department, never lead to the executive boardroom; other ladders, say within the finance department, do provide the possibility. And organizations differ in the degree to which it is possible for an individual to change from one ladder to another. These kinds of internal segments and differential closeness to outsiders are all relatively simple elaborations of the current model. While the modifications are logically simple, our current results suggest that the modification might have quite complicated and substantial consequences for both organization and individual.

A fifth major direction for making the current model more realistic would be to relax the assumption of population homogeneity. We have, in the current case, treated all individuals at a given level in the hierarchy as having the same probabilities of promotion. The notion that promotion possibilities for individuals differ according to "time in grade," and according to internal ladders and segments may go a long way toward more realistic representation of individual's chances. In addition, however, one might well suppose that channels of opportunity are differentially open, depending on characteristics of individuals (race, gender, education, language, presentational style, etc.). While full exploration of such effects would be more effectively accomplished with a mixed continuous and discrete state language, we could represent multiple subpopulations by race, age, gender, etc. in the same fashion as time-in-grade or ladder differences.

Sixth and finally, we might suppose that the processes of mobility are a good deal less "rational" than our model represents. Organizations may be slow to perceive the existence of vacancies, may perceive vacancies where none exist, or may create vacancies prospectively (rather than as delayed responses). Once a vacancy exists there may be substantial delay in filling it and there may be considerable error and noise in the process of selecting individuals. As we have suggested on numerous occasions, the dynamic behavior of many systems can be dramatically altered by the presence of noise, delay, and bias. "Intendedly rational" systems often become unwieldy and irrational in the presence of such informational problems.[8] There is little reason to expect that patterns of mobility within organizations are immune to such effects.

The Mobility Matrix

One of the most commonly used analytic tools in the study of patterns of social stratification is a cross-tabulation that describes the frequencies of movements between a set of origin statuses and a set of destination statuses. The densities of cases in regions of such a "mobility matrix" can be seen to represent a map of the degree and form of mobility chances in a population, and hence are a telling summary of the overall rates of upward and downward movement, short and long distance movement, propensity to "status inheritance," and permeability and impermeability of the several strata.[9]

The notion of a process with multiple origin statuses, multiple destination statuses, and reciprocal movements back and forth among origins and destinations, of course, is far more general than its application to "social mobility." Voters may move back and forth among the states of being Democrats, Republicans, and Independents;

nation states may move from "peripheral" to "semiperipheral" to "core" positions in the world political economy; workers may move back and forth between employed and unemployed status; families may move from one geographical location to another and (sometimes) back again. All of these problems (and, of course, many others) can be thought of as involving the movements of individuals back and forth between "origins" and "destinations."

The process that the mobility matrix summarizes is a relatively straightforward extension of the the simple chains that we have been considering in this chapter. The "origin" and "destination" statuses in a mobility matrix can be thought of as a single set of system states, observed at two points in time. In our dynamic formulation of the same process, we see the number of persons at each status level as varying continuously over time. The frequencies of movements between each origin and each destination in the mobility matrix are interpretable as transition probabilities. In our dynamic formulation, these transition probabilities become rates of "flow" of individuals among statuses. The basic structure of such a system is shown as Figure 9.8.

The main difference between the type of mobility process captured in the mobility matrix and those that we have discussed so far in this chapter is in the connectivity among the states. In both of our previous examples, transitions occurred in a single direction—age increased but never decreased, persons were promoted but not demoted. In the mobility matrix, movements are possible in both directions between each pair of statuses. As a result of this increased connectivity, the range of possible careers is much greater in mobility matrix than in the other simple chains. Nonetheless, the basic structure of the system of multistate origin to destination mobility is an easy extension of the models 'that we have considered previously.

Developing the Baseline Model

A basic dynamic model for the kinds of multistate transitions described by mobility matrices is quite easy to construct. The system has as many states as there are origins and destinations, the quantities in each state are "conserved," and changes in system levels are the simple sum of movements into the state from other states and movements out of the focal state to other states. If we were describing a system of two strata (say "white collar" and "blue collar"), we could write the basic equations as follows:

L   WC.K = WC.J+(DT)(BCWC.JK−WCBC.JK)

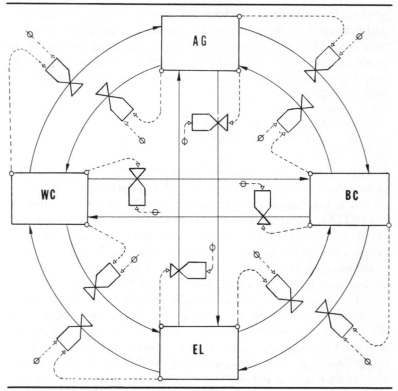

Figure 9.8: Mobility matrix.

L   BC.K = BC.J+(DT)(WCBC.JK–BCWC.JK)

These two statements are straightforward accounting: The number of white-collar persons at time K (WC.K) is equal to the number of such persons at the previous time point plus the number moving from blue collar to white collar over the time period JK (BCWC.JK), less the number moving from white collar to blue collar over the same period (WCBC.JK). The same two flows also describe the changes in the blue-collar population, but take the opposite signs.

Change in the number of white-collar persons between the two time points depends on the rates of movement from blue collar into white collar and rates of movement from white collar to blue collar. In the most basic of mobility models, these rates are governed by "transition probabilities" that express the odds that an individual in a given origin status will move out of that status to a given destination in a fixed time period. The number of actual movements from an origin to a destination, then, depends on the transition probability of such a movement, the number of persons "at risk" (i.e., the number in the origin status), and the length of time that the people are exposed to the risk. For our two-state model, we could specify these rates with the following statements:

    R   WCBC.KL = PWCBC*WC.K
    R   BCWC.KL = PBCWC*BC.K

These statements say simply that the rate of movement from white collar to blue collar over the period from K to L (WCBC.KL) is equal to the constant probability of such a move (PWCBC) times the number at risk (WC.K); the rate of movement from blue collar to white collar over the period (BCWC.KL) is equal to the constant probability of such a move (PBCWC) times the number at risk (BC.K). There is one constraint to be noted here. The quantities PWCBC and PBCWC are probabilities, and hence can logically vary only between 0 and 1. In a model with larger numbers of origins and destinations, the persons in any origin status are constantly "at risk" of making a transition to any of the destination statuses. The sum of these "risks" or transition probabilities is also constrained to be less than or equal to unity. These constraints are perhaps more clearly seen in a model with more statuses, such as the five-state model that we will use as our baseline here. The DYNAMO code for such a five-state model is given in the Appendix.

Behavior of the Baseline Model

The dynamic behavior of first-order Markov processes such as the one we have created here is well understood, and is the same whether there are two, five, or any number of states.[10] Such systems have stable equilibria that are approached asymptotically; the values of the states of the system at equilibrium depend only on the transition probabilities— not on initial conditions, and the value of any state at any point in time is a function of its value at the previous point in time times the relevant transition probabilities (or, alternatively, is a function of the initial value, the length of time that the process has been operating, and the transition probabilities).

These properties can easily be deduced by simulation, as well as by direct solution of the equations of the system (though the latter is more elegant and general). If we simulate the five-state system as shown in the Appendix (with 100 persons in each stratum initially, and all transition probabilities set constant at .2) the system remains in a stable equilibrium. That is, the number of persons in each stratum does not change from period to period, though they are not the same people, as individuals are constantly changing statuses.

If we leave the transition probabilities constant, but change the initial conditions, the system ultimately returns to the same state as in the baseline, but does so after periods of time that vary with the difference between the initial conditions and the equilibrium. This property is illustrated by the results in the top panel of Table 9.4. In this panel we report the number of persons in the fifth stratum after various elapsed times for three scenarios: (a) the system has its equilibrium distribution at the start, (b) there are 50 rather than 100 persons in the fifth stratum at the start, and c) there is only a single person in the fifth stratum at the start.

The first column of the top panel shows that the system remains in equilibrium once equilibrium is established. This statistical equilibrium exists despite the fact that 10% of the people in stratum five leave the stratum each time period, because they are replaced by outflows from other strata. The second and third columns of the top panel report scenarios where numbers of persons smaller than the equilibrium number are initially in stratum five. The behavior of these two series demonstrates the tendency of the system to asymtopically approach its equilibrium. The speed with which this approach occurs, of course, depends on the magnitude of the transition rates—the more people are moving around, the faster the system approaches its steady state.

The first experiment suggests that this system has a a stable equilibrium, and that this equilibrium condition does not depend on the numbers of persons in each status initially. The second panel of Figure 9.4 shows the results of another series of experiments that explore the consequences of varying transition rates rather than system levels. In the first series we define stratum one as an "absorbing state." That is, persons flow into this stratum, but do not leave it. In the second column we set the outflow rate for the first stratum to 5%, or one-half of the outflow rates of the other strata; the third column sets the outflow rates of stratum one equal to those of the other strata (that is, 10%); the last column shows outflow rates from stratum one that are twice the outflow rates of the other strata.

This second series of experiments demonstrates the other basic property of first-order Markov processes—that the equilibrium distribution of cases across statuses does depend on the transition rates. Where the first stratum is an absorbing state (column one), eventually all of the 500 individuals end up in it. This occurs rather slowly because

TABLE 9.4
Baseline Mobility Matrix Experiments

Differing Initial Conditions	Numbers of Persons in Stratum Five Initial		
Elapsed Time	100	50	1
2	100	82	65
4	100	94	87
6	100	98	95
8	100	99	98
10	100	100	99

Differing Transition Rates	Numbers of Persons in Stratum One Outflow Rate			
Elapsed Time	0%	5%	10%	20%
0	100	100	100	100
2	173	130	100	62
4	232	147	100	57
6	281	156	100	56
8	321	161	100	56
10	354	164	100	56
15	411	166	100	56
20	446	167	100	56

of the large number of sequences of moves that are possible in each point in time. Where the outflow rates of a stratum are less than those of another, the stratum will asymptotically approach a level that is larger than the other. Where the rates are equal, equilibrium numbers are equal, where rates are less, final numbers are less. In all cases, the paths that levels follow toward their equilibrium levels are exponential.

These results are hardly original, but they are important. Formally, systems of this type have stable equilibria, these equilibria depend upon the transition rates and not on the initial conditions, and the levels tend to approach their equilibrium conditions by smooth exponential time-paths.

We can also state these conclusions somewhat less formally. There are many systems that approximate the ideal type of movements occurring back and forth among many states, where the chances individuals making transitions from their current status to another status is constant over time and the same for all individuals in the status. Systems of this type tend toward stable numbers of cases being in each status (even though lots of cases may be making transitions), and the relative numbers of cases in the various statuses depend solely on the odds of the various changes occurring.

Extensions of the "Mobility Matrix"

The baseline mobility matrix model is relatively simple in the number of levels, their connectivity, and the control structures governing rates of flow among the states. There are, however, several ways in which the baseline model could easily be modified to make it more useful for analyzing social mobility processes and for other systems of bidirectional flows among multiple origins and destinations.

As a model of processes of status mobility, the baseline is probably most seriously deficient in that it assumes that all of the people composing the flows are homogeneous. This follows from the specification that the chances of a given individual's undergoing mobility are the same as those of every other individual with the same origin status. There are many cases in which we might want to distinguish among the persons in the various statuses according to other characteristics, both because we can presume that they are not really homogeneous with regard to mobility chances, and because our interest may focus on the composition of the population of persons occupying statuses.

We might suppose that the mobility chances of males and females in entry-level positions are not identical in a large organization; our interest might well be in the ratio of males and females in executive positions that are the outcome of the dynamics of mobility. Similarly, we might suppose that people in a given status are at decreasing (or, more rarely) or increasing risk of undergoing transition the longer that they have been in the status—that is, the "population" is "heterogeneous" with respect to duration in the state. There is considerable theory and evidence suggesting, for example, that, after a time, the chances of further promotion decline with tenure in a position in many large organizations (that is, those who are going to be promoted are promoted early, those who remain behind are less likely to ever be promoted).

The baseline mobility model can be extended to deal with heterogeneity of transition probabilities by both traits and duration rather easily—though we will not do so here. The method for doing so is tedious, but relatively straightforward. If one is interested in taking into account gender differences in mobility in a three-state "matrix," six rather than three system states are created. Some of the logically possible flows, of course, cannot exist: Low-status female persons have zero probability of undergoing a transition to become middle-status males; their chances of attaining middle-level status, however, may now be modeled as different from those of low-status males. Duration dependence of transition rates can similarly be captured by creating chains of transitions within each status that represent heterogeneity by duration (for example, new low-status persons, low-status persons of average tenure, low-status persons of longer than mean duration). In some cases the first- and third-order delay functions provided by DYNAMO (or others designed by the theorist using macros) can capture this form of heterogeneity quite compactly.

As a model for theorizing about social mobility, the baseline developed above is deficient in a second way. In the current model we follow the spirit of Markov models in assuming that transition probabilities for individuals are fixed functions with respect to time (though, as we have just seen, they may differ across individuals). In real systems, the number of positions (or vacancies) at various levels may well change over time—increasing or decreasing all rates of movement into or out of statuses. Indeed, most studies of social mobility at the societal level suggest that the largest part of all status changes can be accounted for by changes in the "structure" of opportunity. Again, there would be little difficulty in adapting the baseline-mobility matrix model to take into account such structural change, though we will not do so here. In the current model, rates are modeled as dependent upon constant transition probabilities and the numbers of persons in the origin statuses. To take into account opportunity structures, more complex rules could be written that take into account the number of vacancies as well as the number of candidates.

Chains as Building Blocks

The models that we have examined in this chapter are extremely general and important. We have developed our examples, perhaps somewhat self-indulgently, from the fields of stratification and demography in sociology. Simple chains coupled by differing kinds of control systems, however, are central in the concerns of all of the social sciences. Indeed, from the abstract systems perspective that we have taken, many of the problems about which very diverse social scientists theorize have much the same structure.

"Chain" models involve the rates of movements of conserved quantities among networks of states. A moment's reflection suggests that many central social science problems can be (and, in fact, have been) usefully thought of in this way.

The dynamics of economic relations involve the flows of human and physical capital, money, and natural resources among "statuses." The "circulation of capital," the production "process," and exchanges between buyers and sellers can all be readily conceived as flows of quantities (be these quantities money, people, capital, or resources) among states (where the states may reflect qualitative characteristics or ownership or both). Indeed, the starting point for both macro and micro economic theory is with these basic "accounting systems" of flows of money, people, and things: Raw materials are extracted, transported, transformed, sold, and eventually discarded; human resources are employed, endowed with training and experience, and retired; money is acquired through exchange with customers, and transferred to workers and suppliers. The chains needed to usefully capture the dynamics of economic systems can be considerably more complicated (in terms of numbers of states, connectivity among them, and in control systems) than the basic models that we have examined in this chapter. These more complicated systems, however, are built up from the same kinds of simple chains that we have considered here.[11]

Many of the central theoretical concerns of political science are also built upon "accounting" of conserved flows. Most obviously, the shifts of voters and legislators from support to opposition for policies and candidates can be usefully thought of as a "chain" of states. Political phenomena are often thought of as systems composed of flows of information, influence, and resources among individuals, parties, and governments. Again, the mobility models developed in this chapter are probably a bit too simple to capture the dynamics of most political systems without substantial modification. Simple chains of conserved flows of persons, votes, and resources, however, lie at the core of theorizing about political behavior.[12]

While it may at first seem more natural to think of the application of simple chain models to "macro" phenomena such as population movements, economic production, or voter support; phenomena at the "micro" level can also be usefully conceived of as composed of "chains" of states. One very obvious and important application is in studying the microstructure of social relations. Many social structures can be thought of as networks of individuals (or firms, families, nations, etc.) connected by "relations" involving conserved flows (individuals exchange emotional support, firms exchange personnel and money, and so on). The dynamics of such networks can be captured rather nicely using relatively simple models.

With relatively little modification, then, "simple" chain models of various numbers of states, forms and degrees of connectivity, and complexity of control can be widely applied to basic and important problems across the social sciences. As we have seen throughout the chapters in this section, a wide array of important forms of social dynamics can be modeled with these "simple" models. Simple chains are of great importance for another reason as well. All models of greater complexity are built up out of simple chains. It is a necessary, but not a sufficient condition for understanding the dynamics of the more complex systems that we understand the dynamics of simple chains.

Models composed of single chains, regardless of their complexity, however, are not sufficient to capture the dynamics of many systems. In the next section we will consider how theories of greater complexity are built up out of coupling together "simple" chains with more complex control structures; just as the current chain models are composed of single states coupled with increasing complex control structures. The behavior of "chains" requires the understanding of single states and rates, but is not wholly reducible to the component parts; the behavior of more complex systems requires an understanding of each of the chains of which they are composed, but they also have unique possibilities that are not wholly predictable from their parts.

Notes

1. The three kinds of systems that we will examine here are well known and widely studied by statistical and mathematical approaches, as well as by simulation methods. Our treatment of these systems is not intended to make original contributions to the substantial bodies of theory and analysis that exist with regard to each; rather, the intent is to see these important dynamic processes as the outcomes of relatively simple chain models.

2. Basic demographic processes are presented in any number of excellent texts, including Keyfitz (1977), Shryock, Siegel, and Associates (1976), Bogue (1969), Cox (1959), and Hauser and Duncan (1959).

3. For purposes of accurate projections over lengthy periods of time, such simplifying assumptions and the accuracy of the integration algorithms are of great consequence. The population predictions presented in this chapter should be taken only as illustrative of general patterns and dynamics. They should not be taken as serious population projections.

4. Data are calculated from tables presented in United States Bureau of the Census (1985).

5. For some interesting and more sophisticated modeling of fertility dynamics and their consequences, see Keyfitz (1971, 1975).

6. The classic work on vacancy chains is that of Harrison White (1970). Recent elaborations have extended the model in interesting ways; see particularly Stewman (1975), Rosenbaum (1979), and Stewman and Konda (1983).

7. Explorations into the effects of changes in system size and shape have been extensively explored by many analysts, among them Anderson and Warkov (1961), Blau (1970), Hummon (1971), Kassarda (1974), Kennedy (1962), and Land (1970, 1975).

8. Problems of information delay, distribution, and distortion have been a major topic of interest to theorists of organizations. See, for some particularly interesting examples, Ackoff (1959), Bavelas (1950), Bonini (1963), Cohen and Cyert (1965), Cyert et al. (1971), Cyert and March (1963), Emery and Trist (1960), Katz and Kahn (1966), Kochen and Deutsch (1980), Marshall (1967), and Simon (1947).

9. There is a large literature on such processes in sociology, particularly with regard to the intra-and intergenerational changes in individual's occupational prestige. A flavor of some of the mathematical and statistical approaches to problem can be found in Blumen (1966), Boudon (1975), Ginsberg (1971), Mayer (1972), McFarland (1970), McGinnis (1968), Singer and Spilerman (1974, 1976), and Spilerman (1972a, 1972b).

10. See, for detailed discussions of Markov processes, Bartholomew (1983) (for a mathematical treatment) or Leik and Meeker (1975) (for an applied treatment).

11. See particularly Forrester's (1961) model of the firm, and Meadows and Robinson's (1985) discussion of macroeconomic models.

12. Two very useful macropolitical models are offered by Brunner and Brewer (1971) and Ilchman and Uphoff (1969).

APPENDIX 9.1. Population Age Structure Model

```
* SIMPLIFIED DEMOGRAPHIC MODEL
NOTE BASELINE DATA ARE USA 1980
NOTE                 THE NUMBER AGES ZERO TO ONE IS
NOTE                 DETERMINED BY THE BIRTH RATE, WHICH IS A
NOTE                 FUNCTION OF THE NUMBER AGES 15-44.
L        P01.K = P01.J+(DT)(BR.JK-ISR.JK-IDR.JK)
R        BR.KL = FERT*P1544.K
C        FERT = .0342
R        ISR.KL = P01.K*.98711
R        IDR.KL = P01.K*.01289
NOTE ISR IS INFANT SURVIVAL, IDR IS INFANT DEATHS
L        P14.K = P14.J+(DT)(ISR.JK-CSR.JK-CDR.JK)
R        CSR.KL = (P14.K/4)(.99936)
R        CDR.KL = (P14.K/4)(.00064)
NOTE CSR IS CHILD SURVIVAL, CDR IS CHILD DEATH RATE
NOTE                 LEAVING RATE IS SIMPLIFIED TO BE 1/4 OF
NOTE                 NUMBER IN THE LEVEL AT EACH POINT IN
NOTE                 TIME.
L        P514.K = P514.J+(DT)(CSR.JK-ASR.JK-ADR.JK)
R        ASR.KL = (P514.K/10)(.9969)
R        ADR.KL = (P514.K/10)(.00031)
NOTE ADOLESCENT SURVIVAL AND DEATH RATES ASR, ADR
L        P1544.K = P1544.J+(DT)(ASR.JK-PSR.JK-PDR.JK)
R        PSR.KL = (P1544.K/30)(.99854)
R        PDR.KL = (P1544.K/30)(.00146)
NOTE PRIME-AGE SURVIVAL AND DEATH RATES PSR, PDR
L        P4564.K = P4564.J+(DT)(PSR.JK-MSR.JK-MDR.JK)
R        MSR.KL = (P4564.K/20)(.99044)
R        MDR.KL = (P4564.K/20)(.00956)
NOTE MIDDLE-AGED SURVIVAL AND DEATH RATES MSR, MDR
L        P65.K = P65.J+(DT)(MSR.JK-AGDR.JK)
R        AGDR.KL = P65.K*.05668
NOTE DEATH RATES FOR AGE 65+, AGDR
S        TPOP.K = P01.K+P14.K+P514.K+P1544.K+P4564.K+P65.K
NOTE TOTAL POPULATION IS COMPUTED
```

```
N              P01 = 3269600
N              P14 = 13078400
N              P514 = 34942000
N              P1544 = 105203000
N              P4564 = 44503000
N              P65 = 25550000
NOTE INITIALS ARE SET AT USA 1980 VALUES
SPEC           DT = .25/LENGTH = 100/PRTPER = 5/PLTPER = 1
PRINT          P01,P14,P514,P1544,P4564,P65,TPOP
PLOT           P01/P14/P514/P1544
PLOT           P4564/P65/TPOP
RUN
```

APPENDIX 9.2. Vacancy Chain Model

```
*              SIMPLE VACANCY CHAIN MODEL
NOTE                      This model is an example of a simple vacancy chain
NOTE                      with three levels: "Entry" level (EL), "Middle"
NOTE                      level (ML) and "Senior" level (SL).
L              EL.K = EL.J+(DT)(HIRE.JK-PREM.JK)
NOTE                      HIRE IS THE NUMBER HIRED INTO ENTRY
NOTE                      POSITIONS
NOTE                      PREM IS THE NUMBER PROMOTED TO MIDDLE
NOTE                      LEVEL
R              HIRE.KL = MAX(DISC1.K,0)
NOTE DISC1 IS THE DISCREPANCY BETWEEN THE NUMBER OF
NOTE                      ENTRY LEVEL PERSONS AND THE "GOAL" OR
NOTE                       DESIRED NUMBER.
A              DISC1.K = EGOAL-EL.K
NOTE                      THE GOAL FOR ENTRY LEVEL NUMBERS IS 600
NOTE                      PERSONS
C              EGOAL = 600
R              PREM.KL = MAX(DISC2.K,0)
NOTE                      THE RATE OF PROMOTION FROM ENTRY TO
NOTE                      MID LEVEL IS SET EQUAL TO THE DISCREPANCY
NOTE                      BETWEEN THE NUMBER OF PERSONS AT THE
NOTE                      MIDDLE LEVEL, AND THE GOAL FOR THAT
NOTE                      LEVEL.
A              DISC2.K = MGOAL-ML.K
NOTE                      THE GOAL FOR MID LEVEL IS SET TO 300.
C              MGOAL = 300
NOTE                      THE MIDDLE LEVEL IS NOW DEFINED.
L              ML.K = ML.J+(DT)(PREM.JK-PRES.JK)
NOTE                      THE NUMBER OF PERSONS AT THE MID
NOTE                      LEVEL IS AUGMENTED BY PROMOTIONS FROM
NOTE                      BELOW (PREM) AND DECREMENTED BY
NOTE                      PROMOTIONS TO THE SENIOR LEVEL (PRES).
R              PRES.KL = MAX(DISC3.K,0)
```

A	DISC3.K = SGOAL–SL.K
NOTE	PROMOTIONS FROM MID TO SENIOR LEVEL
NOTE	DEPEND ON THE DISCREPANCY (DISC3)
NOTE	BETWEEN THE NUMBER AT THE SENIOR LEVEL
NOTE	(SL) AND THE GOAL FOR THAT LEVEL (SGOAL).
C	SGOAL = 100
NOTE	THE SENIOR LEVEL IS NOW DEFINED
L	SL.K = SL.J+(DT)(PRES.JK–RR.JK)
NOTE	SENIORS ARE AUGMENTED BY PROMOTIONS
NOTE	FROM MID LEVEL (PRES), AND DECREMENTED
NOTE	BY THE RETIREMENT RATE (RR).
R	RR.KL = SL.K/5
NOTE	RETIREMENTS ARE A CONSTANT 20% OF THE
NOTE	SENIORS INITIALIZATION OF LEVELS
N	EL = ELI
C	ELI = 600
N	ML = MLI
C	MLI = 300
N	SL = SLI
C	SLI =100
NOTE	SUPPLEMENTAL INFO: PROMOTION CHANCES.
S	PROMO1.K = PREM.KL/EL.K
S	PROMO2.K = PRES.KL/ML.K
NOTE	OUTPUT SPECIFICATION
SPEC	DT = .1/LENGTH = 25/PRTPER = 1/PLTPER = 1
PRINT	EL,ML,SL,RR,PROMO1,PROMO2
PLOT	EL/ML/SL
PLOT	PROMO1/PROMO2/RR
RUN	

APPENDIX 9.3. Five-State Mobility Matrix

*	FIVE-STATE MOBILITY MATRIX WITH BIDIRECTIONAL FLOWS
NOTE	THE NUMBERS IN THE FIVE STATES ARE DEFINED
L	S1.K = S1.J+(DT)(R21.JK+R31.JK+R41.JK+R51.JK–R12.JK–R13.JK
X	–R14.JK–R15.JK)
L	S2.K = S2.J+(DT)(R12.JK+R32.JK+R42.JK+R52.JK–R21.JK–R23.JK
X	–R24.JK–R25.JK)
L	S3.K = S3.J+(DT)(R13.JK+R23.JK+R43.JK+R53.JK–R31.JK–R32.JK
X	–R34.JK–R35.JK)
L	S4.K = S4.J+(DT)(R14.JK+R24.JK+R34.JK+R54.JK–R41.JK–R42.JK
X	–R43.JK–R45.JK)
L	S5.K = S5.J+(DT)(R15.JK+R25.JK+R25.JK+R45.JK–R51.JK–R52.JK
X	–R53.JK–R54.JK)
NOTE	
NOTE	LEVELS ARE INITIALIZED WITH CONSTANTS
NOTE	SI1 . . . SI5

```
NOTE
N          S1 = SI1
C          SI1 = 100
N          S2 = SI2
C          SI2 = 100
N          S3 = SI3
C          SI3 = 100
N          S4 = SI4
C          SI4 = 100
N          S5 = SI5
C          SI5 = 100
NOTE
NOTE                       OUTFLOW TRANSITION RATES ARE DEFINED
NOTE                       AS CONSTANT PARAMETERS TIMES THE
NOTE                       NUMBERS IN THE ORIGIN STATES
R          R12.KL = PARM12*S1.K
R          R13.KL = PARM13*S1.K
R          R14.KL = PARM14*S1.K
R          R15.KL = PARM15*S1.K
NOTE
R          R21.KL = PARM21*S2.K
R          R23.KL = PARM23*S2.K
R          R24.KL = PARM24*S2.K
R          R25.KL = PARM25*S2.K
NOTE
R          R31.KL = PARM31*S3.K
R          R32.KL = PARM32*S3.K
R          R34.KL = PARM34*S3.K
R          R35.KL = PARM35*S3.K
NOTE
R          R41.KL = PARM41*S4.K
R          R42.KL = PARM42*S4.K
R          R43.KL = PARM43*S4.K
R          R45.KL = PARM45*S4.K
NOTE
R          R51.KL = PARM51*S5.K
R          R52.KL = PARM52*S5.K
R          R53.KL = PARM53*S5.K
R          R54.KL = PARM54*S5.K
NOTE
NOTE                       THE PARAMETERS ARE NOW SET. NOTE THE
NOTE                       CONSTRAINT THAT THE SUM OF THE OUTFLOW
NOTE                       RATES FROM A GIVEN STATE MUST BE LESS
NOTE                       THAN OR EQUAL TO UNITY. FOR EXAMPLE
NOTE                       PARM12+PARM13+PARM14+PARM15 MUST BE
NOTE                       LESS THAN OR EQUAL TO UNITY.
C          PARM12 = .2
C          PARM13 = .2
C          PARM14 = .2
C          PARM15 = .2
NOTE
```

```
C               PARM21 = .2
C               PARM23 = .2
C               PARM24 = .2
C               PARM25 = .2
NOTE
C               PARM31 = .2
C               PARM32 = .2
C               PARM34 = .2
C               PARM35 = .2
NOTE
C               PARM41 = .2
C               PARM42 = .2
C               PARM43 = .2
C               PARM45 = .2
NOTE
C               PARM51 = .2
C               PARM52 = .2
C               PARM53 = .2
C               PARM54 = .2
NOTE
NOTE                    OUTPUT SPECIFICATION
NOTE
SPEC            LENGTH = 18/DT = .10/PRTPER = 1/PLTPER = 1
PRINT           S1,S2,S3,S4,S5
PRINT           R12,R13,R14,R15
PRINT           R21,R23,R24,R25
PRINT           R31,R32,R34,R35
PRINT           R41,R42,R43,R45
PRINT           R51,R52,R53,R54
PLOT            S1,S2,S3,S4,S5(0,100)
RUN
```

Part III

Complex Action and Interaction

In the second part of this volume we considered processes that could be represented by systems with a single state, or by systems of relatively small numbers of states formed into "chains." The range of dynamic phenomena that can be represented by such "simple" systems is surprisingly broad, and includes most of the kinds of processes normally studied by mathematical and statistical means. Nonetheless, there are many phenomena that are not representable by systems of the types that we've discussed so far, and we must now turn to more complex models.

The systems that we've considered so far have been used to represent the dynamics of single individuals or single populations. This is obviously not good enough for many applications in the social sciences that involve multiple actors: persons, business firms, clans, nations, political parties, etc. The dynamics that we have considered have represented actors (individuals, variables, or aggregates) responding to "internal" stimuli, or to their environments. We have not, however, considered dynamics of *interaction* among multiple "smart" actors.

The elements of systems thinking that we discussed in part one of this volume are the building blocks of the single-state systems that we discussed in the first portion of part two. These "single-state" systems, in turn, are the building blocks of the somewhat more complex "chain" models that we've just considered. Not surprisingly, the more complex models that we will discuss in this section use "chains" as their basic building blocks, and achieve their greater complexity by coupling chains together with control systems.

The kinds of systems that we will consider in this third section are useful for representing patterns of social interaction among multiple actors, or among the "parts" of differentiated systems. In Chapter 10 we will examine two nations competing in an arms race; in Chapter 11 we will examine the relationships between an individual and their network of social support. Each of these dynamics call for systems of multiple actors in dynamic interaction. In Chapter 12 we will examine two alternative views of the political economy of capitalist nations. The models developed to represent these systems describe a single actor (a society) that is composed of multiple institutional subsystems in dynamic interaction (economy, state, and cultural sectors). These models also serve as examples of the range of phenomena that can be approached with increasingly complex dynamic systems models.

Social Action and Interaction

The models examined so far might be termed "closed-system" models, in that they deal with the behavior of single aggregates or single individuals (persons, organizations, societies, etc.). Social action does often resemble such "closed-system" situations in which individuals act independently, or simply respond to environmental stimuli. Where such an assumption is reasonable, each individual is the same as every other one, and we can understand the behavior of each actor and all actors by modeling one. A good deal of social action, however, cannot be represented in this fashion. In many cases individual's actions are not merely responsive to a stable environment and to their own states. In many cases individual actors interact with the environment (which may be composed of many other actors). The models we've examined so far are concerned with social action (i.e., action that is based on learned meanings and goals and takes others into account), but have not really considered social interaction (i.e., where actors are mutually responsive to each others acts through systems of shared meanings).

Each of the models discussed so far has a second limitation for describing many forms of social behavior. In each of the cases we've considered, only the simplest forms of "coupling" and "feedback-control" have been considered. In trying to create useful theories of human behavior, we must confront the fact that another part of what we mean by "social" behavior is often based on extremely complex systems of monitoring, calculation, and goal setting—that is, social interaction is often quite "smart" in the sense that we have used the term in this volume. Most of the models that we've examined so far have been quite simple in this regard, involving either direct and straightforward "dumb" control or relatively simple "goal seeking." Many patterns of social action cannot be adequately represented with such simple tools.

Models of "social" action, by definition, are based on actors' responses to stimuli as they perceive them and attach meaning to them. In the models we've examined so far, we have (implicitly) assumed that actor's perceptions, assigning of meanings, and choices among strategies were identical and not problematic. For example, we ignored the process by which individuals perceive messages (or fail to, or distort), the calculations of costs and benefits that they may make according to their own values and preferences in deciding to adopt an innovation or not, and the problems and delays that they may encounter in imple-menting change. For many purposes, of course, it is perfectly fine to make assumptions about these processes and treat them as "black boxes" that generate an expected distribution of outcomes (the probability of adoption in a period of time). But sometimes we might prefer to focus our attention on theorizing about variance in these processes of social cognition and decision making at the individual level.

Systems Complexity

The limitations of the kinds of models that we have been considering so far can also be seen from a "general systems" perspective. The kinds of processes that we have considered are, in the terms used here, not highly complex. That is, they involve relatively few states, these states are coupled in simple patterns (usually single chains), and the mechanisms of control have been relatively simple—often being easily describable by very simple linear equations.

The models that we have considered thus far are predominantly of "closed" systems. That is, the models reflect the working out of the consequences of the initial conditions where only the levels of the states of the focal system have effects on the realizations of the processes. Of course, as we have pointed out, such models could be made into "open" systems by allowing for exogenous changes of various sorts. However, we have not attempted to model interaction between the focal system and others—that is, processes in which the actions of each actor become the environment to which the other actors respond.

The linkages among states in the models we have examined so far are also relatively simple. For the most part, the states of the models that we have been considering are governed by direct material flows (as in people moving from one age group to another) and simple laws describing information effects (e.g., the flow of people from one level of a hierarchy to another is governed by the "information" of the number of vacancies at the higher level). In most social interaction, we might imagine that the linkages are more complex, more contingent, and more filled with error, selective perception, and distortion than are the "flows through chains" types of models.

The models that we will consider in the next several chapters are of considerable complexity in that they couple multiple "chains" together by means of (often quite complicated) flows of information. The range of dynamic behaviors that such models can produce is virtually unlimited. And the complexity of phenomena that can be modeled by putting together simple chains is limited only by imagination and resources. With the consideration of the "linked chain" models in this section, we will have in hand all of the "templates" of system types that one may need in order to undertake the building of theories about phenomena of any degree of complexity.

10

A Two-Party Game: Arms Race Escalation

A good deal of theory about social dynamics is concerned with situations that involve limited numbers of self-referencing actors in goal-directed interaction. The "actors" involved may be individuals, groups, organizations, or more extended forms; they may be "self-referencing" in a wide variety of ways; and, they may "interact" by responding directly to other actors or more indirectly by responding to environmental conditions created by other actors.

In principle the dynamics of interaction of any degree of complexity can be captured by coupling together the simple chains we examined in the previous chapter. In the current chapter we will take a couple of short but important steps in the direction of increasing complexity. First, we will have multiple actors (in this case only two, to keep it simple) who directly interact with one another. Second, we will make the actors a bit "smarter" than they have been in previous models in terms of the amounts of information that they take into account in formulating action plans.

The model that we will develop in this chapter is very similar to many others in various social sciences in that it deals with interaction among small numbers of goal-oriented actors. While we will be concerned with the particular two-party game of armed escalation, the current model can also serve as a template for formulating models about interactions in a small group context, among firms in a market, among governments, and many other similar situations in which actors interact in the pursuit of goals.[1]

Arms Races and Other Games

Social scientists have been interested for some time in a problem that contains many of these kinds of dynamics of adjustment to the states of both one's own and others' systems: arms races and escalations of conflict between parties. It takes a certain degree of perversity to group models dealing with arms races into the same category of "games" as "the prisoner's dilemma" or chess. Nonetheless, as theoretical systems, the problems are similar. Escalation models are good examples of "smart" interaction between or among parties in that they are fully dynamic and each party monitors the self, the environment, and other actors. The particular context that we will consider—arms races—is, of course, substantively important. It also differs from many other models in the "game theoretic" tradition in that the interaction is positive sum (or, in the case of arms races, negative sum). This is not a necessary part of such models. For our purposes, it is sufficient that arms races be reasonably thought of as essentially similar to most two or multiactor "games" of this type: Each actor has goals, monitors their own and others' actions, and continuously modifies and updates strategy based on changing conditions.

There are very substantial literatures that present and analyze formalized "games."[2] Formal mathematical models for many relatively simple games have been created, and the problem of escalation and competition between two actors has been subject to particularly close scrutiny. The model of escalation in the interaction between two actors that we develop below as a "systems dynamics" model has also been extensively analyzed by mathematical means and subjected to empirical testing.[3] We will begin by building a simple model of competitive interaction between two actors that is formally identical to these mathematical models. After we explore its properties we will then turn to some of the additional possible specifications that our analysis of the simple model suggests. In particular we shall be concerned with the consequences of informational distortions and delays in complex dynamic systems.

Developing the Baseline Model

Let us suppose that there are two actors (X and Y) and that each possesses a stock of arms. Arms are created by transforming natural resources at some rate over time, and become obsolete or useless after a time and are discarded. Our system then is composed of two "subsystems"—the actors, each of which is characterized by a "state space" composed of a single chain of material feed-forward relations—raw materials are transformed into arms are transformed into scrap. These parts of the model can be diagrammed as in Figure 10.1.

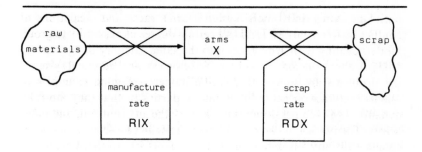

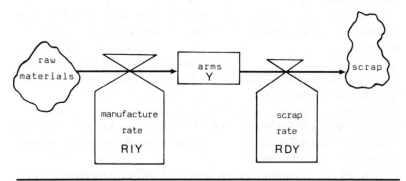

Figure 10.1: Chains for arms race model.

We are deliberately keeping the baseline model quite simple in a number of ways so that we can understand the basic dynamics of this interaction before moving to elaborations. We are assuming that only two actors are involved in the interaction, we are assuming that each actor's resources are unlimited, and we are assuming that "scrap" is a "sink." None of these assumptions are necessary, but they are useful to keep the model to its bare-bones structure.

From looking at Figure 10.1 it is apparent that the system thus far can be represented as two "level" equations, each having two associated rate components (that is, rates of transformation of raw materials into arms, and rates of discard from the stock of arms to scrap). The level equations are:

L   X.K = X.J+(DT)(RIX.JK–RDX.JK)
L   Y.K = Y.J + (DT)(RIY.JK–RDY.JK)

where X and Y are the current levels of arms of the two competitors.

Let's now examine the control structure surrounding each of these chains, leaving aside—for the moment—how the chains are coupled together. Take note of the strategy here, for we are following the same approach as we did in the development of simpler models: First divide the problem into subsystems, then identify the chains that couple the states within each subsystem, then examine the control structure of each process. Only after each of the "parts" is assembled are they be coupled together.

The level of arms in each subsystem controlled by two decisions: decisions about rates of arms construction and decisions about rates of scrapping. We will assume that the important and interesting policy decisions are "smart," or "goal oriented and self referencing," and involve how rapidly arms will be built. The process of scrapping arms will be treated as a simple physical process of constant decay of the stock of arms:

R   RDX.KL = MAX(A1*X.K,0)
C   A1 = .1

That is, the rate of decline in arms for actor X (RDX) will be equal to 10% (A1) of the current level of arms (X), but not less than 0. The same, of course, holds for actor Y.

The "smart" decision making about the building of arms is more complicated, and involves the monitoring of information. In order to make each of these systems "dynamically self-referencing," it is necessary that some mechanisms be specified that describe how actors monitor their own statuses. There are several possibilities: The level of resources available could be monitored; the level of existing armaments could be monitored; the level of scrap could be monitored; the rate of transformation of resources into armaments could be monitored; or, the rate of transformation of armaments into scrap could be monitored. In real world arms races actors probably monitor all of these states and rates and combine the information in complex ways. We will keep the baseline model simple by assuming that each actor monitors their own stock of arms, and does so without distortion or delay.

"Smart" decision making also involves the comparison of the monitored state (in this case, one's level of arms) to some goal. Actions are then based on perceived discrepancies between the actual and desired state of the levels. We will make the assumption that actors goals are constants, and exogeneously determined. The most common such assumption is that each party desires superiority to the other:

A   DLAX = KX*YP.K
C   KX = 1.05

That is, actor X's desired level of arms (DLAX) is equal to 105% (KX) of the arms it perceives its opponent to possess (YP) at any point in time. Actor Y formulates its goals in the same fashion.

The information that each actor has about its own level of arms (X) is compared to the desired level of arms (DLAX) to produce a perceived arms gap, which serves as the basis for action:

A   GAPX.K = DLAX.K-X.K

The internal control system for each actor then can be summarized as in Figure 10.2.

There is nothing new in this model so far. Each actor's "subsystem" is a single chain of three states governed by two rates—both of which reference the level of arms, and one of which is "dumb" (scrapping) and the other "smart."

Now we come to the key step. In order for this model to be a true "dynamic interaction," each actor must be paying attention to (monitoring) some aspect of the other's system, and adjusting its behavior to meet its goals in light of the changing behavior of the other. Again there are choices. What aspects of the other's system is monitored? How accurate and speedy is the monitoring? What role does the monitored information play in decision making?

We will begin by assuming, like most of the existing models of escalations, that each actor monitors the level of arms of the other. This is, of course, somewhat unrealistic, for the levels of the opponent's available resources and the rates at which the opponent is building arms are also probably monitored. We will also assume, for our baseline, that each actor has accurate and up-to-date information about the level of the others arms:

A   YP.K = Y.K

That is, actor X perceives actor Y's arms (YP) as identical to their true current levels (Y).

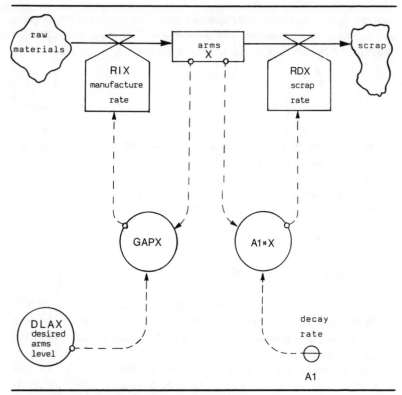

Figure 10.2:   Control structure for arms production.

With this simple step in the specification, we have coupled the two actors together into a more complex system. By making the desired level of arms of each actor a result of the goals of the focal actor, the current state of the focal actor's system, and the current state of the other's system (as the focal actor perceives it), the two chains interact. We can represent the full model by elaborating our diagram slightly, as in Figure 10.3.

The general structure of the diagram in Figure 10.3 is now familiar. It, like all of the others to be presented in the remainder of the volume, consists of "subsystems" composed of simple chains that are coupled together by flows of monitored information.

As we have built it, the model—while highly interactive and dynamic—is still very simple. A great deal of elaboration could be done on each of its parts to make it more realistic. Some of these alternatives

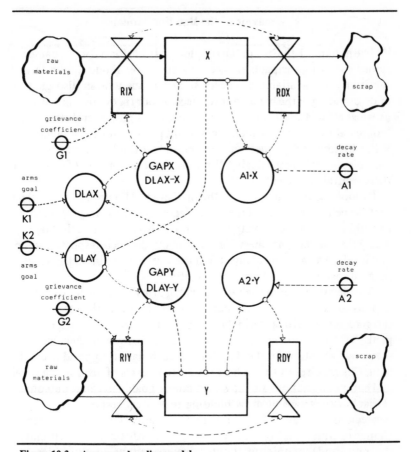

Figure 10.3:   Arms race baseline model.

have, in fact, been explored in the theoretical and research literatures on arms races, and we will explore and discuss some of the possible extensions later on. For our current purposes, however, the model that we've specified is sufficient: It shows two actors, each conscious of their own condition and the condition of the other, each with goals (which we have specified as being incompatible), interacting over time. In principle, such a model can serve as a starting point for the formalization of theories having to do with more actors, more complex state spaces for each, and more complexly coupled interactions. Before moving toward such complicated models, however, there are some interesting dynamics to be explored in the baseline model.

Behavior of the Baseline Model

The dynamic behavior of the simplest possible forms of this game are rather easy to anticipate. Answers to questions about equilibria and sensitivity are available by direct solution, but we can also gain an understanding of the behavior produced by our theory by simulating it, as we shall in a moment. But let's think through the problem before looking at the results. What factors might produce different outcomes? What factors and connections are most "central" in the network of variables describing the theory? What are the consequences of modifying these central variables?

By looking at the diagram of the final model (Figure 10.3), it is clear that the behavior of each of the chains is governed primarily by decisions to build arms. The decision to build arms is also the point in the diagram where the two nations "meet" or are connected—their resources, scrap, and levels of arms don't connect, but the level of arms in each is a factor in the decisions to build arms by the other.

The decisions about the rates at which arms are to be built, in turn, depend on several things: the current level of arms in the focal nation, the perceived level of arms in the competitor's nation, and each nation's goals. To anticipate the dynamic behavior of this system then, we must focus our attention on the decisions in each nation to build arms. In turn, this requires us to ask how the current levels of arms in the focal and competing nations and how the nations' goals determine outcomes.

Each actor's rate of arms building is a direct response to the gap between its own level of armament and the level it desires. The rate of change in arms building in each nation, then, is directly proportional to the magnitude of this difference. The magnitude of the difference depends in turn on past levels of arms building and on the goals of that actor. Differences in the goals of the actors, then, would seem to be critical to the dynamic behavior of the system. If each actor desires superiority to the other (KX and KY > 1), escalation results. If each actor should desire inferiority to the other (KX and KY < 1) a "race" downward will result. If the actors have different goals, say one desiring superiority while the other is satisfied with inferiority in arms, or if the two actors desire exact parity, then stability over time would be implied.

According to our logical analysis of the diagram of the theory, the levels of arms in the two nations and the goals of the two parties are the keys to the dynamic behavior of this system. To explore the effects of these factors, let's design a series of experiments that vary the levels of arms, and vary the goals of the actors while holding other factors constant. The levels of arms possessed at any point in time will be set to be equal, favor actor X over actor Y, or vice versa. The goals of the actors can also have several configurations: X and Y may seek superiority, each may seek equality, or each may seek to have fewer arms than the other.

Along one dimension our two actors, X and Y, divide 200 units of arms either equally, or with a 3-to-1 superiority for one side or the other. Along another dimension we vary the goals of the X and Y (labeled KX and KY), which are expressed as their desired levels of arms as a percentage of the arms of their opponent. We create four alternative scenarios of the goals: Both actors desire equality, both actors desire superiority, both actors desire inferiority, or one actor desires superiority while the other desires inferiority. In Table 10.1 below, the levels of arms present in each camp after 25 cycles of the model are reported.

The basic results of these simple interaction games are relatively easy to anticipate and understand: (1) where both actors have the goal of equality with the other, the equilibrium result is equality at a level between the two starting points (here it is 100), (2) initial differences in the levels of arms are rapidly adjusted away by increases in the arms of the initially inferior player and declines in the arms of the initially superior player, (3) where both actors desire superiority to the other, "escalation" or exponential growth occurs, (4) where both actors desire to reduce their arms to be less than those of those of their competitor, the "arms race" leads downward, again regardless of initial levels. In general, whether the characteristic behavior of the model is exponential growth, exponential decline, or stability depends on the sum of the goals of the actors and the ratio of these goals to each other.

These experiments give a good understanding of the characteristic behavior of the baseline model. A stable level of armaments is achieved where both actors desire equality, or where both desire inferiority. Where both desire superiority, or the balance between the desire for superiority by one is not exactly balanced by a desired inferiority on the part of the other, unstable situations result. Where both desire superiority, exponential growth ensues; where goals are unequal, either unbounded growth or bounded decline ensue, depending on the ratio of the goals. The levels of arms of the actors at the beginning of the race make little difference in the baseline model: The equilibrium levels of the processes are the same regardless of initial equality or inequality.

An Extension: Delays

There are a number of ways that the baseline model could be extended and made more realistic. In the next section we will briefly

TABLE 10.1
Baseline Escalation Model Results at t = 25
Initial Levels of Arms

Goals	X = 100 Y = 100	X = 150 Y = 50	X = 50 Y = 150
KX = KY = 1.00	X = 100 Y = 100	X = 100 Y = 100	X = 100 Y = 100
KX = KY = 1.05	X = 350 Y = 350	X = 348 Y = 348	X = 348 Y = 348
KX = KY = .95	X = 29 Y = 29	X = 29 Y = 29	X = 29 Y = 29
KX = 1.05 KY = .95	X = 99 Y = 95	X = 98 Y = 93	X = 101 Y = 96

discuss some of the possibilities. One particular modification of the basic game, however, is worth considering in some detail because of the importance it has for understanding the dynamics of most social interactions.

In the interactions among human actors, delays and distortion in perception, communication, and action are usually present and can have substantial consequences. In very simple systems the consequences of delays and distortions are relatively easy to anticipate (as in our discussion in the first part of this volume). In complex systems with feedback, however, the consequences are not always so obvious. Now that we have a firm grasp of the basic dynamics of a two-actor escalation game we can modify our basic model to begin to understand how such imperfections affect outcomes.

There are many kinds of delay and distortion that occur in interactions. Actors may fail to perceive signals being sent, may be slow in decoding them, and may lose part of the message (or add noise to the message). Once a message is received and decoded it takes time for the actor to make decisions. Indeed, the more complex the organization of the actor the more likely it is that there will be a lengthy delay between perception and action. Once a course of action has been decided there are frequently delays (and sometimes errors as well) in implementation. To these "imperfections" in the capacities of each actor we must add another factor. When two actors, each "imperfect," base their actions on the behavior (including signals given off) of the other, the errors, delays, and distortions in interaction are multiplied by the interaction: A incorrectly perceives what B is doing, makes a response that B perceives as inappropriate, which causes A to respond differently, etc. Such cycles of misperception and consequent inappropriate action may make for clever comedy, but may be somewhat less amusing when the interaction in question may lead to a nuclear exchange. What might the consequences be if such delays and distortions were introduced into our escalation-interaction model?

To explore this question, let us first calculate two "baseline" scenarios. We will assume that each actor has perfect information about the other and is able to respond immediately and completely (as we have been assuming thus far). We will further assume that each actor desires a 5% supremacy over the other and has unlimited capacity. When an actor has more arms than he needs at a given point in time he does not get rid of them—except for scrapping obsolete ones—but does not build more. In the first baseline scenario the two actors each begin the game with 100 units of arms. In the second baseline scenario actor X begins with 150 units and actor Y with 50.

As in our analyses in the previous section, starting the actors with equal levels of arms and equal desires to have superiority over the other results in an exponential increase in the levels of arms of each and an exponential increase in the gap between the level of arms that each has and the number that it would deem satisfactory. Starting with 100 units of arms each actor has acquired 331 units by the 25th time period and is acquiring arms at a rate of 50 units per unit time. This is the classic problem of escalation, as we have studied it above.

Initial inequality of arms compounds the problem. Where the actors begin with equal desires to superiority but radically unequal initial levels (X has 150 units initially to Y's 50), both the level of arms accumulation and the rates of accumulation for both actors are accelerated. By the 25th time point both actors have acquired 394 units of arms and are building arms at a rate of 60 units per year at this time under the leader-follower scenario.

Now let us suppose that there are no delays or errors in each actor's perceptions of their opponent's level of arms, but that it is not possible to immediately respond to perceived gaps. That is, let us suppose that it takes some time to actually build the arms after it has been decided that they are necessary. For current purposes we will use a simple first-order exponential delay with a period of three time units (roughly, the actor responds in such a way as to close the gap over a period of three units):

R   RIX.KL = DELAY1(MAX(G1+GAPX.K+RDX.JK,0),3)

That is, X's rate of arms building (RIX) is a first-order exponential delay of average length of three units (DELAY1,3) of the larger of two quantities. X builds arms at a rate sufficient to satisfy its feelings of grievance or bellicosity (G1), to replace arms that have depreciated (RDX), and to close the gap it perceives between its current arms and its goal (GAP). Arms, once created, are not destroyed even if they are not "needed" (note the use of the MAX function to represent this effect).

When the actors begin the game with equal levels of arms, the effect of a delay in producing new arms is to reduce the final levels of arms. The exponential pattern of growth and growing gaps, however, persists. When the actors begin the game with unequal arms, however, the pattern of dynamic behavior is dramatically affected by a delay in arms production. The actor who is far behind initially undertakes a massive building program to attempt to close the gap. However, since the arms are not immediately delivered, the opponent does not immediately perceive the threat, and initially takes no action to maintain his superiority. As the program of building on the part of the initially inferior actor begins to reach its full realization, the initially superior actor finally perceives the threat and begins his own building response. However, since it takes time for these arms to be delivered, the first actor—who was initially inferior—reaches his goal of superiority and stops building. The resultant pattern is one of dampening cycles in perceived gaps on the part of both actors and an unstable upward arms race—as is shown in Figure 10.4.

It is also notable that the instability introduced by the delays in building not only distorts the dynamic pattern but also the final realization of the series. By the 25th time point in this scenario the total arms possessed by each actor are much greater (570 units) and the rate of building of new arms is somewhat greater (77 units per unit time) than in the equal initial-arms scenario. Thus we are led to an interesting result: In the presence of initial equality, delays in response lead to a lower final accumulation and no change in time pattern; in the presence of initial disequilibrium, delays in building lead to an acceleration of the arms race, and to cyclical instability in the time trace.

It also seems likely in an interaction of the type that we are modeling that actors may not have access to perfect information about the status of the other. Indeed, in arms races (and other forms of competition), actors may find it in their interest to disguise their true strength (or weakness), and hence gain an advantage over the other. Let us suppose that each of the actors in our game is able to hide information, so that the true levels of arms in each system become apparent to the other actor only with delay. This delay can be modeled with the statement:

A   YP.K = DELAY1(Y.K,3)

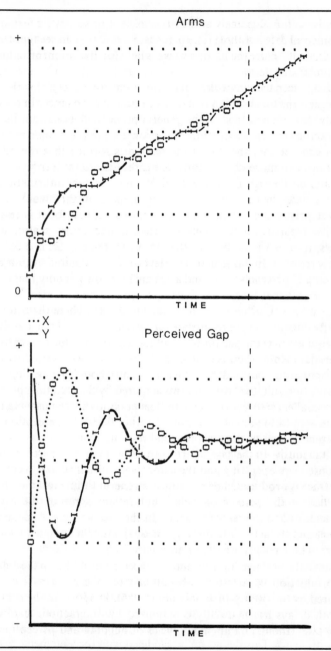

Figure 10.4: Delay in response in leader-follower model.

That is, actor X perceives the level of Y's arms with a first-order exponential delay of three time periods. So that we can see the effect of this kind of "perceptual" delay, we shall, for the moment, allow no manufacturing delay.

In the scenario in which our two competitors begin with equal resources, the major effect of a delay in perceiving changes in the arms level of the other is to slow the general process of escalation. Because each actor sees only a portion of the increase in the other's arms in a given time period, the (false) impression is formed that the other is building arms more slowly than is the case. Each actor formulates their own building program on the basis of this incorrect information and hence creates less ambitious building plans than they would with a correct perception. Since the level of arms actually built is less, the perceived gap is cumulatively reduced. While arms escalation still occurs, it occurs linearly, and the rate of increase in arms building is greatly reduced. In this scenario the level of arms acquired by time point 25 is only 138 by each actor, and arms are increasing at only 16 units per year.

The effects of a "perception" delay are similar where the actors are initially unequal. These results are displayed as Figure 10.5. The degree of inequality in the initial positions of the actors is not fully perceived by either, dampening their responses and dramatically slowing down (but not eliminating) the tendency of each to "overshoot" in adjusting to the other. As a result, the levels of arms acquired by the 25th time point are much smaller (160) than those in the leader-follower scenario where the delays were located in the "response" rather than the "perception."

In real systems both perceptual and response types of delays operate simultaneously. In the case where both forms of delay—perceptual and response—are operating and the actors were initially equal, a complex time trace is produced. The arms race is generally quite retarded by the presence of the perception delay, but retains some of the cyclical character due to the response delay. In the case where both delays are present and the actors are initially unequal, another complex response occurs. These results are shown in Figure 10.6.

Due to the initial inequality and the "acceleration" due to the delay in the production of arms, a substantial stockpile of arms has been acquired by the twenty-fifth time point (285). In addition, the presence of both delays has markedly destabilized the interaction, leading to continuing (though dampening) cycles of building and perceptions of "gaps."

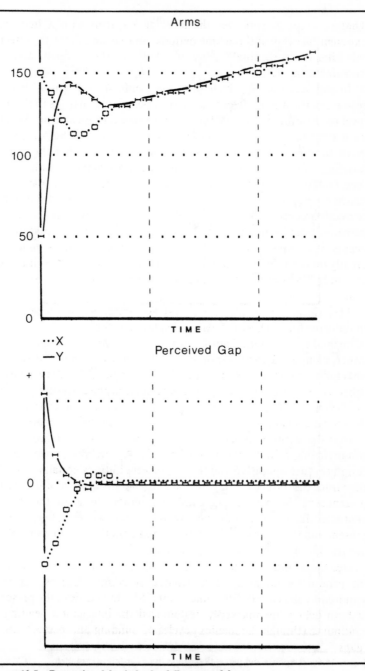

Figure 10.5: Perception delay in leader-follower model.

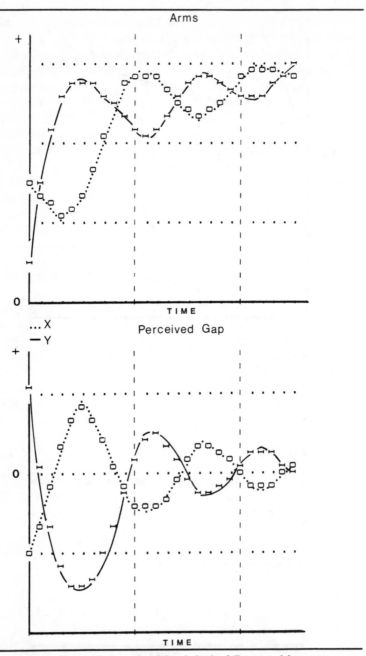

Figure 10.6:   Response and perception delays in leader-follower model.

A summary of the results of these experiments with perceptual and response delays is shown as Table 10.2.

We can reach a number of conclusions about the effects of delays on the dynamics of competitive interaction from these results. In the case of a system in which the actors are initially equal, delays in perception and response always result in lowering the rate of growth. Where the actors are initially unequal, however, the effects of delays are not so predictable. Response delays in this circumstance actually accelerate the process of escalation. Under the particular rules of this game, competition between actors who are initially unequal generates more heated races than does competition between equals. The presence of any delay in a system not in "balance" tends to produce the general pattern of overcompensation and cyclical behavior in the time paths of both actors. In this game, the cycles dampen with time in all cases. Where the presence of both delays in the system, however, dramatically slows the rate at which the cycles dampen—that is, misperception and slowed responses tend to reenforce one another in creating problems of adjustment.

We are obviously still very far from an empirically adequate theory of competitive interaction with this model. The results of even such a simple game, however, are interesting—and not entirely obvious. The primary lesson to be taken from this simple extension of the basic model, for our current purposes, is that the delays, misperceptions, and errors and slowness of response by actors in interaction can be highly consequential for both the final realizations and time paths of interactions. Such problems of communication and action are extremely common in human action systems, and should therefore be part of the list of things that theorists of social dynamics must specify in the process of theory building.

Some Directions for Dynamic Theories of Competition

The primary purpose of constructing and analyzing the particular theories of two-actor competition that we examined in this chapter is as an illustration and exploration of the dynamics of social interaction. As a theory of arms races specifically, one can readily imagine a number of important ways in which the current model could be extended and made more realistic. We will not pursue these elaborations here (the reader may wish to, using the model provided in the Appendix as a starting point), but some of the major possible directions are worth noting.

Let's first consider the mechanics of arms production. A number of

TABLE 10.2
Outcomes of Competitions with Delays

	Levels at t = 25	*Rates at t = 25*
Scenario: Actors Initially Equal (X = Y = 100)		
No delays	331	50
Response delay	241	33
Perception delay	139	16
Both delays	139	15
Scenario: Actors Initially Unequal (X = 150, Y = 50)		
No delays	394	60
Response delay	569	77
Perception delay	285	32
Both delays	160	18

simplifying assumptions have been made that might be relaxed. We have assumed, for example, that all arms are identical. More complex models (like those used by nuclear strategic defense planners) might prefer to model the levels of several types of arms, perhaps having relationships of substitutability (more ICBMs and less bombers, etc.). The differing types of arms might have differing delays, differing efficacy, and be subject to differing mechanisms of goal setting. The decision-making process then becomes quite complex, as different mixes of arms can be selected—resulting in an optimization problem.

In the same vein, we have assumed that the stock of arms becomes obsolete at a constant rate and that obsolete arms are automatically replaced. We might instead suppose that arms have a useful "half-life," so that the rate of obsolescence depends on the rate of building at prior time points. The scrap rate might be regarded as manipulable as a result of policy—accelerated to slow the accumulation of arms, or slowed to achieve higher levels of current force. If multiple types of arms were considered, differential obsolescence of different weapons types would have to enter the decision-making matrix.

We have also not considered the problem of resource constraints and resource competition. The rate of possible increase in arms and the total amounts of arms that can be built may well be limited by the resources available. The possibilities here are quite interesting. In addition to absolute limitations imposed by resource availability, the costs and delays of production may differ between actors due to these factors. The competition for scarce resources between armaments and alternative products calls for a more realistic picture of the political processes of our actors. There may be some levels or rates of arms production that are not politically feasible, just as some levels and rates are not physically feasible within natural resource constraints.

Our simple game also makes a series of highly simplified assumptions about the informational aspects of the system, as well as about the material. One can easily imagine alternative specifications about what is monitored, how the information is processed, and how decisions are made.

In the current model, each actor monitors only their own current level of arms and the current level of arms of their opponent. We might suppose that real decision makers have access to more information than this. They might also pay attention to the rates of building of themselves and their opponent and the rates of obsolescence, so that they make decisions on the basis of their projections about the behavior of the other—not merely on the basis of the observed behavior. Our decision makers might also take into account their perceptions of the resource limitations and limitations on the rates of arms building possible for themselves and their opponents in making projections.

In the previous section we examined the effects of simple first-order delays in the perception of and response to the opponent's actions. The results were rather dramatic and, in a few cases, somewhat unexpected. The kinds of delays and distortions we considered above however, are only a very small part of the range of possible informational imperfections that occur in such systems. In addition to simple delay, organizational systems often contain delays that vary randomly or systematically with levels of the system (e.g., the more highly developed the technology, the shorter the average perceptual delay). Informational systems are often "noisy," as well as filled with delay. Such noise can be quite destabilizing in the dynamics of interaction—as it is sometimes amplified, as well as dampened. Real bureaucratic decision makers also may take considerable periods of time in making decisions—quite independently of delays in perception and delays in response. As we have seen in the example above, multiple delays in a system can have the consequence of amplifying distortion and slowing the realizations of equilibrium tendencies.

To all of this complexity about how information is really handled in competitions between actors, we should add an additional very troublesome possibility—that the actors are "intelligent" in how they deal with information problems (research on organizational decision making, however, does not always support the view that bureaucratic actors deal intelligently with such problems).

Consider a problem that currently exists in the arms race between the United States and the Soviet Union. Given the speed and accuracy of certain new missile types, deployment near the national boundaries of the other actor reduces the available response time in the event of a first strike. Being aware of the limited response time (that is, correctly perceiving the degree of information processing delay in their own system) each actor must adopt a more rapid decision-making method than the one currently used (a highly specific and routinized plan with executive veto). Each actor is tempted to program the decision making into a microprocesser to meet the challenge. To make such a change, however, eliminates discretion and judgment from the decision-making process and may result in an "incorrect" response if any "noise" gets into the monitoring and decision-making system. Since both actors are quite aware that their systems for monitoring the behavior of the other (i.e., whether the other has, in fact, begun an attack) are slightly unreliable— that is, they are aware of the existence of noise—each faces a dilemma. Where lies the greater risk: in the new information processing technology that is inflexible and hence subject to error due to noise, or in the old technology, which is flexible and less sensitive to noise errors but is too slow? We have, unfortunately, no answer to offer. The point for those who would theorize about social interaction, however, can be taken: Actors are sometimes aware of, and seek to take into account, informational delays and distortions in designing systems and making decisions. The introduction of such a high level of self-awareness into the models of escalation considered here could produce systems with dramatically different dynamics.

We have only considered the simplest possible ideas about goal formation in the current model. We might first explore the consequences of assuming more complicated goal setting algorithms on the part of our actors. Leaders may not simply desire superiority, but might desire to not see existing gaps narrowed. The goals may also be made a function of other factors—and hence dynamic rather than static. For example, actors may be less interested in superiority, and become willing to settle for equality as the levels of arms of each reach very high levels, or as the strain of building arms becomes too great (either as a function of limitations of physical or of political resources). One can also imagine that goal setting becomes "intelligent." For example, an actor that falls too far behind in the race may capitulate—ending the game. Or, possibly, actors may adjust their goals due to internal political considerations (i.e., nations may become more aggressive if they are suffering from problems of internal order) or the behavior of the other (e.g., being willing to accept a lesser degree of superiority when the opponent is not closing an existing gap).

Lastly, and importantly, our "game" is quite limited in that it takes into account only two actors, and assumes that the two actors are quite similar. Real arms races are often multiparty games, and the different actors usually face quite different configurations of constraints. Expanding the game to include multiple actors and allowing the actors to differ in both their material and informational systems presents no technical problem for constructing theories. The complexity of such models, however, expands by law of combinations, not additively. For each new actor the relations between that actor and all others in the game must be specified: In a two-actor game, there is one such relation; in a three-actor game, three; in a four-actor game, six, etc. The addition of more actors may also realistically be expected to change the nature of the game in fundamental ways. Each actor must now monitor, make sense of, and respond to multiple stimuli—a far more complex and indeterminant task. Where all of the actors in such games are connected, each additional complexity, delay, or distortion also multiplies through the system, producing still greater uncertainty.

The possibilities for elaborating and exploring theories of relatively simple dynamic interactions among even relatively similar and simple actors are numerous. Far from being intimidated by the range of possibilities, however, theorists should see these possibilities as a research agenda. By decomposing scenarios of social interaction into the language of subsystems, states, rates, and coupling, even the most complex forms of interaction are analyzable in formal terms.

Conclusions

Social interaction in general is complex, relative to the simple action models considered in the earlier chapters. In an interaction each of the parties monitors both the status of their own system and the system of the others. The information derived from the mutual monitoring is used by each actor, in conjunction with its own goals to formulate actions—which in turn provide the basis for action on the part of others. Social interactions are necessarily symbolic. Each actor must perceive, interpret, and formulate goals and plans within the constraints of its own system of meanings. But social interactions are also necessarily physical. It is the action of each party that creates the field that is monitored and interpreted by the other. The dynamics of social interactions are, consequently, determined by both the material and informational aspects of the system and its parts.

As the model of the very simple interaction developed in this chapter suggests, there is no basic difficulty in using the language of systems to describe, formalize, and analyze the dynamic behavior of social interaction. Indeed, patterns of social interaction can be seen as being built up of the coupling together of actors through the exchange of information. The actors may be many or few; they may each be characterized by simple or complex state spaces; the connections among the actors may be simple and sporadic or dense and multifaceted. All such systems of interaction are potentially decomposable, and their characteristic dynamics analyzable.

In the specific model developed in this chapter we've paid particular attention to the role played by delays in systems. The reason for this emphasis is that where concern focuses on dynamics rather than statics, such imperfections in perceiving, organizing, and responding to information can have major consequences. We have tried to make several simple but important points about the effects of delays in models of interaction. Depending on their nature and location in the systems, delays can act either to dampen or to amplify. The presence of multiple delays in a system can lead to unanticipated results as the delays may either reenforce distortions or dampen them. The presence of delays in interactions can result in extreme complexity and instability, as the imperfections of information and consequent response are reenforced in the dynamic interaction.

Notes

1. Theories involving the dynamics of smart interaction among relatively small numbers of actors have been highly developed in a number of disciplines. In addition to formal "game theory" (see note 2), the analysis of small-group dynamics and social exchange have extensively developed models that have many similarities to those described in this chapter. The interested reader might want to look at some of this work; some places to start are Bartos (1972), Blau (1964), Camilleri et al. (1972), Caplow (1968), Cohen (1962), Coleman (1972), Davis (1967), Davis and Leinhardt (1972), Fararo (1972), Holland and Leinhardt (1977), Hopkins (1964), Komorita (1974), Malone (1975), and Simpson (1973).

2. "Game Theory" is a set of particularly well-developed formalizations of interactions such as those described in this chapter. For some of the interesting applications of formal game theory models, see Ackoff (1959), Bloomfield and Padelford (1959), Brams (1975), Luce and Raiffa (1957), von Neumann and Morganstern (1947), Raiffa (1970), Rapoport (1966), Rapoport and Chammah (1965), Thrall et al. (1954), and Shubik (1964 and particularly 1984).

3. The arms race model in this chapter is based on the work of Lewis B. Richardson (1960), and the extensive literature that has developed surrounding his original model. For an introduction to the rather extensive theoretical, mathematical, and statistical literature on escalations, see Abelson (1963), Alker and Brunner (1969), Boulding (1962), Brody (1963), Brody and Benham (1969), Cappello (1972), Coe (1964), Hollist (ed., 1978), Pruitt (1962), Rapoport (1957, 1960), Saaty (1968), Schelling (1963), Schrodt (1978), Shubik and Hansford (1965), Singer (1958), Smoker (1965), and Waltz (1967).

APPENDIX 10.1. Arms Race Model With Delays

```
*                ARMS RACE MODEL, BASED ON RICHARDSON'S THEORY
NOTE
NOTE                        ***** ACTOR X *****
NOTE
L         X.K = X.J+(DT)(RIX.JK–RDX.JK)
N         X = XI
C         XI = 100
NOTE                        Arms increase at RIX and depreciate at RDX.
A         DLAX.K = KX*YP.K
NOTE                        Desired arms are equal to KX of Y's perceived arms
A         YP.K = DELAY1(Y.K,3)
NOTE                        X perceives Y's arms with 1st order delay.
A         GAPX.K = DLAX.K–X.K
NOTE                        The gap between desired and current arms.
R         RIX.KL = DELAY1(MAX(G1+GAPX.K+RDX.JK,0),3)
NOTE                        X's rate of arms building is equal to the whole
NOTE                        of the gap between desired and actual arms
NOTE                        plus an amount due to "grievance" (G1).
NOTE                        Building, however, takes an average of 3 units of
NOTE                        time to accomplish.
R         RDX.KL = MAX(A1*X.K,0)
NOTE                        The rate of exhaustion of arms is A1.
NOTE                        PARAMETERS FOR ACTOR X ARE SET:
C         A1 = .1
C         KX = 1.05
C         G1 = 0
NOTE
NOTE                **ACTOR Y'S SYSTEM IS SIMILARLY DEFINED**
L         Y.K = Y.J+(DT)(RIY.JK–RDY.JK)
N         Y = YI
C         YI = 100
A         DLAY.K = KY*XP.K
A         GAPY.K = DLAY.K–Y.K
A         XP.K = DELAY1(X.K,3)
R         RDY.KL = MAX(A2*Y.K,0)
R         RIY.KL = DELAY1(MAX(G2+GAPY.K+RDY.JK,0),3)
NOTE                        PARAMETERS FOR ACTOR Y
C         A2 = .1
C         G2 = 0
C         KY = 1.05
NOTE
NOTE                        OUTPUT SPECIFICATIONS
SPEC          DT = .1/LENGTH = 25/PRTPER = 2/PLTPER = 1
PRINT         Y,X,RIY,RIX,GAPY,GAPX
PLOT          Y,X
PLOT          GAPY,GAPX
RUN
```

11

Individuals and Groups:
Stress, Coping, and Social Support

In the previous chapter we have examined models in which "chains" are coupled together in increasingly "smart" ways. The structure of the arms-race model is, in systems terms, only slightly more complex than those of the models considered in previous chapters. As a theory of social action, however, it is different in important ways. Rather than having a single system or actor, the arms race model has two actors; rather than representing social "action," the model represents a social "interaction." In the arms-race model, the kind of social action that is captured is somewhat more complex. In the escalation game, each actor is aware of the other and formulates strategy based on its own goals and its perceptions of its opponent's actions. In this model, the behavior of each actor depends on the behavior of the other—that is, rather than simple "action," the model captures a process of "interaction."

Models that capture the dynamics of "interaction" are of central importance in social science theory. Many of the key issues in international relations and international political economy are centered on the processes of interaction (be the interaction economic, cultural, political, or military) among nations. The behavior of economic (and other) organizations over time is often examined as patterns of interaction between the focal organization and other organizations in its environment. Much theory of general social psychology, small group processes, and the family and intimate relations is explicitly concerned with the dynamics of interaction between individual persons. In a more abstract vein, most "game theory," whether pure theory or applied to political, social, or economic action is explicitly concerned with

Author's Note: The work reported in this chapter is the joint product of David L. Morgan and Robert A. Hanneman.

processes of interaction in the sense that we have used the term here.[1]

The essentials of models of "interaction" are quite straightforward. Interaction requires more than one actor, that actors be aware of each others' actions, and that they dynamically adjust their own behavior (and possibly their own goals) over time, taking the behavior of the other into account. The dynamics of such systems are inherently more complex than those of "closed" or "open" systems because the stimuli that each actor is responding to is continuously shifting as a consequence of the actions of the other—and hence, indirectly, its own past actions.

The processes of interaction that social scientists describe in their work are often quite complicated. Actors' perceptions of their environments (including particularly the behavior of other actors), are frequently regarded as highly problematic. Unlike simplistic models of "rational action," most theories of interaction suppose that actors may have great difficulty in obtaining information about relevant aspects of their environments. The amount and quality of information they obtain varies over time and as a consequence of their positions in networks of interaction. Most interaction models suppose that information about the environment and other actors is variably understood and interpreted by actors, depending on processes of socially conditioned cognition. The behavior of actors in response to stimuli, as perceived, may also be quite variable, depending on the goals actors hold, their expectations about the behavior of others in response to their acts, and the resources they have available. In short, the processes underlying "games" or "interactions" among actors are often regarded as being quite complex and worthy of study in themselves.

In this chapter we will begin to explore some of the possibilities for modeling these more complicated dynamics. We use as our example a particular theory of "stress buffering" drawn from the literature on social networks, social support, and mental health. The structure of the system that we will use to construct this model, however, is potentially of much wider applicability. In principle the model could be extended to include any number of actors. It can be elaborated to embody still more complex hypotheses about perception, cognition, and action, and the actors could as easily be organizations (governments, firms, etc.) as individuals and groups. The "smarter" interaction that is characteristic of the system describing "stress buffering" may be of interest in itself for the application to other similar interaction processes. The model also suggests the richness and flexibility of the theories that can be systematically developed using the approaches advocated in this volume.

The Problem: Stress Buffering and Social Support

In the course of everyday life individuals are subjected to "stressful life events." Most of these events are quite minor and are easily dealt with without seeming to cause any permanent damage or disability. You are aggravated by having to wait in a line to purchase groceries, your boss yells at you, you find that you have too much work to do and too little time to do it in, the children are difficult, and on and on. By the next morning when you wake up the events are largely forgotten and you feel no worse or better than you did before they happened.

In addition to these everyday happenings, we are all subject to less frequent but more severe stresses arising from "major" events: deaths of loved ones, loss of jobs, dissolution of marriages, etc. Most of the time most people are able to cope effectively with the stress from these "big" events as well, but often they leave emotional scars, and often we are temporarily partially disabled by them.[2]

Considerable theoretical and empirical effort has been focused on the question of the processes by which individuals are able to cope with "stressful life events," and why some individuals appear to suffer less short-term and long-term disability as a consequence of these events. Among the many contributions to the theoretical and research literature on this subject are a number of works that emphasize the role played by "support networks" in aiding individuals to cope with stressful events. The fundamental hypotheses of these works are highly plausible and, at a general level at least, supported by statistical analyses of cross-sectional and panel data. At many points in our development of the model in this chapter we will make quite arbitrary assumptions about the time forms of relationships. Researchers in the field of social support have only recently begun to specify over-time models, and hence provide only limited guidance about this part of the theory.[3]

All of the major theories have a number of common features. They suggest that the effect of stressful life events on the ability of individuals to maintain normal functioning is mediated both by the individual's coping resources and by characteristics of the individual's "support networks"—that is, other individuals and institutions that can provide resources to assist the individual in coping with the distress arising from stressful life events. The more resources that the individual has available personally or in its networks, the more likely it is that the impact of stressful events on individual functioning will be kept within manageable limits.[4]

Feed-Forward Effects

As researchers have sought to account for the effects of social support and individual coping, they have advanced increasingly complex theoretical models of the processes of interaction that occur in stressful situations. Various authors have suggested three quite different mechanisms by which the relationship between an individual and its support network can produce more effective coping with stress and less loss of functioning.[5]

First, it is suggested, certain characteristics of support networks reduce the probability that stressful events will occur for the focal individual and thus prevent the occurrence of stressful life events. To choose but one example, individuals who are part of a family-run business (a "network" of a sort), may be less likely to endure the stress accompanying being laid off or fired from a job. Second, if stressful events occur, the degree to which they produce actual "distress" in the focal individual also depends upon the nature of the support network. Again, to choose a simple example, a frequent churchgoer may experience less distress from the death of a spouse than an individual who is not connected to a network of coreligionists. This, it is argued, is because the close network buffers the focal individual by interpreting the event and defining the reality in such a way as to make coping easier. The assertion by one's reference group that the death of a spouse is "God's will" and that the focal individual is expected to "be strong" may go a long way toward reducing the degree of distress perceived by the affected individual.

Third, in addition to these mechanisms of "prevention" and "buffering," support networks are seen as providing compensating resources and support to help restore functioning once a stressful event has occurred. Again, to choose an obvious example, an injury that produces physical disability is probably somewhat more easily endured if the disabled person has helpful neighbors and friends who provide assistance so the disabled person may remain home, rather than being placed into some direct-care residential facility. Persons with resource-rich support networks can more easily "compensate" for some of the economic and other costs of stressful events and hence have their levels of functioning more fully and quickly restored.

In addition to "prevention," "buffering," and "compensation" through network support, individuals also deal with stressful life events by mobilizing their own personal resources to cope. Most theorists hypothesize that the focal individual is also able to "prevent," "buffer," and "compensate" for stress by a set of mechanisms parallel to those provided by the social network.

Individuals who possess high levels of personal resources are more likely to "prevent" the occurrence of stressful life events than those with fewer resources. Individuals who have certain cognitive sets of skills may be better able to "buffer" the stress induced by events when they do occur. And, individuals who possess more personal resources (material and psychic) are more able to mobilize them to compensate for losses of functioning due to stressful events.

We can take all of the ways in which individuals and their social networks are connected to stress and functioning discussed thus far and represent them diagramatically, as in Figure 11.1. The theory, to the degree that we have developed it thus far, suggests that both individual "coping" and social network "support" affect individual functioning in several ways. The resources of individuals and individual's networks may act to "prevent" environment hazards from affecting the focal individual. When such events do occur, both individual and group resources can be called upon to "buffer" the intensity of the resulting distress. And once distress has resulted in the loss of functioning, both individuals and the social networks may act to "compensate" and restore the individual to normal functioning.

Feedback Effects

There are a number of ways in which the theory is still quite incomplete. In particular, we've not paid much attention yet to the nature of the control structures that connect individual functioning to "prevention," "buffering," and "compensation," or to the connections between individual's resources and coping or between network resources and support.

We might hypothesize that the "prevention" effects are more or less automatic, that is, they are governed by "dumb" control mechanisms. Prevention of untoward events by both the network and the focal individual operate without monitoring, goals, or conscious decisions. But "buffering" and "compensation" effects are probably somewhat more complicated.

Buffering by the focal individual may be usefully thought of as occurring more or less automatically.[6] The meanings that we attach to events, and how "stressful" we find them are mediated by personality and cognitive structures that operate automatically and instantaneously. On the other hand, the buffering of stressful events by the support

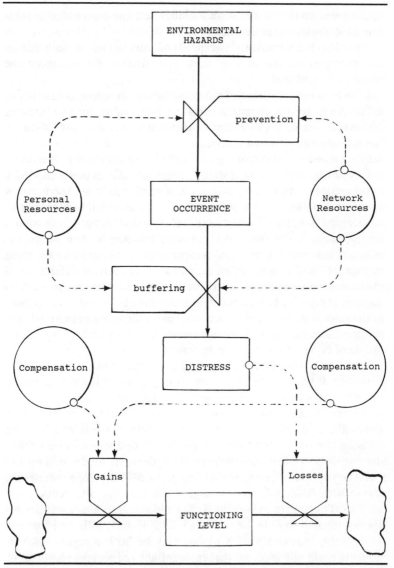

Figure 11.1: **Stress, coping, and social support: feed forward connections.**

network is not so automatic. In order to engage in buffering activities, the support network must be aware that a stressful event has occurred, decide that buffering is an appropriate response, and act. That is, the support network must monitor event occurrence, make decisions about action based on this information, and then act. The degree of awareness of event occurrence, the decisions that the support network makes about taking buffering actions, and the speed and intensity of the implementation of buffering acts may all vary considerably, depending on the nature of the network.

Efforts by both the affected individual and his or her support network to "compensate" for distress and restore functioning are also far from automatic. We might hypothesize that these processes are based on "smart" control. Affected individuals can be thought of as monitoring their own level of functioning and mobilizing personal resources to restore functioning to a "goal state"—normality. The support network's compensatory actions are governed by a similar process: The network monitors the functioning of the affected individual, compares this functioning to a "goal," and mobilizes resources ("support") to restore the individual's functioning. Of course, the speeds with which the intrapersonal and interpersonal compensation processes operate might be expected to be quite different, and to operate with different goal levels. The capacity of both the focal individual and the network to respond to perceived functioning problems may be thought of as limited by the resources available to each. We have added the implied feedback and control mechanisms discussed here to Figure 11.2 (along with a couple of others, to be discussed below).

As we have specified it so far, the system is rather a "smart" one, consisting of two negative feedback loops (the use of individual coping and network support) to overcome the effects of exogenous stressful events. But there is one last complication that we must consider that makes the dynamics of this particular model more interesting and realistic: Not only do stressful life events induce distress, but they may also simultaneously reduce the capacity of the individual and his or her social network to respond. A disabling physical injury, for example, not only causes "distress" for the focal individual but also reduces the individual's capacity to cope by limiting mobility, taking away discretionary income (due to loss of work and medical bills), and so on. Analogously, the death of a spouse may be both a highly distress-inducing event and an event that substantially reduces the resources of the focal individual's support network, because the spouse is usually a central figure in individual's support systems.

There are two additional connections in Figure 11.2 that we have not yet discussed. These connections are relatively straightforward. For both the individual and for the network, there is a connection between the level of compensatory effort and the resources available. Not surprisingly, both individual and group efforts at restoring functioning

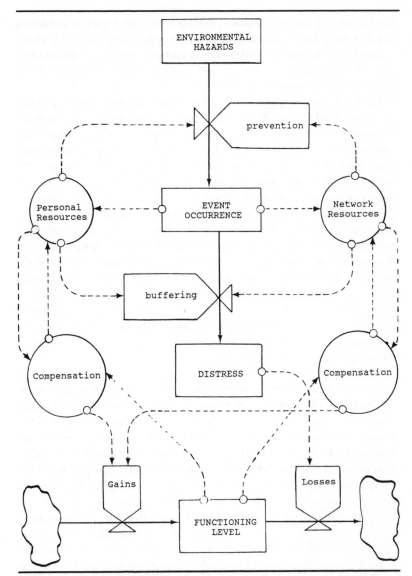

Figure 11.2: Stress, coping, and social support: feed forward and feedback connections.

are limited by available resources and the speed with which they can be mobilized. When resources are used for the purpose of coping or supporting, they are removed from the stockpile of those available to respond to future events. In our model we do not deal in any detail with the source of either personal or network resources which are regarded, for simplicity's sake, as self-renewing.

The dynamic processes represented in Figure 11.2 are, in the terms we have been using, rather complex (though, as we will discuss a bit later, the current formulation is really just a starting point). The system consists of two "smart" actors: the focal individual and the social network. Each of these actors is aware of the actions of the other (though they are not necessarily timely or accurate in their perceptions), and each formulates strategies and behaviors on the basis of the continuously changing interaction between them. This particular dynamic system is one that is "equilibrium seeking," but is composed of a substantial number of effects that may or may not allow the realization of the goal of maintaining individual functioning in the face of stressful life events. Indeed, now that we have formulated the various hypothesized processes into a dynamic system, our theoretical work has just begun. We must now translate the system into a model, and then use the model to explore the limitation and implications of our ideas.

Developing the Baseline Model

Functioning

As we have discussed it above, the whole stress, coping, and social support system revolves around the level of functioning of the focal individual. This is the quantity that is decremented by stressful life events and restored by the compensatory action on the part of the focal individual and of the network. So that we can model continuous rates of change in functioning, we will treat it as a level variable, and indicate it by the letter F.

```
L     F.K = MAX(F.J+(DT)(FIR.JK–FLR.JK),0)
N     F = FI
C     FI = 100
```

In these three statements we first state that the level of functioning at a later point in time is equal to the level at the previous point in time plus integrated effects of factors acting to increase functioning (the functioning increase rate, FIR), less factors acting to decrement the functioning rate (functioning loss rate, FLR). Since we would suppose that functioning does have a fixed lower limit (i.e. "dead" or complete loss of function), we use the MAX function to limit the values that the level can take to positive ones.[7] The second statement sets the initial level of functioning equal to a constant called FI, so that we can easily modify this value for reruns of DYNAMO simulations. The third statement sets the initial value to 100 units of functioning. This simple statement, of course, completely begs the issues of the meaning of "functioning" at a conceptual level and how it might be indicated in empirical research—both difficult issues, but neither of which are critical to the development of the abstract theoretical model.

In the theory that we have been developing, losses of functioning are the direct consequence of "distress" (DIS) resulting from (buffered) stressful events. We can specify the functioning loss rate (FLR) as:

$$\text{R} \quad \text{FLR.KL} = \text{MAX}((\text{PARM1*DIS.K}),0)$$
$$\text{C} \quad \text{PARM1} = 1.0$$

In the first statement we set the rate of functioning loss equal to the larger of either some proportion (PARM1) of the level of distress, or zero. That is, functioning loss is some function of the level of distress, but cannot be less than zero. In the absence of strong theory, we will assume that functioning losses are directly proportional to distress (i.e. PARM1 = 1.0). Future modeling efforts might make different assumptions at this point, particularly about the time shape of this effect. For example, it might be that distress results in loss of functioning only with delay. And it might be supposed that the degree and form of the delay might vary depending on the level of the distress, the kind of event that is inducing the distress, or other independent variables. Such alternative assumptions about the size and time shape of PARM1 could be expected to be highly consequential for the behavior of the system because of their closeness to the level of functioning—the quantity that is central to the whole system.

The rate at which functioning is increased is slightly more complicated, because such increases are the result of both individual compensatory "coping" and compensatory "social support" from the network. If we call the level of individual compensatory coping effort "C" and the level of compensatory social support "SS," the functioning increase rate can be specified as:

$$\text{R} \quad \text{FIR.KL} = \text{MAX}((\text{PARM2*C.K}) + (\text{PARM3*SS.K}),0)$$
$$\text{C} \quad \text{PARM2} = 1.0$$
$$\text{C} \quad \text{PARM3} = 1.0$$

The first statement specifies that the rate of functioning increase must be nonnegative and that it is the sum of coping and social support, each modified by a parameter. Again, for simplicity, we will assume that these parameters are unity; that is, that the effects of changes in coping and social support on functioning are immediate and proportional to the changes in coping and support. Again, we see a place at which the theory could use some future development. The magnitude and time shapes of the effects of coping and social support on levels of functioning might very well be thought of as differing in intensity, being nonlinear in form, and being nonlinear in time. For example, one might suppose that individual coping is more efficacious than group support in restoring functioning (that is, that PARM2 is greater than PARM1); one might suppose that both effects are realized only with delay; and, possibly, that the time shapes of the two effects are different and have different average delays. Different assumptions about these factors would be highly consequential for the overall behavior of the system because of their immediate effect on the level of functioning.

Life Hazards, Stressful Events, and Distress

One of the important theoretical advances in the stress and coping literature is the recognition that individual's characteristics and social positions can prevent and buffer the negative consequences of stressful events on individual's functioning. In order to build a model that takes these "preventive" and "buffering" effects into account, we must distinguish between life hazards, the occurrence of stressful events, and the distress induced by the occurrence of events. It is useful to think of these quantities as a "chain" of states, as shown in Figures 11.1 and 11.2.

Let us first suppose that the actual occurrence of life events is generated by some process exogenous to the model. One such process that will be used later on is the following:

```
A    S1.K = EXOG.K
A    EXOG.K = 10.0+PULSE(MAG,5,30)
C    MAG = 100
```

Let "S1" stand for the intensity or seriousness of events occurring at a given time. The first statement (which is not strictly necessary) sets this quantity equal to the output of some EXOGenous process. For the current run, we suppose that stressful events are decomposed into a constant or chronic level of "background" stress (equal to 10 units) and a single powerful event of peak intensity of "MAG" units that occurs at time point 5 (here, MAG is set to 100 units), and is repeated 30 time points later. As with the other parts of the model, there are alternative ways that this exogeneous "hazard" might be specified. In addition to examining "transient response" by use of a PULSE, we might very well also want to specify constant exogenous stress (to examine the equilibrium tendencies of the model), or random shocks drawn from various distributions (e.g. equiprobability, normal, Weibull).

The degree to which environmental hazards are translated into stresses affecting our focal individual are theorized to be limited by "preventive" factors. The intensity of the prevention depends upon the resources of the focal individual and the resources of the social network of which the individual is a part. Let us call the intensity or stressfulness of events that actually occur for our focal individual "S2." We can represent this part of the process as:

A   S2.K = MAX(S1.K-PARM4*NR.K-PARM5*PR.K,0)
C   PARM4 = .025
C   PARM5 = .035

The intensity of the stressful events reaching our focal individual (S2) is equal to the level of hazard (S1) less a prevention effect of the social network (PARM4) that is proportional to the resources of the network (NR), less a prevention effect of individual characteristics (PARM5) that is proportional to the level of individual resources (PR). The MAX function is again used to assure that the level of stress received is not a negative quantity. The two parameters here, PARM4 and PARM5, reflect the efficacy of individual and network characteristics in preventing untoward events. For our baseline, we have assumed that individual resources are slightly more efficacious than network resources.

These assumptions, like many others in our baseline, are clearly too simple (though they go well beyond existing theory). More sophisticated thinking about this part of the problem might suggest that prevention effects act with delays that are different in both form and length between the individual and the network. The intensity of the prevention effect might be thought of as nonlinear with respect to individual and network resource levels; perhaps there are decreasing marginal returns in prevention to increased resources. Or perhaps the magnitude of the prevention effect depends on the magnitude of the stressor or on other independent variables. While we will not explore these possibilities here, the formalization of the model has helped to identify new issues in the theory that require further thinking.

We have now reached the point in the process where unfortunate events are occurring for our focal individual. The degree of "distress" induced by these events, however, is also regarded as variable—

depending on how effective the individual and the social networks are in "buffering" their impacts. We can represent this buffering in a fashion similar to that of prevention:

A   DIS.K = MAX(S2.K−PARM6*NR.K−PARM7*PR.K,0)
C   PARM6 = .025
C   PARM7 = .035

As with prevention, we use the MAX function to assure that buffering cannot reduce distress (DIS) to a negative quantity. The degree of buffering is modeled as the sum of individual and group effects, each directly proportional to the resource level of the source.

For simplicity, we have assumed that individual buffering and social network buffering are both "automatic" or "dumb" systems. More complicated formulations are again quite easy to suggest. We might suppose that individual buffering is automatic, but that network buffering requires monitoring, decision, and feedback. And, as with prevention effects, we might suppose that the buffering effects of individual resources and group resources operate at different speeds, have differing time shapes, and have different and nonlinear relationships with the resource levels of the individuals and the network. These assumptions are consequential for the behavior of the system, but are necessarily left for future theoretical research.

This completes the picture of how environmental hazards are converted, by means of prevention and buffering by individuals and their networks, into the personal distress that reduces individual's levels of functioning. We now turn our attention to the processes that seek to restore well-being.

Individual Compensatory Coping

Individual's responses to stressful events are highly variable. While we will not seek to specify exactly what individual resources and skills are relevant to coping, we can build a general model of the process of individual coping efforts. At the general level, individual coping is a smart feedback system in which the individual becomes aware of changes in their own level of functioning, evaluates these changes as a problem, and mobilizes personal resources (both material and psychic) to restore functioning. Individual coping responses to stress are limited by the level of resources available to the individual and by the capacity of the individual to mobilize these resources.

The first step in the process is self-monitoring of the level of functioning. For our baseline model, let's use the simplest possible specification of this part of the process:

A   FAI.K = FUNCT*F.K
C   FUNCT = 1.0

The first of these statements says that the level of functioning apparent to the focal individual (FAI) is equal to the actual level of functioning (F), times a parameter (FUNCT).

In this case, we treat the process of self-perception as completely unproblematic, involving no delay, bias, or noise. Of course self-perception is not really so simple, and one might wish to elaborate on this portion of the model. For example, individuals probably do suffer delay in perceiving change in their own functioning, and there may very well be "noise" and unreliability in their perceptions. The extent and form of the delay, the signal-to-noise ratio, and systematic upward or downward biases in self-perceived functioning may differ across individuals, and may depend on the level of individual resources and/or current levels of functioning. It may be, for example, that individuals who possess high levels of coping resources are likely to perceive functioning problems more quickly and correctly than individuals with lower levels of resources.

The response to perceived functioning problems by the individual depends on the comparison of these perceptions to goals or desired levels of functioning. We must then specify where these "goals" come from, and identify how the discrepancy between these goals and the perceived functioning level are defined. There are many interesting possibilities here, but we will, at least for baseline purposes, use one of the simplest:

A   FGI.K = CLIP(100,FAI.K,100–FAI.K,0)
A   FDISCI.K = MAX(FGI.K–FAI.K,0)

The first of these statements says that the functioning goal that the individual holds for their self (FGI) is equal to 100 or to the current perceived level of functioning (FAI), whichever is larger. That is, individuals seek to maintain a level of functioning that is no lower than their current level or the baseline level of 100. The second statement says that the functioning discrepancy apparent to the individual (FDISCI) is the simple difference between the functioning goal (FGI) and the perceived current level (FAI), but may not be a negative quantity. That is, individuals do not view functioning at levels higher than their goal levels as problematic.

Again, we make no claim that this particular specification of the process is the proper specification. The processes by which individuals set goals for their own functioning is a separate and interesting problem that we will not pursue here. Individual's goals might change over time as a function of group support, past functioning performances, individual resources, or perhaps even adjust for stressful events by temporarily discounting the level of demands that individuals make on themselves. We have regarded the functioning discrepancy as a simple linear difference between goal and perceived functioning. Again, more complex views are possible. For example, small discrepancies may receive little weight, medium-sized discrepancies may be regarded as very serious, but very large discrepancies might be viewed as hopeless. This kind of view could lead to nonlinearities in individual response to stress that show increasing marginal responsiveness up to a threshold, but then resignation and complete absence of coping in the presence of severe stress.

Once the individual has perceived a functioning problem and identified its seriousness by comparison to goals, resources are mobilized to reduce the discrepancy. Individual's responses, however, are limited by available coping resources. For our baseline model, let's represent this part of the process as follows:

A	C.K = PARM8*CLIP(CRL.K,DC.K,DC.K–CRL.K,0)
C	PARM8 = .25
A	DC.K = FDISCI.K
A	CRL.K = MAX(PARM9*PR.K,0)
C	PARM9 = .03

The first of these statements says that the level of coping effort (C) is equal to a coping response limit (CRL) if the desired coping response (DC) is greater than the coping resources limit; if not, then the response is equal to the desired coping response. Whichever quantity is selected, it is delayed by a response time parameter (PARM8). More simply, the level of coping effort is equal to the desired coping effort, but cannot exceed the resources available. In either case, there is a delay in mobilizing resources. The third statement is actually redundant in this model, simply relabeling the desired coping effort as equal to the full magnitude of the functioning discrepancy. The fourth and fifth statements define the coping response limit (CRL) as equal to 3% of the available personal resources (PR). The extent to which an individual is able to respond to stress is limited by the individual's available coping resources. Individuals with generally low levels of personal resources, or individuals who have suffered acute loss of resources due to a stressful event are less able to restore their own functioning by "coping."

As with the other parts of the model, when we make our theory completely explicit by embodying it in a set of formal statements, its limitations become very clear. Without doubt, far more complex, realistic, and interesting specifications of how individuals respond to perceived functioning discrepancies could be attempted. One must, however, start somewhere, and simple initial models are to be preferred because we can comprehend their behavior.

For the purposes of our baseline, we will conceptualize the reproduction of personal coping resources and the limits that these resources place on coping in a rather simple fashion. First, we define the level of personal resources and initialize the quantity:

L $PR.K = PR.J+(DT)(PRIR.JK-PRLR.JK)$
N $PR = PRI$
C $PRI = 100$

Here, the level of personal resources (PR) is increased by a personal resources increase rate (PRIR), and decreased by a personal resources loss rate (PRLR).

Losses of personal resources occur as a consequence of stressful life events occurring for the focal individual:

R $PRLR.KL = MAX(PARM10*S2.K,0)$
C $PARM10 = 1.0$

That is, the resource loss in a period of time (PRLR) is equal to some proportion (PARM10) of the life stress that has occurred (S2.K) or zero, whichever is greater. While the parameter in question could be made a function of other variables, we will treat it as a constant in our baseline model.

The definition of the process that restores personal resources is slightly more complex:

R $PRIR.KL = PARM11*MIN(IRD.K,10)$
A $IRD.K = MAX(PRI-PR.K,0)$
C $PARM11 = 1.0$

The second statement here calculates an individual resources discrepancy (IRD) that is equal to the difference between the initial level of resources and the current level, but restricted to be a positive number. The first statement then specifies that the personal resource increase rate (PRIR) is some percentage (PARM11) of the discrepancy, but cannot exceed 10 units per unit of time. This is a very simple model of the process of the renewal of personal resources, and further work could contribute to a far more realistic and subtle model. Since the renewal of personal resources is not our central concern here, we will live with the oversimplification.

We have now specified how individuals respond to perceived loss of functioning by mobilizing coping resources. The model that we have put forward is a familiar smart feedback system, but one in which response is limited by available resources—which, in turn, depend on the occurrence of stressful life events.

Social Network Compensatory Support

In addition to "preventing" untoward events and "buffering" the negative consequences for functioning that follow from them, individual's social networks are a source of resources that can be mobilized to restore a stressed person to normal levels of functioning. Our model supposes that the processes of compensatory social support operate very much like those of individual responses to stress. That is, actors in the network of which the individual is a part monitor the functioning of the focal individual, compare this performance to expectations, and mobilize resources in support of the focal individual when there is a perceived discrepancy between the expected and perceived functioning level of the individual. As in the case of individual coping responses, network support response is limited by available resources, and network resources may themselves be damaged by the occurrence of stressful events.

We can quickly develop this portion of the model as analogous to the individual coping process. First, the level of functioning (F) is monitored and filtered by some function (FUNCT2) into a level of functioning as perceived by the network (FAN):

A   FAN.K = FUNCT2*F.K
C   FUNCT2 = 1.0

We will, at least initially, assume that there is no delay, bias, or noise in network perceptions of individual functioning, and that these perceptions are independent of the levels of functioning and network resources. In practice, of course, we would presume that the speed and accuracy of the network's monitoring of the focal individual might very well depend upon the strength of the network and operate more slowly than individual's monitoring of their own functioning.

Once the network has perceived the functioning of the focal individual, the level is compared to the functioning goal held by the network for the focal individual (FGN), and discrepancies between the observed and goal state noted (FDISCN):

| A | FGN.K = CLIP(100,FAN.K,100−FAN.K,0) |
| A | FDISCN.K = MAX(FGN.K−FAN.K,0) |

As with individual's goals and perceived discrepancies, we have presumed that the network seeks to restore the individual to the baseline level of 100, or to the level in the previous period—whichever is higher. We also presume that discrepancies of functioning are perceived by the network as a simple linear difference between goals and perceived functioning.

The network's responses to functioning discrepancies are set equal to either a fixed proportion (PARM13) of the existing discrepancy (DSS) or to the same proportion of the maximum available network resources (SSRL). The latter, in turn, is a constant proportion (PARM13) of total network resources (NR):

A	DSS.K = FDISCN.K
A	SSRL.K = PARM12*NR.K
C	PARM12 = .02
A	SS.K = PARM13*CLIP(SSRL.K,DSS.K,DSS.K−SSRL.K,0)
C	PARM13 = .25

As in the individual's coping response process, we have supposed that response is delayed somewhat (PARM13), and that it is limited by available resources. In this case, we have limited the maximum possible response to be equal to 2% of network resources in any period of time (PARM12).

The network resources available at any point in time (NR) are a function of a self-renewal process (NRIR) that restores losses in network resources (NRLR) after the occurrence of stressful events:

L	NR.K = NR.J+(DT)(NRIR.JK−NRLR.JK)
N	NR = NRI
C	NRI = 100

Losses of network resources occur as a direct function of stressful events (S2):

R   NRLR.KL = PARM14*MAX(S2.K,0)
C   PARM14 = 1.0

Network resources are replenished in direct proportion to their discrepancy from their initial levels, but limited to a maximum renewal of 10 units per unit of time:

A   NRD.K = MAX(100–NR.K,0)
R   NRIR.KL = PARM15*MIN(NRD.K,10)
C   PARM15 = 1.0

Initially, at least, we will presume that the parameters, as well as the structure of the network social support system are identical to those of individual coping. The only difference between individual and network responsiveness in the baseline model then, is that the network is limited to 2% of its resources as an upper limit on response, while the individual may allocate up to 3%. Again, this is an unrealistic set of assumptions and suggests a place where further work is called for to clarify how the dynamics of social network support differ from those of individual coping.

With the connection of the group to the individual, we have now completed the translation of the theory into a baseline model. The complete DYNAMO program for this model is provided in the Appendix. As we have pointed out at a number of places in this process, we have made among the simplest possible assumptions about many of connections, and much more elaborate and realistic assumptions could be made. Before we begin to explore these possibilities, however, we need to understand the performance characteristics of our baseline.

Behavior of the Baseline Model

With a theory as complex as the one embodied in our baseline model, the dynamic properties of the system are not entirely obvious. It is quite important, therefore, to explore the behavior of the baseline model carefully before proceeding to experiments and elaborations. As we discussed in an earlier chapter, it is most important to grasp the equilibrium tendencies and bounds of the system, and to explore it's transient response to shocks as ways of getting a feel for its range of possible behaviors.

For our first experiment we will put the system in what we believe to be its equilibrium condition and see if (1) our notions about the equilibrium condition are correct and (2) whether the system remains at the initial levels in the absence of shocks. For our second experiment we will subject the system in equilibrium to a mild exogenous shock and see whether it returns to equilibrium, finds a new equilibrium, or becomes unstable. Both of these experiments are performed by simulation using the program as shown in the Appendix.

In this simulation, the system is set initially to a functioning level of 100, personal and network resource levels are set at 100, and personal and individual resource renewal rates (.035 and .025) are set at levels sufficient to cope with the level of chronic stress (which is set at 10 units per unit of time). These levels are likely to produce equilibrium behavior because all discrepancies between functioning and goals, and between resource levels and goals are zero. The level of chronic hazard in the environment (10) should be within the "carrying capacity" of the system at full resources, such that such hazards do not result in distress because of the operation of prevention and buffering. At the tenth time point, the system is subjected to a stressful life event of peak magnitude 100, so that the transient response characteristics of the system can be explored. An event of this magnitude, while noticeable, is not likely to exceed the equilibrating capacity of the system (if indeed it does equilibrate), and hence provides a test of the "normal" coping and social support response to acute distress.

The results of these baseline experiments are shown in three panels of Figure 11.3.

All of the trace lines remain stable for the first 10 time points, demonstrating (a) that when there are no discrepancies between functioning and resource levels and their goal states, no change occurs, (b) that the system in equilibrium tends to remain in equilibrium, and (c) that the "prevention" and "buffering" processes are filtering out environmental hazards so that no distress is occurring (see the last panel of the figure).

The transient response to stressful events is also what we might have anticipated. After the event, discrepancies are created between the perceived level of functioning and the goal state held for functioning by both the focal individual and the network (see the functioning curve in (11.3). These discrepancies are reduced exponentially (at 25% of the remaining discrepancy in each time period) by both individual compensatory coping responses and compensatory social support responses (second panel). Individual coping has a greater effect than social support because we had specified that individual coping was limited to 3% of the personal resource base while social support was limited to 2% of the

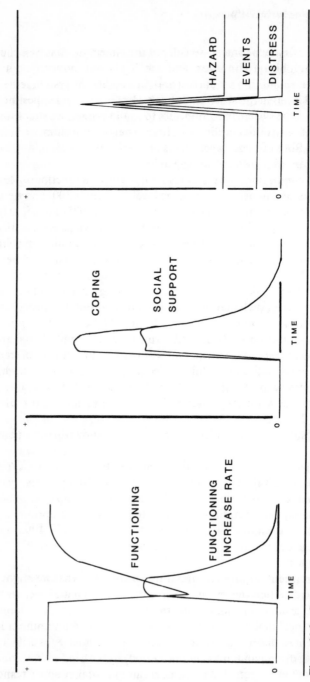

Figure 11.3: Stress, coping, and social support: baseline model.

network resource base. This results in a "ceiling" on network support response to the stressful event.

In a second set of experiments (not shown in detail here), the reaction of the system to differing initial conditions of personal resources, network resources, and functioning were explored. As we had specified in building the system, when resource or functioning levels are initially below the goal state, positive action occurs to restore them to the goal level. When the levels of any of the resource or functioning levels exceeds the goal state, no action one way or the other occurs. That is, functioning below the goal level results in return to the goal level; functioning above the goal level remains stable at its initial level. In the current model, however, chronic stress will gradually down resources or functioning that exceeds the goal levels of 100 units, since no coping occurs when functioning is already above the goal level.

An Experiment: Finding the Equilibrium Bounds

The baseline system succeeds in restoring functioning to its goal level in the face of minor and transient stressful events. But is the system capable of dealing with all levels and kinds of stress? That is, does it always attain equilibrium at "full functioning?" To explore this question, we conducted two additional experiments. In the first we progressively increased the magnitude of the acute stressful event until a level was found at which the system could no longer "cope" (obviously an experiment that one can perform with a simulation, but not with people). In the second experiment we subjected the system to a chronic new stress of substantial magnitude (10 units); that is, we changed the level of stress occurring in each time period from the background level of 10 to a new level of 20.

Acute Stress

As it turns out, it takes a quite severe acute event to drive the system beyond its equilibrium bounds (that is, to drive functioning to the level zero, where coping and social support cease, resulting in a "low level equilibrium trap"). In Table 11.1, we show the minimum resource levels and minimum functioning levels resulting from shocks of various peak magnitudes occurring at t = 10.

An acute event must have a peak magnitude of between 225 and 250 in intensity to reduce the functioning of the focal individual to zero and bring the restorative coping and social support processes to an end.[8]

TABLE 11.1
Baseline Model Responses to Acute Stress

Peak Magnitude of Shock	Minimum Level of Functioning Reached	Minimum Level of Resources Reached
10	98.6	94.6
20	96.2	93.5
40	91.2	89.7
60	86.0	84.4
80	80.5	79.2
100	75.0	74.0
150	57.4	68.4
200	31.9	47.8
225	14.9	41.3
250	0.0	34.8
300	0.0	21.7

Note that it is not necessary for personal resources or network resources to be reduced to zero for complete loss of functioning to occur in this scenario.

Increasingly serious events create increasingly longer recovery times as coping and network resources are destroyed by the events. In Figure 11.4, for example, some results are shown for a stressful life event of peak magnitude 225.

In the first panel the level of functioning is shown. Note that functioning continues to decline for a period of time after the stressful event. This is because so many personal and network resources have been destroyed by the event that coping and social support are not even sufficient to deal with the "chronic" stress of everyday events. Because, in our specification, both personal and network resources are self-generating at relatively high rates; however, resources sufficient for coping and support are eventually accumulated and functioning begins a long but exponential climb back toward the goal state.

Severe acute stress, then, not only can drive a system to a point where it is no longer able to restore equilibrium, but severe stresses also substantially reduce the rates at which recovery occurs.

Chronic Stress

While the system is quite capable of dealing with even very high levels of acute stress, it is far less able to recover functioning in the face of chronic or continuing stress. Indeed, if the level of chronic stress exceeds the "carrying capacity" of the system (which is a function of the rates at

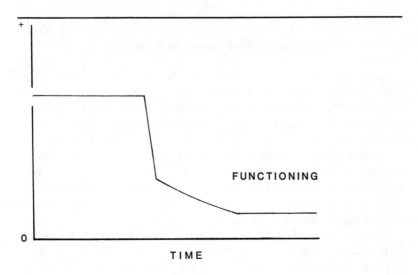

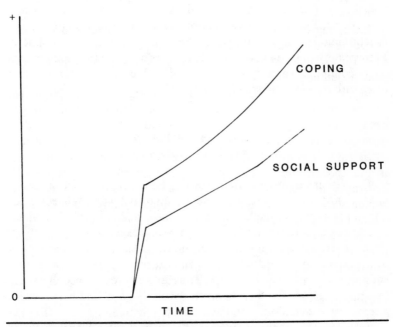

Figure 11.4: Stress, coping, and social support: extreme stress.

which personal and network resources are regenerated), a linear downward trend in functioning results until the individual ceases to function.

In one simple experiment, when the level of chronic stress was raised from 10 to 20 units per unit of time at time point 10, the level of functioning was driven to zero by time 20. Given the parameters of the baseline model, personal and network resources are capable of "refreshing" themselves at a rate sufficient to cope with chronic stress levels of between 10 and 15 units, but cannot recover when subjected to continuing shocks of greater magnitudes; network and personal resources continue to be destroyed at rates faster than they can be created, the capacity to cope or render social support is thereby reduced, and functioning declines until death occurs.

The baseline model with its highly simplified assumptions is capable of producing some interesting behavioral patterns. It appears to be an adequate representation of the general theory in that it produces equilibrium-seeking coping and social-support responses to stressful events. More than this, however, we have found (by intuitively guided "sensitivity" testing) that the system does have equilibrium bounds, and that the time shapes of its behavior are sensitive to resource levels, functioning levels, and the magnitude and time shape of shocks. Perhaps most important, the model produces behavior that is interesting in its complexity and appears to mimic some of our intuitions and observations about stress and coping.

Two Experiments: Resource
Strength and Perception Delay

The baseline model is a useful starting point for theoretical analysis, but is clearly too simple in a number of important ways. While it is not our purpose in this chapter to explore these possibilities in any great detail, let's look into two of them with simple experiments.

In the stress and coping model the individual is protected by two sets of processes, one based on their own efforts at coping, the other on support from their social network. Thus far we have assumed that these two processes operate in very much the same ways, and hence act as alternative mechanisms for maintaining functioning. This assumed equivalence is probably quite unrealistic. In particular, the strengths of individual's personal and network resources are highly variable, and personal coping may be much more efficacious than social support because of more accurate and rapid perception and faster mobilization of resources. Let's briefly explore some of the implications of these differences between individual coping and network social support for the speed of individual's recovery from acute stress events.

Resource Strength

For a first experiment, we subject our focal individual to a stressful event of peak magnitude 100 at time point 5 and measure the level of functioning attained some time later (time point 20). In this experiment, as in our baseline model, individual coping is regarded as more efficacious than network support by allowing a higher proportion of available personal resources to be used for coping (3.5%) than network resources (2.5%). The question that we ask here is how well individuals recover if they are themselves weak or strong (implemented by varying personal resources from 50 to 100 to 150 units as starting values), and if they are members of resource-poor or resource-rich social networks (implemented by varying network resource starting values from 50 to 100 to 150 units). The results of these experiments are shown in Figure 11.5.

The results of this experiment are rather easy to anticipate with a bit of thought, but nonetheless rather important. Because the mobilization of personal resources can occur with greater intensity than that of network resources, the "main effect" of varying personal resources is greater than of varying network resources. Much more important to note, however, is the strong "interaction" effect of personal and network resources. Individuals who are both weak themselves and have poor network resources have a far more difficult time recovering from acute stresses than would be predicted simply on the basis of the sum of the effects of poor personal resources and poor network resources; that is, being simultaneously weak in both sets of resources increases risk of poor coping multiplicatively, not additively.

The implications of this experiment are twofold. First, and again quite obviously, since personal coping is more effective than network support in this model, better returns in functioning are achieved if personal rather than network resources are strengthened. Second, and less obviously, because of the interaction of personal and network resources, the returns in functioning to increased resources depend upon the existing distribution of resources. If, for example, personal and network resources are about equal, then the greatest returns in increased functioning come from increasing individual resources. If, however, either personal or individual resources are at extremely low levels, greater returns in overall functioning are attained by assuring at least

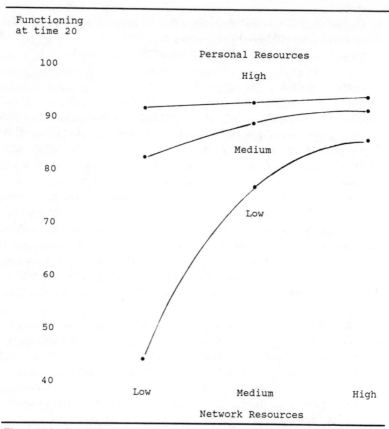

Figure 11.5: **Personal and network resources effects on functioning recovery.**

minimal levels of both personal and network resources. These unequal "marginal returns" to investment in personal or network resources are the natural consequence of the interaction of the two types of resources in maintaining functioning, and are similar (indeed, they are mathematically equivalent to) "production frontier" analysis in economic theory.

Perception Delay

Personal and social-network resources may also differ in their effects on individual functioning because of the speed with which these resources can be mobilized. While individual coping might be presumed to occur quite rapidly, network responses usually take longer. Networks may not monitor the functioning of an individual member very closely (perhaps varying by the centrality of the individual in the network), may take some time to "decide" that support is necessary, and may be slower in mobilizing and delivering resources.

To get some sense of the importance of these kinds of delays, we performed another experiment with our baseline model responding to a stress event of peak magnitude 100 at the fifth time point. In this experiment a third-order exponential delay was introduced in the network's perception of change in individual functioning, and the average length of the delay was varied from one to seven time periods.

As anticipated, network delay in perceiving that individual functioning had declined (and also delays in perceiving that it is improving as a result of individual coping) does slow network social support response and reduce the speed of the recovery from the stressful event. Somewhat surprisingly, however, functioning is quite insensitive to changes in network perception delays. With an average delay of one time period, functioning had returned to a level of 89.63 by the twentieth time period. With a much longer delay of average length of seven, functioning recovery was only very slightly reduced, attaining a value of 89.23 by the twentieth time period. Thus, while the effect is in the expected direction, and while network social support responses are fairly strongly affected, overall functioning is rather insensitive to network perception delay in this particular scenario. Of course, additional delays in processing information and responding would have further effects, but these are also unlikely to have much impact. And changes in other parameters of the baseline model could interact with network response times in such a way that greater sensitivity to delay might be apparent in alternative models. In the current model, however, we must conclude that the intensity, rather than the speed, of personal and network responses to crisis is far more important.

Directions for Further Elaboration

The simple experiments that we have conducted here give some sense of the variety of behavior that the baseline model can produce and also aid us in identifying areas where further elaboration of the theory might be productive. While the baseline specification is capable of producing a wide range of behaviors, many of which seem intuitively reasonable, it is obviously oversimplified. More realistic models could be suggested that are capable of an even wider range of responses. Among these possibilities are a number that call for some additional conceptualization and some that call for making the current model more complex and dynamic.

Our experiments suggest that the duration and time shape of stress events are critical to system performance, even more so than the simple "seriousness" or maximum stress intensity induced by the events. In particular, events with substantial duration appear to be far more detrimental than short episodes, even when the short episodes are extremely stressful. While this conclusion is dependent upon the particular specification of the personal and social network resource renewal processes specified in the baseline model, it does suggest a fruitful direction for further research. Most current work in this area has focused simply on event intensity—consistent with the cross-sectional and static biases of existing theory. If we are to be concerned with dynamics, however, the current results suggest that duration and time-shape may be far more consequential. This in turn suggests that stressful events need to be classified in terms of duration and time-shape, as well as intensity.

Our analysis suggests a second aspect of "stressful life events" that is quite consequential and hence is worthy of further research. In our experiments we have made very simple assumptions about the ways that events impact on personal and social network resources. We have assumed that events have equal impacts on personal and on social network resources, and that all stressful life events have substantial impacts on resource levels. These assumptions are quite consequential because they result in limitation of the resources available to an individual to cope or to a network to provide support during stressful events. Obviously, not all events have equal impacts on individual and on network resources. Some events are highly consequential because they reduce individual's resources and hence call for greater network support; other events may be highly consequential because they weaken the connection between individuals and their social networks. In understanding whether individual coping or social-network support is the more useful response to depressed functioning we must more carefully specify the nature of the precipitating event in terms of its consequences for personal or social network resources. Widowhood, for example, is usually a major blow to the personal support network, but may not necessarily reduce personal coping resources. Unemployment, in contrast, reduces income substantially, but may not have great effects on the strength of network ties.

We might also consider some changes at the level of modification in the basic structure of the model. In the baseline model we have assumed that individual and personal resources are "self-generating" and that stressful events destroy accumulated resources but not the capacity to produce resources. This assumption is questionable in terms of what we believe we know about responses to stress, and is extremely consequential for the behavior of the model. If stress events not only reduced the levels of personal/network resources, but also the capacity to produce new resources, the tendency of the system to seek equilibrium at its initial level could well be lost. In fact, we believe intuitively that some stressful events not only are costly in terms of personal and network support resources, but also reduce the capacity of the individual and the network to generate resources—as in permanent physical disability or the death of a spouse. Again, events differ qualitatively as well as quantitatively in these effects, and these differences deserve more research because of the fundamentally different dynamic behavior of systems that have self-regenerating resources and those that do not. In many regards, we suspect that the baseline model is far too "optimistic" in its specification, and more realistic models would suggest poorer coping and more enduring disability as more realistic outcomes of many types of events.

At a number of points in the baseline model we have made simplifying assumptions that certain parameters are constants. Most notably we assumed that the capacity of personal and network resources to renew themselves were constant; the speed and accuracy of monitoring of functioning was regarded as constant; the goals of individuals and their networks for levels of functioning were regarded as constants; and the speed and intensity of responses to perceived functioning discrepancies were fixed. None of these specifications is necessary, and all are somewhat suspect. One major direction for further elaboration of the baseline would be to make each of these constants a dynamic rather than a fixed quantity. Changes of these types are also highly consequential in that they create new "loops" that are not present in the baseline model; because they have this fundamental character, their consequences for the behavioral tendencies of the model are not directly deducible—and might differ substantially from the baseline.

Suppose, for example, that the capacity of personal and social networks to generate resources changed with the level of resources accumulated. If richer individuals or networks were able to renew a larger proportion of their resources in a period of time than resource-poor persons or networks, then the discrepancies between "rich" and "poor" present in the baseline would be exacerbated. At the lower end, it would take far longer for badly stressed individuals to recover from extreme events than the current model suggests.

One might also suppose that the accuracy and speed of functioning monitoring was dynamic rather than static. It might reasonably be hypothesized, for example, that members of resource-poor networks must devote more effort to maintaining their own functioning and thus are slower to perceive functioning changes than individuals in rich networks. The delay time in network perception of individual functioning, then, might increase as the resource level of the network decreases. In a parallel fashion one might suppose that the proportion of resources that an individual could mobilize for coping or that a social network could spare for rendering support varied positively with the level of personal or network resources. Both of these more dynamic possibilities would seem to suggest further discrepancies in the recovery times of "rich" and "poor" individuals.

One last possibility for greater dynamic flexibility is to allow "goals" to vary as a function of other variables—causing the system to be always "chasing" a changing equilibrium point. For example, we have supposed that individuals seek to rise no higher in functioning than their initial condition. We might suppose that individuals seek growth rather than stability; that richer individuals have higher goals than poorer people; or, perhaps, that individuals "adjust" their goals to accept, at least temporarily, lower levels of functioning in the face of stress. This last possibility represents yet another form of coping, in that goals are softened (and hence discrepancies between goals and functioning lessened) in response to stressful events.

There are two rather different directions suggested here, and let's pause for just a moment to be sure that the distinction is clear. On one hand, the baseline model can be much more fully explored by varying the kinds of stimuli to which it is subjected, and by varying the parameters governing its response to these stimuli. We have only scratched the surface of the possible areas of "sensitivity" analysis that could be conducted with the baseline. On the other hand, we have also proposed the possibility of some more fundamental changes in the structure of the model itself—that is, in the nature of the connectivities among quantities. In particular, the model could be made far more "dynamic" than it currently is by changing constant parameters into effects that vary as a consequence of system levels. Changes of this latter type make the system more "complex" in that the connectivity of the system is increased and the number of "constants" reduced and "variables" increased. While the system that we have designed here is quite "smart" relative to existing theories of stress and coping, it could—and probably should—be made still more self-referencing and smarter.

Conclusions

In this chapter we have developed and partially explored a model of a relatively complex and "smart" social system. The model is similar to the earlier "arms race" model in that it involves the dynamic interaction between a focal actor and an environment. In the current case, however, the connections between the actor and the environment are much more complicated and contingent than in the earlier model, reflecting higher degrees of awareness and interaction, rather than reaction, on the part of the actors.

The model that we have developed in this chapter is intended to mimic the behavior of individuals coping with the distress induced by exogeneous life events, and the role played by individual's social networks in this process. This particular substantive problem, of course, is of limited interest—though we all suffer stress and attempt to cope. The stress-coping-support model, however, is far more general when considered as an abstract "system." In this model we have two actors, each facing internal constraints (resource limitations), interacting on the basis of their own goals (desired levels of functioning), in ways that cause each to continuously monitor the interaction and adjust their behavior as a result of the actions of the other and their own past actions. While the details would differ very greatly, one can readily imagine using the current model as a template for developing theoretical analyses of such smart interaction between government officials and the mass public; between profit seeking firms interacting across markets; or between kin or ethnic groups. Social action and interaction, considered as dynamic systems, have a great deal in common across substantive areas. And the basic models that we develop to analyze dynamics in one area can often be usefully applied as starting points in other areas.

As we have developed it in the current chapter, the model of stress-coping-support dynamics has been kept deliberately "simple." That is, while it is much more complex than existing statistical or mathematical models of such dynamics, it is still far from representing the full richness of qualitative accounts of such interactions. There is no technical barrier to extending the model to attempt to capture more of the texture of real events. We have proposed only two actors in the system, but there is no reason why we could not have many separate actors. Indeed, rather than an abstract "network," we could model the specific sectors of the network (e.g., family, coworkers, social service personnel, etc.) or even the individual actors in the network. We have not distinguished among types of events or types of resources, coping, and support. Again, there is no technical reason why one should not separately model the dynamics of, for example, chronic versus acute stress events or distinguish between the dynamics of material and emotional resources. As we discussed in the previous section, there is no necessary technical reason that so many parts of the system be governed by "constants," and the behavior of the model could be made far more complex and dynamic than we have.

The reasons that we have not pursued these possibilities further are quite straight forward. First, of course, there is a limit to how much our reader can tolerate. While the current model is very general and interesting in the abstract, more detailed applications to stress and coping are better left to a specialized work. Second, and more important, the current model is complex enough to suggest the wide range of applicability and the quite striking behavioral possibilities of even quite simple "smart" models. And third, with increased complexity comes decreasing analyzability. The current model, for all its simplifying assumptions and caveats, is still complicated enough to generate some unexpected results and new insights. While we have continuously urged that theorists construct more complicated (as well as more systematic) models, there are very real limits of how much complexity of theory is useful. If one cannot even approximately understand the implications of one's own theory, it is too complicated. The current model has that possibility if pushed too much further.

Notes

1. For a survey of recent advances and applications in game theory applications in the social sciences, see Shubik, (1984a) and (1984b).

2. There is a large literature on assessing the magnitudes of stressful life events. A good introduction to the literature on the measurement of event magnitude and the consequences of events for physical and mental health can be found in Brown and Philliber (1981), Holmes and Masuda (1974), Holmes and Rahe (1967), and Rabkin and Struening (1976).

3. The leading examples of efforts to apply statistical models to over-time data in the study of change in functioning are Thoits (1982) and Cronkite and Moos (1984).

4. Some exemplary empirical studies connecting the strength of networks with stress buffering include Dean and Lin (1977), Gore (1985), LaRocco et al. (1980), and Pearlin and Schooler (1978).

5. For reviews of the numerous competing and partially overlapping models of the relationships among stress, coping, and social support, see House (1981), Thoits (1982), and Wheaton (1985). In this chapter we follow the terminology and development of House (1981).

6. Individuals, of course, may display considerable variability in their ability to buffer stress by cognitive mechanisms. One major thrust of programs for the treatment of stress disorders involves the application of cognitive therapy. See, for example, Taylor (1983).

7. Though we have not done so in the current model, a CLIP or SWITCH could be added in the current model to stop all further change in either functioning increase or loss when the current level of functioning was driven to zero.

8. This result depends on the fineness of the integration. For the results in this chapter, each time unit was divided into four parts for the purpose of integrating rates of change (i.e., $DT = .25$).

APPENDIX 11.1. Stress, Coping, and Social Support Model

*	STRESS, COPING, AND SOCIAL SUPPORT MODEL
NOTE	
NOTE	FUNCTIONING
NOTE	
L	F.K = MAX(F.J+(DT)(FIR.JK–FLR.JK),0)
N	F = FI
C	FI = 100
NOTE	
R	FLR.KL = MAX((PARM1*DIS.K),0)
C	PARM1 = 1.0
NOTE	
R	FIR.KL = MAX((PARM2*C.K)+(PARM3*SS.K),0)
C	PARM2 = 1.0
C	PARM3 = 1.0
NOTE	
NOTE	STRESS AND DISTRESS
NOTE	
A	S1.K = EXOG.K
A	EXOG.K = 10.0+PULSE(MAG,5,30)
C	MAG = 100
NOTE	
A	S2.K = MAX(S1.K–PARM4*NR.K–PARM5*PR.K,0)
C	PARM4 = .025
C	PARM5 = .035
NOTE	
A	DIS.K = MAX(S2.K–PARM6*NR.K–PARM7*PR.K,0)
C	PARM6 = .025
C	PARM7 = .035
NOTE	
NOTE	COPING
NOTE	
A	FAI.K = FUNCT*F.K
C	FUNCT = 1.0
NOTE	
A	FGI.K = CLIP(100,FAI.K,100–FAI.K,0)
A	FDISCI.K = MAX(FGI.K–FAI.K,0)
NOTE	
A	C.K = PARM8*CLIP(CRL.K,DC.K,DC.K–CRL.K,0)
C	PARM8 = .25
A	DC.K = FDISCI.K
A	CRL.K = MAX(PARM9*PR.K,0)
C	PARM9 = .03
NOTE	
L	PR.K = PR.J+(DT)(PRIR.JK–PRLR.JK)
N	PR = PRI
C	PRI = 100
NOTE	

```
R        PRLR.KL = MAX(PARM10*S2.K,0)
C        PARM10 = 1.0
NOTE
R        PRIR.KL = PARM11*MIN(IRD.K,10)
A        IRD.K = MAX(100-PR.K,0)
C        PARM11 = 1.0
NOTE
NOTE                     NETWORK SUPPORT
NOTE
A        FAN.K = FUNCT2*F.K
C        FUNCT2 = 1.0
NOTE
A        FGN.K = CLIP(100,FAN.K,100-FAN.K,0)
A        FDISCN.K = MAX(FGN.K-FAN.K,0)
NOTE
A        DSS.K = FDISCN.K
A        SSRL.K = PARM12*NR.K
C        PARM12 = .02
A        SS.K = PARM13*CLIP(SSRL.K,DSS.K,DSS.K-SSRL.K,0)
C        PARM13 = .25
NOTE
L        NR.K = NR.J+(DT)(NRIR.J-NRLR.JK)
N        NR = NRI
C        NRI = 100
NOTE
R        NRLR.KL = PARM14*MAX(S2.K,0)
C        PARM14 = 1.0
NOTE
A        NRD.K = MAX(100-NR.K,0)
R        NRIR.KL = PARM15*MIN(NRD.K,10)
C        PARM15 = 1.0
NOTE
NOTE                    OUTPUT SPECIFICATION
NOTE
SPEC        DT = .25/ LENGTH = 25/PRTPER = 1/PLTPER = 1
PRINT       F,PR,NR
PLOT        F = */FIR = +/FLR =.
PLOT        C = */SS = +
RUN
```

12

Systems and Subsystems: Alternative Views of Societal Dynamics

Analysts concerned with large-scale and long-term changes in political, economic, and cultural structures have frequently put forward explicitly dynamic theories.[1] These theories are particularly interesting to us in the affinity that they display for the types of systems dynamics models that we have advocated in this volume. In this chapter we will examine parts of the thinking of two such theorists: Vilfredo Pareto and Karl Marx, each of whom developed quite complex and rigorous views of societal change that are readily transformed into formal systems models. The models and analyses in this chapter are based on earlier work with Charles Powers (on Pareto) and Randall Collins (on Marx).[2] Without their extensive knowledge of these writers and their substantial work in building formal dynamic models, the current chapter would not have been possible. The weaknesses, oversimplifications, and errors in the current chapter, however, should not be attributed to these collaborators.

The purpose of this exercise is not to advocate the views of either Marx or Pareto, but rather to illustrate some of the directions that can be taken in developing more complex models of social dynamics. The models of Marx and Pareto, at least as we interpret their writings, share a number of important similarities, display some interesting contrasts, and are very suggestive about how models for representing quite complex systems can be effectively developed. Most importantly, each writer conceptualizes societies as systems of "subsystems" and sees social change as driven by the internal dynamics of the parts and by the coupling together of the parts into the whole. Social action, as in the stress-coping-support model, is seen as a consequence of the dynamic tendencies of each subsystem (i.e., the focal individual and the social network as "subsystems") and of the interaction of the subsystems. The subsystems of Pareto and Marx are structurally the same as those in previous models. Conceptually, however, they are quite different. In the models in earlier chapters the "subsystems" have been individual actors (nation states, political parties, persons undergoing stress, etc.). In the work of Marx and Pareto, the "subsystems" are sets of general variables or institutional sectors rather than individual actors. While the two theorists see the nature of these connections and their dynamic implications quite differently, they share a common systems/subsystems way of thinking about social change.

This way of thinking about complex phenomena is central to the systems method for building theories about complex phenomena, whether one is concerned with economic, political, cultural, sociological, or psychological dynamics. The approach also holds with equal value whether one works at the "micro" level, the "macro" level, or seeks to build models integrating the levels of analysis. The essence of the approach lies in disassembling extremely complex dynamics into much simpler parts and simple relations among the parts. By building and understanding the behavior of each part of a complex system of action and understanding the relations between each of the parts, one gradually constructs an approximate understanding of the whole system. This method of disassembling complex systems into simpler subsystems that can be understood does not necessarily imply that an exact understanding of the whole system is possible. But without understanding of each part and the relations among parts there can be no understanding at all of the complex patterns of behavior that systems composed of linked subsystems can produce.

Marx and Pareto are intriguing writers precisely in the complexity of the system behaviors that are implied by the seemingly quite simple subsystems and simple connections among them. The central dynamic models of each author are relatively easy to formalize, and are quite similar in structure—though not in implications.

The Problem: The Dynamics of Economic, Political, and Cultural Change

Karl Marx and Vilfredo Pareto were centrally concerned with the sources and implications of cyclical crises in the Western European societies as they underwent the early stages of industrialization, cultural "modernization" or "rationalization," and political democratization. In observing the European societies of the mid-nineteenth century, both analysts were struck by the booms and busts in economic activity, the cycles of political crises (not infrequently resulting in revolutionary violence), and the usually less violent, but nonetheless important intellectual and cultural crises and movements of the era. From similar observations, however, the two theorists distilled quite different views of the causes and implications of these events.

Marx, whose work is much more widely known, saw the fundamental sources of these crises in the exploitation of workers by capitalists arising from the institutions of private capital and wage labor. The internal dynamics of economic production under capitalism, Marx argued, led to increasingly serious episodic crises until the capacity of the system to recover was exceeded and revolution occurred. The crises of political and "ideological" institutions of society were seen as largely secondary and driven by the crises in the economic system. The (admittedly highly simplified) picture, then, is one of a system that cycles between growth and contraction of production, gradually losing its capacity to recover as the crises deepen. Ultimately, the collapse of the relations of production in the economic sector result in a revolutionary crises that changes the entire economic, political, and cultural systems of the society.

Pareto's views of the sources and consequences of the episodic crises of the Western societies were quite different. Rather than seeing fundamental contradictions in the "system" and tendencies toward ultimate disequilibrium, Pareto saw the crises of society as problems of adjustment and temporary excesses in economic, political, and cultural institutions. Rather than tending toward ultimate contradiction and destruction, the "crises" of society were actually the visible signs of institutions being adjusted and returned to their "normal" conditions by feedback processes.[3] The fundamental tendency of the system of modern society was toward stability and equilibrium; crises implied adjustment and stability rather than contradiction and instability.

Pareto's views of the mechanics of society, as well as his views of the meaning of its crises, were also different from those of Marx. Both saw societies as composed of interdependent economic, political, and cultural institutions (or subsystems). Both recognized, to varying degrees, that each institutional sector had its own internal logic and dynamism. And both argued that the crises and changes in each institutional sector was a source of strain, crisis, and change in other sectors. Marx, however, clearly placed a much greater weight than Pareto on the role of the economic system in determining both short-term and (particularly) long-term system behavior. The linkages from the economic subsystem to the cultural and political subsystems in Marx's theories are highly developed, but the "feedbacks" from these systems to the economic sector are not given great attention or weight. Pareto, in contrast, has a more fully developed view of the internal dynamics of political and cultural institutions, and gives considerable weight to the the effects of political and cultural changes on the behavior of the economic subsystem of society.

In the writings of Marx and Pareto we have interesting similarities and dissimilarities. For current purposes, the two theories are of particular interest because they are examples of models composed of multiple interacting subsystems (i.e., the "economic," the "political," and the "cultural" institutional sectors). The authors differ somewhat in their views of the internal dynamic tendencies of each subsystem and of the nature of the connectivity among the subsystems, and these differences produce strikingly differences in the dynamics implied by their theories.

Pareto's Societal Dynamics

Pareto's view of the structure of society is one of interconnected subsystems of material production, cultural production, and political control. Each of these subsystems is governed by an internal dynamic of negative feedback, and the three societal subsystems are coupled together in a further set of feedback relations. A simplified representation of these connections is shown in Figure 12.1.

The political cycle or subsystem is characterized as moving between centralization and decentralization of power, with excesses in either direction generating resistance that drives the subsystem toward balance. The cultural subsystem displays cyclical movement between traditionalism and acceptance of innovation. Excesses of either traditionalism or of innovativeness are seen as creating problems of alienation or anomie that act to drive cultural conditions toward more less extreme values. The economic subsystem, as well, consists of a negative feedback loop. Investment in capital goods gives rise to increased production; as production increases larger and larger shares are given over to consumption rather than savings; eventually there is insufficient investment to sustain growth and economic contraction occurs, driving the system back toward its origin. Similarly, in periods of depression the consumption share declines and the investment share increases, eventually generating sufficient capital to begin the recovery of productive capacity.

The three subsystems of Pareto's societal dynamic are coupled together in ways that partially reenforce and partially inhibit the internal dynamics of each. Traditionalism in popular beliefs tends to legitimate centralization, and at the same time to encourage economic

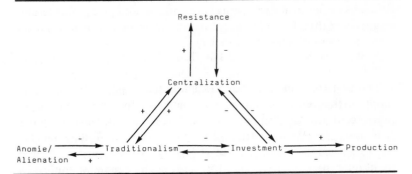

Figure 12.1: Pareto's societal dynamics.

development by increasing the propensity to save. The centralization of political power tends to reenforce traditional value orientations and at the same time discourages economic entrepreneurship. Economic expansion affects the dynamics of politics and culture by tending to create liberalism of popular belief and promoting decentralization of power. Taken together, the institutional sectors of society are seen as largely mutually reenforcing, while the dynamics within each sector act to limit the realizations of this largely positive cycle among the sectors.

Politics: Cycles of Centralization and Resistance

Pareto argues that the politics of any society tend to oscillate between the extreme concentration of power (centralization) and extremes of decentralization, with extremes in either direction engendering sufficient resistance to arrest and reverse trends. Once a system begins to move toward either centralization or decentralization, it develops momentum and, if no resistance were encountered, would continue until an unstable condition resulted. However, as either centralization or decentralization becomes increasingly severe, resistance rises rapidly. Eventually this resistance is sufficient to stop the momentum of the political trend and turns it around. Once the trend has been reversed, momentum builds in the opposite direction. We can capture these basic dynamics by specifying centralization/decentralization as a conserved level coupled to resistance in a (nonlinear) negative loop. For reasons that we will explain as we proceed, the DYNAMO code necessary to capture this process is a bit complicated. Let us begin with the level of centralization, its initialization, and the components of the rate that drive changes in centralization:

L   C.K = C.J+(DT)(DC.JK)
N   C = CI
C   CI = 0
R   DC.KL = CC.JK+CR.JK+CT.JK+CP.JK

The first three of these equations are quite familiar by now, and simply define centralization as a level affected by a rate (DC.JK, for "delta centralization"). This rate is defined as a sum of the four processes: Changes in centralization are driven by centralization itself (CC), by changes in resistance (CR), by changes in the level of traditionalism in the cultural sector (CT), and by changes in the level of economic productivity (CP).

The effects of cultural and economic conditions on changes in the concentration of political power are conceptualized very simply:

R   CT.KL = PARM3*T.K
C   PARM3 = .03
R   CP.KL = PARM4*P.K
C   PARM4 = -.06

That is, each increase in traditionalism (T) reenforces tendencies toward centralization by a proportional (PARM3) amount, while each increase in economic productivity (P) inhibits tendencies toward greater centralization by a proportional (PARM4) amount.

Pareto argues that changes in the level of political centralization display a form of inertia or momentum. That is, once a movement toward centralization begins, it tends to continue of its own force; once a movement toward decentralization occurs, the system will continue to move in that direction. We have captured this effect by making changes in centralization (DC) a function of past changes, using the following code:

R   CC.KL = PARM1*SMOOTH(DC.JK,1)
C   PARM1 = 1.25
C   CC = CCI
C   CCI = 0

The first statement says that one component of the rate of change in centralization (CC) is a function (PARM1) of SMOOTHed (that is, first-order exponentially delayed) prior changes in centralization (DC). The second statement, defining the value of PARM1, indicates that, all else being equal, current changes in centralization will be 1.25 times the changes that occurred in the previous period: Change accelerates. The use of the SMOOTH function in the first statement, and the use of the initialization (N and associated C) statements for this rate are necessary to make the system identified. If an intermediate "level" of changes in centralization was not created (by means of the SMOOTH function), and if this was not given a starting value, then we would be in the situation of attempting to calculate the starting value for the rate of change from its level at the same time as we were attempting to calculate the starting value for the level from its rate.

The final factor generating changes in centralization is resistance to extremes of concentration or deconcentration of power. To capture this process the first step is to this component of the rate of change in centralization (CR) as a function (PARM2) of the level of resistance:

R   CR.KL = PARM2*R.K
C   PARM2 = -1.0

The major nonlinearity in the theory lies in the way that resistance (and hence induced changes in centralization) depend upon the level of centralization itself. Pareto argues that, within quite broad limits around some "goal" level, there is little resistance engendered by the condition of centralization or decentralization of the system. However, as the discrepancy between the actual level of centralization or decentralization and the "goal" or "normal" level of centralization increases, increasing resistance is encountered. We can capture this part of the process with the following statements:

A   CD.K = CG-C.K
C   CG = 0
A   R.K = TABLE(RTAB,CD.K,-100,100,10)
T   RTAB = -51.2/-25.6/-12.8/-6.4/-3.2/-1.6/-.8/...
X   .1/.2/.4/.8/1.6/3.2/6.4/12.8/25.6/51.2

The first two statements define a "goal state" for centralization (CG) and calculate the discrepancy (CD) between the current level of the system and this goal. The remaining statements define the amount of resistance as an exponential function of this discrepancy. If, for example, centralization reached a value of -100 (that is, extreme decentralization), resistance would be equal to -51.2. When this is multiplied by the parameter (PARM2, above) reflecting the effect of resistance on centralization change (-1.0), the effect is to drive centralization back toward zero. Resistance is shown by the table statement to be an exponential function of the degree of discrepancy: Small discrepancies engender almost no resistance, but the level of resistance increases at an increasing rate as the discrepancy increases.

The political subsystem of society, as we read Pareto, is quite dynamic in and of itself, as well as responsive to trends in the economy and culture. Across broad ranges of values, the political system is governed by momentum—systems tending toward centralization or toward decentralization continue to do so. Beyond critical thresholds of political centralization and decentralization, however, political crises occur and processes are set in motion the reverse the momentum of historical processes. Cycles of politics then come not from "delay" or from "self-referencing feedback," as in some of the earlier examples that we have considered, but rather from a continuous tendency of society to exceed the boundaries of "normalcy" that results in episodic crises that reestablish order.

Culture: Cycles of Traditionalism and Anomie

The subsystem that generates cycles in popular sentiments and beliefs are very similar in structure to that of the political system. In Pareto's model, beliefs have a tendency to move in self-generating ways toward greater traditionalism or toward greater liberalism. Some "cultural resistance" in the forms of alienation and anomie are generated by changes in popular beliefs, but this resistance becomes sufficient to reverse the direction of cultural trends only when extremes of traditionalism or liberalism are attained. Like the political system, the cultural system is "self-regulating," but maintains its equilibrium by proceeding from crisis to crisis. The DYNAMO code for the cultural sector is an exact parallel to that of the political sector. First we define the level of traditionalism/innovativeness (T) as a function of a compound rate (DELTAT).

```
L     T.K = T.J+(DT)(DELTAT.JK)
N     T = TI
C     T = 0
R     DELTAT.KL = TT.JK+TA.JK+TC.JK+TP.JK
```

The rate of change in traditionalism depends upon past changes in traditionalism (TT), on changes in "cultural resistance" (i.e., alienation or anomie, TA), changes in political centralization (TC), and changes in economic productivity (TP). The effects of political centralization, economic productivity, and alienation/anomie are specified quite simply:

```
R    TA.KL = PARM6*A.K
C    PARM6 = 1.0
R    TC.KL = PARM7*C.K
C    PARM7 = .05
R    TP.KL = PARM8.P.K
C    PARM8 = -.12
```

As in the case of the political system, the self-generating mechanism of change in culture is specified as a function of smoothed past changes in culture:

```
R    TT.KL = PARM5*SMOOTH(DELTAT.JK,1)
C    PARM5 = 1.25
N    TT = TTI
C    TTI = 0
```

And the relationship between extremes of traditionalism/innovativeness and cultural resistance is specified as one of exponential increase in resistance (A) as the level of the system (T) moves further and further away from its goal state (TG):

```
A    TD.K = TG-T.K
C    TG = 0
A    A.K = TABLE(ATAB,TD.K,-100,100,10)
T    ATAB = -51.2/-25.6/-12.8/-6.4/-3.2/ . . .
X    .1/.2/.4/.8/1.6/3.2/6.4/12.8/25.6/51.2
```

The basic structure of the cultural subsystem of society, then, is the same as the political. Over time, cycles, first of traditionalism and then innovativeness, sweep through the world of ideas. Each trend has its own internal logic and momentum and, if left unchecked, would drive culture beyond reasonable bounds. When culture becomes extremely traditional, however, crisis ensues in the form of alienation, leading to movements toward greater intellectual freedom. Trends in this direction, if they continue too far from the "normal," engender cultural resistance in the form of anomie. The cultural sector of society hence cycles back and forth between crises of extremes, always seeking, but rarely achieving, a stable balance.

Economy: Cycles of Growth and Contraction

Pareto's analysis of economic dynamics was somewhat more elaborate than those of politics and culture, but has a very similar logical structure. Economic production is based on the accumulation of productive capital, and those factors that increment or decrement the capital stock are central to Pareto's theory of economic dynamics. Generally, capital accumulates and productivity grows when the level of investment exceeds the rate of depreciation of the existing stock of capital. Economic decline ensues when there is insufficient investment to match the rate of depreciation. The forces determining these rates of investment and depreciation are somewhat complex.

Let us begin our specification of this part of the theory by defining a system level for the stock of productive capital:

> L   K.K = K.J+(DT)(IR.JK–DR.JK)
> N   K = KI
> C   KI = 0

That is, the stock of capital is conserved, accumulates as the result of investment rates (IR), and declines as the result of depreciation rates (DR). Using an arbitrary metric, we define the initial level of capital as zero units, and allow capital to take on negative as well as positive values.

Pareto's model is of its greatest subtlety in describing the processes that lead to changes in investment rates and depreciation rates. As investment increases, the capital stock of the system increases, giving rise to rapidly expanding productivity. As productivity expands, however, smaller and smaller shares of this product are reinvested, and "consumerism" begins to run rampant. Eventually the capital stock is depleted to the point at which it can no longer support high consumption levels, and contraction begins. Movements toward growth and contraction are accelerated by biases in the nature of the capital stock resulting from emphasis on capital or consumer goods. As productivity expands and there is an increasing emphasis on the production of consumption goods, the inherent rate of depreciation of the capital stock increases. In periods of decline the opposite pattern occurs: With increasing emphasis on the production of capital goods comes decreases in the depreciation rates of this stock. Thus the partially self-generating growth (or decline) of economic production is arrested and turned around by changes in the depreciation rates of the capital stock, generating another negative feedback loop.

This part of the system is slightly more difficult to capture. First, let us define the level of productivity (P) of the system as a constant (reflecting technology and organization) times the level of capital:

A   P.K = PRMULT*K.K
C   PRMULT = 1.0

For our current purposes, we will set this multiplier at a constant of unity.

Pareto's view of economic dynamics is one of goal-referencing control. Both the rate at which new investment occurs and the rate at which the depreciation of existing productive capital occurs depend upon how far the system is from some baseline level of productivity. We will define this goal as PG, and set it equal to zero, and we will calculate the production discrepancy (PD) between the current state of the system at any point in time (P) and this goal.

A   PD.K = PG-P.K
C   PG = 0

We are now ready to define the ways in which the capital stock changes upward (by investment) and downward (by depreciation) with respect to the distance that the system is from its "goal" state. First, the rate of depreciation of capital:

R   DR.KL = DS.K*K.K
A   DS.K = TABHL(DTAB,PD.K,-100,100,20)
T   DTAB = .9/.64/.50/.38/.28/.20/.14/.09/.05/.02/0

The first of these statements defines the actual amount of depreciation (DR, in units of capital per unit of time) equal to a "depreciation share" (DS) times the existing capital stock (K). The next two statements define the depreciation share as a nonlinear function of the production discrepancy (PD). When production is 100 or more units above the system goal, almost all goods are nondurable, and depreciation of the capital stock is extremely high (.9). When the current level of production is at the system goal (P = 0), the depreciation share is .2 (which is equal to the investment share at this level, as we shall see below). When production is far below the system goal, depreciation rates fall to zero, according to the function assumed. Differential rates of depreciation of the existing capital stock, then, are one of the forces in Pareto's economy seeking to drive the system to its "goal" level.

The dynamics of investment in productive capital are even more important in Pareto's system than his hypotheses about depreciation. Pareto sees political and cultural conditions as acting on the economy primarily by their effects on the propensity to invest:

A   IST.K = PARM9*T.K
C   PARM9 = -.01
A   ISC.K = PARM10*C.K
C   PARM10 = -.02

The investment share effect from traditionalism (IST) is seen as a function of cultural trends. High levels of traditionalism tend to inhibit investment, while high levels of cultural innovativeness and liberalism (negative values of T) tend to promote investment. The effect of political centralization on investment shares (ISC), according to Pareto, is to inhibit private investment in productive capital.

Aside from these additional effects of the cultural and political sectors, the investment rate is determined in the same way as the depreciation rate. That is, when production is low relative to the systems "baseline" or "goal" level, a very high share of all new production goes to investment; when production exceeds the "goal" the rate of investment drops below the 20% necessary for simple replacement of depreciating capital. These ideas are represented by a set of equations that parallel those stated above for depreciation. The first equation is somewhat more complex because of the need to limit gross investment to fall between zero and 100 units.

R   IR.KL = MIN(MAX(((IS.K*P.K)+IST.K+ISC.K),0),100)
A   IS.K = TABHL(ITAB,PD.K,-100,100,20)
T   ITAB = 0/.02/.05/.09/.14/.2/.28/.38/.50/.64/.9

Pareto's economy is more complex in some ways than his cultural or political sectors due to the differential effects of variables on rates of increase (investment) and rates of decrease (depreciation) in the fundamental level (capital) of the subsystem. On the other hand, the economic sector does not contain the same dynamics of self-generating momentum toward growth or decline that are characteristic of cultural and political movements. As a consequence, Pareto's economy is more determined by other sectors than determinative of other sectors of the society, quite in contrast to the vision of Marx.

Simulation Experiments with Pareto:
Subsystem Coupling

One of the most interesting aspects of Pareto's thinking, from the point of view of formalizing and exploring theory, is its clearly modular nature. That is, the dynamics of the system depend both on causal processes occurring within each institutional subsystem, and on the forms and strengths of the linkages among the subsystems. It is not possible to explore the full implications of the Paretian model here, for the range of possible behaviors of the model is very large and its sensitivities and equilibrium conditions are extremely complex. The model does, however, provide a nice illustration of some of the behavioral consequences of linking subsystems into larger systems—an issue that arises in analyzing all complex theories. Before attempting to understand the overall behavior of a model with linked subsystems, one should explore the behavioral tendencies of each of the parts. Understanding the behavior of subsystems is necessary, but not sufficient to understanding the behavior of the fully linked system.

Scenario 1: An Uncoupled System

In developing the Pareto model we noted that the political and cultural subsystems are characterized by self-generating momentum (positive feedback) as well as by resistance (negative feedback); the economic system, in contrast, contains only negative feedback processes (both investment rates and depreciation rates drive the system toward its "goal" condition). We would expect therefore, that the basic behavioral tendencies of the cultural and political systems would be rather different from those of the economic. To explore the implications of each of the subsystems in isolation, it is necessary to "uncouple" them and to set the system in motion. Uncoupling is accomplished by setting the parameters of the processes governing feedback among the subsystems equal to zero (the entire PARETO model is appended to this chapter):

```
C    PARM3 = 0
C    PARM4 = 0
C    PARM7 = 0
C    PARM8 = 0
C    PARM9 = 0
C    PARM10 = 0
```

To get a quick grasp of the behavioral tendencies of each of the subsystems, we can initialize them at different levels. We will set the political system "out of equilibrium" by giving it an initial value different from its "goal" state. The cultural system, which has the same dynamics as the political, will be initialized at the "goal" value of zero. Comparison of the behavior of these two subsystems will give us a good feel for the tendencies of the rather complicated dynamic processes of both of these subsystems. Since the economic system contains only negative feedback processes, it can be expected to remain at its goal state (zero) when it attains it; the only interesting question about the dynamics of the economic subsystem, then, is the speed and time-path that the system follows in seeking this equilibrium. To explore this question we will initialize the economic system at a considerable distance from its goal state of zero.

```
C    CI = 90
C    TI = -25
C    KI = 100
```

Plots of the results of this experiment over a 20-period run are reported in the three panels of Figure 12.2.

The political and cultural subsystems of the model (panels a and b of Figure 12.2) display the expected oscillation between extremes. Accelerating movements toward centralization, decentralization, traditionalism and cultural innovation generate acute crises of resistance, alienation, and anomie. The cultural and political subsystems, seen in isolation, move back and forth between extremes and crises.

In this experiment the political system was initialized at a considerable distance from its goal state, while the cultural system was initialized at its goal state. The political system begins oscillatory behavior immediately, while it takes the cultural system quite some time to reach levels at which the strong cyclical pattern begins. This suggests an important result: As we have specified these systems, they do not attain equilibrium once equilibrium is disturbed (the cultural system moves away from its goal state because its initial rate of change was set as a nonzero quantity in this experiment). Thus, while these systems are held within broad boundaries by external constraints, they do not tend toward a stable equilibrium. It is important to note, however, that this result depends upon the magnitudes of the positive and negative feedback processes in each subsystem. Low values of the "momentum" parameter, combined with high values of negative feedback from resistance or aliena-tion/anomie are capable of producing subsystems that approach their goal states.

The behavior of the economic subsystem (panel c of Figure 12.2) is also as expected. Since this subsystem contains only negative feedback processes the system moves toward its goal state (zero) over time. As the level of capital approaches (exponentially) the goal state, the intensity of the feedback also lessens exponentially. This subsystem, like many

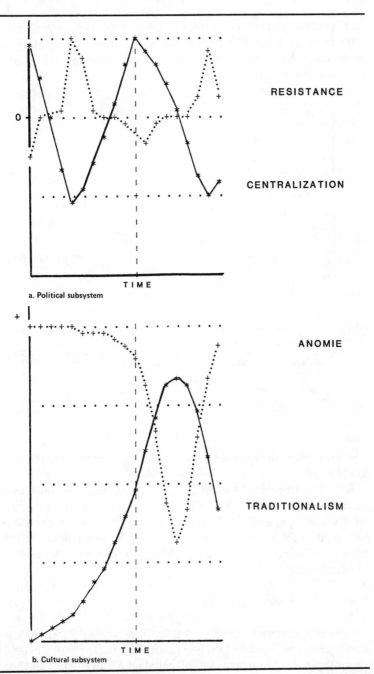

a. Political subsystem

RESISTANCE

CENTRALIZATION

TIME

ANOMIE

TRADITIONALISM

TIME

b. Cultural subsystem

Figure 12.2:   Pareto baseline model, uncoupled.   *(continued)*

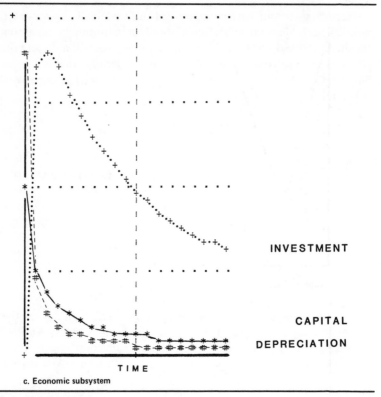

c. Economic subsystem

Figure 12.2 Continued

others that we have examined, seeks a stable equilibrium, and remains in equilibrium once attained.

With the important caveat that cyclical behavior occurs in the cultural and political sectors only in the presence of relatively strong "momentum" parameters, the behavior of each of the Paretian subsystems is as predicted when viewed in isolation. For a next step, let's examine what happens when these subsystems are coupled together into a larger system.

Scenario 2: A Coupled System

The range of possible behaviors of the fully coupled Paretian system is very great, and cannot be analyzed in detail here. To illustrate some of the most plausible outcomes we will couple the subsystems and choose starting values that represent an ideal-typical pattern of system levels.

According to our earlier theoretical discussion of the model, the political and cultural subsystems stand in a mutually reenforcing (positive feedback) relationship to one another. We will represent these effects with parameters of .05, a "medium" magnitude that is considerably less than the size of the effects occurring within each of the subsystems.

    C   PARM3 = .05
    C   PARM7 = .05

Pareto also suggests that political centralization and cultural traditionalism act to limit economic growth by inhibiting investment. For our example, we will suppose that these effects are considerably smaller than the connections between politics and culture, and smaller than the effects within each of the subsystems.

    C   PARM9 = −.01
    C   PARM10 = −.02

Finally, we will suppose that the economic subsystem has relatively powerful constraining effects on both politics and culture. As Pareto suggests, we will specify that periods of economic boom tend to weaken both cultural traditionalism and to lead toward decentralization of the polity.

    C   PARM4 = −.15
    C   PARM8 = −.12

To get a feel for the consequences of this coupling together of the subsystems, let's create something of an "ideal typical" society by specifying initial conditions for the level of centralization, traditionalism, and accumulated capital.

    C   CI = 75
    C   TI = 25
    C   KI = −25

This "society" is in a traditional phase: The level of political centralization is quite high and is supported by (and supports) a traditional cultural system. Broadly consistent with these levels of centralization and traditionalism, the level of economic productivity is somewhat below the "goal" state of zero. The behavior of this system over 50 time points is reported in Figure 12.3.

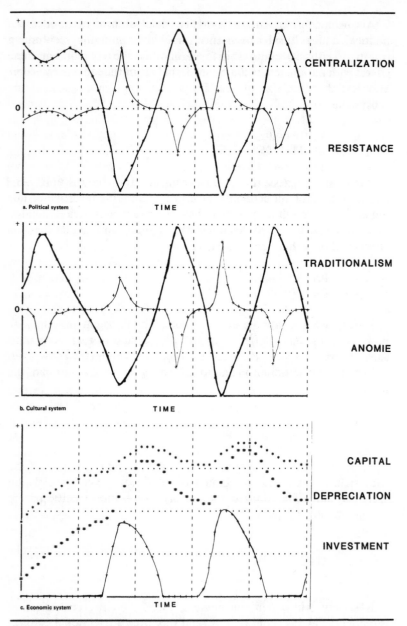

Figure 12.3: Pareto baseline model, coupled.

The behavior of the coupled system is broadly similar to the sum of its uncoupled parts (due to the relatively weak linkages among subsystems relative to the magnitudes of the linkages within subsystems). There are, however, some important consequences of linking the subsystems to one another.

The political and cultural subsystems display the same general patterns of cyclical movements (with periods of about 20 time points from trough to trough) as in the uncoupled model. The slow initial adjustment of each of these subsystems can be traced to the reenforcing effects of the low productivity of the economic sector. After initial adjustment, both subsystems center on, but never attain, their goal states. And, though the tendency is slight, the crises of each subsystem are becoming more extreme as time goes on. This tendency is probably a consequence of the mutually reenforcing feedback between the cultural and political sectors.

The behavior of the economy is the most dramatically affected by being coupled to the other societal subsystems. In the first experiment, above, we demonstrated that the economy in isolation simply moves toward its goal state at a constant rate of change. In the presence of stimuli from the cultural and political sectors, however, the economy displays cyclical behavior and (after the initial disequilibria are worked out) a very slight tendency toward upward drift. The creation of cyclical movements in the economy as a direct result of cultural and political cycles is theoretically significant in itself, and also create further stimulus to the deepening of cultural and political cycles (due to the relatively strong feedback from economic to political and cultural change).

It is also important to note, despite the induced boom and bust cycles of the economy, that the economy (and other subsystems) move toward centering on their goal states. That is, overall the model seeks (but probably never attains) its goal states in each subsystem—regardless of initial conditions. The economic system, as the clearest example, displays more growth than recession in its cycles until the goal state is approximated. After the general goal level is attained, economic cycles move about equally between booms and busts. In the cultural and political sectors the first cycles are held at levels of traditionalism and centralization rather far from the goal states. After a quite short period, however, these cycles come to center on the system "goals."

The most important lesson to learn from this experiment is that the sum of the parts of a dynamic system can be considerably less, or more, than the whole—depending on how the parts are coupled. We can see this lesson even more clearly in exploring and tinkering with the ideas of Karl Marx on the "system" of modern capitalism.

Marx's Societal Dynamics

Most of us are more familiar with the ideas of Karl Marx, at least in broad outline, than with those of Vilfredo Pareto. Central to Marx's theory is a relatively complicated and self-propelling dynamic in the economic sector of society by which the rational profit-maximizing activities of individual capitalists create conditions that lead to the destruction of capitalism as a whole. While economic "contradictions" are central to the analysis, Marx does not ignore the cultural and political institutions of society. Indeed, while it is the economic system that creates revolutionary conditions, these conditions must be converted into revolutionary action against the state by self-conscious class actors to lead to the destruction of the capitalist system. Marx's system is much like Pareto's in general structure (though very different in detail), for it can be thought of as composed of economic, cultural, and political "subsystems" that are linked together by dynamics of positive and negative feedback.

Economy: Production, Reproduction, and Exploitation

Marx's analyses are richest and most fully developed in describing the dynamics of economic production and reproduction in capitalist systems. In simplified and schematic form, the structure of the economic subsystem can be diagramed as in Figure 12.4.

Economic actors are seen as divided into two classes: capitalists who control the "means of production" and workers who do not and consequently must sell their labor for wages. In addition to these two groups, there is also a "reserve army" of unemployed persons who both provide services that "reproduce labor" (e.g., homemakers and child rearers), and act as a source of cheap labor that capitalists use to hold down wages.

The processes of economic production and distribution are also quite straightforward. Goods are produced when the capital and technology controlled by capitalists are combined with wage labor. These goods are either sold on markets, with the proceeds being distributed as wages and profits, or are not sold and become "overproduction." Profits are used to "reproduce" capital and to invest in new technology, while wages are used to purchase the goods and services necessary to "reproduce" labor.

There is nothing very unusual in Marx's ideas about the nature of economic actors and the movements of capital, commodities, and money. Where Marx's theory does diverge radically from other classical models is in the way that the dynamic forces of the economy and their

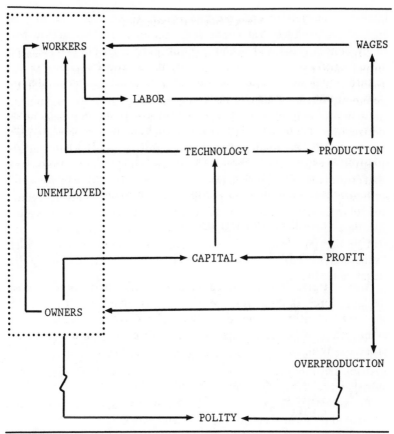

Figure 12.4: Marx's societal dynamics, economy.

consequences are conceived. Capitalists, who seek to maximize profits in the face of competition with one another, exploit workers by paying them less than the full value of their labor. This "surplus value" is then used to invest in further increases in capital—and particularly in capital that will displace labor. As a result of labor displacement and exploitation, demand for production grows less rapidly than the productive capacities of the capitalist economy—the unemployed and the wage workers do not have the money to purchase the products of their own labor. As a consequence, sales decline and price competition cuts into the rates of profits of capitalists. As profits decline, less efficient (and/or less exploitive) capitalists are driven into the working class or the ranks of the unemployed. In the short run, the economy recovers as competition lessens, investment by the remaining capitalists increases, and laborers are reemployed. However, with each cyclical crisis of overproduction and underconsumption capital becomes increasingly concentrated and the production process displaces more and more workers in favor of machines. As these processes continue, the cultural and political conditions for revolution become more and more favorable until the system is overturned.

As in the Paretian economy, the central level is that of the economic subsystem is that of capital (CAP). We will be concerned only with the factors that impact on the rate of capital investment (CIR), ignoring the question of depreciation. We must specify a number of things before we can return to the capital investment rate, however. First, we define and initialize the stock of productive capital—"the means of production."

    L   CAP.K = CAP.J+(DT)(CIR.JK)
    N   CAP = CAPI
    C   CAPI = 100

Also central to processes of economic production and reproduction is the labor force. In the simplest version of this model, we see labor as a conserved quantity that may be displaced (DLAB) as a result of changes in the system. We must wait just a bit before discussing the displacement process as well.

    L   LAB.K = LAB.J+(DT)(-DLAB.JK)
    N   LAB = LABI
    C   LABI = 100

Capital and labor are combined in the process of production according to the following function:

    R   PROD.KL = LAB.K*EXPLB*CAP.K*TECH

Note that the rate of production over a period of time is a multiplicative function of the supply of capital (CAP) and the supply of labor (LAB). That is, for production to occur, both factors must be present. The volume of production of labor is shown as depending on the rate of exploitation (EXPLB), that is, the ratio of the hours worked to the hours for which workers are paid the full value of their production. Production, then, is the result of both "socially necessary" labor (the amount of labor time necessary to reproduce labor power) and "surplus value" that arises directly from the exploitation of labor. The contribution of capital to production is also weighted (by a factor called TECH), that reflects the productivity of capital. For the purposes of developing a simplified baseline, we will regard both of these "multipliers" as fixed, though in Marx's own thinking and in some of our examples below, these quantities are dynamically related to other system states.

C EXPLB = 1.5
C TECH = 1.1

Once goods have been produced, they may either be sold or left unsold if demand is insufficient. The unsold portion, or "overproduction" can be defined as:

L OVP.K = MAX(0,OVP.J+(DT)(PROD.JK–SLS.JK))
N OVP = OVPI
C OVPI = 0

According to this specification, overproduction cannot be a negative amount, is conserved, and accumulates to the extent that production (PROD) exceeds sales (SLS).

Continuing the circuit, sales may be defined as the sum of consumer demand (DEM) and investor demand (in the form of PROFITs):

R SLS.KL = DEM.K+PROFIT.K

Demand is perhaps not an ideal label for the concept in the preceding statement for in Marxian economics it does not refer to a quantity determined by the movements of prices on a free market. Rather, demand (DEM) is defined as the volume of production necessary to reproduce existing capital (RPRDCP), labor (RPRDLB), and technology (RPRDTC).

A DEM.K = RPRDLB.K+RPRDCP.K+RPRDTC.K

The amount of production necessary to reproduce capital, labor, and technology is set equal to their contributions to the total volume of production, since Marx argues that all surplus production is the consequence of the exploitation of labor:

A RPRDCP.K = (CAP.K/(LAB.K+CAP.K))*(LAB.K*CAP.K)
A RPRDLB.K = (LAB.K/(LAB.K+CAP.K))*(LAB.K*CAP.K)
A RPRDTC.K = LAB.K*CAP.K*EXPLB*(TECH-1)

All production beyond that which is necessary to reproduce the system is PROFIT, and is derived entirely from the exploitation of labor. PROFIT, then, is equal to the difference between the volume of production necessary to reproduce labor and the actual volume of production. Or, alternatively, it is equal to the exploitation rate times the level of labor:

A   PROFIT.K = RPRDLB.K*(EXPLB-1)

To close the system and make it dynamic we must finally describe the factors that give rise to the displacement of labor by machines and the laws that describe changes in the level of capital. These two final equations are:

R   DLAB.KL = LAB.K*(TECH-1)
R   CIR.KL = PROFIT/(RPRDCP.K/CAP.K)

The first of these statements shows labor being displaced by machines at a constant rate. This will serve for our purposes here, but is a considerable simplification of Marx's thinking on this point. Part of the cyclical nature of the capitalist crisis in Marx theory stems from a dynamic linkage between capitalist's propensity to displace workers and the rate of profit. The second of the statements above is considerably more complex looking than the simple idea it expresses. The capital investment rate (CIR) is simply equal to PROFIT in this model, but profits—which are expressed in units of production—must be translated back into units of capital by use of the ratio RPRDCP/CAP. Again we oversimplify Marx's thinking in assuming that capitalists do not waste or hoard profits; our capitalists, bent on profit maximization—and hence their own doom—immediately reinvest all of the surplus that they have exploited from laborers.

Karl Marx's conceptualization and theory of the dynamics of economic production under capitalism is a remarkable intellectual achievement (to which we have done considerable violence in the course of the current simplified presentation). The driving forces of profit maximization and the exploitation of labor move the system toward crises of overproduction and underconsumption. These tendencies, however, are only the starting point for the theory of the demise of capitalism. The economic crisis of capitalism must be translated into a cultural and political crisis for revolution to occur.

*Culture and Politics: Classes,
Class Conflict, and the State*

In various places in his work Marx offered observations on the forces and processes that translated economic crisis into political action. Despite the richness of these insights and accounts, however, he did not develop his thinking on ideology and politics as a rigorous dynamic system—as he did with the economy. Our model of these parts of Marx's system are consequently less complex than those of the economy. The general argument can be captured rather well in a diagram (Figure 12.5).

This portion of the model does not display any internal self-generating dynamic, as do the Paretian accounts of politics and culture. Rather, the dynamics of politics are solely determined by the dynamics of economics. Control of the state is the result of political and ideological conflict between capitalists and workers; to this conflict the parties bring capacities that are determined by the condition of the economy. The political and ideological power of the capitalist class is largely a function of the class's size and, more importantly, the financial resources that it controls. Worker's power, on the other hand, is primarily a function of numbers, but is increased by capital intensification (that concentrates workers), and by high unemployment and overproduction that contribute to delegitimation of the current regime and mobilization against it. Thus all of the factors underlying class conflict and control of the state apparatus are ultimately traceable to the economy.

Because the cultural and political subsystems are such simple functions of economic conditions, it is quite easy to translate this portion of the model into formal language. We begin by focusing on the number of workers:

L   LABN.K = LABN.J+(DT)(FAILCP.JK–DISPLB.JK)
N   LABN = LABNI
C   LABNI = 1000

The number of laborers (LABN) is a conserved quantity that is increased over time by the addition of failed capitalists (FAILCP), and decreased by laborers who are displaced (DISPLB) into the "reserve army of the unemployed." The number of unemployed is also quite simply calculated as the accumulation of displaced laborers:

L   UNEMP.K = MAX(0,(UNEMP.J+(DT)(DISPLB.JK)))

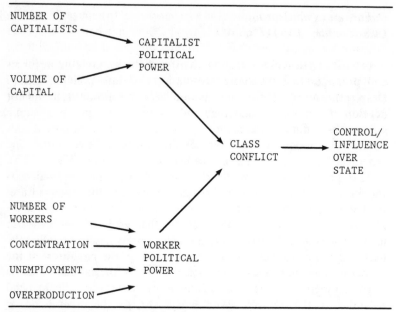

Figure 12.5:   Marx's societal dynamics, class conflict.

> N   UNEMP = UNEMPI
> C   UNEMPI = 0

The rate of displacement of workers into the pool of unemployed (DISPLB) is modeled, in our baseline, as a simple function of constantly changing technology; this specification is an oversimplification of Marx's ideas, for Marx tied the rate of change in technology dynamically to the rate of profit.

> R   DISPLB.KL = LABN.K*(TECH.K–1)

Changes in the numerical size of the capitalist class are somewhat more complex. Over time capitalists are displaced ("proletarianized") as a consequence of the falling rate of profit and consequent concentration of capital.

> L   CAPN.K = CAP.J–FAILCP.JK
> N   CAPN = CAPNI
> C   CAPNI = 200

The rate at which capitalists fail is proportional to changes in profits. Unfortunately, the DYNAMO language does not contain a special function for lagged past changes (though one could be built with the macro facility). We get around this problem by creating a set of temporary "levels" containing information about past profits (PRTF) and current profits (OUT), and setting the failure rate proportional to the ratio of the two:

R   FAILCP.KL = (1-(PRFT.JK/OUT.JK))*CAPN.K

With these statements we have specified how the numerical sizes of the three class actors—capitalists, workers, and unemployed—are tied to changes in the performance of the economy.

Class conflict and the political domination of the interests of one class over those of the other, however, depend on the mobilization of the power resources of these classes. The political power of the classes are specified in our model as:

A   CAPMOB.K = CAPN.K*CAP.K
A   PROLMB.K = MAX(0,(1+(10*(LABN.K+(UNEMP.K*2)))*
X   (RPRDTC.K/20000)*(OVP.K/10000)))

The power of the capitalist class is equated with the numbers of capitalists (CAPN) and the amount of the capital resources that they control (CAP). The expression for the power of the proletariat (PROLMB) is more complex, and includes effects of the size of the class (LABN) plus a measure of the concentration of capital (RPRDTC), a measure of the level of accumulated overproduction (OVP), and the level of unemployment (UNEMP). The relative magnitudes of these effects and the form of their combination are, we must admit, quite ad hoc, as Marx is not specific on these issues.

The nature of "the state," its relation to the balance of power between classes, and its role in reproducing economic and cultural relations are all issues of extensive debate among Marxist scholars. In keeping with the spirit "baseline" models, we will specify the relation between control of the state and class conflict very simply, though we will experiment with this part of the model a bit, later on.

A   STATE.K = CLIP(1,2,CAPMOB.K,PROLMB.K)

That is, control of the state apparatus belongs to whichever class has the higher level of political mobilization at a point in time.

The political conflict between classes for control of the state apparatus is consequential in Marxian thinking because the power of the state (coercive, legal, and ideological) is a central lever for maintaining or modifying the basic property and class relations of society. To illustrate the insights available from the Marxian model we will examine, by means of theoretical experiments, some of the consequences of shifts in state control in the next section.

Simulation Experiments with Marx: State and Revolution

Marx is quite clear on how the fundamental contradictions of the economic system of capitalism create the conditions necessary for political revolution and the "class nature" of the state. Marxian analysis is considerably less well developed with regard to the nature of the "feedback" relationship between the state and economic relations. That is, while we are quite clear on how the economic subsystem determines the political-cultural subsystems, we are less clear on how the political-cultural systems affect economic institutions. As a way of becoming sensitive to the implications and possibilities of analysis using formal models of complex coupled subsystems, we will very briefly explore some alternative ideas about these state to economy linkages.

Scenario 1: Revolution and Aftermath

In the baseline model that we developed in the previous section, the state plays no active role in determining economic dynamics. The state is not exactly "neutral" in this model, in that it acts to maintain the institutional patterns of capitalism by not interfering with the operation of capital and labor markets. There are, however, no explicit state actions to regulate competition among capitalists, support the unemployed, subsidize capitalist development, or redistribute product. This is quite an unrealistic view of the role of the state under capitalism, but is a useful starting point for thinking about the consequences of politics for economics. As a first step in understanding the consequences of our own theory—as embodied in the model that we have just developed—let's examine the consequences of this view of the role of the state by means of a simulation experiment.

In the three panels of Figure 12.6 the results of a simulation of the baseline model are reported.

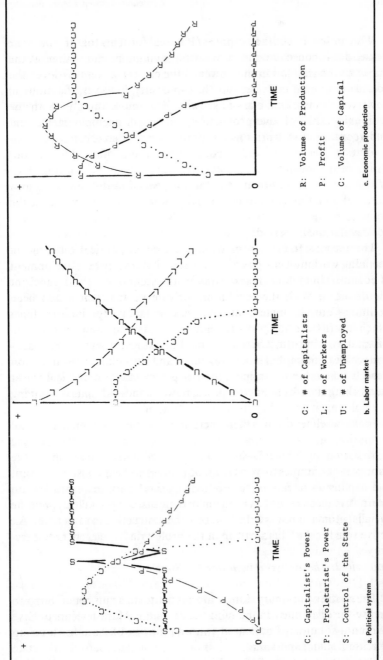

R: Volume of Production

P: Profit

C: Volume of Capital

c. Economic production

C: # of Capitalists

L: # of Workers

U: # of Unemployed

b. Labor market

C: Capitalist's Power

P: Proletariat's Power

S: Control of the State

a. Political system

Figure 12.6: State and revolution.

311

We can see from the first panel (Political System) that the baseline model does indeed produce a political revolution. For a time at the outset of the simulation the power of the capitalist class grows as the volume of capital increases. At the same time, however, the political power of the working class is growing even more rapidly. With the economic crisis of overproduction, increased unemployment, and underconsumption, working-class power exceeds that of capitalists, and revolution occurs (followed by counterrevolution, followed by consolidation of the revolution), and state control shifts to the working class. With the revolution private capital disappears, as does the capitalist class—eliminating capitalist political power. Note, however, that the political power of the working class also is shown to decline in the postrevolutionary period.

The reasons for this somewhat unexpected political outcome of declining working-class power can be found in tracing the development of economic and labor market trends (the second and third panels of Figure 12.6). With the revolution, private profits (which had been declining) are eliminated entirely, because labor exploitation—from which profits are derived—is eliminated. As a consequence of the elimination of profit, however, capital investment (beyond reproduction) ceases, the capital stock stagnates, and the volume of production steadily falls as labor continues to be displaced. As the numerical size of the working class declines, its political power wanes—despite continuing unemployment and labor force concentration.

In the baseline scenario then, there appears to be a dilemma. Political revolution brings the elimination of the capitalist class and ends the exploitation of labor. Despite this, the economic condition of the population continues to worsen, as the processes of capitalist investment and expansion of economic productivity have been disrupted but no alternative mechanism has been put in their place. This is clearly not the socialist utopia that was to follow from the destruction of capitalism. An active role for the "dictatorship of the proletariat" is clearly necessary.

Scenario 2: The Active Revolutionary State

The postrevolutionary state could choose to do a number of things to resolve the dilemmas of managing the economy. Marx appears to have favored a solution of increased consumption and leisure for labor to increase demand and absorb excess production. Alternatively, the state could appropriate the "excess" production (that is, the production arising from labor exploitation) and use it for nonproductive purposes— conspicuous consumption, bureaucratic growth, or military adventurism.

Finally, and perhaps most realistically, the state could take on the role of managing investment, demand, and factor allocation.

If we supposed that the state appropriated the overproduction of system and directed it toward productive investment, postrevolutionary economic growth, rather than decline is the result. The simulation reported in Figure 12.7 displays the consequences of state reallocation of half of the accumulated overproduction to new investment. In this scenario, rapid growth is the consequence of the redirection of previously wasted resources into new production. While technological displacement continues, worker's political power continues to increase over time with increasing capitalization and "unemployment." Of course, under socialist distributional principles, unemployment is a socially desired state in which citizens are able to engage in leisure and cultural pursuits while being supported by the wealth produced by the collective economy.

With only slight manipulation of the rate at which overproduction is reinvested, a steady state, rather than exponential growth can be produced in the postrevolutionary epoch. This pattern is shown in the simulation shown as Figure 12.8. This simulation suggests the plausibility of another postrevolutionary vision. By careful management of the pace of development, the state is able to substitute technology for labor while maintaining levels of material productivity (at levels slightly below the prerevolutionary peak), and stabilize the political mobilization of the working class. Rather than a superheated path toward "socialist development," the postrevolutionary society is one of economic and cultural/political stability at a high level of material and intellectual well-being.

If an "active" rather than a passive socialist state is able (at least in our idealized models) to produce a range of desirable outcomes, could an active capitalist state do the same?

Scenario 3: The Welfare State

In all of the models that we have examined so far, we have presumed that control of the state was an all-or-nothing proposition, and that state policy was a direct and immediate reflection of the policy preferences of the dominant class. With these assumptions, the model invariably produces revolution, an event that did not empirically occur in the systems the model was intended to mimic. The empirical failure of the Marxian model could be traced to many roots, but one of the most obvious is in the oversimple conception of the class nature of the state and state policy. In all of the Western societies the state has become far

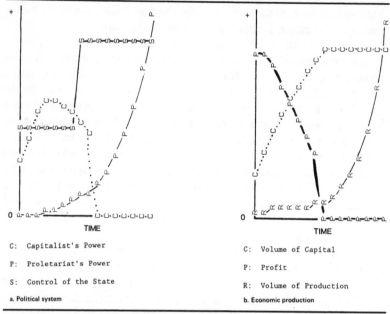

C: Capitalist's Power
P: Proletariat's Power
S: Control of the State

a. Political system

C: Volume of Capital
P: Profit
R: Volume of Production

b. Economic production

Figure 12.7: Postrevolutionary growth.

more active in economic management than the original Marxian model
supposes; and many of the policies that it has pursued have been
intended to benefit the working, rather than the owning, classes.

A quite simple modification of the baseline model is able to capture
parts of these realities about the behavior of the "welfare state." Let us
suppose that the state is responsive to proportional shifts in the relative
political strengths of classes, rather than pursuing the interests of the
single dominant class in an unalloyed fashion. That is, let us suppose
that the modern state is "smarter" in monitoring changes in quantitative
shifts in the political mobilization of groups, and formulates policy that
is directly and immediately responsive to these shifts.

Let's suppose that the welfare state has become a "smarter" system in
a second way—the state has become more closely coupled to the
management of the economy. In our baseline model the state either
supported the interests of capital by doing nothing or pursued the
interests of labor (after the revolution) by ending exploitation. Rather
than these simple but crude policies, let us suppose that the state has
become directly active in managing movements of supply and demand—
that is, the Keynesian state. Rather than waiting for the revolution and
socializing all investment (as in the previous scenario), our "welfare"

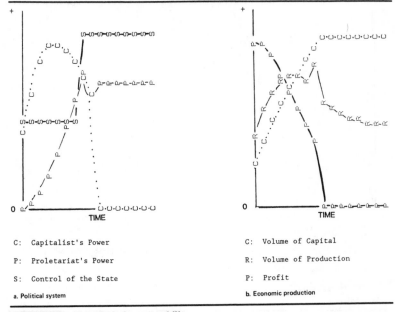

C: Capitalist's Power

P: Proletariat's Power

S: Control of the State

a. Political system

C: Volume of Capital

R: Volume of Production

P: Profit

b. Economic production

Figure 12.8:   Postrevolutionary stability.

state takes a share of the overproduction of the system (perhaps by taxation) and reinvests it in productive activities to produce employment. The stronger the working class relative to the capitalist class, the larger the proportion of the surplus invested in such activities. In the welfare state, then, private capitalists coexist with a partially socialized investment process. Private investment responds to economic imperatives, public investment to political imperatives. The system is smarter, but does it work?

In Figure 12.9 results of one run of the "welfare state" version of the Marxian model are shown. The entire model (which is the same as the basic model, but includes a modified state control equation and a job-creation process not in the basic model) is given in the Appendix.

These results give quite a different impression of the nature of economic and political dynamics under capitalism than do the results of the baseline model. The most notable result is, of course, that the economic crisis and political revolution are averted by an active state policy of employment creation. Indeed, the welfare state appears to work remarkably well—both capital and labor factors of production become fully utilized, unemployment is reduced, and importantly, the balance of political power between the two classes is maintained.

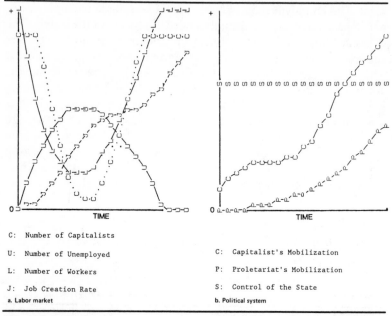

C: Number of Capitalists

U: Number of Unemployed   C: Capitalist's Mobilization

L: Number of Workers   P: Proletariat's Mobilization

J: Job Creation Rate   S: Control of the State

a. Labor market   b. Political system

Figure 12.9:   Welfare state.

As seemingly rosy as this picture may be, it does not tell the whole story. While the welfare state model is able to avert the immediate crisis and generate growth, all is not well. As the unemployed are drawn back into the ranks of the working class and the surplus overproduction seized and reinvested by the state, the conditions for the political mobilization of the working class are compromised. Despite increasing numeric strength and increasing concentration (due to continued technological change), the political mobilization of the working class relative to that of the capitalist class is eroded by welfare state policies. As a consequence, state activity to create employment slows down and unemployment again grows, setting off a new round of political conflict and policy change. Inherent in the logic of the welfare state then is also a cycle of "dialectical" and "contradictory" dynamics.

There is a still deeper problem in the welfare state model as formulated here. The state takes an active, and in the short run effective, role in employment and investment management. It does not, however, do anything about one of the fundamental long-run causes of the political-economic crisis: the displacement of human labor by technology. The welfare state is able to maintain stability, in the current scenario, only by continued rapid expansion of public sector employment. This employment is, in fact, a form of disguised unemployment, and depends critically on the unbounded expansion of the system. The continued substitution of technology for labor in the production process can be sustained only if the state takes an active role in employing those who are displaced. It may continue to do so only to the extent that the system continues to produce "overproduction" that the state may use for job creation. The system can continue to create surplus only so long as there are no limits to continued expansion. Thus we are led to a second fatal contradiction of the welfare state: The welfare state, no less than the "capitalist" state is fundamentally dependent on continued growth and expansion. The linkage drawn by Lenin between capitalism and colonialism is only displaced and disguised by the welfare state—not eliminated.

Conclusions

In this chapter we have examined two rather complex models of the dynamic relations among the "subsystems" of whole societies. There are a number of things that can be taken from these exercises, some of greater interest to particular audiences, some of more general importance.

Sociologists, political scientists, and economists all lay claim to both Pareto and Marx as important figures in the development of theory in their disciplines. The examples in this chapter were chosen, in part, because they are common across these fields, and because the ideas of Marx and Pareto remain vital in each. Among the virtues of the "systems" approach in general, and of the formalization of theories as dynamic models in particular, is an increased capacity to communicate ideas across disciplinary boundaries. The versions of the ideas of Marx and Pareto offered here are hardly the last things to be said on the subject. Hopefully the formalization of the models and the explorations of their implications by simulation methods will stimulate further inquiry in all of the disciplines.

The formal models of both theories are somewhat imposing by the time we are finished with them (i.e., the DYNAMO code contained in the appendixes). And, it would be less than honest to suggest that they were easy to create or unproblematic in development and experimentation. A second major reason for picking on models of this complexity for our closing examples is, quite simply, to demonstrate that they can be done. One of the main themes of this entire book has been that the gap between "formal models" and "social science theory" is far wider than it needs to be. By attempting to capture some of the richness and complexity of full-blown theories of large and complex processes in formal models, the intent has been to demonstrate that the systems method and formal modeling languages do allow the representation of theories of sufficient complexity to be of interest. By experimenting with the models, the intent has been to demonstrate that some of the virtues of rigorous analyzability inherent in formal models can be applied (if only in the sense of "approximate" solutions) to quite complicated theories.

The theories of Marx and Pareto are also the most "complex" "systems" that we have examined in this volume. In systems language, these models represent relatively complex artifacts because they contain many elements, the elements are linked in complicated ways, and the control structures governing the dynamics of the systems contain complex functions that are nonlinear in both multiple variables and time. These models are examples of systems that are "complex" primarily as a consequence of the nature of their control structures, just as the models at the end of the second section of this volume were "complex" because of the larger number of states that they describe. The "degrees of freedom" (i.e., range of possible behavioral outcomes) of models of the type that we have examined in this chapter are very great, and pose major challenges of specification and further theoretical research for social scientists.

Notes

1. For some interesting works on large-scale systems composed of multiple and interacting subsystems, see Andreski (1968), Baumgartner et al. (1976), Boulding (1970, 1978), Brunner and Brewer (1971), Cole et al. (1973), Deutsch et al. (1977), Forrester (1973), Guetzkow (1962), Guetzkow and Valdez (eds., 1974), Hamilton et al. (1969), Hughes (1980), Meadows et al. (1974), Meadows and Meadows (1973), Meadows et al. (1973), Mesarovic and Macko (1969), Mesarovic and Pestel (1974), and Pattee (1973, 1975).

2. For a more complete discussion of the work of Pareto, and its translation into a formal model, see Powers and Hanneman (1983) and works cited therein. For a more extended treatment of Marx's model, see Hanneman and Collins (1986) and works cited therein.

3. Very similar conceptions of societal systems and societal dynamics can be found in the work of a leading sociological theorist who was substantially influenced by Pareto: Talcott Parsons (1957, 1966).

APPENDIX 12.1. Pareto's Societal Dynamics Model

```
*                     PARETO MODEL
NOTE                  ***** CENTRALIZATION AND RESISTANCE *****
NOTE                  CENTRALIZATION
```

```
L          C.K = C.J+(DT)(DC.JK)
N          C = CI
C          CI = 75
R          DC.KL = CC.JK+CR.JK+CT.JK+CP.JK
R          CC.KL = PARM1*SMOOTH(DC.JK,1)
C          PARM1 = 1.25
N          CC = CCI
C          CCI = 1
R          CR.KL = PARM2*R.K
C          PARM2 = 1
R          CT.KL = PARM3*T.K
C          PARM3 = .05
R          CP.KL = PARM4*P.K
C          PARM4 = -.15
NOTE                RESISTANCE
A          CD.K = CG-C.K
C          CG =0
A          R.K = TABLE(RTAB,CD.K,-100,100,10)
T          RTAB = -51.2/-25.6/-12.8/-6.4/-3.2/-1.6/-.8/-.4/-.2/-.1/0/
X                .1/.2/.4/.8/1.6/3.2/6.4/12.8/25.6/51.2
NOTE                ***** CULTURAL SECTOR *****
NOTE                TRADITIONALISM
L          T.K = T.J+(DT)(DELTAT.JK)
N          T = TI
C          TI = 25
R          DELTAT.KL = TT.JK+TA.JK+TC.JK+TP.JK
R          TT.KL = PARM5*SMOOTH(DELTAT.JK,1)
C          PARM5 = 1.25
N          TT = TTI
C          TTI = 1
R          TA.KL = PARM6*A.K
C          PARM6 = 1
R          TC.KL = PARM7*C.K
C          PARM7 = .05
R          TP.KL = PARM8*P.K
C          PARM8 = -.12
NOTE                ALIENATION AND ANOMIE
A          TD.K = TG-T.K
C          TG = 0
A          A.K = TABLE(ATAB,TD.K,-100,100,10)
T          ATAB = -51.2/-25.6/-12.8/-6.4/-3.2/-1.6/-.8/-.4/-.2/-.1/0/
X                .1/.2/.4/.8/1.6/3.2/6.4/12.8/25.6/51.2
NOTE                ***** ECONOMY *****
NOTE                CAPITAL AND PRODUCTION
L          K.K = K.J+(DT)(IR.JK-DR.JK)
N          K = KI
C          KI = -25
A          PD.K = PG-P.K
C          PG = 0
```

```
NOTE                    DEPRECIATION
R               DR.KL = DS.K*K.K
A               DS.K = TABHL(DTAB,PD.K,-100,100,20)
T               DTAB = .9/.64/.50/.38/.28/.20/.14/.09/.05/.02/0
NOTE                    INVESTMENT EFFECTS FROM CENT. AND TRAD.
A               IST.K = PARM9*T.K
C               PARM9 = -.01
A               ISC.K = PARM10*C.K
C               PARM10 = -.02
NOTE                    INVESTMENT RATE
R               IR.KL = MIN(MAX((((IS.K*P.K)+IST.K+ISC.K),0),100)
A               IS.K = TABHL(ITAB,PD.K,-100,100,20)
T               ITAB = 0/.02/.05/.09/.14/.2/.28/.38/.50/.64/.9
NOTE                    ***** OUTPUT SPECIFICATION *****
SPEC            DT = .25/LENGTH = 50/PRTPER = 1/PLTPER = 1
PRINT           C,R,T,A
PRINT           K,IR,DR
PLOT            C = */R = +
PLOT            T = */R = +
PLOT            K = */IR = +/DR = #
RUN
```

APPENDIX 12.2. Marx Model: Welfare State Variant

```
*                   MARX MODEL
*               WELFARE STATE VARIANT
NOTE ************************************************
NOTE *ECONOMIC PRODUCTION AND REPRODUCTION *
NOTE ************************************************
NOTE                    Overproduction
L               OVP.K = MAX(0,(((OVP.J+(DT)(PROD.JK-SLS.JK))
X                   -(JOBCR.JK*OVP.J)))
N               OVP = OVPI
C               OVPI = 0
NOTE                    Rate of Production
R               PROD.KL = LAB.K*EXPLB.K*CAP.K*TECH.K
NOTE                    Level of labor exploitation
L               EXPLB.K = CLIP(1,EXPLB.J,PROLMOB.K,CAPMOB.K)
N               EXPLB = EXPLBI
C               EXPLBI = 1.5
NOTE                    Production multiplier from Technology
A               TECH.K = 1.1
NOTE                    Rate of Sales
R               SLS.KL = DEM.K+PROFIT.K
NOTE                    Profit is equal to surplus value
A               PROFIT.K = (RPRDLB.K)(EXPLB.K-1)
NOTE                        Demand is the reproduction cost of the factors of
NOTE                        production: labor, capital, tech.
```

```
A           DEM.K = RPRDLB.K+RPRDCP.K+RPRDTC.K
NOTE            The cost of reproducing labor is equal to the
NOTE            labor share of total productivity of capital and
NOTE            labor, leaving aside technology and exploitation.
A           RPRDLB.K = (LAB.K/(LAB.K+CAP.K))(LAB.K*CAP.K)
NOTE            The cost of reproducing capital is defined in a
NOTE            parallel fashion.
A           RPRDCP.K = (CAP.K/(LAB.K+CAP.K))(LAB.K*CAP.K)
NOTE            The cost of reproducing technology is defined as
NOTE            equal to the technology share in total production
A           RPRDTC.K = (LAB.K*CAP.K*EXPLB.K)(TECH.K-1)
NOTE ******************************************************
NOTE * LEVELS OF THE FORCES OF PRODUCTION *
NOTE ******************************************************
NOTE            The amount of labor time is reduced by technology
NOTE            but incremented by job creation policies
L           LAB.K = MIN(LABI,((LAB.J+(DT)(-DLAB.JK))+(JOBCR.JK*
X           LAB.J)))
N           LAB = LABI
C           LABI = 100
NOTE            The rate of job creation depends on the relative
NOTE            political mobilization of the classes
R           JOBCR.KL = MAX(0,(POWR(PROLMOB.K/CAPMOB.K)))
C           POWR = 5
NOTE            The rate of displacement of labor by technology
NOTE            is proportional to the productivity of tech.
R           DLAB.KL = LAB.K*(TECH.K-1)
NOTE            The level of capital is defined
L           CAP.K = CAP.J+(DT)(CIR.JK)
N           CAP = CAPI
C           CAPI = 100
R           CIR.KL = PROFIT/(RPRDCP.K/CAP.K)
NOTE ******************************************************
NOTE * CLASS DEMOGRAPHICS, MOBILIZATION, AND POWER *
NOTE ******************************************************
NOTE            The numbers of capitalists
L           CAPN.K = MIN(CAPNI,(CAPN.J-FAILCP.JK))
N           CAPN = CAPNI
C           CAPNI = 200
NOTE            Failure rate of capitalists is calculated by
NOTE            creating current and past rates of profit
NOTE            and by setting failures proportional to changes
NOTE            in the rate of profit
R           FAILCP.KL = (1-(PRFT.JK/OUT.JK))(CAPN.K)
L           ACPRFT.K = PRFT.JK
N           ACPRFT = ACPRFI
C           ACPRFI = 2500
L           OUT.K = ACPRFT.J
N           OUT = OUTI
C           OUTI = 2500
R           PRFT.KL = MAX(PROFIT.K,.001)
```

NOTE	The political power of capitalists is defined:
A	CAPMOB.K = CAPN.K*CAP.K
NOTE	The numbers of workers
L	LABN.K = MAX(0,(MIN(LABNI,(LABN.J+(DT)(MAX(0,(FAILCP.JK))
X	–DISPLB.JK)))))
N	LABN = LABNI
C	LABNI = 1000
NOTE	Labor displacement by technology, in units of
NOTE	laborers, mitigated by job creation.
R	DISPLB.KL= MAX(0,((LABN.K*(TECH.K–1))–(JOBCR.JK*LABN.K)))
NOTE	The level of unemployment
L	UNEMP.K = MAX(0,(UNEMP.J+(DT)(DISPLB.JK)))
N	UNEMP = UNEMPI
C	UNEMPI = 0
NOTE	The political power of labor is defined:
A	PROLMOB.K = MAX(0,(1+(10(LABN.K+(UNEMP.K*2)))*
X	(RPRDTC.K/20000)*(OVP.K/10000)))
NOTE	Control of the State is defined
A	STATE.K = CLIP(1,2,CAPMOB.K,PROLMOB.K)
NOTE	**
NOTE	* OUTPUT SPECIFICATIONS *
NOTE	**
SPEC	DT = 1/PRTPER = 5/PLTPER = 2/LENGTH = 90
PRINT	CAPN,FAILCP,CAPMOB,LABN,PROLMOB,JOBCR
PLOT	CAPN/LABN/UNEMP
PLOT	CAPMOB/PROLMOB/STATE/JOBCR
PLOT	OVP/PROD/PROFIT/CAP
RUN	

13

Conclusions

It is easy to become absorbed by the details and possibilities of some of the theories that we have been examining. We certainly hope that these examples are stimulating to a wide range of social scientists. But we also hope that the detailed development of formal models and the theoretical experiments that have been conducted with these models are generally instructive in a methodology of theory building and evaluation. In closing, we should take a step back from the particulars and return briefly to the larger agenda that motivates the examples of theoretical research that we have developed in this volume.

The broader motivation underlying this volume is to reorient the way that social scientists theorize. Large bodies of social science theory describe structures and conduct analysis by the method of comparative statics; we have sought to emphasize the utility of theoretical work that focuses explicitly on processes and dynamics. A good deal of social science theory is expressed in "everyday" language, and some is expressed in formal mathematics. We have sought to emphasize the utility of formal, but nonmathematical languages as a tool for the expression of social science theories. Many theorists in the social sciences regard their work as done when they have presented general propositions. We have sought to show that there is a great deal to be gained by programs of theoretical research. To this end, the conceptual schemas of general systems theory and the method of computer-assisted simulation have been emphasized here.

Each of these emphases—on dynamics, on formalisms, and on theoretical research—offer considerable advantages as ways of "doing theory" in the social sciences. And, each emphasis suggests some new directions and challenges for social scientists.

Statics and Dynamics, Structures and Processes

The naming and classification of phenomena and the development of understanding by comparing phenomena are critical enterprises. Our literatures devote extensive attention to such issues as forms of government, kinds of markets, personality types, forms of kinship relations, and types of societies. Great insights are obtained by attempting to understand the affinities among the elements of such "structures" by making comparisons among examples of them. Comparative "statics" are central to the social scientific enterprise.

There are, however, even deeper questions for social theorists: working out general principles of how structures come about, how they are maintained and changed. Theories of the processes by which changes are causally connected to one another—theories of dynamics—should also have a central place in social science theory. In some disciplines there has been considerable progress in developing theories of dynamics, in other disciplines there has been somewhat less. One of the goals of this volume has been to demonstrate that theorizing about dynamics can be pursued with the same rigor and richness that characterizes formulations of comparative statics in the social sciences.

Greater emphasis on theories of dynamics has profound implications for the ways that many social scientists think about problems, and for the kinds of explanations and evidence that they use. The method of understanding by static comparison calls for rich and thick description; exercises in verification based on comparative statics call for the classification of populations (or samples) of phenomena in cross-section. Understanding is achieved when the patterns of covariation among the traits defining phenomena fit together in consistent and replicable ways.

An emphasis on dynamics calls for different thrusts in explanation and verification. "Structures" come to be seen as the momentary and temporary realizations of the actions of (usually multiple) ongoing dynamic processes. The variability of phenomena is seen to be the result of different conjunctures of common underlying processes. Exercises in verification of theories of dynamics acquire a distinctly "historical" flavor under both controlled conditions (as in a laboratory experiment where the same dynamic process is replicated across subjects) and uncontrolled conditions (as in the study of the rise and fall of empires). It is the capacity of the hypothesized process or processes to produce, predict, and postdict trends and sequences that becomes central to evaluation of the theory.

The greater attention to dynamics that is advocated in this volume, then, leads to both theories and empirical research that have somewhat different flavors than a good bit of current work in many social science disciplines. Many empirical researchers and methodologists in all of the social science disciplines, however, are already headed in the direction of greater emphasis on dynamics and the analysis of over-time realizations (some, of course, have always maintained this emphasis). The methods in this volume enable, and challenge, social science theorists to move in this direction as well.

Formalism: Language and Theory

The DYNAMO language for stating theories about dynamics has received a great deal of attention in this volume. The reason for this emphasis is that the DYNAMO language seems, to the author at least, a very powerful tool for talking about the kinds of things that social scientists talk about.

Because the language has a limited vocabulary and syntax, there is much less ambiguity (for both the theorist and the audience) about what is being said when the formal language is used. Yet, as I hope we have demonstrated, the highly structured language allows for the effective statement of quite complex ideas from the entire range of social scientific inquiry. Hopefully the use of such a language will ease communication across disciplinary boundaries in the social sciences, and allow greater cooperation and mutual learning.

The DYNAMO language deserves the attention that we have given it for a second and related reason: It is a special-purpose language for describing continuous state-continuous time dynamics. Not only does the syntax of the language aid in structuring the theorist's thinking, but it allows for the easier statement of extremely complicated multivariate and over-time relations. Theories stated in everyday language can approximate this complexity, but lack clarity and precision. Theories stated in formal mathematical form can approximate both the complexity and precision of DYNAMO models, but are incomprehensible to most social scientists. The DYNAMO language is also noteworthy because of its compatibility with the conceptual schemas of much social science discourse. The grounding of the language in general systems theory, and its strong differentiation between "material" and "informational" quantities is very consistent with the ways that many (though certainly not all) social scientists think and talk about problems.

We hope that we have demonstrated the value of the use of formal language in creating, stating, and doing research on social science theories with the examples in this volume. To the extent that the reader is convinced of this value, a new item can be added to the agenda of the social science theorist: the development of "smarter" formal languages for describing social relations. While DYNAMO is an extremely powerful and useful language, it is only a tool for discourse; new tools should be developed as the need arises. Languages having the same virtues of user friendliness and strong syntax can certainly be developed for application to other kinds of social science problems, and, to some extent, have been. At the time of this writing, the particular problems of mixed continuous and discrete state models, mixed continuous and discrete time dynamics, and network relations models (e.g., for mental schemas, structures of kinships, structures of markets, patterns of political and social conflicts and exchanges for many actors over space and time) seem most in need of development of language.

Theoretical Research

For better or worse, social scientists often distinguish between "doing theory" on one hand, and "doing research" on the other. "Doing theory," I would contend, is much closer to "doing research" than is often realized. By both the general organization of this volume, and by the particular examples presented, I have tried to suggest that there is a good deal of "research" to be done on theories themselves.

A central concern of all social science theorists should be the clear explication of their ideas, and analysis of their internal consistency, limits, and implications. In "everyday language" theories and propositional inventories, rules of logic and deduction are used to accomplish this task. In mathematically formalized theories, methods of direct solution are often applicable. For theories of dynamics that involve large-state spaces and complex and nonlinear and contingent relations among traits and over time, however, exact solution is often impossible. In this volume we have emphasized the use of computer-assisted simulation as one method to derive approximate solutions to complex theories where other methods are insufficient to the task.

But should theories in the social sciences be so complex that we must resort to such approximate methods for understanding them? Simplicity and generality are, of course, to be greatly desired in social science theory. The very simple theories in the first and second parts of this volume are capable of describing the dynamics of very wide ranges of important economic, political, and cultural phenomena—and are often quite comprehensible by deduction and/or direct solution. But, in dealing with social dynamics in even very simplified and abstracted ways, the complexity of our theories can rapidly get out of hand. The exercises in the third section of this volume are both extremely simple models and of sufficient complexity to be explicable only by formal methods.

It is not the intent of this volume to suggest that social scientist's theories strive for greater complexity as an end in itself. But, as the concepts of "general systems" and "complexity" used in this volume suggest, even many quite "simple" social dynamics are too complicated to understand fully without assistance. Computer-assisted simulation in "theoretical research" can be understood as a research tool—one of several—that can and should be used to explicate and analyze our own theories. Social science theorists should not deliberately seek to create complicated theories, but neither should they shy away from them when they are necessary. Hopefully this volume has contributed to theorists' tool kits as they undertake these tasks.

References

Abelson, Robert P. (1963) "A 'derivation' of Richardson's equations." Journal of Conflict Resolution 7 (March): 13-15.

Abelson, R. P. (1967) "Mathematical models in social psychology," in L. Berkowitz (ed.) Advances in Experimental Social Psychology, Vol. 3. New York, Academic Press.

Abelson, R. P. (1968) "Simulation of social behavior," in G. Lindzey and E. Aronson (eds.) The Handbook of Social Psychology, Vol. 2. Reading, MA: Addison-Wesley.

Ackoff, R. L. (1959) "Games, decisions and organization." General Systems 4: 145-150.

Alfeld, Louis E. and Alan K. Graham (1976) Introduction to Urban Dynamics. Cambridge: MIT Press.

Alker, H. R. and R. D. Brunner (1969) "Simulating international conflict: a comparison of three approaches." International Studies Quarterly 13: 70-110.

Allison, Paul D. (1984) Event History Analysis: Regression for Longitudinal Event Data. Newbury Park, CA: Sage.

Anderson, T. R. and S. Warkov (1961) "Organizational size and functional complexity." American Sociological Review 26: 23-28.

Ando, Albert, Franklin M. Fisher, and Herbert A. Simon (1963) Essays on the Structure of Social Science Models. Cambridge: MIT Press.

Andreski, S. (1968) Military Organization and Society. New York: Pantheon.

Arrow, Kenneth J. (1956) "Mathematical models in the social sciences." General Systems I: 29-47.

Ashby, W. Ross (1952) Design for a Brain. London: Chapman & Hall.

Ashby, W. Ross (1958) An Introduction to Cybernetics. New York: John Wiley.

Ashby, W. Ross (1962) "Principles of the self-organizing system," in H. von Foerster and G. W. Zopf, Jr. (eds.) Principles of Self-Organization. New York: Pergamon.

Bailey, Norman T. J. (1957) The Mathematical Theory of Epidemics. New York: Hafner.

Ball, M. A. (1985) Mathematics in the Social and Life Sciences: Theories, Models and Methods. New York: John Wiley.

Barnes, J. A. (1972) Social Networks. Reading, MA: Addison-Wesley.

Bartholomew, David J. (1973) Stochastic Models for Social Processes (2nd ed.) London: John Wiley.

Bartos, Otomar J. (1972) "Foundations for a rational-empirical model of negotiation," pp. 3-20 in Joseph Berger et al. (eds.) Sociological Theories in Progress, Vol. 2. Boston: Houghton-Mifflin.

Baumgartner, T., Tom R. Burns, D. Meeker, and B. Wild (1976) "Methodological implications of multi-level processes for social research." International Journal of General Systems 3.

Bavelas, A. (1950) "Communication patterns in task-oriented groups." Journal of the Acoustical Society of America 22: 725-730.

Bayless, L. E. (1966) Living Control Systems. San Francisco: Freeman.

Bellman, R. (1961) Adaptive Control Processes: A Guided Tour. Princeton, NJ: Princeton University Press.

Berge, Claude (1962) The Theory of Graphs and Its Applications. New York: John Wiley.

Berger, Joseph, B. Cohen, T. Conner, and M. Zelditch, Jr. (1966) "Status characteristics and expectation states: a process model," in J. Berger et al. (eds.) Sociological Theories in Progress. Boston: Houghton-Mifflin.

Berger, Joseph, Bernard P. Cohen, J. Laurie Snell, and Morris Zelditch, Jr. (1962) Types of Formalization in Small-Group Research. Boston: Houghton-Mifflin.

Berrien, F. Kenneth (1968) General and Social Systems. New Brunswick: Rutgers University Press.

Bertalanffy, Ludwig von (1968) General System Theory: Foundations, Development, Applications (Revised ed.). New York: George Braziller.

Blalock, Hubert M., Jr. (1961) Causal Inferences in Nonexperimental Research. New York: Norton.

Blalock, Hubert M., Jr. (1967) Toward a Theory of Minority-Group Relations. New York: John Wiley.

Blalock, Hubert M., Jr. (1969) Theory Construction: From Verbal to Mathematical Formulations. Englewood Cliffs, NJ: Prentice-Hall.

Blalock, Hubert M., Jr. (1971) Causal Models in the Social Sciences. Chicago: Aldine.

Blau, Peter M. (1964) Exchange and Power. New York: John Wiley.

Blau, Peter (1970) "A formal theory of differentiation in organizations." American Sociological Review 35: 201-218.

Bloomfield, L. and N. Padelford (1959) "Three experiments in political gaming." American Political Science Review 53: 1105-1115.

Bogue, Donald J. (1969) Principles of Demography. New York: John Wiley.

Bonini, C. P. (1963) Simulation of Information and Decision Systems in the Firm. Englewood Cliffs, NJ: Prentice-Hall.

Blumen, I. (1966) "Probability models for mobility," pp. 318-334 in P. Lazersfeld and N. Henry (eds.) Readings in Mathematical Social Sciences. Chicago: Science Research Associates.

Boudon, Raymond (1975) "A model for the analysis of mobility tables," in H. M. Blalock et al. (eds.) Quantitative Sociology: International Perspectives on Mathematical and Statistical Modeling. New York: Academic Press.

Boulding, Kenneth E. (1956) "Toward a general theory of growth." General Systems I: 66-75.

Boulding, Kenneth E. (1962) Conflict and Defense. New York: Harper & Row.

Boulding, Kenneth E. (1970) A Primer on Social Dynamics. New York: Free Press.

Boulding, Kenneth E. (1978) Ecodynamics: A New Theory of Societal Evolution. Newbury Park, CA: Sage.

Brams, Steven J. (1975) Game Theory and Politics. New York: Free Press.

Braun, M. (1975) Differential Equations and Their Applications: An Introduction to Applied Mathematics. New York: Springer-Verlag.

Bremer, S. A. (1977) Simulated Worlds: A Computer Model of National Decision-Making. Princeton: Princeton University Press.

Brody, R. A. (1963) "Some systematic effects of the spread of nuclear weapons technology: a study through simulation of a multi-nuclear future." Journal of Conflict Resolution VII: 663-753.

Brody, R. A. (1963) "Varieties of simulations in international relations research," in H. Guetzkow et al. (eds.) Simulation of International Relations: Developments in Research and Teaching. Englewood Cliffs, NJ: Prentice-Hall.

Brody, R. A. and A. H. Benham (1969) "Nuclear weapons and alliance cohesion," pp. 165-175 in D. G. Pruitt and R. C. Snyder (eds.) Theory and Research on the Causes of War. Englewood Cliffs, NJ: Prentice-Hall.

Brown, L. A. and S. G. Philliber (1981) "The diffusion of a population-related innovation: the planned parenthood affiliate." Social Science Quarterly 58: 215-28.

Brunner, Ronald D. and Garry D. Brewer (1971) Organized Complexity: Empirical Theories of Political Development. New York: Free Press.

Buckley, Walter (1967) Sociology and Modern Systems Theory. Englewood Cliffs, NJ: Prentice-Hall.

Buckley, Walter [ed.] (1968) Modern Systems Research for the Behavioral Scientist: A Sourcebook. Chicago: Aldine.

Burmeister, E. and R. Dobell (1970) Mathematical Theories of Economic Growth. New York: Macmillan.

Burns, Tom R., T. Baumgartner, and Philippe Deville (1985) Man, Decisions, Society: The Theory of Actor-System Dynamics for Social Scientists. New York: Gordon & Breach.

Burns, Tom R. and Walter Buckley [eds.] (1976) Power and Control: Social Structures and Their Transformation. Newbury Park, CA: Sage.

Busacker, R. G. and T. L. Saaty (1965) Finite Graphs and Networks: An Introduction with Applications. New York: McGraw-Hill.

Bush, Robert R. and Fredrick Mosteller (1955) Stochastic Models for Learning. New York: John Wiley.

Buxton, J. N. (1968) Simulation Programing Languages. Amsterdam: North Holland.

Cadwallader, M. L. (1959) "The cybernetic analysis of change in complex organizations." American Journal of Sociology 65: 154-157.

Camilleri, Santo F., Joseph Berger and Thomas L. Conner (1972) "A formal theory of decision making," pp. 21-37 in Joseph Berger et al. (eds.) Sociological Theories in Progress, Vol. 2. Boston: Houghton-Mifflin.

Campbell, Donald T. (1962) "Blind variation and selective retention in creative thought and other knowledge processes." General Systems 7: 57-70.

Campbell, Donald T. (1965) "Variation and selective retention in socio-cultural evolution." pp. 19-49 in Herbert R. Barringer et al. (eds.) Social Change in Developing Areas. Cambridge, MA: Schenkman.

Cannon, Walter B. (1939) The Wisdom of the Body. New York: Norton.

Caplow, Theodore (1968) Two Against One: Coalitions in Triads. Englewood Cliffs, NJ: Prentice-Hall.

Cappello, H. M. (1972) "International tension as a function of reduced communication," pp. 39-45 in J. A. Laponce and P. L. Smoker (eds.) Experimentation and Simulation in Political Science. Toronto: University of Toronto Press.

Cartwright, D. and F. Harary (1956) "Structural balance: a generalization of Heider's theory." Psychological Review 63: 277-293.

Chorafas, D. N. (1965) Systems and Simulation. New York: Academic Press.

Chow, G. C. (1967) "Technological change and the demand for computers." American Economic Review 57: 1117-1130.

Coe, R. M. (1964) "Conflict, interference, and aggression: computer simulation of a social process." Behavioral Science 9: 186-197.

Cohen, Bernard (1962) "The process of choosing a reference group," in J. Criswell et al. (eds.) Mathematical Methods in Small Group Processes. Stanford: Stanford University Press.

Cohen, K. J. and R. M. Cyert (1965) "Simulation of organizational behavior," in James G. Marsh (ed.) Handbook of Organizations. Chicago: Rand-McNally.

Cole, H.S.D. et al. [eds.] (1973) Models of Doom. New York: Universe.

Coleman, James A. (1964) "Mathematical models and computer simulation," in R.E.L. Faris (ed.) Handbook of Modern Sociology. Chicago: Rand-McNally.

Coleman, James S. (1964a) "Collective decisions." Sociological Inquiry (Spring): 166-181.

Coleman, James S. (1964b) Introduction to Mathematical Sociology. New York: Free Press.

Coleman, James S. (1966) "Foundations for a theory of collective decisions." American Journal of Sociology 71 (May).

Coleman, James S. (1968) "The mathematical study of change," in Hubert M. Blalock and A. B. Blalock (eds.) Methodology in Social Research. New York: McGraw-Hill.

Coleman, James S. (1972) "Systems of social exchange." Journal of Mathematical Sociology 2: 145-163.

Coleman, James S. (1973) Mathematics of Collective Action. London: Heinemann.

Coleman, James S. (1981) Longitudinal Data Analysis. New York: Basic Books.

Coleman, James S., E. Katz, and H. Menzel (1966) Medical Innovation: A Diffusion Study. Indianapolis: Bobbs-Merrill.

Cox, Peter R. (1959) Demography (3rd. ed.) Cambridge: Cambridge University Press.

Coyle, R. G. (1977) Management System Dynamics. London: John Wiley.

Cronkite, Ruth C. and Rudolf H. Moos (1984) "The role of predisposing and moderating factors in the stress-illness relationship." Journal of Health and Social Behavior 25: 372-93.

Cyert, R. M., E. A. Feigenbaum, and J. G. Marsh (1971) "Models in a behavioral theory of the firm," in J. M. Dutton and W. H. Starbuck (eds.) Computer Simulation of Human Behavior. New York: John Wiley.

Cyert, R. M. and J. G. March (1963) A Behavioral Theory of the Firm. Englewood Cliffs, NJ: Prentice-Hall.

Davis, James A. (1967) "Clustering and structural balance in Di-Graphs." Human Relations 20 (May).

Davis, James A. and Samuel Leinhardt (1972) "The structure of positive interpersonal relations in small groups," in Joseph Berger et al. (eds.) Sociological Theories in Progress, Vol. Two. Boston: Houghton-Mifflin.

Davies, James C. (1969) "The J-curve of rising and declining satisfactions as a cause of some great revolutions and a contained rebellion," pp. 690-730 in Graham and Gurr (eds.) History of Violence in America: Historical and Comparative Perspectives. New York: Bantam.

Day, Richard H. (1974) "System simulation: on system dynamics." Behavioral Science 19 (July): 260-271.

Dean, Alfred and Nan Lin (1977) "The stress-buffering role of social support: problems and prospects for systematic investigation." Journal of Nervous and Mental Disease 165: 403-417.

Demerath, Nicholas J. III, and R. A. Peterson [eds.] (1967) System, Change, and Conflict: A Reader on Contemporary Sociological Theory and the Debate over Functionalism. New York: Free Press.

Deutsch, Karl (1963) The Nerves of Government. New York: Free Press.

Deutsch, K. W., B. Fritsch, H. Jaguaribe, and A. Markovitts (1977) Problems of World Modeling: Political and Social Implications. Cambridge, MA: Ballinger.

Dixon, R. (1980) "Hybrid corn revisited." Econometrica 48: 1451-1461.

Dodson, J. A. and E. Muller (1978) "Models for new product diffusion through advertising and word-of-mouth." Management Science 24: 1568-1578.

Doreian, P. and N. P. Hummon (1976) Modeling Social Processes. Amsterdam: Elsevier North-Holland.

Dubin, Robert (1969) Theory Building: A Practical Guide to the Construction and Testing of Theoretical Models. New York: Free Press.

Duncan, Otis D. (1975) Introduction to Structural Equation Models. New York: Academic Press.

Dunn, E., Jr. (1971) Economic and Social Development: A Process of Social Learning. Baltimore: Johns Hopkins.

Dutton, J. M. and W. H. Starbuck (1971) Computer Simulation of Human Behavior. New York: John Wiley.

Easton, David (1958) A Systems Analysis of Political Life. New York: John Wiley.

Easton, David (1965) A Framework for Political Analysis. Englewood Cliffs, NJ: Prentice-Hall.

Emery F. E. (1969) Systems Thinking: Selected Readings. Baltimore: Penguin.

Emery, F. E. and E. L. Trist (1960) "Socio-technical systems," in C. W. Churchman and M. Verhulst (eds.) Management Sciences: Models and Techniques, Vol. 2. Pergamon.

Emery, F. E. and E. L. Trist (1965) "The causal texture of organizational environments." Human Relations 18: 21-32.

Emshoff, J. R. and R. L. Sisson (1970) Design and Use of Computer Simulation Models. New York: Macmillan.

Eyestone, R. (1977) "Confusion, diffusion, and innovation." American Political Science Review 71: 441-447.

Fararo, T. J. (1972) "Dynamics of status equilibriation," in J. Berger et al. (eds.) Sociological Theories in Progress, Vol. 2. Boston: Houghton-Mifflin: 183-217.

Federico, Pat-Anthony and Paul W. Figliozzi (1981) "Computer simulation of social systems." Sociological Methods and Research 9 (May): 513-533.

Flament, C. (1963) Applications of Graph Theory to Group Structure. Engelwood Cliffs, NJ: Prentice-Hall.

Foerster, H. von and G. W. Zopf, Jr., [eds.] (1962) Principles of Self-Organization. New York: Pergamon Press.

Forrester, Jay W. (1961) Industrial Dynamics. Cambridge: MIT Press.

Forrester, Jay W. (1968) Principles of Systems. Cambridge: MIT Press.

Forrester, Jay W. (1969) Urban Dynamics. Cambridge: MIT Press.

Forrester, Jay W. (1973) World Dynamics. Cambridge: MIT Press.

Forrester, Nathan B. (1973) The Life Cycle of Economic Development. Cambridge: MIT Press.

Foster, C., A. Rapoport, and E. Trucco (1957) "Some unsolved problems in the theory of non-isolated systems." General Systems 2: 9-29.

Gilbert, E. N. (1966) "Information theory after 18 years." Science 152: 320-326.

Ginsberg, R. (1971) "Semi-Markov processes and mobility." Journal of Mathematical Sociology 1: 233-263.

Goodman, Michael R. (1974) Study Notes in System Dynamics. Cambridge: MIT Press.

Gordon, G. (1969) System Simulation. Englewood Cliffs, NJ: Prentice-Hall.

Gore, S. (1985) "Social support and styles in coping with stress," pp. 263-278 in S. Cohen and S. L. Syme (eds.) Social Support and Health. New York: Academic Press.

Gray, V. (1973) "Innovation in the states: a diffusion study." American Political Science Review 67: 1174-1182.

Griliches, Z. (1957) "Hybrid corn: an exploration in the economics of technological change." Econometrica 25: 501-22.

Grinker, R. R. [ed.] (1965) Toward a Unified Theory of Human Behavior. New York: Basic Books.

Guetzkow, Harold (1962) "Inter-nation simulation: an example of a self-organizing system," pp. 72-92 in M. C. Yovits, et al. (eds.) Self-Organizing Systems. Washington DC: Spartan.

Guetzkow, H., et al. [eds.] (1972) Simulation in Social and Administrative Science: Overviews and Case-Examples. Englewood Cliffs, NJ: Prentice-Hall.

Guetzkow, H., P. Kotler, and R. L. Schultz (1972) Simulation in Social and Administrative Science. Englewood Cliffs, NJ: Prentice-Hall.

Guetzkow, Harold and Joseph J. Valdez [eds.] (1981) Simulated International Processes: Theories and Research in Global Modeling. Newbury Park, CA: Sage.

Hage, Jerald (1972) Techniques and Problems of Theory Construction in Sociology. New York: John Wiley.

Hage, Jerald (1980) Theories of Organizations: Form, Process, and Transformation. New York: John Wiley.

Haire, M. (1959) "Biological models and empirical histories of the growth of organizations," pp. 272-306 in M. Haire (ed.) Modern Organization Theory. New York: John Wiley.

Hall, Arthur D. (1962) A Methodology for Systems Engineering. Princeton, NJ: Nostrand.

Hamblin, Robert L. (1971) "Mathematical experimentation and sociological theory: a critical analysis." Sociometry 34: 423-452.

Hamblin, Robert L., R. B. Jacobsen, and J.L.L. Miller (1973) A Mathematical Theory of Social Change. New York: John Wiley.

Hamilton, H. R., S. E. Goldstone, J. W. Milliman, A. L. Pugh III, E. B. Roberts, and A. Zellner (1969) System Simulation for Regional Analysis: An Application to River Basin Planning. Cambridge: MIT Press.

Hanneman, Robert A. and Randall Collins (1986) "A dynamic simulation of Marx's model of capitalism," in Norbert Wiley (ed.) The Marx/Weber Debate. Newbury Park, CA: Sage.

Harary, F. (1969) Graph Theory. Reading, MA: Addison-Wesley.

Harary, F., R. Norman, and D. Cartwright (1965) Structural Models: An Introduction to the Theory of Directed Graphs. New York: John Wiley.

Hare, Van Court, Jr. (1967) Systems Analysis: A Diagnostic Approach. New York: Harcourt Brace and World.

Hauser, Phillip M. and O. D. Duncan [eds.] (1959) The Study of Population. Chicago: University of Chicago Press.

Hearn, G. (1958) Theory Building in Social Work. Toronto: University of Toronto Press.

Heise, David R. (1975) Causal Analysis. New York: John Wiley.

Hermann, Charles F. (1967) "Validation problems in games and simulation with special reference to models of international politics." Behavioral Science 12 (May): 216-231.

Hoivik, Tord and Nils Petter Gleditsch (1975) "Structural parameters in graphs: a theoretical investigation." in H. M. Blalock, A. Aganbegian, F. M. Borodkin, R. Boudon, and V. Capecci (eds.) Quantitative Sociology: International Perspectives on Mathematical and Statistical Modeling. New York: Academic Press.

Holland, P. W. and S. Leinhardt (1977) "A dynamic model for social networks." Journal of Mathematical Sociology 5: 5-20.

Hollist, W. L. [ed.] (1978) Exploring Competitive Arms Processes: Applications of Mathematical Modeling and Computer Simulation in Arms Policy Analysis. New York: Marcel Dekker.

Holmes, T. H. and M. Masuda (1974) "Life change and illness susceptibility," pp. 45-72 in Barbara S. Dohrenwend and Bruce P. Dohrenwend (eds.) Stressful Life Events: Their Nature and Effects. New York: John Wiley.

Holmes, T. H. and R. H. Rahe (1967) "The social readjustment rating scale." Journal of Psychosomatic Research 11: 213-218.

Homans, George C. (1961) Social Behavior: Its Elementary Forms. New York: Harcourt Brace Jovanovich.

Hopkins, Terence K. (1964) The Exercise of Influence in Small Groups. Totowa, NJ: Bedminster.

House, James S. (1981) Work Stress and Social Support. Reading, MA: Addison-Wesley.

Hout, Michael (1983) Mobility Tables. Newbury Park, CA: Sage.

Huckfeldt, R. Robert, C. W. Kohfeld, and Thomas W. Likens (1982) Dynamic Modeling: An Introduction. Newbury Park, CA: Sage.

Huggins, W. H. and D. R. Entwisle (1968) Introductory Systems and Design. Waltham, MA: Blaisdell.

Hughes, B. B. (1980) World Modeling: The Mesarovic-Pestel World Model in the Context of Its Contemporaries. Lexington, MA: D. C. Heath.

Hummon, N. P. (1971) "A mathematical theory of differentiation in organizations." American Sociological Review 36: 297-303.

Ilchman, Warren F. and Norman T. Uphoff (1969) The Political Economy of Change. Berkeley: University of California Press.

Jarmain, W. E. [ed.] (1963) Problems in Industrial Dynamics. Cambridge: MIT Press.

Kassarda, J. D. (1974) "The structural implications of social system size: a comparative analysis." American Sociological Review 39: 19-28.

Katz, D. and R. L. Kahn (1966) The Social Psychology of Organizations. New York: John Wiley.

Katz, E., M. Levin, and H. Hamilton (1963) "Traditions of research on the diffusion of innovation." American Sociological Review 28: 237-252.

Kelly, P. and M. Kranzberg [eds.] (1978) Technological Innovation: A Critical Review of Current Knowledge. San Francisco: San Francisco Press.

Kemeny, John G. and J. Laurie Snell (1962) Mathematical Models in the Social Sciences. Boston: Ginn.

Kennedy, J. L. (1962) "The systems approach: organizational development." Human Factors 4: 25-52.

Keyfitz, Nathan (1971) "On the momentum of population growth." Demography 8: 71-80.

Keyfitz, Nathan (1975) "Reproductive value: with applications to migration, contraception, and zero population growth," in H. M. Blalock et al. (eds.) Quantitative Sociology: International Perspectives on Mathematical and Statistical Modeling. New York: Academic Press.

Keyfitz, Nathan (1977) Applied Mathematical Demography. New York: John Wiley.

Kiviat, P. J., R. Villanueva, and J. Markowitz (1969) The SIMSCRIPT II Programming Language. Englewood Cliffs, NJ: Prentice-Hall.

Klir, G. J. (1971) Trends in General Systems Theory. New York: John Wiley.

Knoke, David and Kuklinski (1984) Network Analysis. Newbury Park, CA: Sage.

Kochen, Manfred and Karl W. Deutsch (1980) Decentralization: Sketches Toward a Rational Theory. Cambridge, MA: Oelgeschlager, Gunn, and Hain.

Komorita, S. S. (1974) "Weighted probability model of coalition formation." Psychological Review 81: 242-257.

Krasnow, H. S. (1967) "Computer languages for system simulation," pp. 258-277 in M. Klerer and G. Korn (eds.) Digital Computer User's Handbook. New York: McGraw-Hill.

Kremyanskiy, V. I. (1960) "Certain peculiarities of organisms as a 'system' from the point of view of physics, cybernetics, and biology." General Systems 5: 221-230.

Kruskal, William [ed.] (1970) Mathematical Sciences and Social Sciences. Englewood Cliffs, NJ: Prentice-Hall.

Kuhn, Alfred (1963) The Study of Society: A Unified Approach. Homewood IL: Dorsey Press.

Kuhn, Alfred (1975) Unified Social Science: A System-Based Introduction. Homewood IL: Dorsey Press.

Land, Kenneth C. (1970) "Mathematical formalization of Durkheim's theory of the causes of the division of labor," pp. 257-282 in E. Borgatta and G. Bohrnstedt (eds.) Sociological Methodology 1970. San Francisco: Jossey-Bass.

Land, Kenneth C. (1971) "Formal theory," in Herbert L. Costner (ed.) Sociological Methodology 1971. San Francisco: Jossey-Bass.

Land, Kenneth (1975) "Comparative statics in sociology: including a mathematical theory of growth and differentiation in organizations," in H. M. Blalock et al. (eds.) Quantitative Sociology: International Perspectives on Mathematical and Statistical Modeling. New York: Academic Press.

Lange, O. (1965) Wholes and Parts: A General Theory of Systems Behavior. Oxford: Pergamon.

Laponce, J. A. and P. L. Smoker [eds.] (1972) Experimentation and Simulation in Political Science. Toronto: University of Toronto Press.

LaRocco, James M., James S. House, and John R. French, Jr. (1980) "Social support, occupational stress, and health." Journal of Health and Social Behavior 21: 201-218.

Lave, Charles A. and James G. March (1975) An Introduction to Models in the Social Sciences. New York: Harper & Row.

Lazarsfeld, Paul F. (1954) Mathematical Thinking in the Social Sciences. New York: Free Press.

Leik, Robert K. and B. F. Meeker (1975) Mathematical Sociology. Englewood Cliffs, NJ: Prentice-Hall.

Levin, Gilbert and Edward Roberts (with Gary B. Hirsch, Deborah S. Kligler, Nancy Roberts, and Jack Wilder) (1976) The Dynamics of Human Service Delivery. Cambridge, MA: Ballinger.

Levin, Gilbert, Edward B. Roberts, and Gary B. Hirsch (1975) The Persistent Poppy: A Computer-Aided Search for Heroin Policy. Cambridge, MA: Ballinger.

Levin, M. L. (1962) "Simulation of social processes." Public Opinion Quarterly 26: 483-484.

Lorens, Charles S. (1964) Flowgraphs for the Modeling and Analysis of Linear Systems. (mathematical approach to flow graphs) New York: McGraw-Hill.

Luce, R. Duncan and Howard Raiffa (1957) Games and Decisions. New York: John Wiley.

Luenberger, D. G. (1979) Introduction to Dynamic Systems: Theory, Models, and Applications. New York: John Wiley.

Lyneis, James M. (1980) Corporate Planning and Policy Design: A System Dynamics Approach. Cambridge: MIT Press.

Mahajan, Vijay and Robert A. Peterson (1985) Models for Innovation Diffusion. Newbury Park, CA: Sage.

Malone, T. W. (1975) "Computer simulation of two-person interactions." Behavioral Science 20: 260-267.

Markowitz, H. M., H. W. Karr, and B. Hausner (1963) SIMSCRIPT: A Simulation Programming Language. Englewood Cliffs NJ: Prentice-Hall.

Marshall, W. S. (1967) "Simulating communication network experiments." Management Science 13: 656-665.

Martin, F. F. (1968) Computer Modeling and Simulation. New York: John Wiley.

Maruyama, Magoroh (1968) "The second cybernetics: deviation amplifying mutual causal process," in Walter Buckley (ed.) Modern Systems Research for the Behavioral Scientist. Chicago: Aldine.

Mass, Nathaniel J. [ed.] (1974) Readings in Urban Dynamics: Volume 1. Cambridge: MIT Press.

Mass, Nathaniel J. (1975) Economic Cycles: An Analysis of Underlying Causes. Cambridge: MIT Press.

Mayer, Thomas F. (1972) "Models of intragenerational mobility," pp. 308-357 in J. Berger, M. Zelditch, Jr., and B. Anderson (eds.) Sociological Theories in Progress, Volume Two. Boston: Houghton-Mifflin.

Mayhew, Bruce H. (1984) "Baseline models of sociological phenomena." Journal of Mathematical Sociology 9: 259-281.

Mayhew, Bruce H. (1984) "Chance and Necessity in Sociological Theory." Journal of Mathematical Sociology 9: 305-339.

McFarland, David C. (1970) "Intergenerational social mobility as a Markov process: including a time-stationary Markovian model that explains observed declines in mobility rates." American Sociological Review 35 (June): 463-476.

McGinnis, R. (1968) "A stochastic model of social mobility." American Sociological Review 33: 712-722.

McKelvey, Bill (1982) Organizational Systematics: Taxonomy, Evolution, Classification. Berkeley: University of California Press.

McPhee, W. N. (1963) Formal Theories of Mass Behavior. New York: Macmillan.

McPhee, W. N., N. J. Ferguson, and R. B. Smith (1971) "A model for simulating voting systems," in J. M. Dutton and W. H. Starbuck (eds.) Computer Simulation of Human Behavior. New York: John Wiley.

Meade, N. (1984) "The use of growth curves in forecasting market development - a review and appraisal." Journal of Forecasting 3: 31-41.

Meadows, Dennis L. (1970) Dynamics of Commodity Production Cycles. Cambridge: MIT Press.

Meadows, Dennis L., William W. Behrens III, Donella H. Meadows, Roger F. Naill, Jorgen Randers, and Erich K. O. Zahn (1974) Dynamics of Growth in a Finite World. Cambridge: MIT Press.

Meadows, Dennis L. and Donella H. Meadows [eds.] (1973) Toward Global Equilibrium: Collected Papers. Cambridge: MIT Press.

Meadows, Donella H., Dennis L. Meadows, Jorgen Randers, and William W. Gehrens III (1973) The Limits to Growth. New York: Universe.

Meadows, Donella H. and J. M. Robinson (1985) The Electronic Oracle: Computer Models and Social Decisions. New York: John Wiley.

Meier, R. C., W. T. Newell, and H. L. Pazer (1969) Simulation in Business and Economics. Englewood Cliffs, NJ: Prentice-Hall.

Mesarovic, Mihajlo D. (1961) Systems Research and Design. New York: John Wiley.

Mesarovic, Mihajlo D. (1964) View on General Systems Theory. New York: John Wiley.

Mesarovic, Mihajlo D. (1968) Systems Theory and Biology. New York: Springer.

Mesarovic, Mihajlo D. and D. Macko (1969) "Foundations for a scientific theory of hierarchical systems," in L. L. Whyte et al. (eds.) Hierarchical Structures. New York: Elsevier.

Mesarovic, Mihajlo D. and Eduard Pestel (1974) Mankind at the Turning Point (Second Report to the Club of Rome) New York: E. P. Dutton/Reader's Digest.

Mihram, G. A. (1972) Simulation: Statistical Foundations and Methodology. New York: Academic Press.

Mize, J. H. and J. G. Cox (1968) Essentials of Simulation. Englewood Cliffs, NJ: Prentice-Hall.

Monin, J. P., R. Benayoun, and B. Sert (1976) Initiation to the Mathematics of the Processes of Diffusion, Contagion and Propagation. Paris: Mouton.

Naylor, T. H., J. L. Balintfy, D. S. Burdick, and K. Chu (1965) Computer Simulation Techniques. New York: John Wiley.

Neumann, J. von (1951) "The general and logical theory of automata." L. A. Jeffries (ed) Cerebral Mechanisms in Behavior. New York: John Wiley.

Neumann, J. von and O. Morgenstern (1947) Theory of Games and Economic Behavior. Princeton: Princeton University Press.

Nielsen, F. and R. A. Rosenfeld (1981) "Substantive interpretations of differential equation models." American Sociological Review 46: 159-174.

Orcutt, G. H., M. Greenberger, J. Korbel, and A. M. Rivlin (1961) Microanalysis of Socioeconomic Systems: A Simulation Study. New York: Harper & Row.

Oster, S. (1982) "The diffusion of innovation among steel firms: the basic oxygen-furnace." Bell Journal of Economics 13: 45-56.

Parsons, Talcott (1937) The Structure of Social Action. New York: McGraw-Hill.

Parsons, Talcott (1957) The Social System. New York: Free Press.

Parsons, Talcott (1966) Societies: Evolutionary and Comparative Perspectives. Englewood Cliffs, NJ: Prentice-Hall.

Pattee, Howard H. (1973) Hierarchy Theory: The Challenge of Complex Systems. New York: George Braziller.

Pattee, Howard H. (1975) "The role of instabilities in the evolution of control hierarchies," in T. R. Burns and W. Buckley (eds.) Power and Control: Social Structures and Their Transformation. Newbury Park, CA: Sage.

Patten, Bernard C. [ed.] (1971) Systems Analysis and Simulation in Ecology. New York: Academic Press.

Pearlin, Leonard I. and Carmi Schooler (1978) "The Structure of Coping." Journal of Health and Social Behavior 19: 2-21.

Perrow, Charles (1979) Complex Organizations: A Critical Essay (2nd edition) Glenview IL: Scott, Foresman.

Perrow, Charles (1984) Normal Accidents: Living with High-Risk Technologies. New York: Basic Books.

Pitcher, B. L., R. L. Hamblin, and J.L.L. Miller (1978) "The diffusion of collective violence." American Sociological Review 43: 23-35.

Powers, Charles H. and Robert A. Hanneman (1983) "Pareto's theory of social and economic cycles: a formal model and simulation," in Randall Collins (ed.) Sociological Theory 1983. San Francisco: Jossey-Bass.

Powers, William T. (1973) Behavior: The Control of Perception (systems theory construction) Chicago: Aldine.

Pritsker, A. Alan B. (1973) The GASP IV User's Manual. West Lafayette, IN: Pritsker Associates.

Pritsker, A. Alan B. (1974) The GASP IV Simulation Language. New York: John Wiley.

Pritsker, A. Alan B. and P. J. Kiviat (1969) Simulation with GASP II. Englewood Cliffs, NJ: Prentice-Hall.

Pruitt, D. G. (1962) "An analysis of responsiveness between nations." Journal of Conflict Resolution 6: 5-18.

Pugh, Alexander L. III (1980) Dynamo User's Manual (5th Edition) Cambridge: MIT Press.

Pugh-Roberts Associates, Inc. (1982) User Guide and Reference Manual for Micro-DYNAMO. Reading, MA: Addison-Wesley.

Rabkin, J. G. and E. L. Struening (1976) "Life events, stress, and illness." Science 194: 1013-1020.

Raiffa, Howard (1970) Decision Analysis. Reading, MA: Addison-Wesley.

Randers, Jorgen [ed.] (1980) Elements of the System Dynamics Method. Cambridge: MIT Press.

Rapoport, Anatol (1957) "Lewis F. Richardson's mathematical theory of war." General Systems 2: 55-91.

Rapoport, Anatol (1959) "Uses and limitations of mathematical models in social sciences," pp. 348-372 in L. Gross (ed.) Symposium on Sociological Theory. Evanston, IL: Row, Peterson.

Rapoport, Anatol (1960) Fights, Games and Debates. Ann Arbor: University of Michigan Press.

Rapoport, Anatol (1966) Two-Person Game Theory: The Essential Ideas. Ann Arbor: University of Michigan Press.

Rapoport, Anatol and Albert Chammah (1965) The Prisoner's Dilemma, A Study in Conflict and Cooperation. Ann Arbor: University of Michigan Press.

Rapoport, J. (1978) "Diffusion of technological innovation among nonprofit firms: a case study of radioisotopes in U.S. hospitals." Journal of Economics and Business 39: 108-18.

Reynolds, Paul D. (1971) A Primer in Theory Construction. Indianapolis, IN: Bobbs-Merrill.

Richardson, George P. and Alexander L. Pugh III (1981) Introduction to System Dynamics Modeling with DYNAMO. Cambridge: MIT Press.

Richardson, Lewis B. (1960) Arms and Insecurity. Pittsburgh: Boxwood.

Roberts, Edward B. [ed.] (1978) Managerial Applications of System Dynamics. Cambridge: MIT Press.

Roberts, Nancy, David F. Andersen, Ralph M. Deal, Michael S. Garet, and William A. Shaffer (1983) Introduction to Computer Simulation: The System Dynamics Approach. Reading, MA: Addison-Wesley.

Robinson, L. F. (1972) "How GASP, SIMULA and DYNAMO view a problem," pp. 167-214 in I. M. Kay and J. McLeod (eds.) Progress in Simulation. New York: Gordon & Breach.

Rogers, Everett M. (1983) Diffusion of Innovations. New York: Free Press.

Rosenbaum, R. E. (1979) "Organizational career mobility: promotion chances in a corporation during periods of growth and contraction." American Journal of Sociology 85 (July): 21-48.

Saaty, T. L. (1968) Mathematical Models of Arms Control and Disarmament. New York: John Wiley.

Schank, R. C. and K. M. Colby [eds.] (1973) Computer Models of Thought and Language. San Francisco: Freeman.

Schelling, T. C. (1963) The Strategy of Conflict. Cambridge, MA: Harvard University Press.

Schmidt, J. W. and R. E. Taylor (1970) Simulation and Analysis of Industrial Systems. Homewood, IL: Richird D. Irwin.

Schrodt, P. A. (1978) "Statistical problems associated with the Richardson arms race model." Journal of Peace Science 3: 159-172.

Schroeder, Walter W. III, Robert E. Sweeney, and Louis E. Alfeld [eds.] (1975) Readings in Urban Dynamics: Volume II. Cambridge: MIT Press.

Schutzenberger, M. P. (1954) "A tentative classification of goal-seeking behaviours." Journal of Mental Science 100: 97-102.

Shryock, Henry S. and Jacob S. Siegel, and associates (1976) The Methods and Materials of Demography (condensed ed.) New York: Academic Press.

Shubik, Martin [ed.] (1964) Game Theory and Related Approaches to Social Behavior. New York: John Wiley .

Shubik, Martin (1984a) Game Theory in the Social Sciences: Concepts and Solutions. Cambridge: MIT Press.

Shubik, Martin (1984b) A Game-Theoretic Approach to Political Economy: Game Theory in the Social Sciences, Vol. 2. Cambridge: MIT Press.

Shubik, Martin. and E. A. Hansford (1965) "The Effectiveness of Pacifist Strategies in Bargaining Games." Journal of Conflict Resolution 9: 106-117.

Sigal, C. E. and A.A.B. Pritsker (1974) "SMOOTH: a combined continuous-discrete network simulation language." SIMULATION 21.

Simon, Herbert A. (1947) Administrative Behavior. New York: Macmillan.

Simon, Herbert A. (1957) Models of Man. New York: John Wiley.

Simon, Herbert A. (1965) "The architecture of complexity." General Systems 10: 63-76.

Simon, Herbert A. (1969) The Sciences of the Artificial. Cambridge: MIT Press.

Simon, Herbert A. (1981) The Sciences of the Artificial (2nd ed.) Cambridge: MIT Press.

Simpson, Richard L. (1973) Theories of Social Exchange. Morristown, NJ: General Learning.

Singer, B. and Seymour Spilerman (1974) "Social mobility models for heterogeneous populations," pp. 356-401 in H. Costner (ed.) Sociological Methodology 1973-1974. San Francisco: Jossey-Bass.

Singer, B. and S. Spilerman (1976) "The representation of social processes by Markov models." American Journal of Sociology 82: 1-54.

Singer, J. D. (1958) "Threat perception and the armament-tension dilemma." Journal of Conflict Resolution 2: 90-105.

Smoker, P. L. (1965) "Trade, defence, and the Richardson theory of arms races: a seven nation study." Journal of Peace Research 2: 161-176.

Sommerhoff, G. (1969) "The abstract characteristics of living systems," in F. E. Emery (ed.) Systems Thinking. Baltimore, MD: Penguin.

Spilerman, S. (1972a) "The analysis of mobility processes by the introduction of independent variables into a Markov chain." American Sociological Review 37: 277-294.

Spilerman, Seymour (1972b) "Extensions of the Mover-Stayer model." American Journal of Sociology 78 (November): 599-626.

Stewman, Shelby (1975) "An application of job vacancy chain model to a civil service internal labor market." Journal of Mathematical Sociology 4: 37-59.

Stewman, Shelby and Suresh L. Konda (1983) "Careers and organizational labor markets: demographic models of organizational behavior." American Journal of Sociology 88 (January): 637-685.

Stinchcombe, Arthur L. (1968) Constructing Social Theories. New York: Harcourt, Brace and World.

Takacs, L. (1962) Introduction to the Theory of Queues. New York: Oxford University Press.

Taylor, Shelley (1983) "Adaptation to threatening events: a theory of cognitive adaption." American Psychologist 38: 1161-1173.

Teece D. J. (1980) "The diffusion of an administrative innovation." Management Science 26: 464-70.

Teichrow, D., J. Lublin, and D. Truitt (1967) "Discussion of computer simulation techniques and comparison of languages," SIMULATION 9: 181-190.

Thoits, Peggy A. (1982) "Conceptual, methodological, and theoretical problems in studying social support as a buffer against life stress." Journal of Health and Social Behavior 23: 145-159.

Thrall, R. M. et al. [eds.] (1954) Decision Processes. New York: John Wiley.

Tuma, Nancy Brandon and Michael T. Hannan (1984) Social Dynamics: Models and Methods. Orlando, FL: Academic Press.

Turner, Jonathan H. and Robert A. Hanneman (1984) "Baseline models are not 'finishline' models: a sympathetic critique of Mayhew's strategy." Journal of Mathematical Sociology 9: 283-291.

United States Bureau of the Census (1985) Statistical Abstract of the United States 1985. Washington, DC: Government Printing Office.

van den Berghe, Pierre L. (1963) "Dialectic and functionalism: toward a theoretical synthesis," American Sociological Review 28 (October): 695-705.

Waltz, K. (1967) "The politics of peace." International Studies Quarterly 11: 199-211.

Weaver, W. (1948) "Science and complexity." American Scientist 36: 536-544.

Weymar, F. Helmut (1968) The Dynamics of the World Cocoa Market. Cambridge: MIT Press.

Weiner, Norbert (1948) Cybernetics or Control and Communications in the Animal and the Machine. New York: John Wiley.

Wheaton, Blair (1985) "Models for stress-buffering functions of coping resources." Journal of Health and Social Behavior 26: 352-364.

White, Harrison (1963) An Anatomy of Kinship. Englewood Cliffs, NJ: Prentice-Hall.

White, Harrison (1965) "Stayers and movers." American Journal of Sociology 76: 307-324.

White, Harrison C. (1970) Chains of Opportunity: Systems Models of Mobility in Organizations. Cambridge, MA: Harvard University Press.

White, Harrison C. (1982) "Where do markets come from?" American Journal of Sociology 87: 517.
Whitten, Norman and Alvin W. Wolfe (1973) "Network analysis," pp. 717-747 in John J. Honigman (ed.) Handbook of Social and Cultural Anthropology. Chicago: Rand McNally.
Whyte, L. L., A. G. Wilson, and D. Wilson [eds.] (1969) Hierarchical Structures. New York: Elsevier.
Willer, David (1967) Scientific Sociology: Theory and Method. Englewood Cliffs, NJ: Prentice-Hall.
Wyman, F. (1970) Simulation Modeling: A Guide to Using SIMSCRIPT. New York: John Wiley .

Index

Auxiliary equations, 58, 60, 62; in DYNA-MO diagrams, 59; see also Informational states

Baseline models, 99, 103; and simulation experiments, 93; diffusion, growth, transition, 152; escalation process, 228; mobility matrix, 208; population age structure, 189; stress, coping, and support, 256, 272; vacancy chain, 199

Causal models: see Structural equation models
Causal processes, 17-19; multiple, in levels, 57; reversible, 57
Chain models, 21, 222; career mobility as a chain, 180, 181; definition, 43; diagram of simple chain, 43; input-output matrices, 177; social science examples, 174
Classification, 17, 33, 323
Comparative statics and dynamics, 13, 17, 20, 28, 42, 323-324
Complexity, 37; of chain models, 175; definition, 83; degrees of freedom, 83; DYNAMO diagram example, 101, 179; of multistate chain models, 177; of systems, 32, 95, 98, 104; of theories as systems, 84, 99, 318, 327
Connectivity, 27, 28, 42, 70; in age-structure model, 44; definition, 42; in differential equations, 43; in directed graphs, 43; in flow-graphs, 43; informational, 46; matrix, 43, 50; in multistate chains, 178; in structural equations, 43; in systems dynamics, 43, 51
Contagion processes: as elaboration of diffusion, 159; DYNAMO diagram, 160; DYNAMO model, 171-172; social science examples, 159
Continuous-state continuous-time process, 47, 325

Control, goal referencing, 100, 107, 126; in diffusion models, 148-150; DYNAMO diagram, 100-106; DYNAMO model, 127; DYNAMO model with delay, 134-135, 140-141; examples, 126; experiments, 127-129; structure of, 126
Control, goal setting (or adaptive), 108, 130; dynamics of, 132; DYNAMO diagram, 108; in escalation model, 243; social science examples, 131
Control, self-referencing, 100, 106, 120; delays in, 133; in diffusion models, 146; DYNAMO diagram, 106; DYNAMO model, 121; effects of delay, 132; negative feedback experiments, 124; positive feedback experiments, 122
Control, simple, 99-100, 106; baseline DYNAMO model, 109; in diffusion models, 144; DYNAMO diagram, 99, 106; experiments, 111-114; experiments with delay, 115-119
Control structures, 43, 44; citations, 139; complexity, 100, 105, 106; complexity in chain models, 183; diagram of simple chain, 45; examples in formal organization, 140; examples in stress and coping model, 252-278; feedback experiments, 121-125; feedback and interaction, 139; feed-forward control, 189; see also Control, goal referencing; Control, goal setting; Control, self-referencing; Control, simple
Coupling of subsystems: close-coupling, 173; experiments with Pareto model, 295
Covariation, 17-20
CSSL, 49, 68

Delay, 73; effects in social interaction, 234; in escalation model, 235; exponential delays, 73; exponential delays, first-

About the Author

Robert A. Hanneman is an Associate Professor of Sociology at the University of California, Riverside. His major areas of research interest are in large-scale organizations and political sociology. He is coauthor of *Centralization and Power in Social Service Delivery* with J. Rogers Hollingsworth, and is completing an analysis of the structure and performance of medical care delivery systems in four nations since 1890 with Jerald Hage and Rogers Hollingsworth. He has written a number of articles on the growth of the welfare state, income distribution, and social welfare policy. In addition to his current work on formalization and dynamic modeling, he is also studying military intervention and governmental stability in the contemporary world system.

Notes

Notes

Notes

Notes

Notes

Notes

Notes